BURLEIGH

The Leigh Family Tree. A relief-modelled plaque by Ernest Bailey commemorating the centenary of Burgess & Leigh in 1951.

BURLEIGH

THE STORY OF A POTTERY

by Julie McKeown

BURGESS & LEIGH 1851-1999

BURGESS, DORLING & LEIGH 1999-

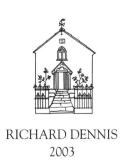

RICHARD DENNIS
2003

ACKNOWLEDGEMENTS

Burleigh, the Story of a Pottery could not have been written without assistance from many individuals and organisations. In particular, I must thank William and Rosemary Dorling for their permission to research and photograph the Burgess, Dorling & Leigh company archives. They have remained constantly welcoming, enthusiastic and generous with their time, as have others at the Middleport Pottery, particularly Susannah Baird and Sue Goulding. Special thanks are due to Steve Davies for sharing his knowledge of the history of Burgess & Leigh and his enthusiasm for its products.

I am especially indebted to Barry Leigh, a direct descendant of the founder and a participant in this history, for reading and commenting on my manuscript.

I am also grateful to long-serving past employees, Ben Ford, Stan and Elsie Johnson and Kath Wilson, for their recollections; David Copeland has been particularly helpful with information on designs produced during his years as Art Director for the company. The descendants of Burgess & Leigh's earlier design team have been equally generous: Ian Bailey and Trudy Jones, son and daughter of Ernest Bailey; Anthony Bennett, son of Harold Bennett; and Helen S. Cooper and Audrey Dudson, family descendants of Charles Wilkes.

Those who have been particularly helpful with research are Rodney Hampson, a very valued reviewer of the early chapters; Bernard Bumpus; and Elizabeth Coupe. Robert Copeland's and Connie Rogers' encyclopaedic knowledge of the *Willow* pattern was especially useful, supplemented by Nancee Rogers' enthusiasm for Burleigh. I am grateful also to Donald Morris for his foresight in photographing the Potteries in the 1960s, and to Dr Malcolm Nixon for sharing his architectural knowledge, humour and oatcakes.

Others who have helped with information and photography include A.D. 1930, Brighton; Verity Claire Andrews, University of Reading; David Barker, Stoke-on-Trent City Council; Maureen Batkin; R. Geoffrey Bell; Derek Bradbury, Burslem Antiques and Collectables; Kelly Bryony, Museum of the Royal Pharmacological Society of Great Britain; Helen Burton, University of Keele; Jim and Gail Cook; Helen S. Cooper; Lucien Cooper, Miranda Goodby and Sue Taylor, Potteries Museum and Art Gallery; Barrie Heath; Dick Henrywood; Robin Hildyard and Kate Rhodes, Victoria and Albert Museum; Louise Irvine; L. & W. Jackson; Wayne Johnson; Joan Jones, Royal Doulton Museum; Chris Latimer, Stoke-on-Trent City Archives; Martin and Shelagh Lister, Invogue Antiques; Jeremy Miln, the National Trust; Kathy Niblett; Chris Nunn; John Potter; Bill Buckley, Potteries Antiques Centre, Burslem; Andrew Pye, Lovers of Blue and White; Jennifer Quérée, Canterbury Museum, New Zealand; David Read, Wood, Goldstraw & Yorath; Scott Rogers; John Shorter CBE; Chris Weatherby; Vega Wilkinson; David Williams of the Charlotte Rhead Newsletter; Pam Woolliscroft, Spode Museum; Terry Woolliscroft; and Peter Wild, Grapha Print.

In the preparation and production of the book I would like to give sincere thanks to Wendy Wort; Sue Evans; Magnus and Buchan Dennis; and particularly Richard Dennis for his enthusiastic support throughout. The patience and encouragement of my husband, family and friends deserve special mention.

Photography by Magnus Dennis
Production by Wendy Wort and Chrissie Atterbury
Print, design and reproduction by Flaydemouse, Yeovil, Somerset
Published by Richard Dennis, The Old Chapel, Shepton Beauchamp, Somerset TA19 OLE, England
© 2003 Richard Dennis and Julie McKeown
ISBN 0 903685 80 9
All rights reserved
British Library Cataloguing-in-Publication Data. A catalogue record for this book is available from the British Library

CONTENTS

INTRODUCTION

Hidden away in the back streets of the Potteries, the long façade of the Middleport Pottery reveals little of the industry which has put plates on tables all over the world since the factory was built in 1888. Certainly, that was my impression in 1977 when, as a junior curatorial assistant at the Gladstone Pottery Museum, I was taken to see how a genuine working Victorian pottery operated. While I learned much that day, some twenty-five years were to pass before I fully appreciated the efforts and skills of the generations of pottery families, which had made Burleigh Ware known *'all over the globe'*.

When I returned to the Middleport Pottery in 2001 to carry out research for this book I was surprised and delighted to find it much as I remembered, with its uniquely evocative atmosphere intact. Stoke-on-Trent City Council had long since taken measures to preserve the Grade II listed bottle oven and site, while the Leigh family's practical disregard for unnecessary cosmetic change, coupled with a lack of funding common to the ceramic industry, had inadvertently preserved much more: nineteenth century potters' workshops; a steam engine; an unusual bath-house, complete with roll-top bath, installed by benevolent employers for those *'working in the lead'*; a Dickensian office with original fixtures and fittings; and stores of copperplate engravings and potters' moulds. But most interesting to me, a substantial paper archive had also survived, hidden in cluttered cupboards, desk drawers and soot-covered corners of the factory. Although a number of exquisite pen and ink design drawings had survived, there was little completed artwork and no beautifully illustrated pattern books of the kind or quantity that more illustrious pottery manufacturers might boast. But the mundane papers, notebooks and battered leather-bound ledgers of Burgess & Leigh were to tell a fascinating story nonetheless.

While the archive revealed some of the personal and distinguished history of the five generations of the Leigh family, sole owners of the pottery from 1912 until 1999, it also - more importantly perhaps - offered a detailed insight into the traditional manufacturing processes and working life of a typical, respectable 'potbank', which reflected British industry in general and the ceramic trade in particular. Founded in 1862 by solid sons of Stoke – one, a money man, Frederick Rathbone Burgess, and the other, a potter, William Leigh - the modest aim of these manufacturers of domestic earthenwares was to produce *'good products at a fair price'*. Their earliest patterns, such as *Willow, Rhine* and *Asiatic Pheasant*, were neither original nor especially fashionable but well-loved, standard designs. Fragile, almost illegible, business correspondence from the 1860s confirmed that the company had quickly built up a reputation for the quality of its fine earthenware, underglaze transfer printed decoration and reliability of supply, all of which appealed to cost-conscious middle classes.

Dusty Victorian 'Day Books' stored on high shelving in the old warehouse also revealed the company's participation in supplying 'matchings', a widespread but little advertised practice of local outsourcing, evidence of the friendly co-operation between rival pottery companies. This 'jobbing' work provided a useful source of income alongside the greater entrepreneurial ambitions of Burgess & Leigh; stacks of 'Foreign Order Books' disclosed a substantial overseas trade with America and territories which reflected the extent of Great Britain's Empire – Australia, New Zealand, India and South Africa. As a result the company was able to build in 1888 its own canal-side, architect-designed factory, the Middleport Pottery, which for many years after was known as the *'Model Pottery of Staffordshire.'* While Burgess & Leigh, in both its buildings and business, mirrored the expansionism of the Victorian age, the company remained modest, unpretentious and down-to-earth, qualities which are typical of the Potteries' people and institutions. Some of the world's finest ceramics continue to be produced in Stoke-on-Trent but for generations of its skilled workers, it is all just another day's work.

In the post-colonial twentieth century, the ceramic industry had to adjust to the difficult trading conditions of the modern age, exacerbated by two World Wars. Company catalogues showed that Burgess & Leigh, like other pottery manufacturers, had to respond rapidly to changes in lifestyle by developing new lines of production; in the recession of the 1920s and the Depression of the early 1930s, it diversified in order to supply an increased demand for novelty in design. Rising to the challenge, it produced some of the most innovative and collectable pottery of the Art Deco period. However, throughout the ceramic style changes of the decades, Burgess & Leigh never lost sight of its strengths: its traditional manufacturing skills and good, reliable products for a middle market. Sometimes, however, it requires more than a good product to succeed and business commentators were eager to analyse why Burgess & Leigh went into receivership in 1999. What my research clearly told me was that as a family firm it had survived longer than many of its rivals, with a superb record of production - and paternalistic care for its employees - over five generations.

Burgess & Leigh's legacy is a proud independence which has preserved not only an architectural gem in the Middleport Pottery but also a truly English product in Burleigh Ware. The company's good fortune was that the Dorlings were able to recognise this when they risked everything to take over the business in 1999. What they also know is that although the pottery now has a significant place in England's heritage industry, Burgess, Dorling & Leigh also belongs to the nation's ceramic industry and must retain a vibrant, commercial, manufacturing presence there. Importantly, the company continues to utilise the traditional skills of local people and is able to maintain a small scale, intimate working environment where every piece of Burleigh Ware is touched by the human hand in the process of its production.

The last few decades have been very difficult ones for the Staffordshire ceramic industry with so much of its production and heritage lost, either transferred overseas or simply gone forever. A particular pleasure in writing *Burleigh, the Story of a Pottery* has been that I have not merely recounted a history but have been able to tell a 'story so far'. While paying tribute to Burgess & Leigh potters and pottery of the past, the final chapter of the story also sends out an optimistic note for the future.

Julie McKeown
April 2003

CHAPTER ONE

THE BACKGROUND AND FOUNDATION OF BURGESS & LEIGH 1820-1868

The story of *Burleigh Ware* is one of potters, potteries and pots. It tells how five generations of potters steered a family firm, Burgess & Leigh, through the changing fortunes of the British ceramics industry; of how the worldwide trade of its nineteenth-century domestic earthenwares enabled the company to build '*the model pottery of Staffordshire*'; and how the launch of the successful brand *Burleigh Ware* in the early years of the twentieth century was to give rise to some of Britain's most significant and collectable Art Deco pots. Happily, the story has not ended as the Middleport Pottery, now home to Burgess, Dorling and Leigh, enters a new and exciting phase of its life in the twenty first century. It begins with the birth of its founders, Frederick Rathbone Burgess in1832 and William Leigh twelve years earlier in 1820.

Background

The Britain into which the founders of Burgess & Leigh were born, although still recovering from the recent Napoleonic Wars, was the most industrialised nation in the world and poised to become the leading manufacturing country. A new king, George IV, had established himself as an enthusiastic patron of the arts and architecture. As Prince Regent, he had encouraged the redesign of a new and stylish Georgian London whose elegant squares and terraces became home to an increasing number of merchants and entrepreneurs made rich by the first phase of the Industrial Revolution. It was largely in the cities in the Midlands and north of England that the new manufacturing industries flourished, places like Birmingham, Liverpool, Manchester and north Staffordshire, the main centre of the English pottery industry and birthplace of Burgess & Leigh.

The six towns, Tunstall, Burslem, Hanley, Stoke, Fenton and Longton, which were federated in 1910 and which since 1925 have comprised the city of Stoke-on-Trent in north Staffordshire, are still known today as the 'Potteries', the only region in England to be named after its trade. A world away from the elegant squares of London, a journalist wrote in the *Monthly Magazine* of 1823:

An engraving of Burslem and Longport, c.1843.

'On entering these towns, the first peculiarity that arrests the stranger's attention is the irregular and straggling style in which they are built; for having most of them sprung up from small beginnings into their present magnitude, in less than half a century, the additions have been made from time to time just as necessity demanded, but without any determinate plan, or the slightest regard to appearance and orderly arrangement. The result has been the strangest confusion that 'tis possible to conceive. Milton's line, 'Wild, without rule or art', was never before half so happily illustrated.'[1]

Pottery ladies in the 1820s. An engraving from *Hone's Everyday Book*, Vol. 2, 1827, recently discovered at the Middleport Pottery.

But the straggling towns had something that more pleasant places did not. Since the late seventeenth century, the area had been the country's foremost centre for ceramic manufacture owing to its favourable geological conditions, close to abundant clay fields and, more importantly, easily accessible outcrops of coal required for pottery firing. As Arnold Bennett, whose fictionalised stories of his home-town made him one of England's greatest novelists of Edwardian times, was to write: *The Potteries is the Potteries because on that precise spot of the surface of the British Empire there were deposits of clay and of quick-burning coal close to the surface. If this was not an invitation on the part of Nature to make pots, what was it?*[2] Thus, generations of families working in pottery production provided the area with a highly skilled local workforce. Although geographically isolated, the opening of the Trent and Mersey Canal in 1777 had facilitated cheap and efficient transportation to and from north Staffordshire; raw materials, such as clays from Dorset, Devon and Cornwall and flints from southern England, were delivered to the Potteries by canal narrowboats, which safely carried a variety of ceramic goods out to the ports of London, Liverpool and Manchester for export overseas.

The technological advances made in the British pottery industry by the early 1800s were to ensure its global pre-eminence throughout the nineteenth century; fine earthenware, stoneware, bone china and stone china were all in regular production and a variety of complex moulded shapes manufactured in different styles of decoration using techniques such as transfer-printing. A few far-sighted manufacturers, such as the Josiahs, Wedgwood and Spode, had already introduced steam power to their works whilst machinery for mass-production, such as the 'jigger' and 'jolley' for making flat- and holloware pottery, were to follow later in the nineteenth century. Small family-run pottery workshops were fast being replaced by the factory system, operating on a division of labour whereby each employee was involved in a single process.

Led by the example set a generation earlier by such 'master' potters as Wedgwood, Spode, Minton, Ridgway and Davenport, a new breed of entrepreneurial potter had emerged, keen to exploit new markets both at home and overseas. Their mass production of consistently fine quality ceramic products satisfied all strata of society, not least the prosperous new middle classes wishing to furnish their homes with pottery that was attractive and economical, fashionable and functional.

Many of north Staffordshire's most successful pottery manufacturers were men of wealth, culture and influence. They offered shining examples, having 'risen through the ranks', to artisans labouring in the growing numbers of potbanks in the area. When Wedgwood, for example, had started his own business in 1759 in Burslem, the 'mother-town' and most important manufacturing centre of the Potteries, there had been some sixty-seven small 'potbanks' there, a number which had increased to over 300 at the time of his death in 1795.[3]

However, increased competition and a fluctuating trade, which was to see numerous depressions during the decades to come, made it a struggle for many small manufacturers to survive. That Burgess & Leigh, now Burgess, Dorling and Leigh, optimistically enters the twenty-first century is testament to the skills and strength of character of the company founders, Frederick Rathbone Burgess and William Leigh.

Early Lives of the Founders

Both Frederick Rathbone Burgess (1832-1895) and William Leigh (1820-1889) were born and spent their early working lives in Tunstall in the Potteries, then a comparatively new and well-ordered town described as *'pleasantly situated on the declivity of a considerable eminence... It is the chief liberty of the Parish of Wolstanton; has many respectable tradespeople in it; and its manufacturers rank high for talent and opulence. From it*

there are some very pleasing prospects, over much of the District, and its vicinity...'[4]

It is not recorded whether William Leigh, born in 1820, ever knew his parents. Orphaned whilst young, he was brought up by an aunt and uncle named Mawdsley[5] whose descendants later married into the Weatherby family of potters.[6] Details of William's early working life are scant. After leaving the Wesleyan Day School in Tunstall, he is thought to have started working either as a potter's printer[7] or a clay thrower for Podmore, Walker & Co.[8] at Newfield Potworks in Tunstall. An ambitious young man, William studied at evening school to gain a position in the offices of the company, eventually becoming Works Manager.[9]

William had already begun his first year of work, aged twelve, when his future partner, Frederick Rathbone Burgess, was born on 22nd November, 1832.[10] Potting was certainly in Frederick's blood; it is probable that his mother, Matilda, was descended from the family of Samuel and John Rathbone, china manufacturers in Tunstall (1812-1835), whilst his father, Richard, himself the son of a potter, was in partnership in the pottery firm Gibson & Burgess, which traded from c.1845 at the George Street Pottery, also in Tunstall.[11] Frederick's early career is not documented although a Frederick R. Burgess was listed in Kelly's trade directory of 1860 as a shopkeeper in Sneyd Street, Tunstall. If one and the same, it was perhaps an unlikely career start for a pottery manufacturer but would have proved good preparation for the business and financial role Frederick was to perform for Burgess & Leigh.

The two co-founders, as is so often the case in a successful partnership, were very different but complementary characters. Although both men were eager to succeed in business, William Leigh from an early age also demonstrated a keen social conscience which was fostered by his regular attendance at one of the Potteries' many Methodist churches. Numerous eminent potters were amongst those elected as church elders and their public spiritedness doubtless inspired William to take an active role within the local community in his later years. An interesting reference to the young William, which throws light both on his background and character, was made in Charles Shaw's autobiography *When I Was a Child*. Originally published as a series of articles in the *Staffordshire Sentinel* in the 1890s, Shaw's memories are of a childhood spent in Tunstall and Burslem half a century earlier when, exacerbated by the Corn Laws, deprivation amongst Britain's working classes was very severe. Shaw's first-hand experience brings to life the harsh conditions of child employment in the Potteries, which were exposed in the government commissioned Scrivens Report of 1843. Under the title, *A Warm Heart Under a White Apron*, Shaw wrote of William Leigh:

> *'One particular Sunday night, when the younger ones were crying for food, and hardly any fire in the grate, there came a knock at the door, and a young potter came in. He knew our family well, and though not related directly, he was so indirectly. He carried signs of being better off than most working potters, as he was, for he had some private means besides his weekly earnings. He was dressed in black, with the usual potter's white apron rolled round his body, just over his waistcoat pockets. It was usual to wear a white apron in those days, even during holidays.... What makes me remember so vividly the position of this*

William Leigh, 1820-1899.

Frederick Rathbone Burgess, 1832-1895.

particular apron, was that after this young visitor had been in the house a short time, and had heard the story of our need, I saw him put this thumb and finger down between his apron and his waistcoat. When he brought them back I saw a silvery gleam between his finger and thumb, and in a very few minutes I saw bread and butter on our table. I always connected the apron with that change on our table, and the feast which followed. This young potter I gratefully remember, too, for another reason. His name was William Leigh. He was then, as in his after life, of studious habits, modest, and upright in all his ways, and whose life had much fragrance and sweetness in it. He found out, from seeing me reading at nights when he came to our house, that I was fond of reading, and up to the time of going to the workhouse he regularly supplied me with books, and these were as precious as the bread he gave us. It was he who first opened to me the great world of literature, and from that day I have known "the world of books is still the world".'

William Leigh would have been in his early twenties at the time of Shaw's childhood. He had witnessed, during the reign of William IV (1830-1837) and in the years following Queen Victoria's coronation, a period of great social and industrial unrest in north Staffordshire. This had culminated in riots provoked by the Chartists (a pro working-class movement for universal male suffrage). At the most violent demonstration, initiated by miners striking for better pay, an angry mob rampaged through the Potteries damaging the property of establishment officials: tax collectors, the police and magistrates. Even members of the church were a target:

'the rector of Longton, a man noted for the excellence of his wine cellar, [who] had advised the poor to use dock leaves as a substitute for coffee… did not have many glass panes left in his windows by the time the riot was over'![12] …'a charge was made by the Dragoons and constables upon the rioters, who then dispersed in all directions, and thus the authority of the law vindicated, and anarchy subdued at Burslem on the memorable 16th of August, 1842'.[13]

Amongst the rioters was a number of potters. Their dissatisfaction with the abuse of power of some of their employers had led them to form numerous unions which during the 1820s-1840s period battled with the master potters' more powerful Chamber of Commerce. Strikes were called on various complex employment issues, many of which were to rumble on, unresolved, well into the next century. They included the 'truck' system (payment in kind); minimum selling prices (based on a 'scale' of manufacturing 'rates' for each article, according to size, shape, body and decoration); and the allowance system (which reduced potters' wages when trade was poor). The 'yearly bond' (an annual hiring system which tied a potter to his employer for twelve months irrespective of whether there was paid work for him) was abolished in 1866. However, standardisation of pottery trade sizes and piece rates (a system of sizing and counting individual articles to the 'dozen' to determine the wages of different operatives)[14] remained a bone of contention between master potter and his employees for many years; in 1908 it was written *'The whole system of Potter's Arithmetic is antiquated and absurd, an anomaly and a nuisance, and altogether unreasonable, but no steps yet have been taken to abolish or supersede it.'*[15] (The 'count-to-the-dozen' was used at the Middleport Pottery until the late 1970s and is still in use in some potteries

'Potters' arithmetic… an anomaly and a nuisance'. Prices paid per 'dozen' articles made to Burgess & Leigh throwers and printers during the 1860s and 1870s.

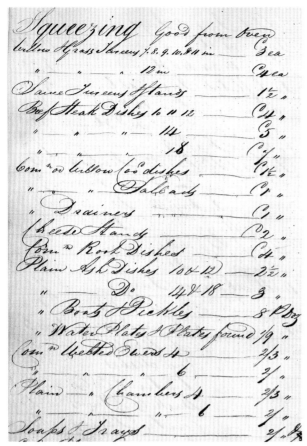

List of prices paid for *'Squeezing'* articles subsequently produced *'Good from Oven'*, c.1860s.

The bookplate of Frederick Rathbone Burgess, c.1860.

'Burleigh' and *'Business'*, entries made in William Leigh's *Index Rerum*, c.1855.

today!) The 'good from oven' ruling (whereby a potter was paid not for his part in the pottery process but only for items which were successfully fired in the kiln) was also a continuing source of discontent which was only finally brought to an end for all sections of the industry in 1964. By the late 1840s, this continuing abuse of labour coupled with fear of unemployment through the proposed introduction of the new jigger and jolley, led a number of pottery workers to join a largely unsuccessful scheme to emigrate to Pottersville, Wisconsin in America.

William Leigh, however, chose to remain in his hometown where experience of potters' hardships was to influence his later role as a compassionate and benevolent employer. The source of what Shaw describes as William's 'private means' is not known but any funds could not have been substantial as subsequent reports make much of his being a self-made man. Indeed, he took the popular Victorian ethos of self-improvement very much to heart. From 1855, he kept a journal, the *'Index Rerum'*, based on a template by a Reverend John Todd from Massachusetts. Now in company archives, this alphabetical *'Index of Subjects'* was *'intended as a manual to aid the Student and Professional Man in preparing himself for Usefulness'*. William's fine copperplate handwriting records numerous quotations and a miscellany of information for future contemplation and edification. Amongst them, mottoes perhaps for the future business style of Burgess & Leigh: *'Be not afraid to work with your own hands and diligently too,' 'A cat in gloves catches no mice'* and, very aptly: *'Be frugal. That which will not make a pot will make a pot lid'*!

As an ambitious young man, it was not long before William was making plans to leave Podmore, Walker & Co. in Tunstall, which from c.1834 also had an additional earthenware works at Swan Bank in Burslem. Indeed it was at the Swan Bank Pottery, near the Wedgwood Institute, that William formed a partnership with a James Whittingham and Benjamin Hancock.[16] By 1857 this company was trading as Hancock, Leigh & Co.[17] manufacturing printed earthenwares but five years later William was again ready to move on. On 5th April 1862 *The Staffordshire Advertiser* recorded that the partnership between the three men was dissolved, the notice being repeated the following week, quoting from the *London Gazette*.

The Central Pottery 1862-1868

Exactly how and when William Leigh came to meet Frederick Rathbone Burgess is not known. However, it was not until 1862, that the two men, aged forty-two and thirty years respectively, entered into a business partnership as earthenware manufacturers trading from the Central Pottery. As its name implies, the pottery was in the middle

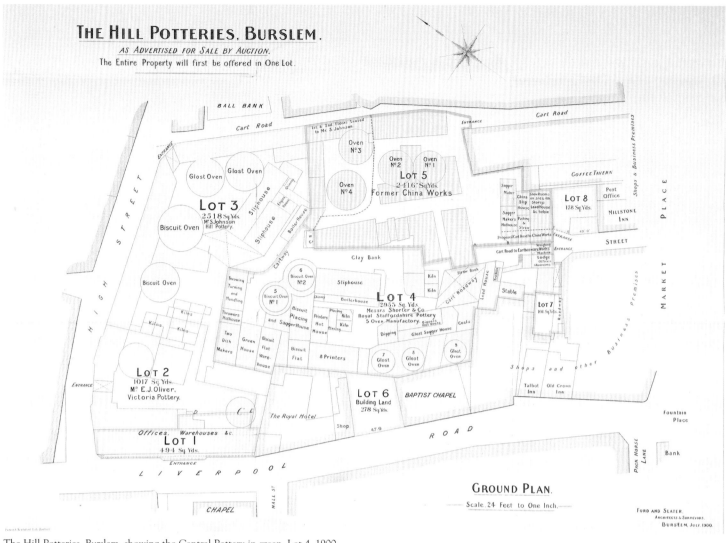

The Hill Potteries, Burslem, showing the Central Pottery in green, Lot 4, 1900.

Messrs. Burgess & Leigh's first bank account book, 1862.

A letter from Burgess & Leigh, 28th July, 1863, to a customer regarding their acquisition of Hulme's patterns.

of Burslem, close to Market Place, and was one of several separate potteries which together made up the Hill Potteries Works. The original occupiers of the Central Pottery are not known but local trade directories indicate that Peter Hopkins & Co., earthenware manufacturers, were succeeded as tenants in c.1842-1843 by T. & R. Boote, specialising then in Parian statuary and vases.[18] Described as having '1 *biscuit, 2 glost ovens, 2 hardening, 1 enamel kiln, frit kiln, slip kiln for 30 tons per week and fixtures – could be enlarged'*, *The Staffordshire Advertiser* had to advertise its lease several times between 1849 and 1850 before the Central Pottery welcomed its next occupants, the earthenware manufacturers Hulme & Booth, in 1851.[19]

1851 was a significant year for Victorian Britain as it hosted the Great Exhibition of Works of Industry of All Nations at the Crystal Palace in London. Attracting more than six million visitors, the exhibition's profits secured a site for the South Kensington (now the Victoria and Albert) Museum. In its bid to promote international trade, it was the first of the International Exhibitions to showcase the pottery industry in north Staffordshire, which at that time employed some 20,000 people in more than 150 established factories.[20] Hulme & Booth, then in their first year of trading, did not exhibit at the Great Exhibition and, indeed, ten years later the partnership had ended, leaving Thomas Hulme as the sole tenant of the Central Pottery. It was not long before Hulme also decided to quit the business and in 1862 Frederick Rathbone Burgess and William Leigh took over his tenancy at the Central Pottery, simultaneously acquiring his patterns, shape moulds and customers.[21] As confirmed by trade directories,[22] the partners immediately started trading under their own company name, Burgess & Leigh.

Today, Burgess, Dorling & Leigh are fortunate in having a sizeable and fairly comprehensive documentary archive. Although significantly lacking in original finished artwork, the material is invaluable in piecing together the history of the company and its wares. All records indicate that the founders were confident and experienced businessmen who quickly established themselves as efficient, reliable manufacturers. It was just as well. In spite of the best attempts to boost trade by holding the International Exhibition in London, 1862 was not a good time to start a business. The Civil War in America had just started and the Staffordshire pottery industry's well-established trade to that country was disrupted as crates full of ware awaiting payment accumulated at Runcorn (the Trent and Mersey canal port) and Anderton (where the Anderton Company, canal carriers, provided warehousing).

Although the state of the American economy was to remain unstable for several years, Burgess & Leigh optimistically joined those potteries (approximately a third[23] of the area's total) which then produced wares for the 'Lancashire trade', that is for export to the USA and other overseas countries through the Lancashire ports of Liverpool and Manchester. Although some export markets demanded special types of ware or designs, for instance, the Americans showed a preference for ironstone and white granite (in effect, cheap earthenware substitutes for French porcelain) there was very little difference then between 'foreign' orders and those produced for the home trade.

The risks of trading with America and other overseas markets at that time were, in fact, arguably less for Burgess & Leigh than for the merchants, the 'middle men', who, whilst taking a commission, also bore much of the costs involved. From the early 1860s, the company was amongst a number of local potteries supplying crates of ware to J. & G. Meakin of Hanley, manufacturers who exported their own and other pottery for sale through their retail outlet in New York. They also took regular orders from Goddard & Burgess of Longton who exported Staffordshire pottery to their New York showroom, which was visited by retailers from all over the USA.

Shipping agents based in the major English ports played an important role as merchants in the pottery import and export trade. In 1863 Messrs Nuttall of Liverpool sent out fifty crates of Burgess & Leigh earthenware to Pernambuco in Brazil. The following year, Thomas Irving, a shipping agent of 17 Gracechurch Street in London, had brought the company the custom of a Mr Pond of Launceston in Tasmania. Crates were regularly sent to shipping agents Morely & Co. of Hull for export to Mr J. Hassall, a dealer in Christiania (now Oslo) in Norway.

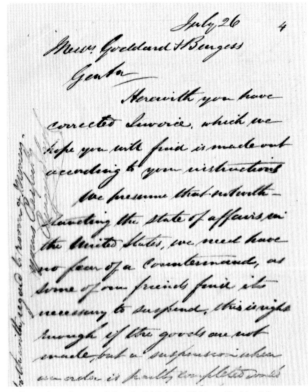

A letter from Burgess & Leigh, 26th July, 1864, to Goddard & Burgess regarding trade with America during the Civil War.

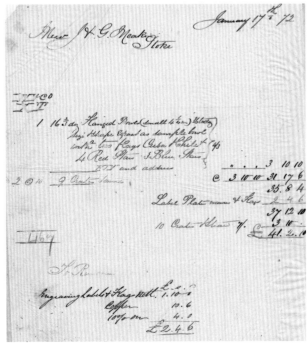

An order for Burgess, Leigh & Co. to supply badged wares featuring the flags of Cuba and Chile, 17th January, 1872.

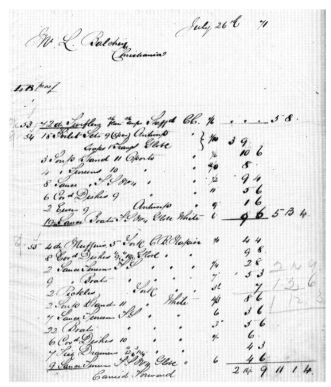

An order dated 26th July, 1871 for wares to Christiania, now Olso, in Norway.

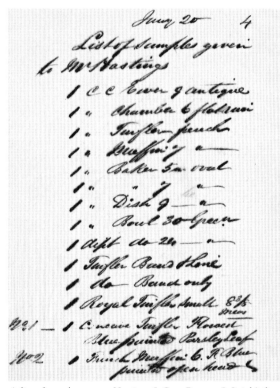

A list of samples sent to Hastings & Son, Burgess & Leigh's first US agents in New York in 1864.

Sometimes, the company received orders directly; in 1864 'terms for earthenware suitable for the Canadian market' were quoted to Mr Blumenthal, a customer inherited from Thomas Hulme. Occasionally, overseas retailers would visit the Potteries themselves to seek out goods for their customers. For instance, the same year, Burgess & Leigh provided photographs and samples for Mr J. S. Hastings of Boston, America. When orders followed within a few months, the company went so far as to appoint Hastings & Son as their New York agents, becoming one of the first potteries with an overseas agency. However, the business relationship was soon strained owing to Hastings' cancellation of orders and Burgess & Leigh's inability then to produce bulk wares in the required time scale. In January 1865, Burgess & Leigh felt 'compelled' to write to J. S. Hastings & Son withdrawing their agency unless new terms could be agreed: that payment should be made to Burgess & Leigh 'in cash in Liverpool or First Class Bills, if in cash five per cent plus two-and-a-half per cent, if in Bills of Exchange only five per cent'; that smaller orders of 'six to eight crates a week' were acceptable; and that 'proper time be given to execute the order'. Should Hastings & Son require a reference, then Burgess & Leigh were able to supply one, stating confidently that they were 'known in New York'.

As a new and positive relationship developed between Britain and America in the later 1860s, attempts were made by the pottery industry to facilitate trade between the two countries by the establishment in Tunstall of a full-time US consul who processed and recorded all invoices. However, overseas trade continued to fluctuate and Burgess & Leigh realised the importance of establishing a reliable UK home market. To this end, they appointed a Mr E. Swann as the company's first commercial 'traveller' or salesman. This may have been Ebenezer Swann, who, until 11th January, 1862, was in partnership with Elizabeth Mills manufacturing china, earthenware and parian in Hanley.[24] Given responsibility for both the London and 'country journeys', Swann would travel wherever possible by train or stagecoach, following the usual practice of hiring 'stock rooms' in hotels up and down the country to which potential retailers would be invited to view – and hopefully stock – the company's latest lines.[25] Swann's early employment was not without hitches and correspondence to him from Burgess & Leigh suggests that he was given to quoting prices somewhat lower than required as well as suggesting new patterns rather than pushing the old ones. Disagreements may have prompted him to leave England for a short time to try his luck in America. During this time a Mr James Burgess (not known to be related to Frederick Rathbone) was taken on to cover the country journeys. However, the recalcitrant Swann must have proved his worth; in 1864 Burgess & Leigh renewed his contract, writing:

'... we guarantee you commission on £300 at five per cent on account that you visit the same towns as you did the last journey and use every possible effort to attain orders at two and a half per cent discount for cash, instead of five per cent, in every case where our neighbours are asking and offering the same or more. The London journey to be taken on commission, as before, but two and a half per cent less discount to be allowed off goods at the old prices... If the country orders account to more than £300, commission to be paid on the whole.'

By 1863, the company was able to boast 180 'ledger accounts' in all areas of the United Kingdom. Swann was at that time a key employee, although the nature of his job did not require him to be based at the Central Pottery with the production staff. An Account Book records that Burgess & Leigh paid out in the spring of 1862 a total of thirty-four wage 'packets' to factory workers. When large well-established potteries employed several hundreds,[26] this number may seem comparatively small. In fact, there may

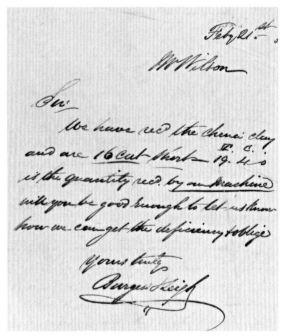

Burgess & Leigh express their concerns over complaints of crazed ware to their traveller, Mr Swann, 1864.

and beakers and associated dressing table items, such as hair tidies, powder boxes and ring trays.

Initially most of the company's earliest shapes would have been acquired from Hulme but there is evidence that outside agencies or suppliers were used to adapt or possibly produce new shapes. A letter addressed to a Mr J. Latham on 3rd August, 1864 saw Burgess & Leigh complaining: _'You have sent us the saucer plate with little alteration in it and no improvement, and… with regard to style, we cannot use it and shall not pay for it.'_

From the outset the company strove to maintain a balance between the cost and quality of their products. Complaints from Primavesi & Son, an important account in south Wales, regarding poor packing and crazing of ware brought profuse apologies from Burgess & Leigh and a determination that such errors should not happen again. Suppliers of poor quality or overpriced raw materials, equipment and designs were rapidly taken to task (as were poor workers). Given the unpredictable nature of pottery manufacture, some inferior ware was inevitably produced, for which there was always a ready market; in common with most manufacturers, Burgess & Leigh sold some 'seconds', _'at a quarter less than best'_, occasionally using it to fill a crate.

When acceptable to the company's high standards, shapes were decorated using a variety of different techniques. What appears to be the company's first pattern book, dating from c.1862-c.1875, has only recently been discovered under several layers of coal dust in a disused part of the factory! Although for the main part unillustrated, this provides a list of the first 1,260 or so named patterns with a brief description of their decoration. As one might expect, utilitarian kitchen- and sanitary wares were usually given either a plain cream-coloured glaze (usually abbreviated to 'C.C'.) or a simple painted band or line decoration. When especially commissioned for the kitchens and dining rooms of institutions such as colleges, hotels, tearooms, mess rooms and hospitals, these wares might also be given a simple printed badge or crest which were recorded in special notebooks. (Broadmoor and Manchester Royal Infirmary hospitals both ordered Burgess & Leigh badged wares during

well have been more employees as, under the 'butty' system of employment, each departmental foreman or woman was responsible for paying a number of assistants or apprentices out of his or her wages. Nonetheless, the impression gained is of a small, tightly run works where employers kept a close eye on their workers, treating them firmly but fairly in return for loyalty, honesty and hard work.

Burgess & Leigh's Early Products

Size and workmen's prices books, estimate notebooks, warehouse orders, and copies of invoices all provide useful guides to the company's early wares. They indicate that from its founding, Burgess & Leigh concentrated their production on sound quality, competitively priced, utilitarian, earthenwares; kitchen wares; dinner- and tea wares; sanitary or hospital wares, (ceramic having proved itself to be an ideally durable and hygienic material for such products); and toiletwares.

Interestingly, it was for its 'toilet sets' that Burgess & Leigh became especially well known and, in the days before every house had a bathroom, they were indispensable items for the bedroom washstand. They usually comprised combinations of jugs or ewers (usually called 'pitchers' in North America) and basins, a slop pail for waste water and a couple of chamber pots. Additional items included soap and sponge dishes, small drinking mugs, toothbrush boxes

Suppliers of china clay are taken to task, 1865.

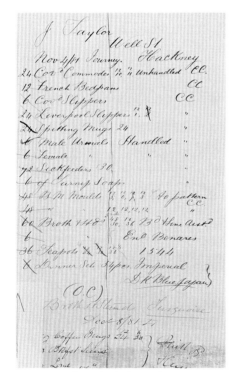

Throwers' price list for 1865 and 1866 showing utilitarian wares produced at the Central Pottery.

John Lockett & Co, Longton, catalogue page showing sanitary and hospital wares of the sort Burgess & Leigh produced from the 1860s. Burgess & Leigh were to take over this company in 1960.

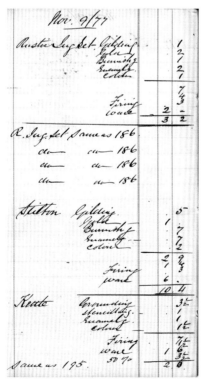

An East London order for hospital wares, 1881.

A breakdown of decorating costs, 1877.

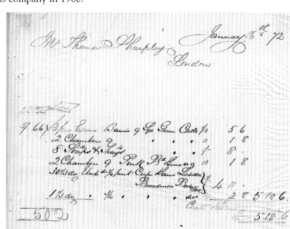

Badged hospital wares for Broadmoor Hospital, 1872.

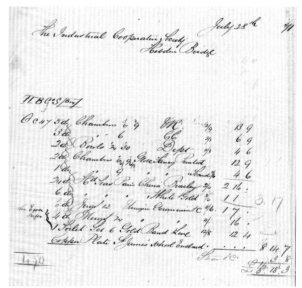

An order for badged wares for St James' School is placed by the Industrial Cooperative Society, Hebden Bridge, in 1871.

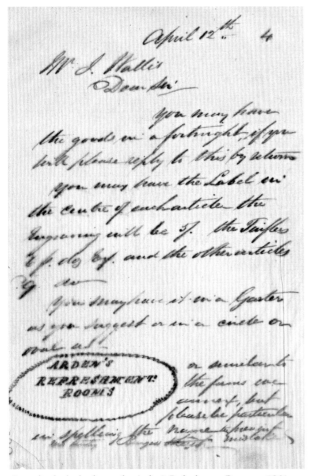

An order for badged ware for Arden's Refreshment Rooms, c.1864.

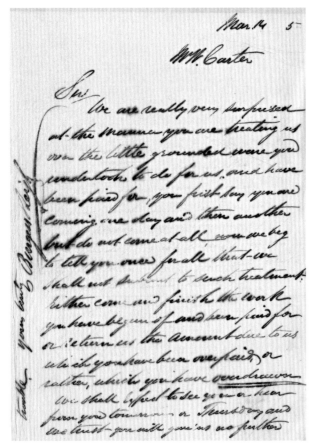

Burgess & Leigh make their displeasure felt to groundlayer, Mr Carter, in 1865.

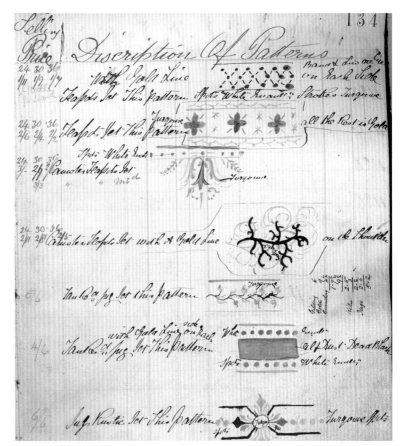

Burgess & Leigh's first pattern book c.1862-c.1875 recently discovered under several layers of coal dust at the Middleport Pottery.

Asiatic Pheasant with its distinctive decorative backstamp incorporating the initials 'B&L'. Illustration is from Burgess & Leigh's Print Record Book, compiled from tissue 'pulls' from copper engravings.

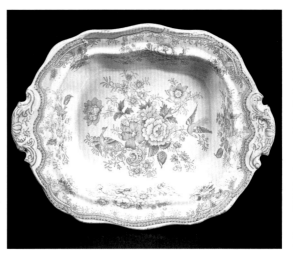

Moulded dish decorated with *Asiatic Pheasant* made by Burgess & Leigh at the Hill Pottery in 1888, 12¼ins x 9½ins (31cms x 24cms). The company first produced the pattern at the Central Pottery in 1862 in pale blue, pink and purple colourways.

Lidstone's ode to Burgess & Leigh published in *'The Thirteenth Londoniad: (Complete in itself) Giving a Full Description of the principal Establishments in the Potteries'*, 1866.[29]

the early 1860s-1870s.) Some items of inexpensive table and kitchen ware might also be 'sponged' (dabbed with a colour-infused sponge); 'checkered' (decorated with a two-toned ground pattern resembling a checkerboard); 'dipped' (decorated with 'slip' or liquid clay); or, occasionally, 'diced' or 'sprigged' with low-relief decoration.

Ranges of dinner-, tea- and toiletware items were more usually decorated with a printed pattern which might also be available with gilding or on-glaze enamel colours (made from metallic oxides and glaze). Amongst other more expensive lines were a few patterns requiring coloured grounds (using powdered colour dusted on to an oiled surface). The Pattern Book records costlier toiletwares featuring *'gold edge and line and footline'* and hand-painted with *'grass and butterflies'* or *'begonias'* by a *'William Hartshorne'* (also recorded in Spode Museum archives as painting groups of flowers for Copeland in c.1869).[27] Another toilet set and *Rustic* shaped jugs were gilded with hand-painted floral subjects by *'Dewsbury'*. These are the only artists' or decorators' names to appear in the Pattern

Book and it is interesting that in October 1864, Burgess & Leigh had written to Swann informing him *'that we have set two experienced enamellers on and wish to keep them, we have also set another jug maker on.'*

A useful source for some of the company's early wares is a poem included in *'The Thirteenth Londoniad: (Complete in Itself) Giving A Full Description of the Principal Establishments in the Potteries'*.[28] This was written and published by the itinerant and opportunist Mr James Torrington Spencer Lidstone in 1866. Though something of a Miltonian epic there are useful descriptions of not only toilet sets; breakfast and teasets; but also jelly moulds (now in production again by Burgess, Dorling & Leigh, from the same moulds); plain and fluted pudding bowls; slop jars; toy (miniature) tea sets; fluted, rice and plain-shaped nappies (small circular or oval baking bowls) and, more exotic to Victorian eyes, a relief-moulded *'Giraffe'* jug.

Pattern names mentioned are: *Fibre* (a 'sheet' or all-over pattern), *Swan, Old Broseley, Paris, Pekin, Lily, Bouquet* and *Asiatic Pheasant*. At that time, *Asiatic Pheasant* was the second most popular blue printed pattern after *Willow* (also made by Burgess & Leigh then). Produced by over sixty different potteries in the nineteenth century, Burgess, Dorling & Leigh is one of only two potteries to manufacture *Asiatic Pheasant* today: the Unicorn Pottery (part of the Wedgwood Group) produce a dark blue version whilst that of Burgess, Dorling & Leigh remains truer to the original pale blue. (Burgess & Leigh also produced it in pink and purple as early as 1862.) Interestingly, it is thought that William Leigh's employer, Podmore, Walker & Co., was the first pottery to produce *Asiatic Pheasant* in c.1834.

Engraving and Underglaze Transfer Printing

It was Josiah Spode who first perfected the technique of underglaze printing in blue on earthenware in 1784. This had followed a fashion for 'blue and white' pottery in imitation of Chinese porcelain, whose importation into Britain was much reduced after c.1799 by the high rate of duty. Early oriental-style patterns, such as *Willow*, had quickly been joined by those with British and European themes. Before the copyright law of 1842, these were copied from a wealth of published sources featuring engraved prints. Patterns depicted views of the Grand Tour and foreign travel; classical subjects; rural pursuits and scenes; botanical and animal studies; and literary and historical scenes. Between 1800 and c.1835, such affordable blue and white patterned earthenwares were immensely popular with all classes of people, both at home and overseas. North America was a particularly profitable market and often had its own printed patterns. Staffordshire potters were not slow to take advantage of this demand, producing a huge variety of useful table and toiletwares.

By the time that Burgess & Leigh started trading, the 'Golden Age' of blue and white wares was over. The introduction during the 1830s of new underglaze colours (predominantly pink, green and brown) had gone some way to extending the market in printed wares but the years up to 1870 had seen a decrease in both their quantity and quality.[30] Fortunately, the later nineteenth century was to see something of a revival of interest, especially in oriental-inspired design. The market was thus still a viable one and Burgess & Leigh set about mastering the traditional skills of underglaze transfer printing.

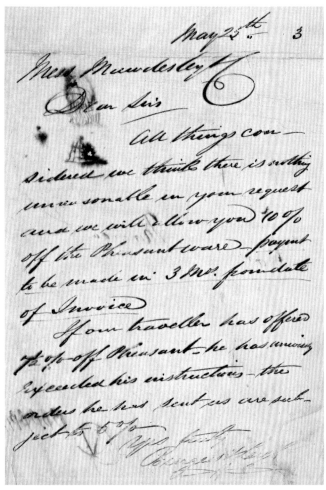

A generous discount is allowed on 'Pheasant Ware' to customer Messrs Mawdesley & Co. on 25th May, 1863.

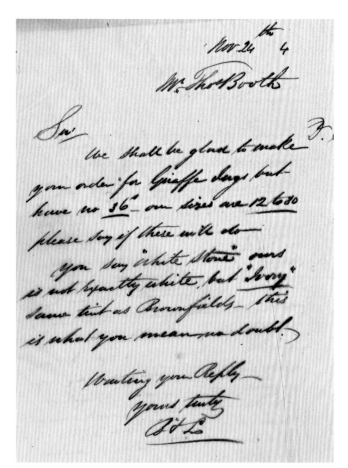

An order for Burgess & Leigh's *Giraffe* jug received in 1864, the year its design was registered at the Patent Office.

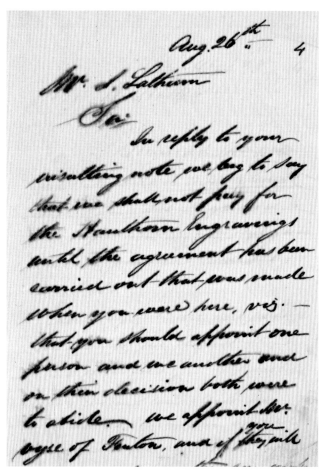

A disagreement between Burgess & Leigh and Mr J. Latham over his engraving of the pattern *Hawthorn* in 1864.

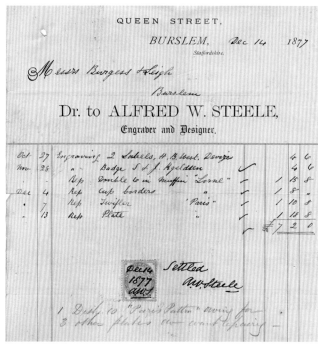

Engraver and Designer Alfred W. Steele submits his bill, December 1877.

This complex process involved many people and businesses but at its heart was the engraver, a highly skilled (and well-paid) artist/craftsman who, using sharp tools, a graver for lines and a punch for dots, cut the pattern into a copperplate. Each pattern had to be engraved to fit whatever shape or shapes of pottery it was required to decorate, no easy matter given the many complex holloware shapes

Printed design for *Etruscan Vases*, a pattern inspired by Sir William Hamilton's eighteenth-century volumes on antique vases.

Etruscan Vases, as illustrated in the Print Record Book.

which might make up a full dinner service. The completed copperplate became the permanent image of a pattern from which many transfers could be printed.

In each pottery producing transfer-printed wares there was a Printing Department with one or more teams comprising a male printer; his female transferrers; a cutter, usually a young girl; and an apprentice, of any age! The process involved the printer rubbing colour (a mixture of metallic oxides with oil) into the copperplate engraving, which he had warmed on a hot plate. A pre-cut sheet of 'pottery tissue' paper, moistened with a soap and water 'size' to render it both flexible and impervious to oil, was then placed on to the copperplate engraving. In the early 1800s, a flat copperplate was used which, with its application of paper tissue, the printer would place on a plank and lever through the two rollers of his press. This forced the colour in the engraving on to the paper, which was then carefully 'pulled' from the copperplate. By the First World War, Burgess & Leigh had also purchased additional 'roller' printing presses whereby the pattern was engraved on to a cylindrical copper roller rather than a flat copperplate. This enabled the printing of continuous sheets of paper 'transfers', a more economical process for larger quantities of ware (when quality was not paramount) which was adopted by most potteries.

In the transferring area, a cutter cut the transfer print into the shape required and passed it to the transferrer. She skilfully positioned each still tacky transfer print on to the porous biscuit (once-fired) ware, ensuring the pattern fitted accurately and neatly to each shape. Being careful to avoid any tearing, her apprentice rubbed down the print with a stiff bristle brush and soft soap to make certain the colour transferred effectively. The paper was then washed off with water to leave only the printed pattern, which was fixed by a further firing in a 'hardening' kiln prior to glazing. Today, Burgess, Dorling & Leigh continue to manufacture using this highly skilled, traditional method.

During the nineteenth century, engravers were much in demand not only to create new patterns but also to copy existing designs or adapt them for different shapes and to repair or replace worn-out copperplates. There was also a flourishing trade in second-hand copperplates. Many were sold on, either privately or through auction, when pottery manufacturers ceased trading. Burgess & Leigh made numerous purchases[31] throughout the nineteenth and twentieth centuries, enabling them to continue reproducing a variety of popular printed patterns.

Pottery manufacturers usually employed their own 'in-house' engraver or team of engravers to design, develop and maintain copperplates. Occasionally, they would also use the services of the many engraving businesses or workshops which had been established in the Potteries and which were later to evolve into general pottery suppliers. Burgess & Leigh initially used outside workers or businesses, the less than satisfactory expertise of Mr J. Latham being sought for the engraving of the *Hawthorn* pattern in 1864.[32] Later, the company also employed their own engraver or team of engravers; according to correspondence from Frederick Burgess dated 1878, the company was *'paying £4 5s 0d per week for engraving on the works'*. Later correspondence also includes a bill from an engraver, Alfred W. Steele of Queen Street, Burslem, and a request addressed to Baddeley & Heath of Burslem for an estimate for their re-engraving of plates in the *Pamona* pattern.

Whilst many potteries, pre-copyright law, could manufacture the same or very similar patterns and models, afterwards they were eager to develop, in addition, their own exclusive designs. Burgess & Leigh were no exception and early examples include those mentioned in the *Londoniad*: *'their peculiar'* tableware pattern, *Premier*. To prevent

Antique-shaped mug, printed *Chariots* pattern on turquoise ground, Greek Key border to rim, gilded, c.1868-1877. Height 8cm (3¼ins).

pirating, Burgess & Leigh joined other pottery manufacturers in registering their original designs (and others whose patents they might have acquired) at the Patent Office in London. Another early tableware pattern to be registered, with number 194537 on 17th January, 1866,[33] was the *Barberini Vase* pattern (so named after the Roman cameo-glass vase, reproduced as *The Portland Vase* in jasper by Wedgwood in 1789). Together with another early pattern, *Chariots*, this was most probably inspired by prints reproduced in Sir William Hamilton's influential books on antique vases published in 1795, a volume of which the company possessed.

Although many of Burgess & Leigh's early copper engravings were inevitably lost or destroyed over the years, a large number are still in the possession of Burgess, Dorling & Leigh. One such is engraved with the name *Kossuth* after the exiled Hungarian revolutionary who visited the Potteries in 1854. This plate also bears the name of the pattern's original manufacturer, Hulme & Booth. On acquiring a new copperplate, the new owner might have his own trade name engraved on it. Alternatively, he might incorporate either his name or initials into the existing backstamp pattern cartouche, which might be included alongside the design on copperplates. Sometimes, however, no manufacturer's mark was used and, with much pirating of patterns, attribution can be problematic. Burgess & Leigh were amongst those companies which did not always mark their early wares. Its first known mark is thought to be a simple 'B & L', either impressed and perhaps including the year of manufacture, or printed and possibly incorporating the word BURSLEM. Later, the company was to take great pride in the variety of its printed marks, some of which included a pattern name.

The Hill Pottery

A new Burgess & Leigh backstamp was engraved soon after 1868 when an expansion in business brought about a move from the Central Pottery. Its state of repair had been a cause for complaint as early as 1863 when the partners wrote to a Mr Hales, with regard to *'the stoppage of the watercourse from our manufactory'*, protesting that *'the stench arising from the water in our cellar is unbearable'*! Five years on, they were glad to take advantage of the vacancy of the adjoining Hill Pottery, also part of the larger site, confusingly known as the

The Hill Pottery, Burslem, rebuilt for Samuel Alcock in 1839 and part-leased by Burgess & Leigh from 1868-1888. (Engraving from J. Ward, *The Borough of Stoke-upon-Trent*, 1843.)

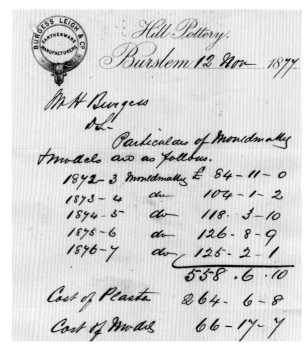

Burgess, Leigh & Co.'s mould-making costs between 1872 and 1877.

Hill Potteries Works. The Hill Pottery had been home from 1828-1859 to Samuel Alcock & Co, successful manufacturers of porcelain, parian and earthenware. There then followed several years when the works were used by a succession of potters; Sir James Duke and Nephews traded there until 1863, followed for a very brief period by Thomas Ford. Richard Daniel took over the works in 1864 manufacturing both earthenware and porcelain but the venture, which traded under the name *'Hill Pottery Company Ltd, late S. Alcock & Co.'*, was short-lived and was put into liquidation in 1867. Thomas Ford again took possession, dividing it into separate china and earthenware works; Alcock and Diggory leased the china department and Burgess & Leigh the earthenware.

It was in 1839, during Samuel Alcock's ownership, that the Hill Pottery was rebuilt at some expense in an extravagantly Venetian style. Described by Ward in *The Borough of Stoke-upon-Trent in 1843* as *'the most striking and ornamental object of its kind within the precincts of the borough'*, it was later fictionalised by Arnold Bennett, in one of his Five Towns novels, *Clayhanger*, as the building which inspired his hero Edwin Clayhanger to become an architect. Alcock's Hill Pottery was praised not only as an impressive building but also for its high standard of organisation; the government commissioned Scrivens' Report of 1843 described it as *'one of the largest and best conducted in the Potteries.'*[34] (Sadly, it was demolished in 1968). By the time of Burgess & Leigh's part-lease of the property, it was no longer modern and undoubtedly less well organised than it had been, a fact which was to influence the two partners when they came to plan the building of their own premises some twenty years later. Interestingly, an area of the Hill Pottery dating back to 1764 had previously been used as a chapel, where the great Methodist minister John Wesley had preached on one of several visits to Burslem. In spite of the Methodist upbringing of at least one of its founders, it was reported in 1881 that Burgess & Leigh had chosen to convert that part of the works into a *'mould chamber'* for the storage of plaster of Paris moulds![35]

A number of those moulds had been purchased from the

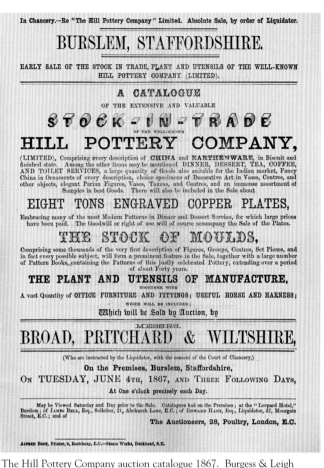

The Hill Pottery Company auction catalogue 1867. Burgess & Leigh acquired various moulds and copperplates at the sale.

Seasons, an early Burgess & Leigh pattern, shown here with 'beehive' backstamp previously used by Samuel Alcock & Co.

Receipt for a recipe for a Parian body, signed by Samuel Alcock, dated July 1861.

Hill Pottery in early June 1867. Then, as a catalogue in Burgess, Dorling & Leigh company archive indicates, a four-day auction saw the disposal of vast stocks of moulds, some eight tons of engraved copperplates and the factory plant and utensils previously owned by Samuel Alcock & Co. It is not known whether or not Burgess & Leigh chose to bid for Lot 764 '*Eight new brooms, 25 coal baskets, window frame and brush*' or, even less likely, Lot 741 '*Brown horse, aged*' but certainly their selection of Alcock moulds was to prove judicious in later years. The purchase of copperplate engravings bearing the 'beehive' mark used by Alcock & Co. (and numerous other continental and English pottery manufacturers) was immediately apparent in Burgess & Leigh's adaptation of the mark to include '*B & L*' and '*HILL POTTERY*' for use on its own printed wares. Also most likely acquired from the time of the company's first lease of the

Hill Pottery was a number of fascinating '*Receipt Books*'; some date back to the 1830s, listing such ceramic recipes as '*Parian body as used at the Hill Pottery, Burslem*'; '*Wedgwood's Beautiful Jasper*' and '*Mr Alcock's Best Flowing Wash*'.

Burgess, Leigh & Co.
The move to the Hill Pottery in 1868 seems to have instigated further changes for the company with Frederick and William being joined that year by a third partner, Frederick Lowndes-Goode. As indicated in the *Londoniad* ode, Lowndes-Goode had been working for the company from as early as 1866 at the Central Pottery. Unfortunately, no further biographical details are known of the new partner. Although he shared a name with the London china and glass retailer, T. S. Goode & Co., there is no evidence that he was related to the family.[36] It is possible that he was

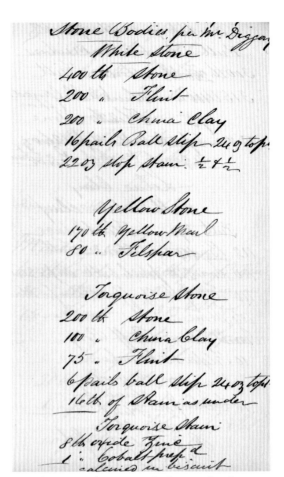

'Mr Alcock's best glazes', from a recipe book acquired on Burgess & Leigh's occupancy of the Hill Pottery in 1868.

More glaze recipes, from a recipe book acquired on Burgess & Leigh's occupancy of the Hill Pottery in 1868.

connected to Lowndes, earthenware manufacturers, who traded during the 1830s-1840s period in Burslem and Stoke.[37] Interestingly, Lowndes-Goode's name was not included in the new company title, Burgess, Leigh & Co., first recorded in *Kelly's Directory* for 1868, although he remained a partner for ten years. On the dissolution of the partnership on 6th April, 1878, he received a payment of just over £3,000 from the company, which, as indicated in subsequent directories from 1879, reverted once more to the name Burgess & Leigh.

The year 1868 had further significance for William Leigh. By then a married man with a family, he not only moved house from Tunstall to Hall Street, Burslem to be nearer to the Works, but was also joined at work by a son. Under their partnership agreement, Burgess & Leigh could bring only one son each into the business[38] and thus Edmund, William's eldest,[39] became the second generation of the Leigh family to join the company.

Quoting an American, Joseph C. Neal, William had written in his Index Rerum: *'The great secret of successful adventure is confidence – a fixed faith in the potency of your star; and he is who deficient in this belief will find it much better to remain at home, or to go ashore, than to tempt the chances of a storm.'*

Fortunately for William, and for the future of Burgess & Leigh, his son Edmund was to prove himself more than ready *'to tempt the chances of a storm'* in the rough seas of the pottery trade!

Envelope addressed to Lowndes-Goode, Burgess and Leigh's partner at the Hill Pottery from 1868 until 1878.

Envelope dated 1873 addressed to Burgess, Leigh and Co, the name by which the firm was known between 1868 and 1878.

CHAPTER TWO

BUILDING EMPIRES: Fathers and Sons 1868-1896

Edmund Leigh, JP, 1854-1924.

Pots and Politics: The Early Career of Edmund Leigh JP (1854-1924)

'Few men spend busier lives than Mr Leigh.'[1]

There seems to be in the history of every successful family business, one person who stands out as a motivating force and a catalyst for its enduring success. There can be no doubt that in the case of Burgess & Leigh, Edmund Leigh was that person. Building on the strong foundations laid by his father, under his dynamic leadership the Burgess & Leigh brand name became known worldwide. His influence was felt not only in the family business but also in public affairs where he made considerable impact on the municipal and political life of Stoke-on-Trent. Indeed, one of his sons was later to reflect that Edmund's life had been *'pots and politics though some might have placed them in reverse order!'*[2]

An invoice of 1871 bearing the confident signature of seventeen-year-old Edmund Leigh.

Born on 26th March, 1854 in Tunstall, Edmund's education at the Wesleyan Day School in Burslem reinforced the ethos of hard work and study which he had learnt from his father. His working life began aged fourteen at the Hill Pottery. Six years after its founding the company's workforce had risen considerably; a wages book for 1868 records the names of some fifty-five claymakers, printers, decorators, kiln firemen, warehousemen and packers who together received a combined payment of £95 18s 0d for the week ending 26th December, 1868. Under their expert tuition, the young Edmund learned all aspects of the pottery trade, knowledge and experience which was to earn him much respect from all those involved in the industry. From these early years he also developed, like his father, a keen concern for the welfare of pottery workers, which was to influence not only his political opinions and interest in industrial relations but also the management of his own business.

In 1872, when he was eighteen years old, and having acquired knowledge of the technical side of manufacture, Edmund became a commercial traveller for the company in order to gain experience of sales and marketing. (It is not known whether Swann was still employed at this time.) Surviving his very first sales trip, the notoriously difficult and remote *'Derbyshire Journey'*, Edmund went on to travel extensively in Britain, apparently with much success. Burgess & Leigh Works Manager, Edwin Kent, was to write of him: *'As a traveller, he was most tactful, often persuading customers to give an order after they had decided they had no orders to give!'*[3]

Edmund's first years with the company during the early 1870s were a period of some prosperity for the British pottery industry as continental pottery production was practically

Flora, an old Davenport pattern produced at the Hill Pottery, illustration from the Print Record Book.

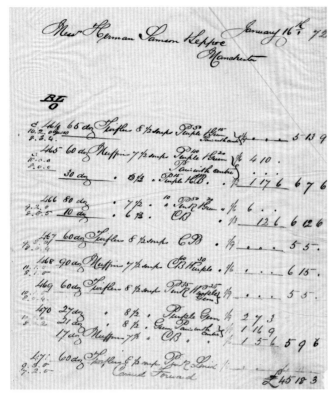

'Twifflers' and 'Muffins' by the dozen, names given in the eighteenth century to variously shaped 8ins- and 6$\frac{1}{2}$ins-plates (20cms and 16 cms).

Analysis of costs for making 300 'Christy Mayonnaise Mixers', 1881.

Extract from a Day Book showing details of Burgess & Leigh's trade in supplying 'matchings' to other local potteries, 1876.

halted by the Franco-Prussian War. Burgess, Leigh & Co.'s range continued much as before although they always showed themselves eager to introduce new shapes and patterns where there was a market. Amongst a list of utilitarian wares, factory notebooks record such diverse items as *Candlesticks*, *Pine Apple Teapots*, *Garden Pots*, *Shrimps*, *Petties*, *Shaving Boxes*, *Beehive Honey Pots*, *Mortars* and *Pestles* and *Dutch* and *Ship* jugs. Invoices and correspondence record the names of other printed tableware patterns Burgess & Leigh could then offer: *Guitar*, *Venetian*, *Flora*, *Rose*, *Amherst Japan*, *Seville*, *Landscape*, *Siam*, *Napier*, *Rhine*, *Louise*, *Greek*, *Manchester*, *Castle*, *Italian*, *Cherry Blossom* and *Lorne*.

The upturn in business was regrettably short-lived and by the mid-1870s the ceramic industry's roller-coaster trade was again depressed. Perhaps as a result of this, the company from around this time until the 1890s operated a successful sideline in providing '*matchings*' for other local pottery manufacturers. This practice of local outsourcing was widespread in the pottery industry. It provided a mutually beneficial trade between normally rival potteries, with smaller firms, such as Burgess, Leigh & Co. and Dudson,[4] willing to supply larger ones with ware which they were unable, for whatever reason, to produce themselves. Sometimes matchings were also supplied direct to individual customers. Entries in archival *Day Books* provide a fascinating insight into this little-researched business, with much borrowing and lending (of moulds and copperplates) to fulfill orders.[5] Each order usually comprised a few odd tableware items to be decorated with a named printed pattern. Some of the wares might also have been marked with the relevant subcontracting company's backstamp.[6] Potteries with whom the company traded included Copeland, Minton, Doulton, Hammersley's and Davenport, as well as lesser-known ones. Burgess & Leigh had supplied matchings whilst at the Central Pottery but only very reluctantly; in correspondence dated October 1864, Burgess & Leigh exhorted their traveller Swann to '*Avoid matchings where you can, we have lost money by them.*' However, in more pressing times the regular income the work provided contributed to Burgess, Leigh & Co.'s growth at a time when it otherwise might have struggled. In 1878 a valuation of the stock, fixtures and utensils at the Hill Pottery added up to £18,840. That same year, the time of Lowndes-Goode's retirement, Burgess & Leigh (the original name to which the company then reverted) had assets of '*£12,280, less liabilities*'.

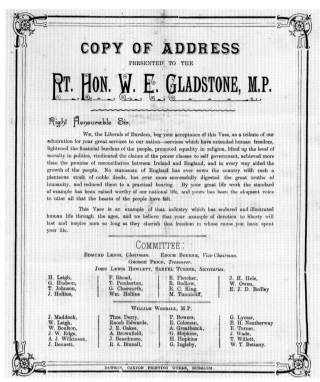

Copy of the speech made by Edmund leigh when, on behalf of Burslem Liberal Club, he presented a vase to Gladstone in 1888.

Plaque, relief-moulded, printed portrait of Gladstone made by Burgess & Leigh, 1898.

During the years spent building up a successful business, William Leigh had not neglected his public duties and had become a person of some standing within the local community and *'exerted a strong though quiet influence upon the municipal life of Burslem'*.[7] Elected Alderman of Burslem Town Council in 1878 with *'no particular class or party to serve'*,[8] William sat on the Cemeteries Committee and on a pottery manufacturers' Board of Employers, dealing with such matters as potters' arbitration cases.[9] He was also Secretary of his local Building Society,[10] a money-lending institution (first initiated in the 1840s by Liberal radicals as a means of effecting Parliamentary reform) which gave male householders the opportunity to purchase freehold land and hence the right to vote.

It was from around 1874 that Edmund, inspired by his father's example, also began to take an active interest in politics. Throughout his life Edmund remained a radical, always *'in the vanguard of progress, a stalwart influence in the onward march of events'*.[11] It was reported: *'You cannot make all men equal but you should endeavour to give them all equality of opportunity. The prosperity of a country is not to be measured by the number of its wealthy men, but by the manner in which its wealth is fairly distributed. These are two cardinal points in Mr Leigh's political and public faith, and they explain very largely his attitude upon many of the vital questions of the day.'*[12]

Unlike his father, Edmund was happy to align himself with a political party. A life-long Liberal at both national and local levels, he was one of the foundation members of the London National Liberal Club, President of both the Burslem Liberal Association and Burslem Liberal Club and Secretary of the Liberal Committee for the North-West Staffordshire division. He supported the Liberal cause at every General Election apart from that of 1922 when he sensationally supported the Labour candidate in protest at the Liberal-Conservative coalition.[13] A loyal follower of Liberal leader and prime minister, W. E. Gladstone, Edmund undoubtedly contributed to the party's local and national dominance during the late nineteenth and early twentieth century. In 1888 Burslem Liberal Club selected him to present a vase to W. E. Gladstone (then in opposition) at his Welsh estate, Hawarden Castle.[14] Inspired by the radical statesman and orator John Bright, Edmund was also an acquaintance in London of the Irish Nationalist Charles Stewart Parnell and, like him, supported Gladstone's Home Rule policy.[15]

Many people thought that Edmund himself might have become a politician and it was reported that:

> *'Had his health been equal to the strain he would have undoubtedly have found a seat at Westminster, for he was requested on several occasions to allow himself to be nominated, and had his name gone forward he would almost certainly have secured election.'*[16] It was widely agreed that *'He would have made an excellent member of Parliament for the Potteries, for he knew and loved the district and its trade, and had a personality that enlisted attention, and he was a clear, forceful and eloquent speaker. He was one of the outstanding personalities amongst the manufacturers. With his visits to London coming as frequently as they always did from his youth, he was very much at home at Westminster.'*[17]

Edmund's reluctance to enter national politics might well have been due to his frequent bouts of ill health although the long-term bronchitis he suffered did not curtail his fondness for either cricket in his youth nor golf in his old age! More likely it was his all-consuming devotion to the Potteries, its industry and its people, which influenced his decision. Whilst participating in local municipal matters, he was, however, more than happy to lend his support to aspiring politicians. His assistance to the campaign for William Woodall as Liberal MP for Burslem, and later Hanley, was rewarded by the presentation to him by Woodall's executors of an engraving, featuring his hero the economist and politician Richard Cobden, entitled *'The Council of the Anti-Corn Law League'*. One of Edmund's most treasured possessions, this picture hung for many years in the sitting room of his home. At William Woodall's own home

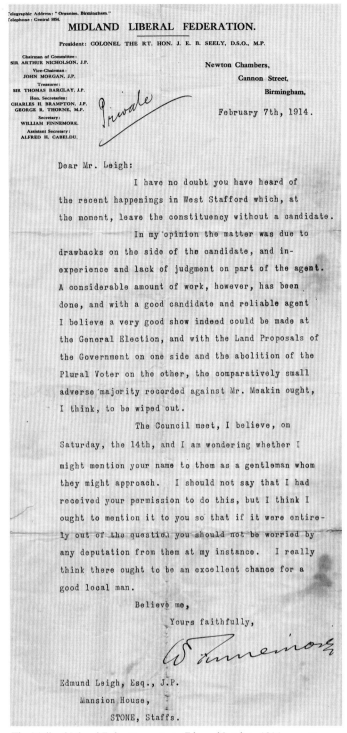

Telegraphic Address : " Organise, Birmingham."
Telephone : Central 5854.

MIDLAND LIBERAL FEDERATION.

President: COLONEL THE RT. HON. J. E. B. SEELY, D.S.O., M.P.

Chairman of Committee:
SIR ARTHUR NICHOLSON, J.P.

Vice-Chairman:
JOHN MORGAN, J.P.

Treasurer:
SIR THOMAS BARCLAY, J.P.

Hon. Secretaries:
CHARLES H. BRAMPTON, J.P.
GEORGE R. THORNE, M.P.

Secretary:
WILLIAM FINNEMORE.

Assistant Secretary:
ALFRED H. CABELDU.

Newton Chambers,

Cannon Street,

Birmingham,

February 7th, 1914.

Private

Dear Mr. Leigh:

I have no doubt you have heard of the recent happenings in West Stafford which, at the moment, leave the constituency without a candidate.

In my opinion the matter was due to drawbacks on the side of the candidate, and inexperience and lack of judgment on part of the agent. A considerable amount of work, however, has been done, and with a good candidate and reliable agent I believe a very good show indeed could be made at the General Election, and with the Land Proposals of the Government on one side and the abolition of the Plural Voter on the other, the comparatively small adverse majority recorded against Mr. Meakin ought, I think, to be wiped out.

The Council meet, I believe, on Saturday, the 14th, and I am wondering whether I might mention your name to them as a gentleman whom they might approach. I should not say that I had received your permission to do this, but I think I ought to mention it to you so that if it were entirely out of the question you should not be worried by any deputation from them at my instance. I really think there ought to be an excellent chance for a good local man.

Believe me,

Yours faithfully,

Edmund Leigh, Esq., J.P.

Mansion House,

STONE, Staffs.

The Midland Liberal Federation write to Edmund Leigh in 1914 requesting permission for his name to be put forward as parliamentary candidate for West Stafford.

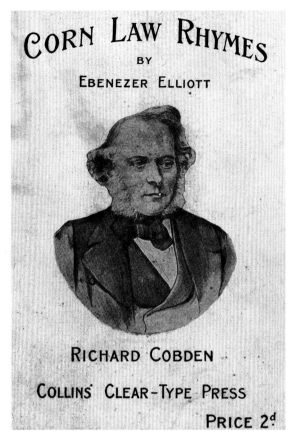

CORN LAW RHYMES
BY
EBENEZER ELLIOTT

RICHARD COBDEN

COLLINS' CLEAR-TYPE PRESS

PRICE 2d.

Edmund Leigh was one of many local potters to support parliamentarian Richard Cobden's advocacy of free trade. On his death in 1865 the flag on Burslem Town Hall flew at half-mast.

in Cobridge, *Bleak House*, Edmund was frequently a member of the political and artistic private gatherings. There he dined (and most probably argued!) with the Liberal MP and British statesman Joseph Chamberlain whose views on tariff reform and Home Rule he did not support.

Undoubtedly, visitors to *Bleak House* would have discussed the beliefs of William Morris (1834-1896), the socialist, writer and designer, whose ideal of a just society was shared by Edmund. Instrumental in founding the Arts and Crafts movement in England, it was Morris' view that, wherever possible, industry should retain individual craftsmanship as a means of preserving aesthetic beauty within functionality, thereby spiritually enriching both

maker and user. Lecturing at the Town Hall in Burslem on 13th October, 1881 on the subject of *'Art and the Beauty of the Earth'*, Morris said:

'You who in these parts make such hard, smooth, well-compacted and enduring pottery understand well that you must give it other qualities besides those which make it for ordinary use. You must profess to make it beautiful as well as useful, and if you did not you would certainly lose your market. That has been the view the world has taken of your art, and of all the industrial arts since the beginning of history...'[18]

It seems likely that Edmund would have been amongst William Morris' audience in Burslem that night and, although not perhaps concurring with Morris' anti-mechanisation stance, he would surely have agreed that Burgess & Leigh pottery always aspired to be *'beautiful as well as useful.'* An account written in the following decade suggested that:

'From the first, the founders... determined to produce a class of ware that should not only be of the best make and material but also of the highest possible artistic merit. This was practically the task they set themselves, and which they devoted all their efforts and intelligence to accomplish.... The aesthetic 'wave' which has passed over the present generation, the cult of the ideal and of form now so universal, and the march of improvement in manufacturing facilities and manipulation, all told in favour of Messrs Burgess & Leigh, and illustrated once more the observation of Shakespeare: 'There is a tide in the affairs of man, which, taken at the flood, leads on to fortune'.'[19]

But, as William Morris would have readily admitted, aestheticism was not a subject frequently discussed in the town halls and taverns of the Potteries and Edmund's local municipal activities were of necessity more prosaic. Nonetheless, he performed such largely thankless duties with enthusiasm and with no apparent desire for self-promotion, it being reported that *'Mr Leigh has twice declined the Mayoralty'*.[20] Before the Federation of the City of Stoke-on-Trent in 1910, each of the six Potteries towns had its own separate municipality. Of these, Burslem was especially regarded and from 1892 Edmund held several positions on its Town Council as a member of the Finance and Sanitary Committees and as Chairman of the Gas Committee. He represented the small town of Kidsgrove on Staffordshire County Council and was appointed Justice of the Peace for the county as well as a borough magistrate for Burslem. He used his public platform to draw attention to his belief in the importance of education; he was an early advocate of technical education for the Potteries area and sat on the Burslem School Board from 1886 until 1894. Although as a young man he was involved in the temperance movement, it seems that his teetotalism was no bar to his becoming in later life a respected Chairman of the Stoke-on-Trent Licensing Committee! Nineteenth-century temperance societies were much encouraged by the Methodist Church and Edmund played an important role in the building of Wolstanton's modern Wesleyan Chapel. A Methodist hymn book[21] was presented to Edmund by the chapel's trustees on his leaving the district in 1908. He had held several lay offices there and was a delegate to the Wesleyan Conference when it met in Burslem.

Edmund also belonged to the quaintly named but nonetheless influential Burslem Association for the Prosecution of Felons, an association set up by prominent local employers to deter theft. The members of this worthy society rewarded themselves with an annual dinner (which still continues), one of which was fictionalised in a novel by Arnold Bennett, perhaps as a result of a conversation the author had with his friend, Edmund Leigh.[22]

Edmund Leigh and Arnold Bennett: *'such persuasive effect'*

There were numerous connections between the Leighs and Bennetts[23] as one might expect from the small, close-knit community of Burslem where the two families lived. During the 1870s, William Leigh had a house in Hall Street less than half a mile from that of Arnold's father, Enoch Bennett, in Dain Street. Both subsequently lived in Newport Street before moving to Waterloo Road, Cobridge, then one of the best residential addresses in the area. Later the families became indirectly related through the second marriage of Edmund's brother-in-law, Ezra Bourne, to Arnold's aunt, Frances Longsdon.

Inevitably, there were also pottery connections. Ezra Bourne, together with Edmund's youngest brother, John Edward Leigh, formed a moderately successful partnership, Bourne & Leigh, which traded until the late 1930s. Frank Beardmore, a brother-in-law of Arnold Bennett, served an apprenticeship at Burgess & Leigh, becoming their country representative in the 1890s. He subsequently founded Frank Beardmore & Co. at the Sutherland Pottery, Fenton, where Septimus Bennett, Arnold's brother, a modeller in the pottery industry, worked for some time.

Edmund and Arnold both attended the same school (although not at the same time, Edmund being the elder by thirteen years). For a short time in the late 1880s, before Edmund moved to *Holly Lodge* in Wolstanton, the two men also lived next door to each other in Waterloo Road: Edmund was at 205 and Arnold, before he left the Potteries in 1889, at 203. Edmund remained a friend and is mentioned respectfully in the author's posthumously published journals. The entry for Tuesday, 7th December, 1909 tells of a visit to Burslem's main bookshop-cum-printer owned by Joseph Dawson, also a registrar: *'Dawson's yesterday morning acquiring stuff for Clayhanger until Edmund Leigh called, and he orated for an hour with such persuasive effect that in the end I volunteered to write a political manifesto for the district; for which afterwards I was of course both sorry and glad!'* It must have proved acceptable as by 11th December, Bennett reported *'Yesterday morning I read my political manifesto to Dawson and Edmund Leigh with great effect. The printing of it was put in hand instantly.'*[24]

Arnold Bennett is known to have created his characters, plots and settings from an amalgam of people, events and places known to him[25] and it seems very likely that the Leigh family provided him with much inspiration. In his article *'Clay in the Hands of the Potter'*, published in the *Windsor* magazine in 1913, Bennett describes a visit he made to his *'uncle's'* pottery in c.1896 in preparation for a novel. Interestingly, one of the photographs accompanying the article showed the exterior of Burgess & Leigh's Middleport Pottery (where the company was to move in 1889). As Edmund arguably might be considered to be Arnold's uncle on account of inter-family marriage, it is possible that it was Burgess & Leigh's pottery which Bennett visited. If so, it may well have been the source for the *'Providence Works'* in *Anna of the Five Towns* which he began writing that year.[26] Certainly, the two works share many characteristics, as do the Hill Pottery and the *'Old Sytch'* in Bennett's later novel *Clayhanger* (although it seems less likely that Edmund Leigh was the model for its eponymous hero, Darius Clayhanger, as has been suggested).

That Bennett used aspects of the Leigh family's life in his novels was certainly a view shared by another friend of Edmund, John Shorter. In a lecture delivered to the Connoisseurs' Club in Sydney in 1926 in which he reflected on a successful career as a potters' agent in Australia, Shorter was to say of Edmund: *'There is, I believe, more than a suspicion that his old schoolmate, Arnold Bennett, utilised many of his characteristics in several of his classics of the Five Towns.'*[27]

The Leigh, Shorter and Wilkinson Connection: A *'trinity of friendship'*

It was John Shorter's brother, Arthur, (also a potter, with a majolica works in Stoke) who was in fact a closer friend to Edmund. Indeed, the two men were also brothers-in-law, both having married sisters of another potter, Arthur J. Wilkinson; Arthur and Henrietta Elizabeth married in the 1870s and Edmund and Jane in February 1880.[28] The three men, Edmund, and the two Arthurs – Shorter and Wilkinson – formed what John Shorter described as a *'trinity of friendship'*. It was, he said, *'for many years… full of vivid events and has left its mark on the history of the Ceramics of North Staffordshire'*. Acknowledging Wilkinson as the natural leader of the trio, he paints a lively portrait sketch of Edmund Leigh describing that his:

Edmund Leigh (centre, back row with hat) with the Shorter family and friends.

'*prominent eyes, square chin, and quiet self possession bespoke his coming mastery of any position he cared to aim for. He lacked the abounding vitality of A. J. Wilkinson, but had the quiet bulldog tenacity, and steady application that always placed him in the forefront in any arguments that required a mastery of facts, figures and dates... He lived a full and generous life, rich in public duties, commercial, industrial and political of the Five Towns.*'

The '*trinity of friendship*' was, however, to be tragically cut short when Arthur Wilkinson fell to his death from a hotel balcony in Switzerland in 1891. He had set up his earthenware pottery, A. J. Wilkinson Ltd, just six years earlier, trading from the Central Pottery, Burgess & Leigh's old works. On his death, it was decided that his brother-in-law Arthur Shorter should manage the works, subsequently known as the Royal Staffordshire Pottery. The business prospered and in 1894 Arthur decided to buy it in partnership with Edmund Leigh. It seems that Edmund's role was as a financial investor only, his major concern being the management of his own pottery. (It was normal practice that inter-marrying potting families continued to do business in a spirit of sometimes less than friendly rivalry with their relatives!) Burgess & Leigh and A. J. Wilkinson Ltd (renamed Shorter & Sons in the early 1900s) were to take similar routes and produce comparable wares until the late twentieth century.[29]

Although Edmund may have had more routine contact with Arthur Shorter in Burslem, it was Arthur's brother, John, in Australia, who arguably had more influence on the future success of Burgess & Leigh. John had emigrated to a sunnier climate for reasons of health, finally settling in Sydney, with a shipment of butter, then in short supply, and just five pounds.[30] Eager to exploit what he knew best, he approached family and friends in the pottery business requesting to act as their overseas agent. Fortunately, he found Edmund's father, William Leigh, one of those prepared to take a risk. He later described William as '*one of the most just and yet generous men I have ever met. In my early Colonial days he gave me their agency and offered me a £1,000 credit on my own word and bond.*'

Business Expansion Abroad

Eager to repay William's trust, John Shorter acted as the company's agent from 1881 until 1889 (when he became sole agent for Doulton & Co.).[31] The appointment of this reliable and dependable family friend was an important factor in establishing the foundations of Burgess & Leigh's successful and enduring trade in Australia. The use of overseas agents was a far-sighted move which did much to increase the company's valuable export trade. Agents' on-the-ground knowledge of their market's requirements and tastes enabled Burgess & Leigh to produce '*many lines expressly.... for colonial and foreign markets*'.[32]

Burgess & Leigh maintained a steady trade with North America where Frederick Rathbone Burgess is reported to have made a business trip in 1887. '*Foreign Order Books*' from that period record that regular shipments of Burgess & Leigh wares went out to Boston, New York and Baltimore on the east coast and New Orleans in the south. From the south goods were transported by the Southern Pacific Railway to Texas and Salt Lake City, Portland and San Francisco on the west coast. Other destinations included Antwerp in Belgium; the Caribbean island of Barbados; and, three especially important future markets, Adelaide in Australia, Cape Town in South Africa and Montreal in Canada. Further far flung outposts of the British Empire receiving Burgess & Leigh wares were Karachi in Pakistan; Rangoon in Burma (now Yangon in Myanmar) and Ceylon (now Sri Lanka) whose government was to place an order in 1891 for a quantity of badged toilet- and kitchen wares.

That such products were so readily and rapidly exported from Middleport to such exotic places would be astonishing to many of Burgess & Leigh's employees. Although Britain's network of canals had already vastly improved transportation to its ports, the Victorian technological revolution meant that orders could now be placed by cablegram or telephone, and goods dispatched around the world by railway and steel-framed steamship with then astonishing speed. Such advances in communication revolutionised global trade for companies like Burgess & Leigh.

Flow Blue for Portland, Oregon, via steamer to New Orleans and by the newly opened Southern Pacific railroad to Texas and the West Coast, 1896.

A pedestal pot and teapot sent together with goods made by A. J. Wilkinson to Cuero in Texas via New Orleans.

Badged toiletwares for the '*Government of Ceylon*', 1891.

An order of *Blue Willow* for New York, 1890.

Mabelle for Montreal in Canada. (The pattern *Mabelle* was named after Edmund Leigh's daughter.)

A page from a *Foreign Order Book* of the 1890s listing identification marks for export crates.

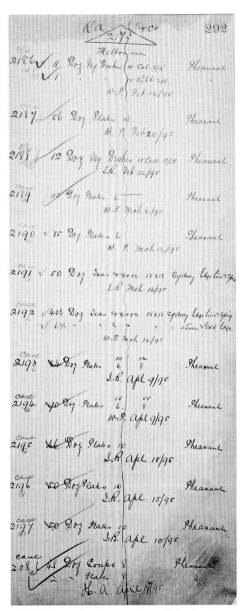

Asiatic Pheasant for Australia, 1895. Orders by the 100 dozen were not uncommon and occasionally as high as 200 dozen.

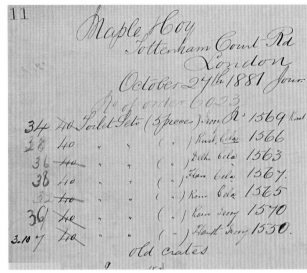

An 1881 order for toilet sets for the well know furniture stores, Maple & Co in Tottenham Court Road. By the end of the nineteenth century, other London department stores stocking Burgess & Leigh wares included Barkers, Dickens & Jones, Lilley & Skinner, Whiteley's and Harrods.

....and Expansion at Home

By the early 1880s, nearly seventy potteries had showrooms in London, mostly operated by agents acting for one or more companies.[33] Burgess & Leigh maintained premises there from at least 1881 when an announcement was made in *The Pottery Gazette* that their new showroom had opened at 16 Thavies Inn, Holborn.[34] Before the appointment of Mr F. Hodgson, Edmund acted as company representative, spending two days in the showroom and the rest of the week visiting customers in the surrounding area. Like his friend Arnold Bennett, he was no doubt eager to leave the Potteries to experience the bright lights of the capital city. However, in Edmund's case, it was to be a temporary move only. He maintained his family home in the Potteries,[35] where it was expected he would return to assist his father, by then in his early sixties, at the Hill Pottery.

Displayed in the London showroom would be a representative selection of the Hill Pottery's decorative tablewares, toiletwares and ornamental wares. An expensive colour advertisement placed in *The Pottery Gazette* in August 1881, the year of the opening of the new showroom,

reveals that pattern numbers had reached 1549. Those illustrated included toilet jugs and bowls in a variety of Japanese 'aesthetic' style patterns on shapes including *Roman* (registered by Burgess & Leigh the year before),[36] *Greek* and *Hawthorn* (also the name of a pattern). Teapots and jugs were available in Jet (black glazed earthenware); *Bamboo*-shaped, or, like *Gypsy*, with a moulded figurative knob to the lid. In the centre of the two-page advert was a large two-handled decorative vase (number 1506) on the *Roman* shape, decorated with an exuberant leaf pattern. Tableware tureens and plates, made on the *Corinth*, *Brunswick* and *Imperial* shapes, featured named patterns like blue *Madras* and the neo-classical style *Kensington*[37] (which had first been registered at the Patent Office in 1875) in bright pink.

Not illustrated but known to have been produced at the Hill Pottery (if not before) was the printed pattern commonly known as *Farmers' Arms*. Variations of this old English design have been produced from the eighteenth century by many potteries, including Sunderland and Liverpool, whose plaques, mugs and loving cups had

Burgess & Leigh's *Kensington* pattern, in bright pink, is included in *The Pottery Gazette* colour advertisement in August 1881.

Hawthorn-, *Greek-* and *Roman*-shaped toilet sets advertised with a *Turin* jug and *Bamboo*-shaped jug, teapot and kettle, 1881.

Kensington, as illustrated in the Print Record Book, with a Hill Pottery 'beehive' backstamp. The pattern was first registered by Burgess & Leigh in 1875.

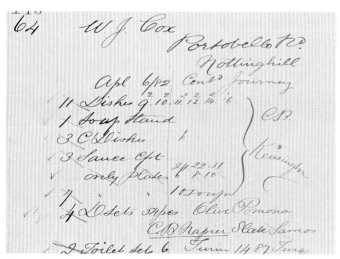

Plus ça change.... Burgess & Leigh pottery was selling on the Portobello Road, Notting Hill, in 1882, this order being for items in the *Kensington* tableware pattern.

Unmarked *Roman*-shaped lidded vase, as shown in Burgess & Leigh's 1881 advertisement, with printed, coloured and gilded rose pattern. Height 17ins (43cms).

Farmers Arms, three loving cups produced by Burgess & Leigh. Nineteenth-century underglaze printed versions, left and middle, are usually marked B&L. The pattern was produced on a variety of shapes until c.2000. Tallest 5ins (13cms).

decorated many a farmhouse wall and kitchen dresser. Burgess & Leigh's version was produced in a wide range of shapes until 1999. Black underglaze prints, with or without enamel colours, were replaced later in the twentieth century by lithographic transfer prints. The design sometimes appears with the following traditional verse:

God Speed the Plough

Let the wealthy and great
Roll in splendour and state
I Envy them not I declare it
I eat my own lamb
My own chickens and ham
I shear my own fleece, and I wear it
I have lawns, I have bowers
I have fruits, I have flowers
The lark is my morning alarmer
So jolly boys now
Here's God Speed the Plough
Long Life and Success to the farmer

Industry Produceth Wealth

Burgess & Leigh's own 'industry' produced considerable wealth from its home market during the 1880s. However, it was arguably the expansion of its overseas trade which accounted for the company's rapid business growth while that of other potteries, including more celebrated ones, declined. When Davenport, Longport's illustrious and long established pottery and porcelain firm, was forced to close in 1887, Burgess & Leigh was able to make purchases from the eleven tons of copperplates and moulds sold at auction, producing patterns and plates which were to reap financial rewards for many years to come.

No longer a small player in the Potteries, the company's business expansion demanded new premises to cope with production. But the partners were no longer content, nor indeed compelled, to compromise on what they wanted, by renting the old and cramped accommodation more usually available to pottery manufacturers in the towns of north Staffordshire. They confidently began to make plans for a modern, architect-designed factory to be built – the Middleport Pottery was set to become Burgess & Leigh's last home.

The Middleport Pottery: the 'Model Pottery' of Staffordshire

The gradual financial collapse of Davenports had brought about the sale in 1886 of Pickford's Wharf,[38] a piece of land previously used for its saggar works and crate yard. Situated in Middleport, a developing area away from Burslem town centre, the main advantage of this site was its excellent communications: the adjacent Trent and Mersey Canal provided cheap and efficient transport to the major ports of Liverpool and Manchester in the north west whilst the proximity of Longport Station on the North Staffordshire railway line gave further links to Britain's cities and ports including Hull in the north east. Recognising the potential of the site, Burgess & Leigh lost no time in acquiring it for their new factory.

The architect entrusted with the design of the new works was Absalom Reade Wood (1851-1922), Edmund's school friend and fellow Methodist, who had qualified under the Stoke-on-Trent architect Robert Scrivener before setting up his own business in 1874 in Tunstall.[39] By the late 1880s, A.R. Wood had several ecclesiastical, domestic and civic commissions to his name, most of which were known to the founders. They would have been particularly interested in the building of the Town Hall in Tunstall, their birthplace, and of St Andrew's Church in Porthill, where both lived for some time. It is interesting that A.R. Wood had never before designed an industrial building and would have readily accepted the commission for a pottery, eager to make a name for himself in a new area. In consultation with the company partners, he therefore set about producing a building which, five years after work commenced in 1888, was still being described as 'the "Model Pottery" of Staffordshire.'[40]

Reporters for the trade press had been quick to comment on plans for the new works and followed its building progress with interest. In April of 1888, *The Pottery Gazette* wrote that '*Messrs Burgess & Leigh's new factory, on the Trent and Mersey Canal is being pushed forward and a large number of hands are employed on the work when "Jack Frost" does not interfere.*' By June it was first noted that the pottery was to be called '*Middleport Pottery*' and that its owners '*hope to take possession and commence operations about March next. This has been a gigantic undertaking but the factory when finished will be replete with all modern machinery and drying appliances.*' Commenting on its advantageous canal-side situation, it reported '*Taking into consideration the cost of carting clays up*

A letter from London finds it way to the Middleport Pottery, Burslem in the 1890s.

An aerial view of the Middleport Pottery, c.1920, showing its layout and advantageous canal-side site.

Across the allotments, a view of the Middleport Pottery during the 1960s. (*Courtesy of Donald Morris.*)

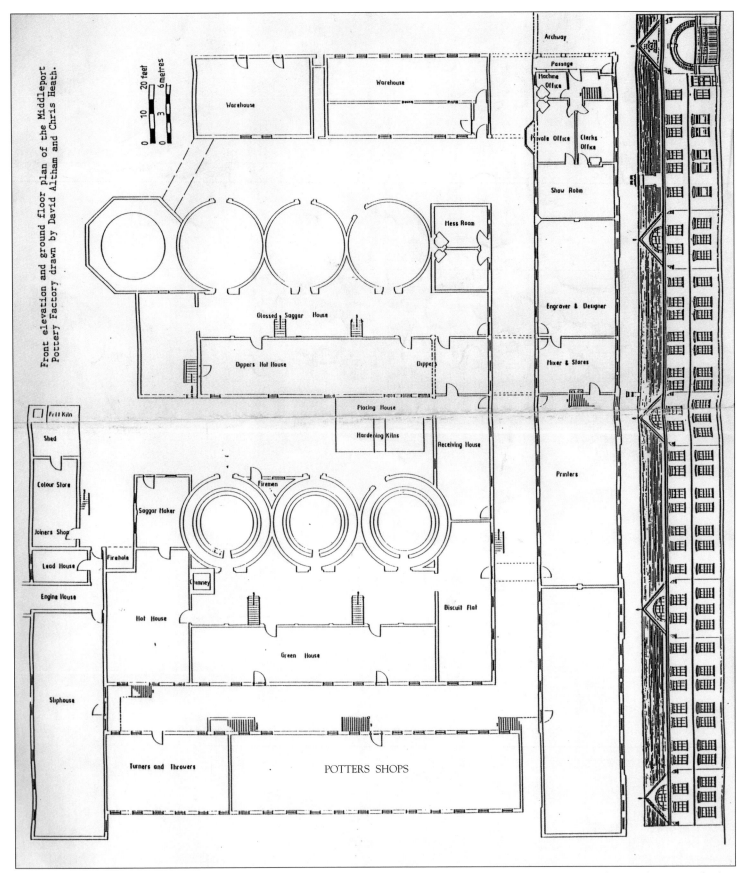

Front elevation and ground floor plan of the Middleport Pottery Factory drawn by David Altham and Chris Heath.

Front elevation and ground floor plan of the Middleport Pottery. (*Stoke-on-Trent Historic Buildings Survey 1984*). The manufacturing process began at the eastern side of the site in the Slip House (shown here bottom left). Production then moved to the Potters' Shops, at right angles, flowing through biscuit and glost bottle oven firing towards the Warehouses (shown at top of page).

June 1, 1889. SUPPLEMENT TO THE POTTERY GAZETTE.

The first know depiction of the new pottery, June 1889.

William Boulton, engineer, of the Providence Foundry, Burslem.
He was elected mayor of the town in the early 1880s.

Engineer William Boulton negotiates terms for supplying and
refurbishing machinery for Burgess & Leigh's 'new works', 25th
February, 1888.

Boulton's bill, 4th March, 1889.

and goods down from the factory, a considerable item will thus be
saved on a twelve months' trade.' In December the factory was
at last 'nearing completion…. They will move early next year'
and finally on 1st April, 1889 came the announcement that
'Messrs Burgess & Leigh vacated Hill Pottery 25th March and
are rapidly settling down to work at Middleport Pottery.'

The same report of April 1889 provided an eagerly
awaited description of the works, promising an engraving of
the factory in the following issue.[41] An advertising and trade
journal of 1893 entitled 'A Descriptive Account of the
Potteries' (illustrated), Messrs Burgess & Leigh, Pottery
Manufacturers, Middleport Pottery, Burslem and an article 'A
Typical Staffordshire Industry, The Middleport Pottery, Burslem'
in the British Journal of Commerce in January 1898 were to
give further accounts of the works. Although not detailed,
these contemporary documents, together with a plan of the
works thought to date from c.1900 and an aerial photograph
taken in c.1920, provide the best description of the original
layout of – what was then – the most modern of potteries.[42]

In architectural style, the Middleport Pottery was far
from radical. The simple red brick, tiled-roofed building
exemplified the Protestant work-ethic values of both its

owners and its architect. Little concerned with external
decoration, it did not share the ostentatious pretensions of
Burgess & Leigh's previous home, the Hill Pottery, but was
essentially utilitarian, its internal organisation based on
maximising efficient production. Having said that, visitors
and employees alike could not fail to have been impressed by
the scale of the building, its two-storey frontage stretching
almost the length of Port Street. Those living in the row of
two-up, two-down terraced houses opposite still look out
today on to the factory's original four gabled bays with
lunette windows. In the fifth and final bay at the far end of
the street, a relief-decorated terracotta pediment announces
the factory's name, 'Middleport Pottery', beneath the owners'
insignia, 'B & L', and the date when building work

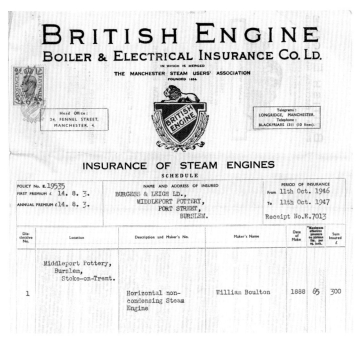

The steam engine remained in use until c.1977. Here, an insurance certificate from 1940.

The Middleport Pottery's horizontal eighteen-inch single-cylinder steam engine made by William Boulton in 1888. Photographed in 2001 before restoration commenced.

began,'*1888*'. Through the arched coach entrance beneath this last bay, with its uninterrupted view to the canal-side, employees rushed in each morning, eager to arrive before the lodge keeper closed the inner 'locking off' gates (thus depriving them of a full day's pay). Visitors to the works, meanwhile, would enter though the door alongside the archway to wait by the lodge keeper's office. Inside, the entrance hall was furnished in pleasant, though modest style, with typically Victorian patterned floor tiles, stained glass windows to the doors and ornamental wrought iron staircase banisters.

Whilst neither the external architectural appearance nor the decorative features of the Middleport Pottery taxed the imagination of the architect too much, the design of the internal layout of the site was a triumph of logic. The luxury of designing a brand new pottery from scratch enabled A. R. Wood to work in consultation with the owners to produce a building tailor-made to their exact requirements. Its design was thus dictated by and followed all the many complex sequential processes of pottery production, from the arrival of raw materials by canal to the dispatch of finished ware by the same route, or by road or rail.

A. R. Wood's plan conformed to the standard Victorian four-sided layout of a pottery, with a group of workshops within an enclosed yard behind a façade. However, what was especially innovative was the siting of the Middleport Pottery's two rows of bottle ovens within parallel workshop ranges so that they formed an integral part of the manufacturing process. Each building range housed a separate department or 'shop', with its own independent access, those on the upper floor having external wooden staircases. The ranges were linked by external cobbled alleyways on the ground floor or by covered 'bridges' between upper storeys. Allowing for both forward (east to west) and sideways movement, no area was far from the next sequential process, facilitating a time-efficient and labour-saving production flow.

The Slip House Range: Preparation of Raw Materials and Clay

Production started at the Middleport Pottery's 120-yard canal frontage with the arrival of raw materials, whose direct purchase and subsequent processing gave Burgess & Leigh better quality control over its finished product. Ball and china clay was delivered by barge from Devon, Dorset and Cornwall, having transferred from sea coaster at Runcorn. It was left outside on the Clay Bank wharf to weather before being carted into the Slip House range, a row of buildings dedicated to the preparation and mixing of raw materials into clay, either liquid (slip) or plastic. Today the external canal-side wall of the Slip House still remains something of a local landmark; spelling *MIDDLEPORT POTTERY*, in three-feet high white ceramic glazed lettering, it provides a permanent advertisement to all those passing by, whether by canal, road or rail. (A later *BURLEIGH WARE* sign was to blow down several times during the latter part of the twentieth century!) At the foremost end of the Slip House range was a frit kiln, for the calcining of materials including stone and flint delivered, ready ground, from nearby Dalehall Mills in which Burgess & Leigh had interests. Adjacent were two storage rooms, one for lead, a component then used in ceramic glazes, and the other for colours, used in decorating. In between these rooms was a workshop for a joiner, bricklayer and plasterer, who were permanently employed to carry out the factory's carpentry and building requirements.

In the centre of the Slip House range was the Engine House, which housed Burgess & Leigh's impressive horizontal, eighteen-inch, single-cylinder steam engine. Fuelled by coal (usually carted to the works from local pits such as Burslem's Sneyd Colliery), the engine's nameplate proudly recorded details of its manufacturer and date of first construction: *W. Boulton, Engineer, Burslem, 1888*. Using a bewildering 'Heath-Robinson' like maze of belts, line shafts, cog wheels and cotton ropes running throughout the pottery, the steam engine provided clean and economical power to drive all the factory's machinery.[43] This was also supplied, either new or refurbished, by William Boulton. Known to Edmund Leigh as a fellow committee member sitting on the Burslem Board of Health, Boulton ran the Providence Foundry in Burslem, then *'one of the most important establishments in Burslem.... the business connected therewith extends to all parts of the country, the firm having for a long time enjoyed a considerable reputation, not only for general foundry and engineering works but especially for the manufacture of all descriptions of machinery and apparatus used in the making of pottery.'*[44]

The Middleport Pottery's steam engine was certainly evidence of Boulton's fine workmanship. Still *in situ* today, it was used until c.1977 (when the Slip House was finally electrified) and would have continued in use had there been anyone qualified to replace Boulton's retiring service engineers! The engine's steam was generated in a huge *Lancashire* boiler, measuring some thirty feet in length and seven feet in diameter, *'calculated to afford a wide margin of steam power'*. Housed in the range just opposite (in the Saggar Makers' Hot House), it was *'fed by an exhaust steam engine or by a donkey pump, the latter being used to supply water to a large cistern fixed above the boiler'*.[45] As well as driving the machinery, the steam engine provided exhaust steam for the heating and drying stoves in all areas of the factory except for the warehouses, which were heated by steam direct from the boiler. Stoves were also used by workers to warm their meals.

The Pottery Gazette's report of the Middleport Pottery in April 1889 drew particular attention to *'the provision made for cooking the meals of the work people and many other comforts provided for the employees by Messrs Burgess & Leigh.'* This is most likely a reference to kitchen-cum-mess room which abutted the now demolished bottle oven closest to the pottery entrance. Britain's 1891 Factory and Workshops Act was to introduce specific regulations governing the provision of employees' meals for those working with hazardous substances such as lead. The inclusion of dining and cooking facilities prior to this legislation is certainly testament to Burgess & Leigh's reputation as a paternalistic, if not progressive, employer. The c.1900 plan of the works indicates that the original mess room may have had a single entrance with a dividing wall providing separate eating areas, for male and female workers, each with its own fireplace. Subsequent factory inventories note the provision of a 'cook-house' or kitchen with a sycamore counter behind which was a gas stove and cooking pots and pans. After the First World War an old army hut was purchased and used as a mess room or canteen until the 1930s when it was given over to production. The kitchen continued to be used, with a cook preparing employees' own food for collection at 'breakfast' and 'dinner-time'. Some retired employees report cooking food themselves on stoves or fireplaces within their

The Middleport Pottery Slip House: filter press operatives at the end of the nineteenth century....

.... and at the beginning of the twenty first.

workshops; others remember meals being brought into the works by wives or by children during their school dinnertime.[46] (Around the time of the Second World War, a purpose-built canteen conforming to more recent factory legislation was erected.)

Before mealtimes, however, there was work to be done and those employed mixing and processing clay in the Slip House would certainly have developed a healthy appetite! As at Bennett's *Providence Works*, the Slip House was located alongside the canal, closest to the steam engine which drove its powerful equipment. Observed in 1889 to be *'roomy and altogether well laid out for convenience and a large business'*, the Slip House initially had two floors, a third storey having been added by 1897.[47] Its ground floor contained the pottery's heaviest machinery, including three blungers, like huge food processors, used to mix clay and water into slip. The slip was then fed by gravity into an underground mixing ark or tank, *'fitted with agitators of improved construction'*. Ready ground flint and Cornish stone were added to the slip before the final mixture was transferred into a storage ark. As the clay slip was required, it was pumped by one of six pumps to the ground floor where a lawn sifter or sieve

Carting clay, view towards the Slip House at the Middleport Pottery with mould-makers' and pressers' shops above. (*Photograph, Rev. M. Graham, 1890s.*)

A flat-presser operates a jigger to make a dish in the Middleport Pottery's Flat Pressers' shop, c.1930.

Clean pinnies, a view towards the Port Street range from outside the Potters' Shops. (*Photograph, Rev. M. Graham, 1890s.*)

At the 'clay end', potters young and old pose outside the Potters' Shops for one of a number of photographs taken at the Middleport Pottery in the 1890s by the Rev. Malcolm Graham. The photographs were used in his book *Cup and Saucer Land*, first published in 1908.

Slip-casting largely replaced pressing at the Middleport Pottery in c.1919. Here, the top Casting Shop in the 1930s, Fred Colclough in flat cap and apron, identified to the far left.

removed any impurities. Three large, wooden (later iron) filter presses removed excess water to produce flat squares of clay. They were then fed into the same number of pug mills, which extruded giant sausage-shaped wads of plastic clay ready for use.

It was noted in 1889 that provision would be made *'in the near future'* for the second storey of the Slip House to accommodate several colour-grinding pans as well as a mill for grinding glaze. Areas here were also used for mould-making, making the multi-part moulds used to reproduce quantities of pottery, and for holloware pressing, making teapots, cups, jugs, bowls and so on, by pressing flat pieces or 'bats' of clay into moulds. Mould-making is a highly skilled three-stage process whereby a hollow block-mould is made from a hand-made prototype model; a case-mould is made from the block-mould; and a hollow working mould is made from the case-mould. The 'master' plaster of Paris 'block and cases' are usually kept for future use and, in this instance, were stored in the long, narrow roof space above the Slip House's second storey, which was accessed by a narrow staircase.

The Potters' Shops: Making Pottery

At right angles to the Slip House were the two-storey Potters' Shops. Here, Burgess & Leigh's diverse range of pottery shapes were made from newly processed clay which was stored, with the necessary moulds, in the basement. The two main methods of making pottery then were throwing and pressing. In the Throwers' and Turners' Shops, closest to the Slip House on the ground floor, items were thrown by shaping a 'ball' of clay with either hands or tools on a rotating potter's wheel. Although a centuries-old technique, Burgess & Leigh had invested in modern hand-operated machinery: a *'patent conical'* potter's wheel and steam lathes which were used for turning (shaving or trimming) items, *'these pieces of machinery…. giving great satisfaction'*.

At the time when the Middleport Pottery was built, most pottery was made by pressing. Different areas for the separate and specialised processes of flat ware and holloware pressing adjoined the Throwers' and Turners' Shops on both storeys. Flat Pressers made plates and saucers in the Flat Shops, whilst Holloware Pressers made cups and similar small shapes in the Cup Shops. Both used modern hand-operated machines: jiggers for flat ware and jollies for holloware which were fitted with plaster of Paris moulds and templates to form the shape required. A Flat Presser might make 1,200 plates on a good day[48] and he had several, usually female, assistants to help him maintain this rate. He also paid numerous 'mould runners', young apprentice boys and girls who had to fetch and carry moulds from each machine. This was a low-paid and thankless job, especially if the presser *'was waiting for you to put another mould on and you hadn't taken off, he used to swear at you and give you a clip up the ear-hole to buck your ideas up'!*[49] Ware was dried in the mould in drying closets powered by two steam-powered *'square and hexagonal stoves, the latter* [known as the 'Dobby'] *being on the revolving principle.'*[50]

The Potters' Shops extended at right angles into part of the Port Street range, with further Holloware Pressers' Shops on ground and first floors. Here men, usually working alone at a slower pace, pressed the larger items of holloware, such as ewers, basins, chamber pots and pails, which together made up Toilet Sets. Described on the factory's first opening as *'a model for manufacturers to study'*, the 175-feet

long shop was fitted with rows of brick-built benches on which flat 'bats' of clay were hammered into two-part moulds. The moulds were strapped together to make up the required shape and placed on to revolving *'whirlers'* with *'strong iron frames'*. The presser would then press the interior of the article to determine the thickness of clay and simultaneously join the two sides together. The inside of the article would be smoothed with various tools, all given wonderfully descriptive nick-names: a *'cow's lip'*, a *'diddler'*, or a *'tommy stick'*! A secondary eight-inch cylinder steam engine at the far, east end of this room drove the rope to run this more powerful machinery.[51]

Once dried and removed from their moulds, ware was taken to the upper storey to be 'fettled' or 'sponged' (smoothed or 'towed' using rough hemp or sponges). Further areas were used for mould storage and to accommodate more pressers. The air in the Pressers' Shops would have been full of the noxious clay dust which caused silicosis, or *'potters' rot'*, a frequently fatal lung disease. Attempts had been made to ensure that these areas were both spacious and, more importantly, well ventilated[52] but the risk to workers' health remained. This was reduced considerably at the Middleport Pottery in c.1919[53] when the use of deflocculants brought about the replacement of pressing by the safer, quicker and more economical method of slip-casting, where liquid clay was poured into moulds.

The Biscuit Range: Saggar Making, Placing and Firing

On leaving the Potters' Shops, the leather-hard or 'green' ware was ready for its 'biscuit' firing which baked it until it was rigid, dry and coarse. The pots were carried on ware boards across the yard, through one of two doors leading to the parallel two-storey Biscuit Range. Here it was stored in the Green House, at right angles to the Hot House above which rose Burgess & Leigh's distinctive 120 feet (36.5 metres) tall chimney. The Hot House was suitably named as, housing the *Lancashire* Boiler, temperatures regularly reached 120°F (49°C).[54] This made it an ideal room in which to dry saggers.

Saggars were different sized and shaped fireclay boxes used to contain and protect ware in the bottle ovens. They were made in the Sagger Makers' Shop, next to the Hot House, from 'saggar marl' which Burgess & Leigh milled themselves from grog (ground used saggers), marl (a rough clay) and water. Flat slabs of this clay were firstly knocked on to a metal-topped bench into different sized oval frames. One of the small sagger making team, known as a 'frame-filler', then wrapped one slab around a wooden drum which acted as a template to form the sides whilst another slab was knocked into an iron ring as a base or bottom, this last task carried out by the famous 'sagger maker's bottom knocker'! One of the company's two sagger makers, placing the drum on to the clay bottom, joined together the bottom and sides. The completed sagger was then dried in the Hot House, prior to firing.

The green ware, ready for its own firing, was packed in saggers, sprinkled with sand or flint to prevent warping. This work was done by a team of male 'biscuit placers' in a placing area between the Green House and ovens or kilns. The Middleport Pottery had three brick-built biscuit bottle ovens of the 'burgundy' type, the kilns or ovens being housed inside an outer protective 'hovel' shaped like a wine bottle. The biscuit ovens, like the glost (used to fire glazed ware), were

Jim Egerton placing items in a saggar for glost firing, 1964. There may well have been a nylon stocking rolled up inside his cap, a useful device when carrying a sagger or wareboard on the head! (*Photograph courtesy of Donald Morris.*)

Fireman Sid Dean adding coal to one of the oven's eleven firemouths around the base of the oven, 1964. (*Photograph courtesy of Donald Morris.*)

Cod Placer Jim Plant (right) supervises the placing of the saggers, some twenty to a 'bung' or stack inside the Middleport Pottery oven, 1930s.

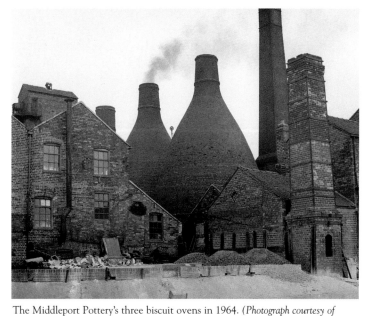

The Middleport Pottery's three biscuit ovens in 1964. (*Photograph courtesy of Donald Morris.*)

Far left: One of the world's last Saggar Maker's Bottom Knockers: Fred Boulton bats saggar marl, 1964. (*Photograph courtesy of Donald Morris.*)

Left: Fred wraps the clay around a wooden drum to shape the sides of an oval saggar, 1964. (*Photograph courtesy of Donald Morris.*)

updraught; the heat and smoke rose up through their tops, some sixty feet (18.3 metres) high above their bases which measured about twenty-eight feet (8.5 metres) diameter. The row of ovens was built along the far side of the Biscuit Range, so that their 'clammins' or small entrances could be accessed from the placing area inside the building. There was also a second, external, entrance to each hovel, around which vast piles of firing coal were stored. Between two of the bottle ovens outside a small covered area provided some protection for the kiln firemen as they worked.

Back inside the Biscuit Range, the 'cod' or head placer would first of all supervise the placing of the heavy saggers, one on top of another, some twenty to a 'bung' or stack, in diminishing circles inside the oven. Each type of ware was appropriately placed according to the oven's uneven temperatures. Newly made saggers were also fired on the top of the bungs, reached by wooden stepladders known as 'horses' or ''osses'. Altogether, around 2,000[55] saggars might be placed in one biscuit oven, with the whole operation taking up to two days to 'set'.

The job of the supervisory kiln fireman was one of the most important, skillful and responsible at the Middleport Pottery as any damage to ware inevitably meant financial losses, not only for the company but also for the fireman's fellow pottery makers who were paid 'good from oven'. Initially, Burgess & Leigh employed just one pottery fireman to fire both biscuit and glost ovens, Thomas Howlett Johnson, who had worked for them at the Hill Pottery. The first of three generations of the same family to work as kiln firemen at the Middleport Pottery, he was given further help in c.1910 when the company took on a biscuit fireman.

The Middleport Pottery was one of the last in the potteries to use coal-fired bottle ovens, the last biscuit ovens still being fired in the 1960s by a process little changed from 1889. It was hot and heavy work and one oven usually took the fireman, night fireman and 'odd man' a total of three days to fire. Once the oven was set, the clammins was bricked up. Then over the first night the odd man would light and very gradually bait (add coal to) the eleven firemouths around the base of the oven. Heat from the fires would be distributed into the oven through 'bags' or short chimneys and underfloor flues. Once the 'smoking' period was over, during which all water was baked out of the clay, the fireman would spend the next two days supervising the firing. Variation of the temperature, which would reach around 1100°C, was obtained by very fine control of the draught, either by opening or closing dampers (firebrick flaps) in the crown (domed roof) of the oven. Progress was monitored by taking trials at different stages of the firing. Prior to the introduction in c.1912 of 'Bullers Rings' (small rings of pottery made to shrink at certain temperatures), this was done either by measuring the contraction of plates placed in open-sided saggers in different parts of the biscuit oven (or observing the length or colour of the flame in glost ovens). Once the firing was complete and the oven cooled, the clammins was broken down and the oven 'drawn' or emptied by the biscuit placers, a particularly hot, dirty and unpopular job frequently filled by casual labour.

Once emptied, the saggers were brushed and repaired whilst the biscuit-fired ware was brushed to remove any dust particles and 'selected' or checked for faults. If acceptable, the ware was stored in the spacious Biscuit Warehouses: flat ware remained on the ground floor in a room parallel to the Port Street range and holloware was carried via one of two internal staircases to first-floor warehouses. An office in the south-east corner of this upper floor was shared by the supervisory Clay Manager and Biscuit Overlooker, an oriel window affording them good vantage points to monitor progress in their areas.[56] Initially a two-storey building, by 1897 the Biscuit Range had had a third-storey storage space added to accommodate the large stock of biscuit ware always kept in readiness.

The Printers' and Decorators' Shops: Pottery Decoration
The biscuit ware was now ready for decoration, most usually by underglaze transfer-printing in the Printers' Shops. As decorating was a comparatively clean process employing women, these rooms, which Bennett described as smelling of '*oil and flannel and humanity*',[57] were housed in the centre of the front Port Street range. A door led directly from the Biscuit Flat Warehouse on the ground floor across the yard to the large Printers' Shop. In 1889 this was furnished with six steam stoves, each serving two printers, on which to prepare the heated colours used in printing; hot plates to keep the copper engraving at the correct temperature; and printers' presses from which the tissue transfers were pulled. Down the centre of the room were '*washing off tubs*' (for removing the transfer print from ware prior to firing) with '*taps etc for each set of workers.*' The floor above had a further Printers' Shop with two stoves (and room for an additional four). By 1893, it was reported that the Printers' Shops employed a total of '*thirty printers, each with a press and three attendants*'. The upper Printers' shop was reached from the first-floor Biscuit Warehouse by a covered bridge, which protected the decorated, but unfired, ware from Middleport's smoking chimneys not to mention the vagaries of the British weather.

The upper floor of the Port Street range had additional painting shops, decorating and gilding rooms, again employing many females. The expensive gold and the various colours used in the decorating processes were stored and mixed in a room next to the ground-floor Printing Shop. The colour used most often was cobalt for blue; but others might include cobalt and manganese for mulberry; chromium and zinc for green; chromium and tin for pink; ferric iron, zinc and chromium for brown.[58] Adjacent was a room for the storage of copper engravings and beyond that a large room, comfortably furnished and decorated with wood panelling and stained glass. This was used by the designer and engraver, the élite of the workforce, whose latest designs could be viewed in the Show Room next door.

Adjacent to, but not yet accessible from, these rooms, were the works' offices. The layout of this area has been much changed over the years, although its Dickensian character remains. Originally, the general office was on the Port Street side, its high desks and stools used by the clerks, sales team and company secretary. A more private office with a large bay window[59] facing the factory was reserved for the company directors. It was suitably furnished with comfortable easy chairs and a large and impressive partners' desk. Still in use today, the desk is believed to have been purchased from Davenport's sale of factory fixture and fittings. As Davenport's many prestigious wares for royalty had included the wedding service for William IV, might it be that its design was discussed and displayed on that very desk?[60] The idea no doubt appealed to the Leigh family's sense of tradition as well as to their own business aspirations!

'*Oil and flannel and humanity*', the Print Shop during the 1930s with Head Printer, Harry Downs, centre.

The general office in c.1930 with, left to right, Winston Brindley, Leslie Stubbs, Miss Mollatt, Miss Hodgkinson, Tom Stevenson Jnr, Wilfie Hope, unknown, and company clerk George Lloyd. Women were only employed in the office following the First World War.

The Dipping House, c.1930, with Tom Stevenson Snr in charge, far left. Protective aprons and caps had to be worn by those working with hazardous lead-based glazes.

The Glost Range: Dipping, Drying and Firing; Sorting, Selecting and Polishing

The office bay window gave the partners a good view of the Middleport Pottery's glost (glazed) range. Prior to glazing (to make it impermeable to liquids), transfer printed biscuit ware first of all had to have a low-temperature firing (around 600°C) in order to burn oil out of the colour. In 1889, two small four-mouth 'hardening-on' kilns had been built, '*on the latest principles with iron doors, etc*' next to the biscuit ovens. A small placing area separated them from the Glost Range's dipping house, a '*long room with iron rack, steam pipes and every modern convenience for saving time and labour*'. There, the dipper would quickly hand-dip the fired printed ware into a suspension of glaze in water in a tub and placed it on a rack to dry. In c.1920 an open-shelved 'mangle' was built located in the dippers' Hot House. This vertical 'paternoster' passed over hot steam pipes which dried the ware as it revolved. It was a huge edifice; the brick-built tower surrounding it stands eighty feet (twenty-four metres) high and is the tallest surviving in the Potteries.[61]

The jobs of the dipper and his assistants were amongst the most dangerous in the factory. Many glazes still contained lead at that time, which gave a wonderful quality and depth of colour to the ware it decorated. However, such an effect was bought at the cost of potters' health and dippers (amongst other pottery workers, such as painters and those working in majolica) were particularly prone to 'plumbism' or lead poisoning. Although it was not made a notifiable disease until 1895, the risks of 'working in the lead' had been well known for some time. Over the years well-intentioned but largely ineffective regulations were introduced, such as ensuring employees took frequent breaks, had regular medical examinations, wore overalls and caps and that they drank a glass of milk each day, a misguided practice which continued well into the 1960s. More effective was 'fritting' *i.e.* a firing process which fused lead-silica with china clay thus rendering a non-poisonous glaze. (Introduced at the beginning of the twentieth century, this precaution continued until the Second World War when measures were taken to replace lead with silica sand.)

Personal hygiene, specifically washing, was also encouraged amongst those working directly with lead based materials and the 1891 Factory and Workshops Acts introduced the first regulations making washrooms (as well as dining rooms) compulsory. Burgess & Leigh again may have been amongst those few philanthropic manufacturers[62] to act ahead of legislation by providing, in the upper storey glost decorating shops, wash basins with additional 'soap fountains' or dispensers (patented by Keeling and Walker).

In addition to the washbasins and lavatories (sited at the corner of the Potting Shops and Port Street range and in the warehouse), the works also, unusually, boasted a bathroom with further communal washing facilities.[63] They were situated in the basement of an extension made in c.1897 to the 'canal end' of the Glost Range. Decorated with white wall tiles and quarry floor tiles, one room housed a roll-top

The dippers' mangle, today.

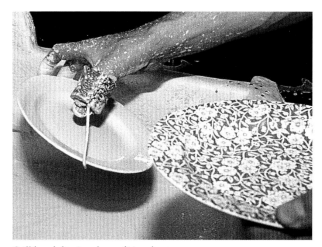

Still hand-dipping the traditional way.

Washing facilities provided in the Wad Cellar at the Middleport Pottery. The bathroom was used by some of the families of those employed by the company until the 1930s. Photographed in 2002.

The Middleport Pottery's glost ovens in 1964. (*Photograph courtesy of Donald Morris.*)

The Packing House as it is today with its large crane for lifting crates of ware on to canal barges. Canal carriage ceased in c.1940.

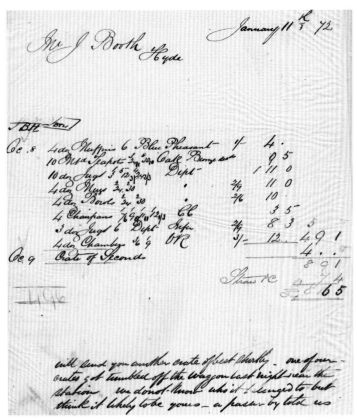

Burgess & Leigh bought in their willow packing crates from local crate makers such as these photographed by the Rev. Malcolm Graham in the 1890s.

Accident in transit? A note to a customer in 1872 indicates that not all deliveries were trouble free.

The site of potters' 'sherdrucks' provides a mine of information for today's ceramic historians. *(Photograph by Rev. Malcolm Graham, 1890s.)*

PACKING CHARGES.

					s.	d.
16 Bar Crate	...	...	...	...	12	6
14 ,,	...	...	...	...	11	6
12 ,,	...	...	...	...	10	6
10 ,,	...	...	...	...	9	6
8 ,,	...	...	...	...	8	6

CASKS.

Sizes	...	Flour	¼ Ton	Middle	½ Ton	Small Tierce
Price	...	2/-	3/4	4/6	6/-	7/6

On return of the empty Crate (carriage paid), a credit note for half the amount is sent which should be returned when remitting.

No allowance made for straw returned.

	No. 1	No. 2	No. 3	No. 4	No. 5	No. 6	No. 7
Hampers (not returnable)	2/-	1/9	1/9	1/3	1/3	1/-	9d.

TERMS:

5% Discount allowed for Cash during the month following date of Invoice.

Seconds Goods are nett and due in one month.

2½% Discount for Cash in 3 months, or on journey at the option.

Afterwards—Strictly Nett and subject to interest at **5%** per annum.

Packing charges per crate, cask and hamper, 1901.

BURGESS & LEIGH

MANUFACTURERS OF GENERAL EARTHENWARE FOR HOME AND FOREIGN MARKETS.

MANUFACTURERS OF JET AND ROCKINGHAM OF BEST QUALITY IN SPECIAL SHAPES AND DESIGNS

MIDDLEPORT POTTERY, BURSLEM, STAFFS.

London Address : Corner of CHARTERHOUSE STREET (next door to Burmantoft's), HOLBORN, E.C.
London Representative—MR. F. HODGSON. Country Representatives { MR. WM. BUTTERS. MR. F. W. BEARDMORE. New York Agents— { R. SLIMMON & CO., 96, Church Street

An engraving of the Middleport Pottery showing the Packing House, far right, which was added in c.1891. *(The Pottery Gazette, 1897.)*

bath and the other a row of eight large relief-decorated wash-basins. Somewhat surprisingly, they were installed in what was called the Wad Cellar, an area used for the pugging of wad clay (used to seal glost saggars), the clay being delivered via an external hatch. The availability of such facilities for those employees working in the dirtiest or most dangerous jobs was another example of the firm's concern for their workers' welfare.

More usually, however, it was pottery, not potters, which was dipped and dried! Mirroring the arrangement in the Biscuit Range, ware was taken from the Dippers' Hot House through to the Glost Placers' House parallel to it. Here glost placers, sometimes assisted by young female 'crankers', would carefully place an assortment of items on 'thimbles', 'spurs' or 'stilts', the refractory supports used in saggars to prevent glazed ware sticking to other surfaces. A 'stilt store' was close by the

Glost Saggar House, itself conveniently sited at the far end of the Glost Range opposite the Saggar Makers' Shop. The full saggars were then placed one on top of the other in bungs – making sure that they were airtight by sealing with wad clay – in one of the four glost ovens.

Originally, there had been just three glost ovens planned, parallel to and symmetrical with the three biscuit ovens. However, it was decided, probably soon after the initial plans had been drawn up, to build a fourth and the factory was thereafter frequently known as 'the seven-oven works'. The building of the fourth glost oven was certainly completed by c.1897 but more than likely added as part of an ongoing building programme in c.1890-1891.[64] Whilst the biscuit firing usually took one week from start to finish, the glost firing was a comparatively quick process. Any one of the Middleport Pottery's glost ovens could be set by glost placers during the day and fired (at around 1090°C) in twenty-four hours. Cooled overnight, it was then drawn on the third day. However, as there might be around five glost firings a week, the job of the glost fireman (latterly Stan Johnson) was still far from effortless. Neither was that of the glost odd man who would have to work in excess of twelve-hour days to earn a decent wage in the pottery industry.

Following the first glost firing which had fused the glaze to the ware, additional on-glaze hand-decoration might be required, such as gilding, ground laying, colour dusting, aerographing, and enamel painting. Then, one or more further low-temperature firings (at around 700°C) would be necessary to fasten the colour or gold to the ware's surface. These small 'muffle' or enamel box kilns were situated next to the 'Number 1' glost oven (closest to Port Street) and not far from an upper-storey Enamelling Shop. From c.1900, the 'Climax', a continuous coal-fired oven, was used for this purpose. It was undoubtedly technologically advanced for its time, there being only one other in the Potteries.[65] Ware was packed not in saggars (which were unnecessary as no flames entered enamel kilns) but in cast iron baskets. These were placed into twenty trucks which were rotated continuously in a circle, making it one of the earliest 'tunnel' ovens of its kind. Correspondence in company archives from a pottery manufacturer in Trenton, New Jersey, wishing to install a similar kiln in his own premises, indicated its 'state of the art' modernity whilst its use by Burgess & Leigh until the early 1950s was testament to its reliability.

The Glost Warehouses

Possibly a full month after it started life in the Slip House, 'clay had vanished into crock'[66] and the decorated ware was ready to make its way to the gleaming Glost Warehouses. These were situated in a two-storey Glost Warehouse range parallel to the glost ovens and extended on the first floor above the office area in the Port Street range. (Additional space was available on the first floor above the Dippers' Hot House.) The Glost Warehouses were relatively comfortable areas in which to work. The Pottery Gazette's Report of June 1899 records that 'both biscuit and glost, leave nothing to be desired, the fitting up of the glost warehouse in particular with pitch pine veneering and tables being an innovation that will save much loss.' Such comfort would have been appreciated by the teams of nimble-fingered 'thimble pickers' and 'sorters', usually female, who sat on small three-legged stools, selecting for re-use any undamaged thimbles or stilts, and also remove any remnants adhered to the ware. Polishing would further

remove or correct any flaws to glost ware.

The upper floor of the designated Glost Warehouse range was fitted with wooden racking which provided separate storage for home and overseas orders. A corner office was used by the Glost Warehouse supervisor; in 1895, Jack Downs had this position, presiding over a team of twenty or so sorters, polishers and packers whose wages for one week amounted to £14 6s 5d. Ware was stored by type; the 1893 'descriptive account' of the Middleport Pottery records a total of five 'warehouses': one for stocktaking and order picking; one for teawares; one for dinner and dessert wares; one for toiletwares; one for 'pheasant' or 'common sets' (the more utilitarian wares and more popular printed patterns including Cottage Pheasant, Dove Rhine and Blue Willow). Areas of the Glost Warehouses were also used in conjunction with the Show Room to display wares to visitors anxious to take home some of Burgess & Leigh's finest earthenware: 'In a word, those desirous of seeing a truly fin-de-siècle museum of the finest things in modern pottery could not do better than ask this courteous firm for permission to have a look at its warehouses.'

The Packing House

Orders duly picked were ready to be packed in the Packing House. This was originally a single storey building[67] which conveniently adjoined the Glost Warehouse range. According to The Pottery Gazette's Report of 1889, 'the ware finally being let down by hoist into the packing house is another new feature to be noted.' The building offered immediate access to the canal for transport by barge, or up to the Port Street entrance for road and rail carriage. The same issue of The Pottery Gazette reported that part of the canal frontage 'will ultimately be a wharf for crates awaiting shipment and straw for packing'. This refers to a new building, described on the c.1900 factory plan as the 'Crate Store, Straw Shed,' which was built parallel to the Glost Warehouse range. It had direct access on to the canal, its other end accommodating a 'four-horse stable and loft over'. (As the building does not appear on the original 1889 engraving of the works but is included on that of c.1893, it is likely to have been built between those years.) The brick built 'Crate Store, Straw Shed' was separated from the pottery's main buildings by the cobbled alley leading from the archway entrance to the canal. In this respect, its planning anticipated and complied with new legislation introduced by the 1891 Factory and Workshop Act which prohibited the storage of flammable material, in this case packing straw, within the main body of factory buildings.

In time, the 'Crate Store' also became used for packing, and became known as the Packing House. The additional space it offered would have been most welcome to the small packing team of just three in 1895. Each packer, seated on the ground, a pile of straw to one side, would quickly and skillfully pack his orders or consignments, brought by boys from the warehouses either in a bung of flat ware or a basket of holloware items. The goods were then packed in returnable wooden crates made locally from small pliant willow branches woven together. An average of 150 crates were packed each week in 1895. This apparently flimsy method of packing resulted in minimal breakage although wares for certain markets might be packed slightly differently with tanks, cases and hogsheads being offered in place of willow baskets or crates.[68] A price list of 1914 advised customers that packing charges were 'at the lowest

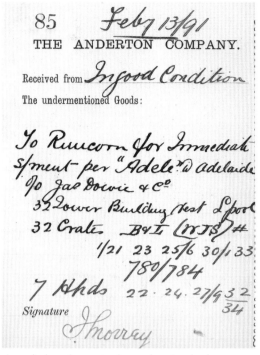

Australia bound, a receipt for canal carriage by the Anderton Canal Company to Runcorn Docks for onward shipment to Adelaide, 1891.

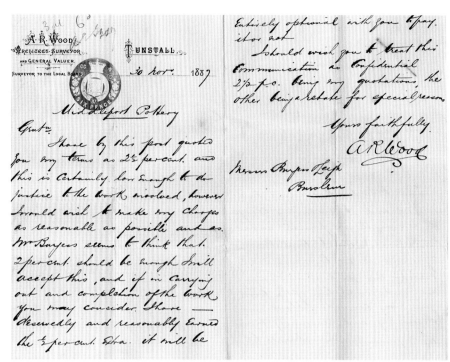

Letter from Middleport Pottery architect A R Wood, 30th November 1889, in which he reluctantly agrees to a reduction in his usual fees.

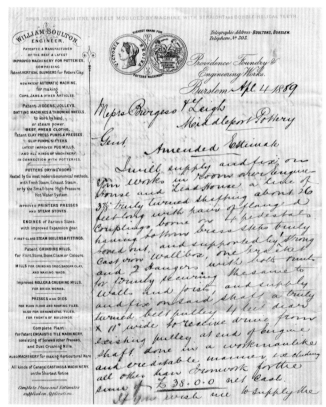

Engineer William Boulton's 'amended estimate', April 4th 1889.

possible rate' whilst for carriage and freight 'Delivery is at the Works, and all charges and costs are at the expense of the purchaser.' Once packed and weighed on the large weighbridge, the larger of two lifting cranes lifted the crated ware on to a canal barge whilst the smaller loaded that due for transportation by road or rail on to a horse-drawn cart for delivery to Longport railway station, nearby. The Middleport Pottery kept horses until the early 1950s, using them for 'shraffing', carting non-recyclable factory rubbish to the company's leased 'shraff' tips (sometimes called 'sherd rucks') across the canal.

Costs

There was seldom any wastage in pottery manufacture. Potters sold faulty wares as seconds, thirds and even 'lump'. By all accounts Burgess & Leigh were especially keen on cost saving. This was illustrated not only in their manufacturing processes but also in the construction of the Middleport Pottery, which may have been the 'model pottery' with all 'mod cons' but was still subject to sensible financial restraints. A letter of 29th November, 1887 from Arthur Ellis, a Burslem Solicitor, confirms that Burgess & Leigh had taken out a mortgage with Parker's Trustees of £8,000 with an interest rate of four per cent to run from 1st January, 1888. With regular repayments as well as insurance on the new factory to pay, the partners were eager to keep costs to an absolute minimum. As is usual in any architectural project, the building underwent numerous alterations and additions, with work ongoing for several years. During that time suppliers and contractors were not allowed any unnecessary additional expenditure, correspondence in company archives revealing that when extra costs were incurred, they were compelled to justify them. Engineer William Boulton wrote in February 1888 that 'I have sent in a very reasonable estimate for the class of work I should do…. This is asking a great sacrifice as I shall do the work in just the same manner…. if I don't get any profit.' He was also requested to refurbish existing machinery from the Hill Pottery wherever possible rather than provide all brand-new machinery. The architect A.R. Wood also had his fees reduced; writing to the company, he stated that while his usual charge was two-and-a-half per cent (of the building), 'Mr Burgess seems to think that two per cent should be enough.' A little grudgingly perhaps, the architect accepted this, 'being a rebate for special reasons.' What those reasons were must remain a mystery!

A further bill from A. R. Wood to Burgess & Leigh, dated 28th August, 1889, confirms the building contractor as William Cooke of Newcastle Street, Burslem, 'established

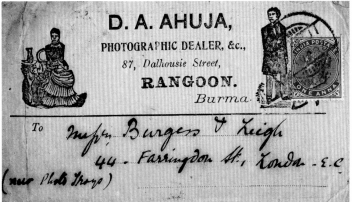

An order from a customer in Burma, addressed to Burgess & Leigh's London Showroom, for photograph trays patented by the company in 1903. Richard S Burgess was an enthusiastic amateur photographer.

1868', and shows charges for the painting, building and estimates for relevant machinery fixtures and fittings for five ranges: 'Slip House Range Colored Green'; 'Potters' Shops Colored Brown'; 'Front Range Colored Yellow'; 'Packing House Range Colored Blue'; and 'Warehouse etc Colored Red'. At that stage and with further additions to make, the total cost was in the region of £7,500.[69] Eight years on, costs had crept up; a balance sheet of Cooke's work,[70] dated 28th September, 1897, lists additional work totalling £8,982 less deductions, the balance due to Cooke being £312. A comparison is provided in The British Architect of August 1887, which quoted tenders for building an eight-oven earthenware pottery at Longport (architect, R. Dain & Son of Burslem and Hanley) to be between £7,245 and £9,437.[71] As one would expect, Burgess & Leigh did not pay over the odds for their seven-oven works! But neither it seems did they always pay on time, as nearly a year later, Mr Cooke was writing directly to Burgess & Leigh requesting 'a cheque in settlement as it is quite time that this was cleared up off our mind'!

The Death of William Leigh

Amidst the excitement of Burgess & Leigh's future plans for the new factory, there was also sadness over the gradual decline in health of the company founder, William Leigh. On 23rd February, 1889, he died aged sixty-nine 'at his residence, 244 Waterloo Road.'[72] William was never well enough to visit the newly built Middleport Pottery, which was to be the lasting testimony of this worthy Victorian pottery manufacturer and his partner. The pottery was not officially occupied until 25th March, a month after he died. However, the company move was gradual and some production work may already have started there. Certainly, one would like to believe the report[73] that William took comfort from seeing smoke rising from the Burgess & Leigh bottle ovens from his home. The Pottery Gazette of 1st March, 1889 reported that with:

> 'his able partner he had succeeded in building up one of the largest businesses in the Potteries. The firm were just removing to a new factory on the Trent and Mersey canal which they have erected and fitted in the most modern style owing to the continued increase in their large business. The funeral took place on Wed 27th ult., the employees following the remains of their kind and always considerate master to his resting place.'

On the announcement of his death at a meeting of the Burslem Town Council, tribute was again paid to his good character: 'his unfailing good temper avoided any undue friction and unpleasantness.'[74] A 'life-long abstainer,'[75] his obituary stated that 'by his perseverance, honesty and uprightness, he had risen to be amongst the most successful manufacturers of the Potteries.'[76]

In fact, William did not live to see the company he had co-founded achieve its greatest commercial success. However, doubtless he had every faith that Burgess & Leigh was safe in the hands of his son and successor, Edmund, and his co-founder and partner of twenty-seven years, Frederick Rathbone Burgess whose own son, Richard Samuel, was to join the company that year.

Richard Samuel Burgess (1858-1912)
and the Death of his Father

Born on 6th December 1858, Richard was thirty-one years old before he joined the company as a partner in 1889. Edmund Leigh had by then worked for the family firm for over twenty years. Although Richard's employment prior to joining Burgess & Leigh has not been documented, his obituary[77] reported that he spent all his working life in the pottery industry. His role within Burgess & Leigh was as a production manager; he 'attended to the manufacturing side of the business, and therefore did not come much into contact with the distributing trade'.

A 'very reserved man', Richard's lifelong hobby was photography and he was 'a remarkably expert operator. This he pursued solely from his love of the art and did not attempt to make it, as he could have done, a remunerative as well as an interesting recreation. He was also a skilled mechanic, and had a workshop of his own in which he spent much of his time when not enjoying himself with his camera.'[78] He was no doubt behind Burgess & Leigh's decision to manufacture photographic equipment; their 'Improved developing trays for photographic film' patented in 1903 drew orders from as far afield as Burma.

Richard's interest in mechanical engineering also extended to the equipment used at the Middleport Factory; although he had no formal engineering training, he is reported to have experimented with and indeed designed a number of pieces of factory kiln equipment for the works including most probably a lifting device for the Climax kiln. It seems that some of his ideas worked better than others: a cooling fan for an enamel kiln only succeeded in blowing dust on to the unfired ware whilst a glaze cylinder he purchased caused persistent problems when iron from its axle contaminated the glaze![79]

Whether Richard viewed these few failures as amusing incidents is not now known. Certainly, he was not without a sense of humour although, if one story is to be believed, it might not have been shared by some of his employees; arriving daily on horseback,[80] it is reported that he used to stand each morning under the archway at the factory entrance greeting a loud 'Good Afternoon' to any bleary-eyed latecomers.[81] However, another anecdote[82] recalls that Richard's own time-keeping was not above reproach and that he was known to spend the odd afternoon enjoying a film at one of Burslem's recently opened cinemas!

Richard had worked at the Middleport Pottery for six years when in 1895 his father died, aged sixty-seven, at the family home, *Oaklands*, in Porthill. Frederick Rathbone Burgess was buried beneath an impressive tombstone in St Margaret's Churchyard, Wolstanton, alongside his wife, Alice Clulow, two years his senior, who had died in 1885 and a child, Robert Clulow Rathbone, who had died in infancy in 1866. He was survived by Richard and a daughter Mathilda Hannah (1859-1925),[83] neither of whom was to marry. With Frederick's death six years after his erstwhile partner and co-founder William Leigh, ownership of the company passed fully to the second generation of Burgess & Leigh.

Burgess & Leigh's First Design Studio: 'Designer' Edwin Leigh (d.1936)

The expansion in business and the move to the Middleport Pottery also saw the establishment of what the ceramic industry today would call an Art or Design Studio. The company's first Art Director or Design Manager was 'Designer' Edwin Leigh, so-called to distinguish him from his employers to whom he was not related. It is not known exactly when he was first appointed but, as he retired in 1929 at a time when people often had the same job for life, it is probable that he joined the Middleport Pottery sometime during the 1890s. One of the few surviving sketches to bear his monogram is dated 1896. Very little has been recorded of his life although a notebook[84] gives an address of Derby Street, Cobridge, Stoke-on-Trent. Written in an elegant and stylish hand, it records various recipes for colours as well as notes on the decoration of wares. A number of unillustrated pattern books in company archives are also in his distinctive handwriting.

Working with 'Designer' Leigh would have been one or more engravers, including possibly George Bateman who records confirm was employed by the company by 1916, then aged fifty-three. 'Designer' Leigh, however, would have had overall responsibility for the design of patterns from a variety of sources: existing copper engravings; patterns or decorative motifs published in folio form (mainly in Europe); possibly his own designs; and designs by freelance ceramic artists, which had either been commissioned or

A page from an inventory of the pottery listing the contents of 'Designer' Leigh's studio, c.1917.

A drawing made by 'Designer' Leigh in the 1890s and bearing his monogram.

submitted speculatively to the Middleport Pottery. (A double-entry bank account book shows a payment of three guineas made in May 1890 for unspecified '*designs*'.)

Several examples of such artists' designs remain in Burgess, Dorling & Leigh company archives. A few (which may or may not have been put into production) bear signatures, not, unfortunately, always legible! Of these, various tableware patterns are signed by an unknown '*Wm E. Dunn*' (possibly a William Dunn, living in Bleak Street, Burslem in 1898) whilst one for a ewer dated July 1890 is marked on the reverse J. Slater, Leveson Villas, Regent Street, Stoke. A Joseph Slater, possibly one of the well-

From the archive: late nineteenth-century drawings for underglaze printed tableware patterns.

Signed undated sketch by Charles Wilkes.

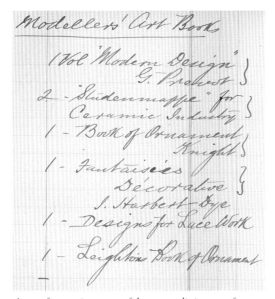

A page from an inventory of the pottery listing art reference books in Charles Wilkes' modelling studio, c.1917.

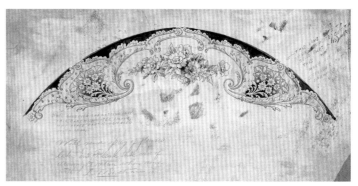

A design for a plate submitted by Louis Thomas Swettenham, a Minton-trained ceramic artist, who produced a number of designs for Burgess & Leigh from the late 1880s to the 1930s.

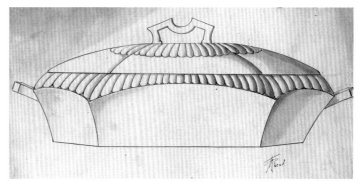

Drawing of a tureen by Frederick Alfred Rhead, neighbour of Charles Wilkes, Liberal associate of Edmund Leigh and father of Charlotte.

known family of ceramicists,[85] is also known to have worked for Samuel Alcock & Co. at the Hill Pottery before going on to Minton (1856-1875).[86]

Another design is signed 'Swettenham'.[87] Variously called Lewis Thomas Swetnam or Louis Thomas Swettenham, this Minton-trained painter, gilder and tile designer (born in 1860) reportedly worked for Royal Doulton from 1886 until 1915 as an etcher. (Etching

involved drawing designs with a metal point on to a wax-coated copperplate which is then dipped into a bath of acid. The acid cannot penetrate the wax but bites into the copperplate where the design has been drawn leaving an outline ready for printing.) Although the skills of etching were not as highly regarded as those of engraving, Swettenham was nonetheless considered to be a fine artist. Charles Noke, Doulton's Art Director, wrote of him: '*Etching for some effects is far more pleasing than engraving, and many of his plates were full of fine details, yet bold, clear and sympathetic in execution. His clever work was always first class.*'[88] Swettenham was to produce numerous designs for Burgess & Leigh although it is not clear whether as a full-time employee or as a freelance artist. (An art reference book remains in company archives inscribed with his name and an address of Nettlebank, Smallthorne, near Tunstall.) Swettenham is recorded as receiving payment of £27 5s 0d for '*wages*', plus £2 15s 0d for '*sundries*' in October 1889,

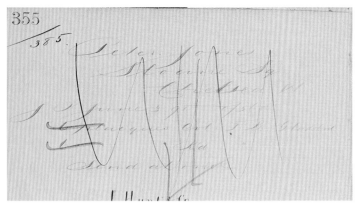

An order for Gladstone commemorative plaques from Peter Jones, 1898. (See pages 25 and 178).

considerable sums which might have been either for designs produced or possibly for a period of employment. He is also recorded as having travelled to London for the company in 1898, the year he designed Burgess & Leigh's portrait plaque commemorating the death of Gladstone. Factory records suggest that Swettenham was in full-time employment at Burgess & Leigh following his departure from Doulton.

A number of archival drawings, including one of a covered vegetable dish, bear the signature of 'F. Rhead'. Frederick Alfred Rhead (1856-1933), artist and designer, was a member of the second generation of a north Staffordshire family of talented ceramic artists,[89] as well as a Liberal associate of Edmund. An assistant to the Minton *pâte-sur-pâte* artist Louis Marc Solon, Rhead designed for Wedgwood and Pinder, Bourne before becoming Art Director for various firms including E. J. D. Bodley, Wileman & Co. (later Shelleys), Wood & Sons and latterly Cauldon Potteries Ltd. It is not known whether Burgess & Leigh produced any of his designs but certainly he had further contact with the company, not least through his famous daughter, Charlotte, who was to make such an impact later.

Charles Wilkes, Modeller

Frederick Rhead was also a good friend of a Charles Wilkes who, following an apprenticeship with Josiah Wedgwood in Etruria,[90] was appointed by the Middleport Pottery Design Studio in 1889. Born on 13th October, 1864 in West Parade, Mount Pleasant in Fenton, Stoke-on-Trent, his father, also Charles Wilkes, worked as a pottery manager in Fenton. Wilkes junior attended the Burslem School of Art (then

Charles Wilkes, Head Modeller, in his studio, c.1930.

housed in the Wedgwood Institute) and later is thought to have taught there for some period of time. Following his marriage, he lived for a time near Frederick Rhead in Lime Cottage, Marsh Avenue, Wolstanton.[91] Later in the 1920s and whilst still employed by Burgess & Leigh, Wilkes joined Frederick Rhead in setting up a small business in two cottage properties in William Clowes Street, Burslem, manufacturing ornamental wares such as wall masks and butterflies. Unfortunately the enterprise failed, most likely owing to the artists' lack of business acumen. Wilkes' marriage produced two children who both worked for the renowned family pottery, Dudson of Hanley: his daughter, May Wilkes, married Hubert, a fourth generation Dudson, and was to work for the firm in an administrative capacity until the early 1940s whilst his son, Frank Wilkes, joined the same firm in 1927 where he proved himself to be a much valued Works Manager.[92]

Charles Wilkes was responsible for new shape design at Burgess & Leigh, working from preliminary sketches to produce an original clay model. A scrapbook from his art school days reveals an academic interest in the history of ceramics with much research from the *Art Journal* and other publications. Remaining sketchbooks and many hundreds of pencil drawings and watercolour sketches reveal him to be a hugely prolific, imaginative and versatile shape designer of table and ornamental wares. Wilkes remained with the company until his retirement aged seventy-two years in 1943. Although his eyesight deteriorated with old age, it did little to halt his continuing interest in art and design. He died in January 1957, at the grand old age of ninety-three. His contribution to Burgess & Leigh should not be underestimated. He was to prove himself adept at responding to changes in a variety of styles, making an effortless transition from the High Victorian, through Art Nouveau to Art Deco.

Burgess & Leigh's Late Victorian Wares

The move to the Middleport Pottery in 1889 did not result in an overnight change of design direction and many of Burgess & Leigh's popular Hill Pottery wares remained in production for some time. However, by 1896 Wilkes' work was already drawing the attention of the trade press which reported:

'Messrs Burgess & Leigh meet the demand for graceful outline and embellishment in all the things they make for everyday domestic use. Their shapes are not the accidental outcome of haphazard experiments, but the development of ideas suggested by the contemplation of art – which, after all, is nothing but the truly beautiful. Messrs Burgess & Leigh have provided that those of us who want beauty in decoration or symmetry in shape, in our tea-pots, jugs, vases and dinner ware, shall have it.'

Ornamental Wares

Wilkes' skill as a modeller was put to good use from the mid-1890s in the further development of ornamental ranges or *'fancy goods'*. Such 'art' wares usually included jardinières and stands (or pots and pedestals), flowerpots, loving cups, pot-pourri jars and a variety of vases. The *Majestic*, an embossed pattern with a scalloped edge, and the *Eclipse*, a twisted fluted shape decorated with a variety of patterns, were two ranges particularly noted in the trade press. Vases were large and ovoid or ewer-shaped with long necks and ornate, sometimes snake-shaped, handles.

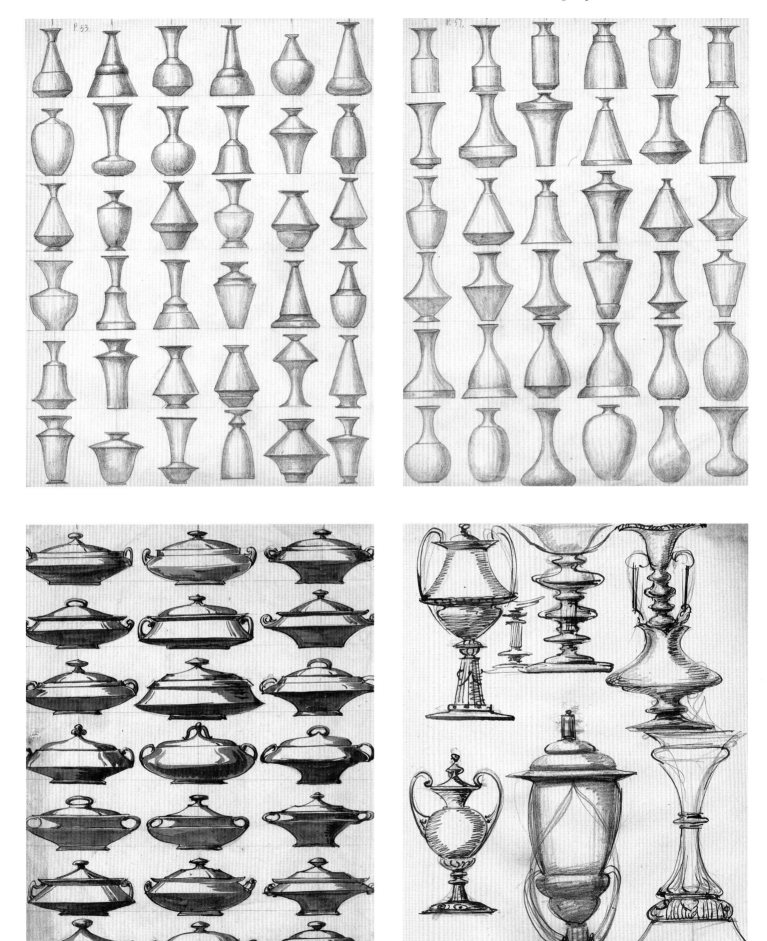

Variations on several themes, examples of the many hundreds of un-dated and un-signed design drawings, attributed to Charles Wilkes, which have been saved by Burgess & Leigh. Here, designs for vases and tureens.

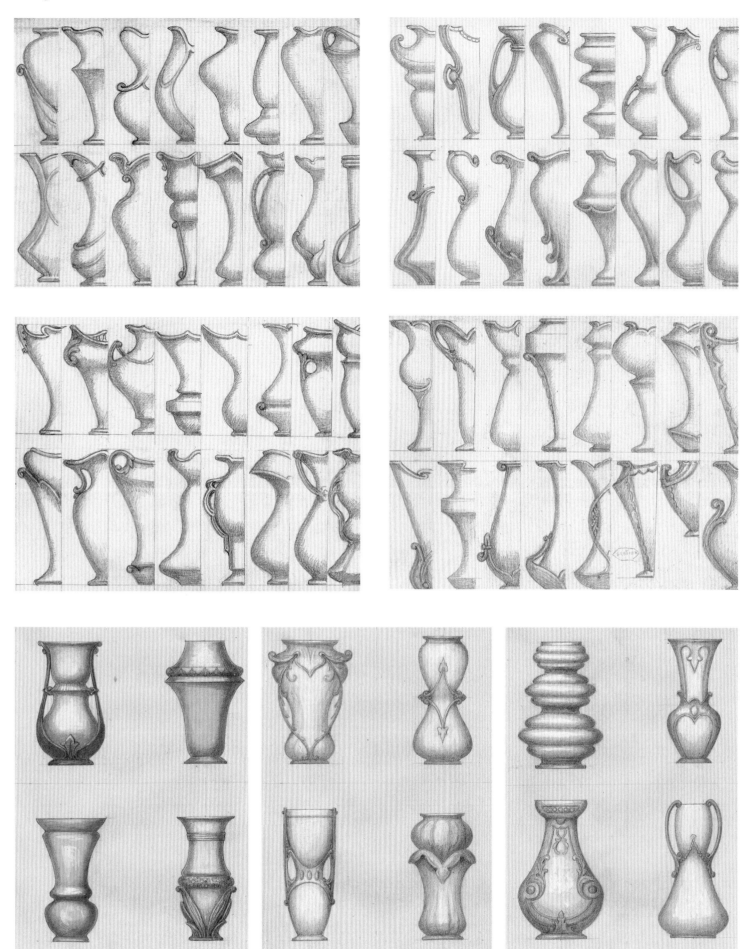

Ideas for vases, drawn in profile and coloured front views. Most of Wilkes' more fanciful designs were never produced by Burgess & Leigh. Wilkes' fanatical interest in shape design included lecturing on the subject at the Burslem School of Art.

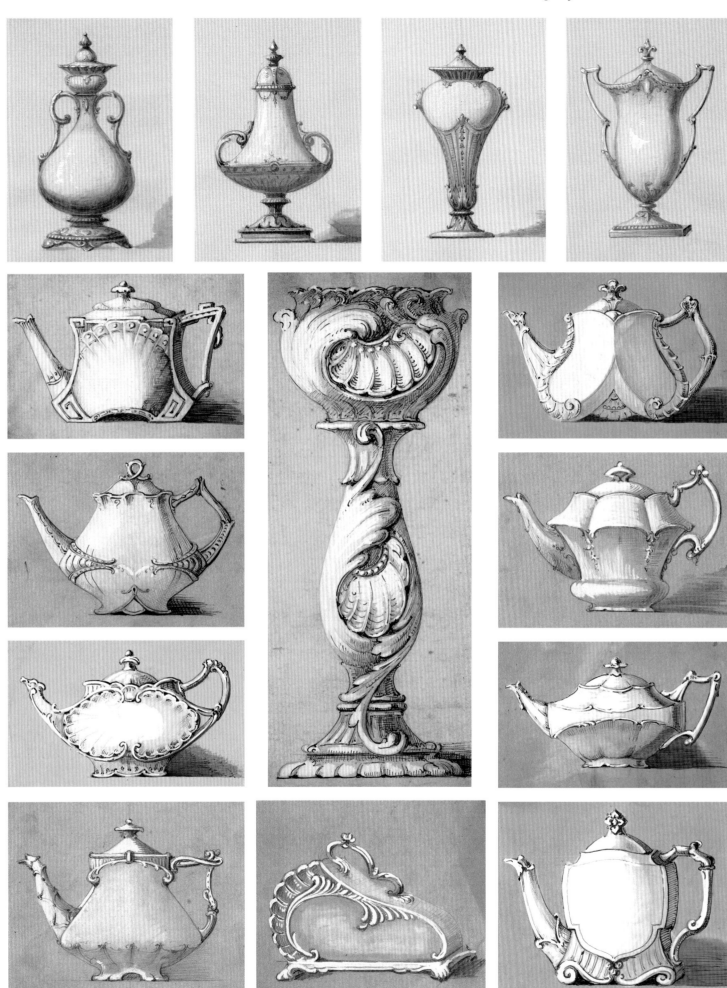

Charles Wilkes or 'Designer' Edwin Leigh? Un-signed pen and ink designs for ornate vases, teapots, a cheese stand and cover and jardinière and stand, c.1890s.

Burleigh

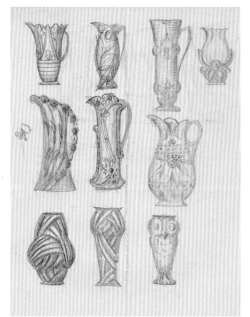 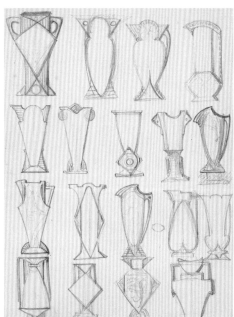 

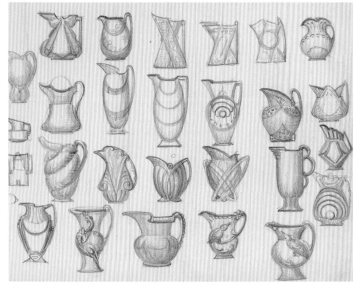 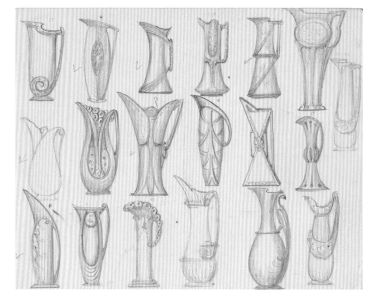

Later designs by Wilkes, including some for 1930s Flower Jugs and teapots.

Drawing for a *Rococo* shape ewer, signed J. Slater, 1890. Compare with the patterns illustrated in the catalogue, shown right.

Every variety of pattern and shape in Burgess & Leigh's ewers and basins from the 1890s.

Toiletwares

During the 1890s, the range of toiletwares expanded considerably and accounted for about half the company's output.[93] The sets, which then comprised a ewer and basin, chamber pot, brush vase, soap box and sponge tray, were available in six-, eight- or nine-piece sets in a wide variety of designs. Shapes were sometimes the same as those for tableware holloware, such as the *London*, *Boston* and *Albany* and featured the same patterns. Some were perfectly plain, for example, the *Trent* or the elegant *Royal* shape, and available with a white glaze or with a simple band and line. Others, like the *Melbourne* and more especially the *New Venetian* and *Rococo*, featured elaborately moulded handles and necks and were decorated with a profusion of floral patterns and gilding. Such opulence in a nine-piece set might have cost in the region of thirty shillings in 1893.

Tablewares

There was also much expansion of Burgess & Leigh's tableware ranges in the 1890s. Some of the old Hill Pottery shapes such as *Corinth*, *Imperial* and *Royal Flute* were continued alongside the introduction of Wilkes' newer ones, for example, *Albany*, *Marlborough* and *Cleveland*. In style, the printed dinner ware patterns of the 1880s-1890s displayed a typically High Victorian eclecticism. Traditional printed patterns remaining in production included *Broseley* and *Willow*; the romantic pastoral pattern *Rhine*, which had been produced by both Alcock & Co. and Davenports; and from 1887 the floral *Kaiser* (also the name of an earlier dinner ware shape) which for obvious reasons had disappeared by the time of the First World War. Some of Burgess & Leigh's

'*Fancy Goods*', an advertisement from *The Pottery Gazette* of 1898 illustrating ornamental wares modelled by Charles Wilkes and two plaques of William Ewart Gladstone who died that year.

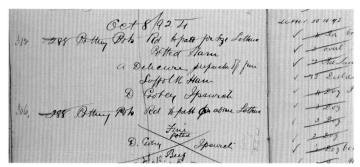

Elaborate badged ware for 'delicious Suffolk Ham', an order from Ipswich, 1892.

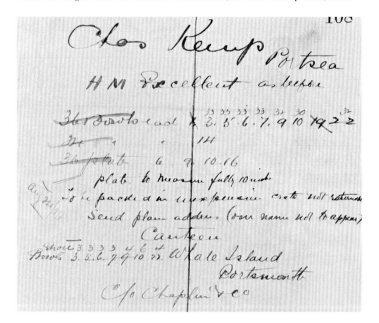

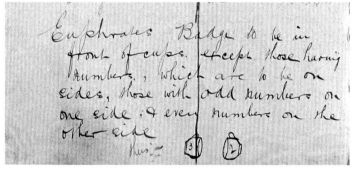

An order for *badged* wares, including numbered cups, for the mess rooms of HMS Euphrates and Excellent, Royal Naval Shore Stations on Whale Island, Portsmouth. The agent, Charles Kemp, requests the Burgess & Leigh name 'not to appear'!

1893 catalogue page illustrating utilitarian wares: plain glazed toilet sets; kitchen wares; and badged- and *Pheasant* tablewares.

Two oriental-style patterns from the 1890s, *Siam*, left, and *Lahore*, right. Larger diameter 9³/₄ins(24.5cms).

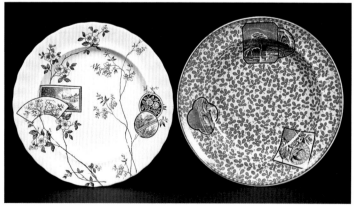

Aesthetic-style patterns made at the Hill Pottery, *Conway*, left, printed in brown and impressed 1888, and an earlier sheet pattern printed in blue with vignettes in brown. Larger diameter 9³/₄ins (24.5cms).

older surface patterns were revitalised when applied to Wilkes' new shapes, such as *Suez*, a Davenport pattern, on the *Albany* shape, and Burgess & Leigh's own neo-classical *Kensington* on the *Marlborough* shape. The Aesthetic style of the 1880s could still be seen in patterns like *Conway* on the *Chelsea* shape and *Norman* on the *Albany* shape whilst the Japanese influence produced patterns such as *Satsuma*, *Nankin*, *Orient* and *Siam*. The names of other patterns, for instance *Lahore* and *Teheran*, evoked Britain's imperial adventures. Designs of fruit and flowers reflected the Victorians' continuing interest in botany: *Fruit* on *Boston*; *Rose*, *Poppy* and *Clover* on the *Cleveland* shape; and the Davenport patterns *Hops* on the *Acme* shape and *Danish Fern* (an abiding Victorian passion) on the *Albany* shape. Animal subjects featured less frequently on Burgess & Leigh's printed patterns, but of these, another Davenport pattern, *Nuts*, featuring a squirrel, was one of the earliest.

Drawing of an aesthetic-style pattern similar to Burgess & Leigh's popular *Rustic* pattern, c.1890.

This pattern from Burgess & Leigh's Print Record Book was also produced by Old Hall in the 1880s and has been attributed to the influential Victorian designer, Christopher Dresser.

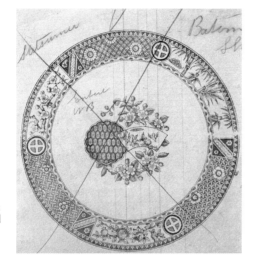

Satsuma, Japanese-style pattern from the Print Record Book c.1885.

The name *Satsuma* was also used for a Burgess & Leigh pattern introduced in the 1920s.

Plate, *Satsuma* pattern printed in brown, diameter 10½ins (27cms). Manufactured by Bates, Gildea & Walker whose printed mark it bears together with a registration diamond of 1879. The company traded from 1878-1881 at the Dale Hall works, Longport. Burgess & Leigh may have purchased their patterns, although it was not unusual for potteries to produce the same patterns at the same time.

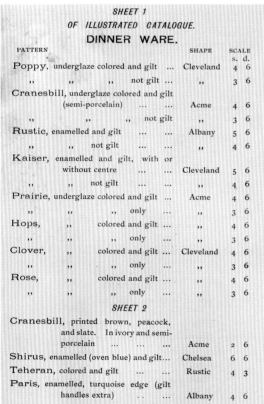

SHEET 1
OF ILLUSTRATED CATALOGUE.
DINNER WARE.

PATTERN			SHAPE	SCALE s. d.
Poppy, underglaze colored and gilt	...		Cleveland	4 6
,, ,, ,, not gilt	...		,,	3 6
Cranesbill, underglaze colored and gilt (semi-porcelain)	...	...	Acme	4 6
,, ,, ,, not gilt	...		,,	3 6
Rustic, enamelled and gilt	...	...	Albany	5 6
,, ,, not gilt	...		,,	4 6
Kaiser, enamelled and gilt, with or without centre	...	...	Cleveland	5 6
,, ,, not gilt	...	...	,,	4 6
Prairie, underglaze colored and gilt	...		Acme	4 6
,, ,, ,, only	...		,,	3 6
Hops, ,, colored and gilt	...		,,	4 6
,, ,, ,, only	...		,,	3 6
Clover, ,, colored and gilt	...		Cleveland	4 6
,, ,, ,, only	...		,,	3 6
Rose, ,, colored and gilt	...		,,	4 6
,, ,, ,, only	...		,,	3 6
SHEET 2				
Cranesbill, printed brown, peacock, and slate. In ivory and semi-porcelain	...	...	Acme	2 6
Shirus, enamelled (oven blue) and gilt	...		Chelsea	6 6
Teheran, colored and gilt	...	...	Rustic	4 3
Paris, enamelled, turquoise edge (gilt handles extra)	...	...	Albany	4 6

Tableware patterns, shapes and price scales, a page from Burgess & Leigh's 1893 catalogue.

Left to right: Lidded tureen, *May* pattern, 1889-c.1903, length 11¾ins (30cms); oval meat dish *Conway*, 1868-1888, length 15¼ins (39cms); and plate *Norman*, 1868-1888, diameter 10¼ins (26cms).

Fruit and flowers, enamelled and gilt printed tableware patterns as illustrated in a catalogue of 1893.

Popular patterns: *Asiatic Pheasant*, *Ferns* and *Rhine*.

Artwork showing the *Poppy* pattern featured on the above catalogue page, top left.

Plate decorated with *Rhine* and printed in dove grey, c.1868-1888. Diameter 10ins (25.5cms).

Rhine in the Print Record Book. Notes indicate that eight flat copper plates and six roller plates were engraved with the pattern to make up a full dinner service.

It is interesting to discover from early records that Burgess & Leigh produced tablewares (most probably unmarked) either depicting children or for use by them. Prints of angelic children engaged in games and pastimes were derived from popular illustraters such as Kate Greenaway.

The most popular items for children to use themselves were simple straight-sided mugs or 'toy cans' which were given as 'gifts for good children' on christenings or other significant occasions. Companies such as Spode had produced these with the children's name either printed, gilded or painted, as early as the 1830s. Burgess & Leigh produced similar mugs and cans from the 1860s until c.1920. Some were decorated with 'educational' prints such as the letters of the alphabet. The company was one of many to reproduce the illustrations of *Dr Franklin's Maxims*, their promotion of self-improvement through industry, temperance and frugality no doubt appealing to the Leigh family's Methodist inclinations. Popular nursery rhymes such as *The House that Jack Built* offered some light relief to the young.

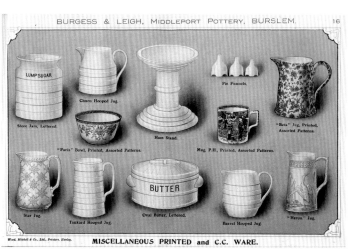

A mug shown printed in black in an early twentieth century catalogue.

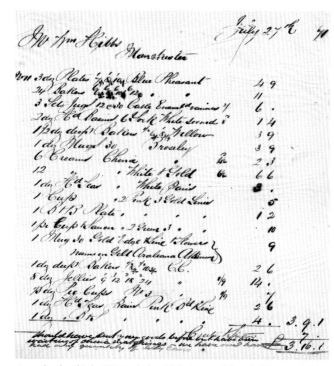

An order dated July 1871 includes '1 Mug', price 9d, with 'Name in Gilt'.

Designs for children from Burgess & Leigh's Print Record Book. Very few of the popular nineteenth-century childrens plates and mugs had factory marks. Cheaply made and probably painted by children. This is the first record of their manufacture in a pottery pattern book.

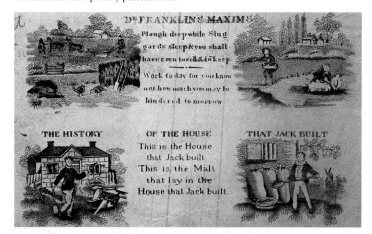

Dr Franklin's Maxims and *The History of the House that Jack Built*, lessons and rhymes for young children, designs for toy cans or mugs from the Print Record Book.

How's Business? Slack! Children at work ....

Beg, Sir and *Expectations*, moral tales for the Victorian child.

The History of The House that Jack Built, a toy can illustrated in an early twentieth century catalogue.

Mary, a typical example of a child's name in a *cartouche*, in a style which Burgess & Leigh made for some fifty years from the 1860s until the early 1900s.

...and at play. Children's games and pastimes were popular subjects for nursery wares.

Catalogue page showing flow blue patterns especially popular in North America, 1890s.

Large Victorian families were able to buy Burgess & Leigh dinner ware in fifty-, fifty-four-, sixty-six-, seventy-six-, and enormous ninety-nine-piece sets, with prices ranging from 12s 11d to £4 11s 9d, depending on quantity and the quality of decoration. Although underglaze printing from copper engravings was the usual method of decoration, records suggest that the company might also have purchased some coloured lithographic transfer prints, which were first produced during the late 1890s in Germany. Underglaze printed patterns were available in a variety of colours and variations: matt blue, dark blue, peacock, brown, sage, slate, pink, dove and black; underglaze coloured; and with and without gilding. 'Flow' or 'flown' blue patterns, in which the blue was encouraged to flow into the glaze giving a soft, blurred effect to the pattern outline, had been popular since the 1840s and this colour option was also offered by Burgess & Leigh, being especially requested by the North American market. Other flow shades introduced included peacock and canton (shades of blue), green, pink, peach (from 1898), and pearl (from 1904).

Non Pareil, a soft flow-blue, multi-scene design (produced by Dixon, Austin & Co. of Sunderland in County Durham from 1820-1840),[94] was introduced by Burgess & Leigh in 1897 and soon became a favourite with the public and trade press (see illustration on page 61):

> 'This is a most effective decoration, and as shown in their special flow blue and gold, makes a handsome dinner set. The effect is not so apparent in a single piece, but the collection at the showrooms makes a fine display. There is much delicacy about the treatment of this decoration, and it is enhanced by the quiet softness of the blue. The same

pattern (and the same colour) is applied to all table accessories, such as dessert sets, dishes, jugs, tea and breakfast sets, teapots, cheese stands and covers etc. This flow blue and gold is of general applicability and looks well on all articles, large and small alike.'

'Suite Ware'

'Suite wares', 'en suite' or 'suited tablewares' could be purchased in addition to the usual dinner, tea and early-morning sets, in the same pattern, an option not then offered by many of Burgess & Leigh's rivals. Later, the company was to have its own *Suite Warehouse* specifically for such items, which were modelled by Charles Wilkes. By the early 1890s, these included fruit and dessert services; single-, double- and triple sweet trays and other designs illustrated in an impressive colour printed sales catalogue of 1893: 'tennis-sets' (comprising a cup and saucer on an elongated oval plate), toast racks, egg-baskets, breakfast cruets, covered butter or marmalade dishes and stands and sardine boxes. In 1896 *The Pottery Gazette* enthused:

> 'We were very pleased to see that Messrs. Burgess & Leigh submit a good selection of cruets, egg-stands, etc. Of course, these are somewhat dearer than the foreign goods which now flood the market. But they are cheap for what they are. We hope to see our manufacturers going more into this trade. There is really no reason why cruets and egg-stands should be almost monopolised by foreign makers'.

The same report also drew a favourable comparison between Burgess & Leigh's new lighter and whiter earthenware body and the more expensive type manufactured in Europe.

Cheese Stands and Covers

Also mentioned were the company's *'already well-established specialty range of cheese-stands and covers'*. The market for Stilton cheese stands had probably been at its height in the 1870s-1880s when Burgess & Leigh produced around twelve different designs including, for example, pattern 199, described in the company's unillustrated first Pattern Book as *'Stilton, enamelled and gilt leaves, Number 10 green and mixt flowers shade 9 in rose colour. Centre yellow, stick work orange and traced on the top in brown. Stand with gilt and rope, gilt line, 11/-.'*

Also from the early years of production and still available in the 1890s were the *London Number 1* and *Wedge* shaped cheese stands; these were available with printed tableware patterns such as the aesthetic-style *Rustic* priced at 3s 6d or 3s 9d. In contrast, the 'Cheshire' Cheese Stand on the *London* shape had a specially designed printed pattern, available in brown, peacock and multi-coloured, of dairy maids in the nearby Cheshire countryside. (So attractive was this design that it was revived in the early 1900s and again in the 1920s.) In a similar style was the *Fables* cheese stand, which, as its name implies, was decorated with appropriate printed illustrations from Aesop's *Fables* (versions of which had been produced by Spode and other manufacturers from c.1830). Allocated pattern number 2170, both pattern and shape were registered with numbers 172863 and 172851 in c.1891.

As competition between manufacturers for novel designs increased, plain round, wedge or triangular shapes gave way to more elaborate forms, such as the shell-shaped stand and the *Rococo* shape, registered with number 221859 in c.1894.

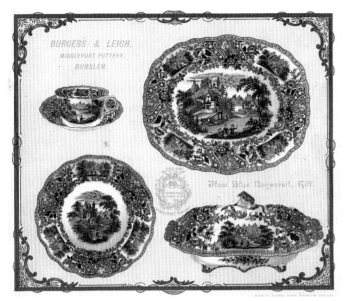

Non Pareil, one of Burgess & Leigh's most popular flow blue multi-scene patterns introduced in 1897.

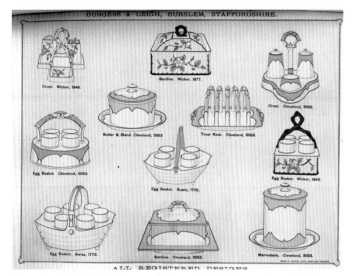

Examples of early Suite Wares made from the 1890s to complement tableware shapes.

Anyone for tennis? Combined cup, saucer and tray sets modelled by Charles Wilkes.

Embossed *Apple Blossom* pattern, 1893 catalogue.

Fables cheese stand and cover. Printed registered numbers, impressed *B&L*, *IVORY* (denoting glaze) 1887 and *ENGLAND*. Height 5ins (13cms).

Drawing for the side of the *Fables* cheese cover. The design was rejected in favour of that shown above.

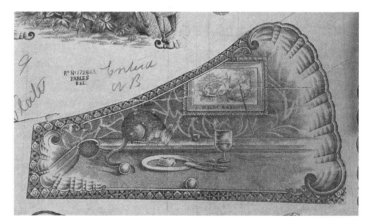

Printed illustration for the *Fables* cheese stand cover.

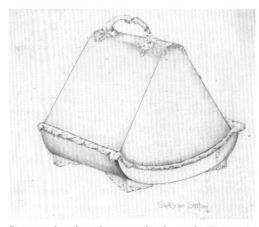

Drawing of a stilton cheese stand and cover by 'Designer' Leigh, signed with monogram.

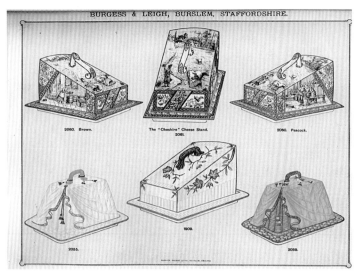

Cheese stands and covers showing the colour variations available in the *Cheshire*, 1893 catalogue.

Pretty dairy maids, illustration from the Print Record Book showing prints used for the *Cheshire* cheese stand and cover produced on the *London* shape.

The Fox and the Raven, drawing for the *Fables* cheese stand cover registered by Burges & Leigh in 1891.

The *Rustic* pattern applied to *London Number 1-* and *Wedge*-shaped cheese stands and covers. They cost 3s. 6d. and 3s. 9d. in 1893. Many examples are unmarked. Height, left, 5ins (13cms).

Illustration of the *Rustic* pattern from Burgess & Leigh's Print Record Book showing a Hill Pottery backstamp.

Moulded and embossed shapes included one resembling wickerwork with a tasselled draped cover (pattern numbers 2055 and 2059); or featuring *Apple Blossom* (2130 and 2131). In 1896 *The Pottery Gazette* illustrated and reported on Burgess & Leigh's "Butterfly" shape.... *It has a very roomy cover and is shown in a variety of decorations. As its name implies, the cover represents a butterfly (rather a large one) with expanded wings.'*

The company continued to produce cheese stands throughout the twentieth century; a notebook of c.1905

records that they were still producing different sizes of their old shapes: *London, Argus, Royal Flute, Queen, Hampton, Kew, Sultan* and *Windsor*. 1930s Pattern Books list the *St Ivel, Chedlet* and *Diploma* cheese stands as well as that produced on the Art Deco *Zenith* tableware shape. From the 1960s, simpler shapes were produced; a circular stilton cheese stand, then made for Habitat hand-banded with *CHEESE* printed in blue, is today produced in numerous underglaze printed patterns.

Artwork for tableware pattern used to decorate the *Hexagon* jug, top left.

Jugs

Individuality of design was also displayed in Burgess & Leigh's large variety of jugs, a number of whose distinctive shapes were registered. The relief-moulded *Giraffe* jug, which had first been registered with the Patent Office in 1864 (number 172876), was to be reproduced (with a modified handle and different colours) many times over the years. It was followed by the *Turin*, registered in 1878, the *Roman* in 1880, and by the 1890s, the *Orient*; the embossed *Athens* and *Cleveland*; and the simpler *Albert*, *Brixton* and *Tankard*. Some jugs, for example, the *Hexagon*, with its elaborately moulded handle, the octagonal *Antique* and the Parian relief-moulded *Heron*, were supplied with 'metal-mounts,' as they had been at the Central and Hill Potteries. Some of these were of the 'swing lid' variety which had been patented by Toft, Wedgwood's chief modeller. Ledgers record that the mounts were fitted by a number of different local firms including Arthur Martin, William Till of Hanley and Mr Clarke of Cobridge. Sizes included 12s, 24s, 30s and 36s (the number denoting size being determined by how

Catalogue page showing a selection of the jugs offered in 1893.

Design for the *Giraffe* jug registered at the Patent Office in 1864.

Early metal-mounted *Giraffe* jug, painted gilded pattern. Embossed diamond registration mark, pattern 581, c.1864.

many of each could be fitted on a potter's board, *i.e.* 12s being the largest). As well as jugs, 'mounted' teapots were also available; Burgess & Leigh had supplied crates of them to a customer in Boston in the USA as early as the 1860s-1870s period. In 1893, the *Richelieu 'patent lock lid'* was being advertised for the home market.

Jet and Rockingham

To compete with other firms, Burgess & Leigh also offered, as it had at the Central and Hill Potteries, a variety of wares, but specifically teapots, in both Jet (black glazed earthenware) and Rockingham (brown glazed earthenware). These specialised wares, which were available in many decorative and gilded patterns, were bought in from other manufacturers, such as Wade & Colclough. Burgess & Leigh had owned shares in one supplier, T.M. Hurd[95] & Co., of the Mayer

Jug, printed *Pansy* pattern, c.1890. Height 7¹/₂ins (19cms).

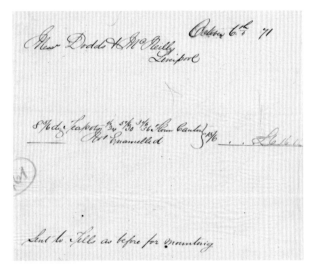

1871 invoice noting that teapots were to be *'sent to Tills'* for mounting. William Till of Hanley was one of several local firms supplying and fitting metal lids to Burgess & Leigh's teapots and jugs.

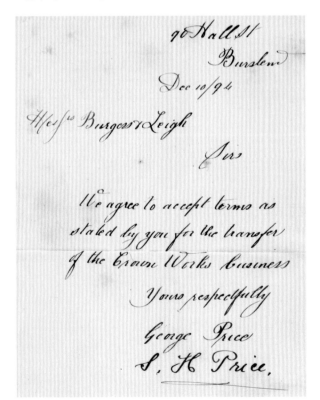

In writing, George and Samuel Price agree to Burgess & Leigh's terms on buying their Crown wares to manufacture Rockingham teapots.

Mug with brown printed floral pattern, as illustrated in an 1893 catalogue in blue. Height 9cm (3¹/₂ins).

Pottery[96] in Sylvester Street, Burslem. In c.1891-1892, following his retirement, Frederick Rathbone Burgess, took over Hurd's. Trading as Frederick Rathbone Burgess & Co.,[97] the company continued to supply Jet and Rockingham to Burgess & Leigh, and possibly other local firms, until c.1900. (As this was five years after Frederick's death, it is probable that his son, Richard, and daughter, Mathilda, continued to take care of and benefit from his remaining interests.)

By 1893 Burgess & Leigh was itself manufacturing Rockingham from a separate pottery, the Crown Works.[98] Situated at the corner of Westport Road and Market Place in Burslem, the Crown Works had, from 1870, specialised in ceramic door furniture, knobs and fingerplates. By 1889 it was occupied by E. J. D Bodley, the china manufacturer who

Page from 1893 catalogue illustrating Jet and Rockingham teapots.

Drawing for *The Geisha* teapot, a typical Japanese-style pattern from the 1890s.

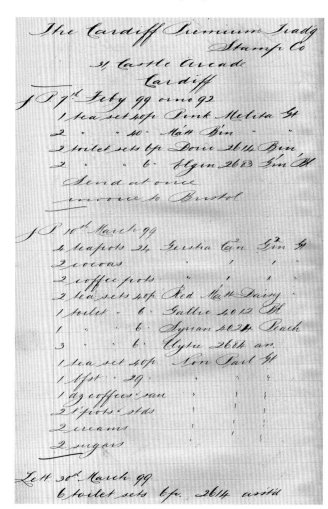

An 1899 order from Cardiff includes *The Geisha* tea-, cocoa- and coffee pots.

From the Print Record Book, showing prints for *The Geisha* teapot including decorative trims for its sides and lid. Registered Shape 223699 and Registered No. 225655

A second version of *The Geisha* teapot pattern from the Print Record Book, c.1895.

Two *Silver*-shaped teapots with printed aesthetic-style patterns – *Rustic* left, and *Suez* right, c.1895 and c.1888. Height approximately 5½ins (14cms).

Illustration of Burgess & Leigh's 1896 'Huntley & Palmers' teapot, Print Record Book.

Tea and biscuits, advertisement for Huntley & Palmers decorated biscuit tins includes their design, top centre, 'adapted' by Burgess & Leigh for their 1896 teapot. (*Photograph courtesy University of Reading Library.*)

Two of Burgess & Leigh's most distinctive teapots and stands. Left, the 1896 'Huntley and Palmers' design and, right, *The Geisha* produced around the same time. The lids impressed B&L. Taller of teapots 8ins (20cms).

had been amongst those co-leasing the Hill Pottery with Burgess & Leigh. Bodley evidently ran into difficulties as his company was bankrupt in 1892 when Burgess & Leigh took over. The venture lasted just three years and in 1895, the year of Frederick's death, the stock, fixtures and goodwill were sold to two brothers, George and Samuel Price. Changing the name of the factory to the Price Pottery, the Price brothers continued manufacturing their famous 'Brown Betty' Rockingham teapots there until 1961 when the company merged with Kensington Pottery (now Price and Kensington).

Teapots

In the mid-1890s it was Burgess & Leigh who were especially *'well known for their great variety of fancy teapots'*.[99] At that time their range included, in addition to the *Richelieu*, with and without *'patent lock lid'*, such shapes as *Fluted, Antique, Derby, Globe, Silver, Bamboo, Queen Anne, Sirdar* and *Tulip*. These were mainly sold separately, to complement their ranges of breakfast and early morning sets and teasets, the latter available on shapes such as *Sydney, Paris, Albany, Royal Flute* and *Minton*. Patterns included *Broseley* and *Willow*, sheet or 'all-over' floral designs, as well as a variety of Crown Derby and

Drawing of the *Daffodil* pattern for an *Antique*-shaped teapot illustrated in the 1893 catalogue, below.

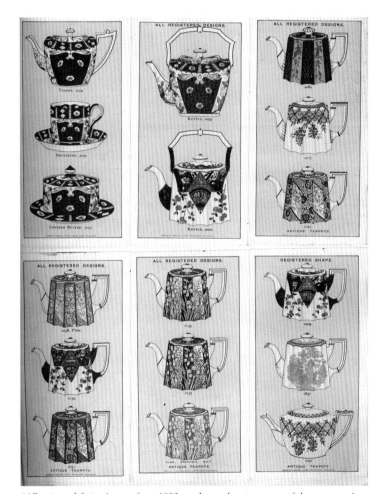

'*All registered designs*', page from 1893 catalogue showing some of the company's range of teapots.

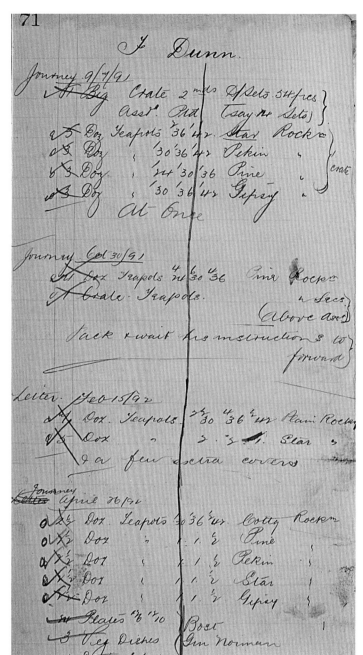

A Devon retailer orders over 500 teapots in nine months, 1891-1892.

Japanese-style patterns which were also applied to tea kettles.

Burgess & Leigh continued to take care to register their most distinctive designs to prevent illegal copying. Teapots were no exception. However, the company was alert, if not opportunistic, to lapses by other firms! This was illustrated when Burgess & Leigh registered in 1896 a design[100] for a teapot identical to that of a biscuit tin manufactured for Huntley & Palmer, the biscuit makers. Huntley & Palmer had unfortunately neglected to register their biscuit tin's design of 1894. On seeing its distinctive shape and colourful pattern of an Indian sporting scene reproduced in teapot

form two years later, they threatened to sue. However, Burgess & Leigh, whilst not perhaps ethically untarnished, had not committed any crime. The case therefore did not come to court, the two firms agreeing that Burgess & Leigh could continue to manufacture the teapot but should change its original multi-coloured printed design to a single-coloured print. Those of today's collectors not fortunate enough to own the original teapot can see it displayed in the Victoria and Albert Museum's New British Galleries, one of a number of Burgess & Leigh pieces in the museum's ceramics collection.[101]

The 'Huntley and Palmer' teapot was typically High Victorian in style, both in its rather elaborate rococo form and in its subject matter, so evocative now of the British Empire. Indeed, the late nineteenth century had seen a further outburst of imperial expansion with many European countries, Great Britain amongst them, acquiring new colonies. This was good news for Burgess & Leigh for whom new territories meant new markets. It, too, was busy making plans to expand its own 'empire' overseas.

CHAPTER THREE

ALL OVER THE GLOBE:
The Beginning of Burleigh Ware 1897-1918

The first price list of the new century.

(3)

	26 pieces			50 pcs.	54 pcs.	56 pcs.	70 pcs.	72 pcs.
	A	B	C					
Plates, 10in. ...	6	6	6	12	12	12	12	12
„ 8in. ..	6	6	6	12	12	12	12	12
„ 6in. ...	6	6	6	12	12	12	12	12
Dishes, 9in. ...	1	1	..	1	1	1	1	1
„ 10in. ...	1	...	1	1	1	1	1	1
„ 11in. ..	...	1	...	...	1	1	1	1
„ 12in. ...	1	...	1	1	1	1	1	1
„ 14in. ...	..	1	1	1	1	1	1	1
„ 16in. ...	...	..	...	1	1	1	1	1
Cov'd dishes ...	2	2	2	2	2	2	2	2
Sauce complete ...	...	...	...	1	2	2	2	2
Boat	1	1	1	1	...	2	...	2
Soup complete...	...	...	...	...	...	...	1	1
Soup plates, 10in.	...	...	...	...	...	...	12	12

61 pieces.
12 Plates, 6 inch.
12 „ 8 „
12 Soups, 7 „
12 „ 8 „
1 Dish, 9 „
1 „ 10 „
1 „ 12 „
1 „ 14 „
1 Boat and Stand
2 Cov'd Dishes
1 Soup and Stand

65 pieces.
36 Plates, 12 12 12
6 8 10 in.
12 Soups, 10in.
6 Dishes 2 1 1 1 1
10 12 14 16 18in.
1 Sauce and Stand
1 Soup Tureen and Stand
2 Vegetable Dishes
1 Sauce Boat

78 pieces.
12 Plates, 6 inch.
12 „ 8 „
12 „ 10 „
12 Soups, 8 „
12 „ 10 „
2 Dishes, 10 „
1 „ 12 „
1 „ 14 „
1 „ 16 „
1 Boat and Stand
1 Sauce Tureen complete
2 Cover dishes
1 Soup Tureen and Stand

For 79 pieces
add 1 Gravy dish

TEA SETS, 21 pieces.
6 Cups and Saucers
6 Tea Plates
1 B. & B.
1 Slop, 1 Cream

22 pieces.
add 1 B. & B.

40 pieces.
12 Cups and Saucers
12 Tea Plates
2 B. & B's.
1 Slop, 1 Cream

BREAKFAST SETS, 29 pieces.
6 Breakfast Cups & Saucers
6 Breakfast Plates
1 Slop, 1 Sugar, 1 Milk
2 B. & B's, 6 Egg Cups

Dinner, Tea and Breakfast, composition of services available in 1901.

As Queen Victoria's long reign drew to a close, the turn of the century anticipated a period of great global change, which would test Edmund Leigh's political and business instincts. The second Boer War in South Africa (1899-1902) and the Russo-Japanese war (1904-1905) severely dented the economic confidence Britain had gained through Victorian imperialism. In the following decade, tensions were to increase further, both at home, with problems caused by social unrest and the issue of Home Rule for Ireland, and overseas, where the Balkan Wars (1912-1913) and an aggressive German foreign policy eventually were to culminate in the First World War.

The late 1890s had seen Edmund give up (though only temporarily) many of his public duties to concentrate on business matters. At home, trade had remained good for Burgess & Leigh; the company supplied many retail outlets throughout the country whilst in London its wares were stocked by such well-known London departments stores as Barkers, Dickens and Jones, Lilley and Skinner, Maple & Co., Whiteley's and, the most prestigious, Harrods.

The continuing growth of business overseas, especially through Shorter's agency in Australia, convinced Edmund to appoint another agency in North America. The McKinley Tariff of 1891, which had imposed a short-lived fifty per cent tariff on US imports, had not dented America's demand for British pottery. The company thus decided in 1897, as Great Britain celebrated Queen Victoria's Diamond Jubilee, to appoint R. Slimmon & Co. of 96 Church Street, New York,[1] an agency also used by Edmund's friend and fellow potter, Arthur Shorter.[2] The US agency confirmed and promoted a longstanding and successful trade with North America which Burgess, Dorling & Leigh continues to enjoy today. Edmund himself travelled extensively in America (and later Canada, Australia, South Africa and Germany) making many loyal friends amongst Burgess & Leigh's retail customers. The President of Geo. F. Bassett & Co. Inc, 'The Dinner Ware House of America' in New York was to write of Edmund: 'His very wide reading and travelling, as well as his sound good sense in judging human affairs, and his deep affection for the better products of American life, especially of President Lincoln, all combined to form many points of interest and contact, that made him a choice companion.'[3]

The added increase in sales through its overseas agencies helped Burgess & Leigh maintain steady and solid progress, with income from sales for the period 1899-1901 amounting to £116,338 12s 3d[4]. However, trade was poor throughout the pottery industry in the early 1900s with much foreign competition. The Coronation of King Edward VII and Queen Alexandra in 1902 was eagerly awaited in the Potteries not least because the manufacture of commemorative wares provided a welcome boost to pottery production.

Third Generation Leighs: William (Henry) 1881-1937; (Arthur) Kingsley 1884-1954; and (Edmund) Denis 1889-1968

Providing support for Edmund at the turn of the century were his three sons, the third generation of the Leigh family to work at the Middleport Pottery. (Mabelle,[5] Edmund's daughter, as a female, would not have been expected to enter the business.) Arnold Bennett's journal for 26th May, 1902 reports a conversation with a relative whose father *'had once pointed out to him that no potting firm, except Wedgwoods, had survived to the third generation. The first generation was of the people, industrial simple; the second, though raised in the social grade, was still plodding and energetic and kept the business together; the third was a generation of wastrels coming to grief.'*[6] Burgess & Leigh were to prove him wrong!

However, it is never easy for an offspring to rise to the exacting standards frequently set by a successful parent and when William, Kingsley and Denis Leigh joined their father they must have felt keenly the expectation of having to continue and build on his success at the Middleport Factory. This burden was undoubtedly lessened by the mutual support of the brothers[7] but, more importantly, by the sensitive leadership and expertise of their father on which they were able to draw for the first twenty years of their working lives.

William was the first and eldest of Edmund's three sons to enter the business, aged seventeen, in 1898. In true Potteries tradition, he followed in the footsteps of his grandfather (after whom he was named) and his father by firstly gaining general experience of the pottery trade on the factory floor prior to acquiring business experience as a traveller in the sales department. He was to spend two years with Harold Holdcroft and R.J. Heath as the company's 'country representative' before replacing in 1908 the valued James Pointing as the firm's city representative in the London showrooms at 44 Farringdon Street.[8]

Kingsley, Edmund's second son, joined the company on

William Leigh 1881-1937, a photograph taken for the society magazine *Eve*, shows William and his sister-in-law enjoying a day at Uttoxeter races, c.1920.

his seventeenth birthday, 1st April, 1901. Both he and William quickly became part of the close-knit environment of the Middleport Pottery. Typical of the good relations between family and firm was William's twenty-first birthday party held at Burslem Town Hall.[9] The company's entire workforce of some 500 attended the occasion which was supervised by the manager of the works, Mr Edwin Kent. Following tea and musical entertainment, Mr Cartledge, a holloware presser who had joined Burgess & Leigh in 1862, presented William with an illuminated address and a gold hunting watch and chain, the case of which was inscribed *'Presented to Mr William H. Leigh by the employees of Middleport Pottery in celebration of his majority with sincerest wishes for his future happiness and prosperity, December 1902'*. William, it seems, was already more than content with his chosen career, speaking then of his first four years at Burgess & Leigh as the happiest of his life. Kingsley was to celebrate his own coming-of-age in 1905 in similar style by receiving a gold watch from the Burgess & Leigh employees.[10] The same year, having already proved himself a more than capable Works Manager, with responsibility for the production side of the pottery, he was appointed Managing Director, the youngest in the Potteries. Denis, the last of the Leigh sons, was to join the Middleport Pottery in 1906, following William in a sales and commercial role.

The third generation, Denis Leigh 1889-1968 left, and Kingsley Leigh 1884-1954.

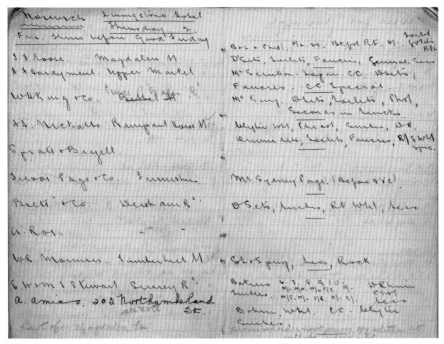

A page from a notebook of '*journeys*' kept by William Leigh in c.1913. During a three week sales trip to the '*Eastern Counties*' he visited fourteen different towns, including Norwich, recording customers' orders.

'*A Familiar Face in the Potting Trade*', Edmund Leigh JP at his magistrates bench, modelled in jug-form by Ernest Bailey in 1951.

Edmund Leigh: A '*Familiar Face in the Potting Trade*'

All the Leigh family must have been proud to see a profile of Edmund in *The Pottery Gazette* of 1st August, 1906, especially as it appeared in the year of the Liberals' landslide electoral victory which ushered in many of the social reforms Edmund had supported over the years. One of a series entitled '*Some Familiar Faces in the Potting Trade: Mr Edmund Leigh, JP*', it provides a fascinating insight into the background and opinions of Edmund, acknowledging him for his public and political service and as a successful pottery manufacturer and spokesman for the industry. The article began:

> '*To be a successful potter in these keen days of competition is no easy matter. To be an active public man, as well as a successful potter, involves an amount of work, and a sacrifice of personal leisure so great, that few manufacturers care to take upon themselves so heavy a burden.*'

Although this burden frequently showed in his health,[11] Edmund was known to be someone of great energy who, whenever he could, used his public profile both in Stoke-on-Trent as well as in '*influential quarters… in the Metropolis,*' to voice his opinions on the pottery trade and to lobby on its behalf. Commenting on the Canal Commission, for instance, he lamented the high railway rates and argued for improved water transport (vital to the Middleport Pottery) through the City Council's involvement in a semi-nationalisation scheme of further canal works. Germany and Belgium used a much superior system of water carriage, insisted Edmund, who was not afraid to voice the unpopular opinion that foreign competitors had many useful methods of manufacture from which Britain might usefully learn.

Edmund's tendency to speak his mind in such a manner made him at times a controversial figure. His views were frequently at odds with other manufacturers in the Chamber of Commerce and later the British Pottery Manufacturers' Federation[12] (known since 1985 as the British Ceramic Confederation which represents manufacturers and material suppliers). Free trade especially was a topic which divided

Edmund, a longtime supporter of Cobden, from some of his fellow potters. Having been asked to speak at the North Staffordshire commercial travellers' annual dinner held at the Grand Hotel in Hanley in December 1905, he had argued eloquently in favour of free trade, it being reported that he '*spoke quite impromptu and without the aid of a single note, but the ability of his oratory was freely admitted by even those who most strongly dissented from what he said*'![13]

The 1906 *Pottery Gazette* profile gave him an opportunity to further voice his opinions on the subject, arguing that:

> '*under free trade, there were thousands of homes in this country, into which effective ornamental pottery now entered, which, he contended, would never have found a place there at all had it not been for the price at which the people had been able to acquire it. [He] entirely rejected protection as a panacea for the ills of the industrial world and suggested that those who sought to better the condition of the pottery trade would do more towards the accomplishment of their desires by reforming our shipping and railway rates, and our consular system, than by agitating for fiscal reform… I believe that nothing would be more disastrous to the real interests, even of the pottery district, than any deviation from the principles of free trade. I think, myself, that the tendency in America will be slowly in the direction of Free Trade.*'

Edmund was not above staging a publicity stunt to draw attention to his beliefs; in protest against an exhibition of 'dumped' foreign pottery, Edmund Leigh and fellow potter, Leonard Grimwade (of Grimwades Ltd later Royal Winton), mounted a display of their own pottery, with a challenge laid down to foreign producers to manufacture and deliver in Britain at competitive prices.

In another controversial stance, Edmund saw no incompatibility between his success as a manufacturer and his support of trades unions. He campaigned equally for the rights of both employer and employee. The profile quoted: '*I have always believed, and I believe now, that it is to the interest of* employers to maintain good relations with the men…. Where they have reasonable ground for complaint, an attempt should be made to meet them fairly. Poorly paid labour is no good to any industry.'

It is surprising that such opinions did not alienate him completely from his fellow manufacturers whom he saw as lacking in 'combined action'. However, it appears that Edmund possessed that rare and respected quality of open-mindedness, of being able to form his own opinion on individual issues without upsetting the opposition!

In the early 1900s Edmund played a significant role in the ongoing debate on leadless glazes in pottery manufacture. Patron of the Arts, Millicent, Duchess of Sutherland, (who lived in nearby Trentham Hall and was shortly to be fictionalised by Bennett as the 'Countess of Chell' in his novel The Card) earned herself the nickname 'Meddlesome Millie' for her attempts to champion the rights of those suffering from the lung disease silicosis or 'potters' rot'. Her report 'On the Dangerous Processes of the Potting Industry' revealed that approximately a quarter of those 'working in the lead' in the late 1890s suffered from lead poisoning.[14] Unusually for one so attentive to the well-being of his employees, whilst Edmund was prepared to advise precautionary health measures, he was against the banning of lead entirely. Having experimented in using leadless glazes on Burgess & Leigh's own products, he came to the conclusion commonly held then that 'small quantities of an inferior quality may be made but anything like the standard of merit which English goods have attained could not be reached.' Negotiating between employers and operatives, he therefore opposed the government's application of the recently formed Workmen's Compensation Act to workers with lead poisoning. It was reported that 'Mr Leigh was able to render the trade a signal service in bringing about so harmonious an understanding between the forces of capital and labour.' (Burgess & Leigh continued to re-assess the problem of lead glazes throughout the years; in 1915, the company took advice from Bernard Moore, the Stoke-on-Trent pottery consultant and manufacturer, who provided Edmund with a recipe for a 'sounder and cheaper' lead glaze.)[15] Also in opposition to some workers, Edmund was generally in favour of the use of labour-saving machinery, seeing its introduction as of long-term benefit to the industry. Whilst potters on the factory floor did not always share Edmund's opinions, like their employers, they respected them and continued to see him as a loyal friend. Mr S. Clowes, General Secretary of the National Pottery Workers' Association was to write that Edmund '…has always given a fair hearing to any request from the workers.'[16]

Art Nouveau: Design at the Middleport Pottery in the Early 1900s

The new century had brought a chance for reappraisal in design and the Burgess & Leigh Design Studio showed itself to be open to new influences. In tableware, it capitalised on the revival of interest in eighteenth-century Adams style, with its festoons and medallions, and in dainty floral design, such as English Rose. A renewed vogue for orientalism saw the revival of Crown Derby Imari style designs as well as the introduction of pseudo-Japanese patterns, such as Tokio and Orient and the revival of the Geisha teapot. But there were also more modern and innovative interpretations of form by Charles Wilkes, such as the Stafford, a 'bold and effective treatment of an artistic shape'.[17]

The most influential style in the decorative arts in the early 1900s however remained Art Nouveau which had originated in the 1890s. In spite of its French name, Art Nouveau 'was the first great international style since the Middle Ages (and the last of course) to which Britain made any perceptible contribution.'[18] With roots in Pre-Raphaelite Art, the Arts and Crafts Movement and Aestheticism, the first true exponent of the Art Nouveau style was the graphic artist Aubrey Beardsley whose illustrations for Oscar Wilde's play Salome were published in the first issue of The Studio in 1893. Characterised by an exuberantly organic and linear elegance of form, 'Le Style Anglais' became synonymous with the name of Liberty, the London store which had defined it in the mid-1890s and continued to promote it successfully at

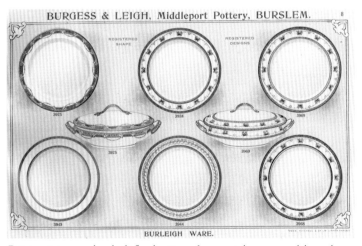

Dainty print, enamel and gilt floral patterns from a catalogue page of the early 1900s.

Imari-style Suite Ware from Burgess & Leigh, early 1900s.

Japanese revival, a pattern featuring oriental figures for export to Paris, illustrated in the Print Record Book.

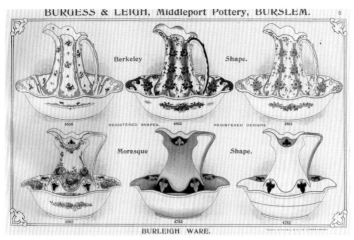

'Not exactly square … and certainly not round', the *Moresque* shape of 1908 illustrated below heavily patterned *Berkeley* toilet sets.

Exuberant Art Nouveau patterns for *Portland*-shaped toilet sets.

home and overseas until the beginning of the First World War in 1914. It is interesting that the English ceramic industry, with the exception of certain larger manufacturers with a tradition of art or studio pottery, such as Doulton, Minton, Moorcroft and Maws, had at the outset largely resisted Art Nouveau as a decorative style.[19] Only in the early 1900s, did smaller potteries, like Burgess & Leigh, decide to embark on a more commercial interpretation.

Over the years leading up to the First World War in 1914, 'Designer' Leigh and Charles Wilkes produced some fine examples of the style especially in toiletwares. A factory notebook of c.1905, which lists the huge variety of shapes Burgess & Leigh produced then, includes a total of thirty-seven different ewer shapes. The *Moresque* toilet sets was described in fulsome Edwardian tone by *The Pottery Gazette* of 1908 as:

'one of the best. The tall ewer is a graceful model – as its name implies – after the Arabesque style. There is much originality – without extravagance – in the basin. It is not exactly square, and it is certainly not round, but is has some of the features of both forms… There is a simple embossed outline which, in the ewer, divides the upper part of the bowl from the lower by a graceful sweep. Otherwise the surface is plain, and is thus free for a variety of decorative effects… the general form of a toilet jug and basin is now practically confined within not very wide limits, considerations of convenience have settled the general outline of the jug, but it is remarkable what variety skillful modellers can impart to it without detracting from its useful features. Many attempts to depart from the outline of a toilet jug, which has been adhered to by most manufacturers for a century, have verged upon eccentricity. But the clever designers at Middleport Pottery have succeeded in giving us many pleasing variations of pure art forms, that enhance, rather than detract from, their artistic effects.'[20]

Decorative ceramic 'art ware' was another area explored in the Art Nouveau style and featured largely in many pottery manufacturers' products in the early years of the twentieth century. Burgess & Leigh were no exception, producing a variety of decorative styles imitating studio pottery; *Faience*, a range of vases and flower pots introduced in 1903, had shaded grounds and hand-painted flowers whilst *Artois*, 'artistically coloured and nicely shaded and gilt',

Ribbons and roses, a pattern from a toiletware pattern book, c.1913.

Florette, a typical Art Nouveau tulip pattern of c.1909 illustrated – and mis-spelt – in the Print Record Book. An elaborate 'B & L Middleport Pottery' backstamp was used from this time.

advertised somewhat bluntly in 1909 as 'original, elegant, effective and cheap,'[21] was applied to a variety of ornamental and tablewares.

The majority of Burgess & Leigh's Art Nouveau tableware designs, however, were decorated with more traditional transfer-printed decoration. Patterns included *Florette* and *Tulipe*, a graceful border pattern which was engraved in 1909 for use on the *Queen* shape. *Briar*, a particularly popular pattern of 1905 was produced in colours including flow blue and gilt and on all tableware shapes as well as fruit dishes, triple trays, marmalade pots, biscuit barrels, toast racks, egg holders and butter dishes. It was,

The *Burleigh* pattern registered in 1903 on the *Oceanic* shape gave birth to the company's famous *Burleigh* brand name.

Plate featuring *Burleigh* in blue, c.1903, diameter 10ins (27.5 cms).

Hot water jug with hinged pewter lid with Secessionist-style 'print and enamel' poppy decoration, c.1910, height 6ins (17.5 cms).

'Telegrams: Burleigh Burslem', 1901 Price List cover detailing the Company's telegram address which prompted the naming of both a pattern and a brand.

however, an earlier Art Nouveau tableware pattern of 1903 which was to have more far-reaching consequences for the company: produced on the new *Oceanic* shape on a semi-porcelain body, its name was *Burleigh*.

'Yes, that is Burleigh Ware'

The memorable contraction of the names Burgess & Leigh used to name the *Burleigh* pattern had previously been used as the company's telegram address. It appealed so much to the directors that they decided to utilise it still further as a brand name. The now famous *Burleigh Ware* brand name was used initially for ranges produced on the company's semi-porcelain body, a type of earthenware which imitated the qualities of porcelain or bone china but was substantially cheaper to produce and buy. Semi-porcelain had been produced at many potteries, including the Middleport Pottery, from the late nineteenth century, with the recipe varying from company to company. However, Burgess & Leigh, in common with each manufacturer, was keen to promote the uniqueness and superiority of its own version. The fine quality of the Burleigh earthenware body was to remain a source of pride for the company.

Immediately, the concept of *Burleigh Ware* captured the public attention and by 1906 *The Pottery Gazette* was stating:

Burleigh Suite Ware, Burgess & Leigh produced similar Art Nouveau-style ranges throughout the First World War, shown here in an undated catalogue from around that time.

"BURLEIGH" BURSLEM

Burleigh Toilet = = =
Burleigh Dinner Sets.
Burleigh Fancy Goods.

"GOOD GOODS"

ensure quick sales and satisfactory profits.

See our **SPRING DISPLAY** and judge for yourselves.

BURGESS & LEIGH,
MIDDLEPORT POTTERY,
BURSLEM.

REPRESENTATIVES:—

Country:—	London:—44, Farringdon Street, London, E.C.
MR. A. H. HOLDCROFT.	MR. J. POINTING.
MR. W. H. LEIGH.	New Zealand:—MESSRS. THOS. WEBB & CO., 28, Fort Street, Auckland.
MR. R. J. HEATH.	Australia:—MR. THOS. W. HEATH, Sydney.

'Good Goods' from 'Burleigh Burslem', an advertisement from *The Pottery Gazette*, 1st January, 1906.

'The name Burleigh Ware stands for something now and dealers appear to realise the fact. When I have seen the name placed conspicuously against the firm's goods in provincial shops it has come home to me that the public also are acquainted with, and appreciate, the ware indicated, and that therefore the dealer finds it to his advantage to advertise the fact that he keeps it.[22] ...The public like to know the name of anything that gives them satisfaction, and when their friends admire their new dinner service, toiletware or suite ware, they are pleased (probably proud) to answer at once: "Yes, that is Burleigh Ware".[23]

'Burleigh Ware is all over the Globe': Australia, New Zealand, America and South Africa

The market branding of Burgess & Leigh products was important in establishing a strong identity to its wares not only in the UK but also overseas where the company was eager to expand its agencies in colonial markets. A survey of its different markets carried out in 1904 found sales for London to amount to £8165; the rest of the home market £16,202; the USA £6,247; Africa £3,973; New Zealand £4,995 and Australia a disappointing £2,593.

Trade in Australia had deteriorated since 1898 when John Shorter ceased to represent Burgess & Leigh and his other pottery firms in order to act exclusively for Doulton. Mr Richards, a home traveller, was sent out by Edmund in early 1900 to review the market[24] and shortly afterwards Harrison & Sons of Paling's Buildings, Sydney, were appointed as the company's new agents. The arrangement proved unsatisfactory and the decision was made to offer the position of agent to John T. Williamson, the Middleport Pottery's office clerk. (First employed as office boy, he was later to become Company Secretary). When Williamson decided to decline for family reasons, he contacted his friend and colleague, Thomas Wood Heath.

The son of Daniel Heath who worked in the Casting Shop, Thomas had joined Burgess & Leigh to work under John Williamson in the office. However, by 1905 he had replaced Sam Oulsnam as the company's representative for the south coast of England.[25] He was to prove himself an effective salesman, records show him to have averaged £8,200 worth of sales annually between 1902-1904, approximately five-and-a-half per cent of the company's total sales. John Williamson's suggestion to Thomas that if he applied for the post in Australia, the 'old man' (Edmund Leigh) would look favourably on him, proved to be correct. In November 1905 Thomas was advanced the sum of £20 to travel to Australia and his wife and new baby followed in the spring of 1906. Thomas' enthusiasm for the job was immediate. Whilst his outward ship docked in Perth, Adelaide and Melbourne, he lost no time in making calls to customers in an attempt to repair the damage done to Burgess & Leigh's good name by its previous agents. Taking over rooms in Palings Buildings, Ash Street, Sydney, he

'TW', Chairman of T.W. Heath & Co. which represented Burgess & Leigh in Australia until 1999, a total of 95 years.

Burgess & Leigh were awarded a silver medal for their '*useful and ornamental earthenware*' at the New Zealand International Exhibition of Art and Industry held in Christchurch in 1906. Here, a photograph of their display stand at the Art Pottery Pavilion of Messrs John Bates & Co. (*Photograph courtesy of R. Geoffrey Bell, John Bares Co. NZIE album 1906-1907.*)

recorded his expenses from London to Sydney as £11 1s 0d. The first goods he received from Burgess & Leigh left the Middleport Pottery on 7th December 1905 by the SS *Gleneslin* and comprised a total of forty-one crates.

Thomas built up a considerable reputation during his early years in Australia as an honest dealer whose '*word was his bond*'. He followed Edmund Leigh's then radical advice to abandon the restrictive and unsupportive wholesale trade and go direct to the retailer: department stores, jewellers and gift shops. Known as Tom or TW in the trade, he forged sound and enduring relationships with retailers. Initially, he remained on Burgess & Leigh's staff, receiving a fairly generous salary, which included regular trips back to England to keep abreast of developments at the Middleport Pottery. However, he was given the option later to form his own company and did so, founding T. W. Heath & Co. in 1909 in partnership with his brother, Daniel. The new company took on additional agencies, operating on commission, but the Heaths' good relations with the Leighs continued on a business and personal level. Edmund visited in 1913 as a representative in the newly formed Australian

Association of British Manufacturers and again in 1921 with his daughter Mabelle. Thomas' son, Sydney, was to follow his father in the business. Staying with his grandfather, Daniel, who had recently retired from the Middleport Pottery in his late seventies, Sydney spent several months with Burgess & Leigh in 1923 under the guidance of sales representative Albert Aldersea. Thomas died in 1963 having completed fifty years' continuous association with Burgess & Leigh. His company, now called Woodheath (NSW) Pty Ltd and operated by two of his grandchildren, Barrie and Tom Heath, represented Burgess & Leigh in Australia and Tasmania from their Sydney headquarters, Burleigh House, up to the end of 1999. T. W. Heath Agencies and their subsidiary Woodheath (NSW) Pty Ltd ceased trading in 2000 after representing and distributing *Burleigh Ware* in Australia for ninety-five years.[26]

Burleigh wares also retained their popularity in New Zealand and were available there through Thomas Webb & Co. who, from c.1905, acted as the company's agent at Fort Street, Auckland, New Zealand. This successful partnership, which was to last over thirty years, was given an early boost in 1906 when Burgess & Leigh 'Manufacturers of the Celebrated Burleigh Ware' exhibited at the Art Pottery Pavilion of Messrs John Bates & Co. of Christchurch at the New Zealand International Exhibition of Art and Industry. Whilst it was Doulton's new art wares which took the exhibition by storm, Burgess & Leigh's display of some 150 items of 'useful and ornamental earthenware', including ewers and basins, tablewares, vases and jardinières (complete with aspidistras!) was good enough to gain them a prestigious Silver Medal.[27]

The company's trade with America expanded in the early 1900s when it won a lucrative contract to supply tableware for sale through Woolworth,[28] which had at that time over 1,000 'five-and-ten-cent' stores across the USA. This possibly marked the peak of production for Burgess & Leigh, which in 1906 employed a workforce of some 600 including two teams of biscuit placers working on two bottle ovens simultaneously. The founders' aim to manufacture 'good products at a fair price',[29] although seemingly modest was by no means easy to achieve. The fulfillment of the Woolworth contract, which gave many thousands of householders worldwide the opportunity to purchase their wares, must have given the company directors and their employees immense pride and satisfaction.

In c.1903 Burgess & Leigh's successful overseas trade prompted the registering of a new trademark: a globe bound by a sash reading variously 'Burgess & Leigh, Burslem' and 'Burgess & Leigh, Middleport Pottery, Burslem'. An advertisement in The Pottery Gazette on 1st April 1910, a record year for the pottery industry, proudly revealed the trademark with the bold declaration: 'The Globe is on all Burleigh Ware, Burleigh Ware is all over the Globe.'

With business improving, William had in 1909 made an

'All over the Globe', an advertisement for Burleigh Ware from The Pottery Gazette, April 1910, boasts a new global brand awareness.

Not what it seems, a Burleigh Silverine teapot, milk jug and sugar bowl, c.1918.

Silverine Ware, an earthenware range decorated with a metallic lustre glaze imitating silver, c.1918.

extensive tour of South Africa, then a relatively new market for Britain's pottery trade. Revealing Burgess & Leigh's competitive spirit in business, a reporter for The Pottery Gazette wrote of William in 1910: 'I hope to have an early opportunity for a short interview with him.... I do not forget (and if I did Mr Leigh would not) that he went out to South Africa in the interests of his firm and not of the pottery trades. But he is not selfish, and will recognise that there is much that he can communicate about our trades in South Africa without giving us the names of his customers!'[30] Whether or not the reporter got his interview is not known, but Burgess & Leigh secured a successful increase in trade in South Africa with the opening two years later of an agency, J. W. Hutty, in Durban.

Celebrations and Commiserations for the Family Firm
It seems however that business had not been the only thing on young William's mind and, on 1st August, 1911, The Pottery Gazette was pleased to report that while in South Africa William had 'took to himself a wife'! As ever, this family occasion was celebrated by the workforce of the Middleport Pottery which on Thursday, 20th July was 'gaily decked out with flags and bunting' (as no doubt it was for the Coronation of King George V and Queen Mary the same year). Daniel Heath, Casting Shop Manager, presided over the event and, following a time-honoured Burgess & Leigh tradition, a long-time employee, Mr J. Wilcox, a presser, presented the happy couple with a silver tea- and coffee service and salver. Characteristically, Edmund, 'hoped that his sons would be able to carry out the succession, and to extend the operations of the firm, but he hoped above all that they would maintain the existing good relations towards the workpeople.'[31] As reported in The Pottery Gazette of 1st August, 1911,

Edmund also took the opportunity of announcing *'that early next year the business would celebrate its fiftieth anniversary. He thought it constituted a record in the Potteries that the present partners of a firm which was established in 1862 should be the sons of the founders'*.

Although Edmund spoke with his usual optimism, his health and that of his wife, Jane, was giving some cause for concern. For several years both had suffered recurring bouts of ill health. Jane had been taken ill in 1907 but recovered after a Christmas staying with Edmund by the sea in Blackpool.[32] Perhaps as a result of sickness, and following the example of the majority of pottery manufacturers, the couple left the smoking chimneys of the Potteries for its more rural outskirts; moving from *The Oaks* in Porthill (their home for twelve years, which they subsequently let to the Red Cross for use as a depot),[33] they settled in *Mansion House* in Stone in Staffordshire, later moving to *Radford House* nearby. Edmund was then aged fifty-four and Jane might have wished to see a little more of her husband whose overseas trips sometimes required him to be away from home for as long as six months.[34] However, she would have surely known enough that there was no such thing then as early retirement in the Potteries! In 1910, with overwork probably to blame, Edmund himself suffered a recurrence of illness and was forced to spend some time recuperating in Southport, the seaside resort in Lancashire.

It was, however, Edmund's business partner, Richard Burgess, whose health proved to be more at risk. Following a complication from a relatively mild illness, Richard died aged fifty-four years on 29th March, 1912 at the family home, Oaklands in Porthill. His obituary in *The Pottery Gazette* reveals that he was respected and well known in the area, although, like his father, he took no part in public life. Survived by his sister, Mathilda, he was buried in the family grave in St Margaret's Church, Wolstanton. On Richard's death, the role of the Burgess family in the firm was to be in

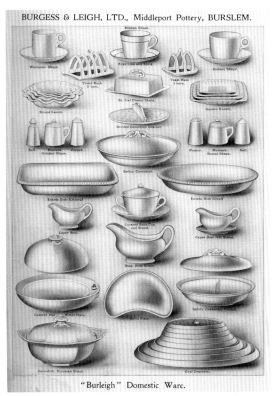

Burleigh plain glazed kitchen wares were first produced in 1862. These examples are illustrated in a catalogue of c.1927.

Catalogue page showing *Royal Flute* tablewares. Although advertised as *'semi china'*, it was in fact earthenware, c.1920.

Richly decorated flower pots were still popular until the end of the First World War.

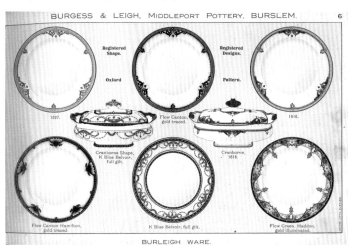

The *Cranborne* tableware shape was introduced in c.1910 and was used for many different patterns including these simple border designs.

name only.[35] Edmund, then aged fifty-eight years, acquired the whole business for the Leigh family but chose to retain the name Burgess & Leigh by which the company was known. That the name survives to this day is, as subsequent Leighs – and Dorlings – would acknowledge, testament to the Burgess family's quiet but considerable contribution to the business.

The Leigh family must have felt especially saddened by the loss in their Jubilee Year,[36] which was marked by the introduction of many new designs including tableware patterns and shapes, suite ware *'all in good taste…. attractive without being extravagant…., a good range of rose bowls (with metal*

Delhi, printed in *Nankin Blue* and shown at an exhibition of pottery at the King's Hall in Stoke-on-Trent, visited by King George V and Queen Mary in 1913.

Chinese Peacock, a 'sheet' pattern first introduced in 1913 and produced today under the name *Bluebird*.

Vases.

Page 15 in Illustrated Catalogue.

Price List of Vases "Chinese Peacock" in the old Nankin Blue.

No.		doz. of 12		No.		doz. of 12	
29	...	8	6	40	...	18	0
30	...	8	6	41	...	30	0
31	...	7	6	42	...	17	0
32	...	15	0	43	...	19	0
33	...	15	0	44	...	15	0
34	...	16	0	45	...	33	0
35	...	13	0	46	...	39	0
36	...	16	0	47	...	22	0
37	...	15	0	48	...	21	0
38	...	19	0	49	...	33	0
39	...	23	0	50	...	18	0

Burleigh Suite Ware. — 1546.
NANKIN BLUE "DELHI."

Page 16 in Illustrated Catalogue.

							s.	d.
No. 73 Teapot, Cranborne	...	...		24's 1/8	30's 1/7			
„ „ Stand, Cranborne	...				7½d. each			
No. 75 „ Ball	...		24's 1/6	30's 1/5	36's 1/4			
„ „ Stand, Ball	...	...			6d. each			
No. 69 Sardine	...	...	...	...			1	9
No. 65 Covered Muffin	...	...	...	...			1	3
Covered Butter	...	...	...	...			1	0
No. 68 Coffee Pot	...	...	...	...			2	3
No. 66 Cocoa Jug	...	...	...	...			2	0
No. 62 Round Bread Tray	...	...	...	...			1	3
No. 76 Cheese Stand, London	...	...	No. 2, 2/6	No. 3, 2/-				
Flower Pot, Stanley ...	...	No. 1, 2/9	No. 2, 2/6					
„ „ Countess	...		2/3					
							s.	d.
Sets Jugs	...	...	...	...			2	3
No. 67 Biscuit Box	...	...	...	...			1	9
No. 72 Marmalade	...	...	...	...			1	6
No. 74 Honey Pot	...	...	...	...			1	3
No. 60 Triple Tray	...	...	...	...			2	3
No. 71 Bacon Dish	...	...	...	...			2	0
Covered Butter (fast stand)	...	...	...				1	3
No. 70 Salad Bowls, round		No. 1, 1/6	No. 2, 1/3	No. 3, 1/-				
No. 64 „ octagon		No. 1, 2/-	No. 2, 1/9	No. 3, 1/6				
No. 63 Oval Bread Tray	...	...	...					1/6
No. 61 Plaques	...	large size 7/6 doz.,	small size 4/6 doz.					

Itemised price list for the *Delhi* range, c.1915.

grids).... pleasing new shapes in toilet services [with] *enamelled patterns of great beauty.... Several good trinket sets...a nice selection of flower pots... a full line of white 'Royal Flute' kitchen ware and C.C.* [cream coloured] *tableware* [and] *a number of bold pedestals and pots, of large sizes with rich decorations.'*[37]

Production of such wares was threatened when a coal strike closed down many potteries in north Staffordshire in the spring but, fortunately, Burgess & Leigh was not amongst them.

In April of the following year the pottery trade was given a boost by the visit of King George V and Queen Mary. Although Middleport Pottery was not amongst the factories they visited, the royal couple was able to see examples of Burleigh Ware exhibited at the King's Hall in Stoke. Prominent on the company's stand were two ranges featuring oriental-style patterns: *Delhi* and *Chinese Peacock*, both printed in *Old Nankin Blue*. A brochure produced by the company described its reproduction of the *'Nankin Blue'* colour, which was *'produced at its best in the fourteenth century (Ta Ming Dynasty)'*, as a *'triumph of the Potter's Art.'* In fact, the company's experiments with reproducing the *Old Nankin Blue* date from around 1900 and a notebook of Charles Wilkes reveals his research on the subject from the *Art Journal* of 1889. Most popular with the public was undoubtedly the *Chinese Peacock* design which, so the

company brochure read, was inspired by *'the old Oriental fable of the Birds' Congress to elect a king. The feeling and treatment of the Design are purely Oriental in character, whilst the shapes of the vases to which the Decoration is applied are from the best Chinese models.'* The design, which became more commonly known as *Bluebird*, remains in production today.

Chinese Peacock was reviewed favourably in a book published under the title *The Staffordshire Potteries As an Empire Asset and An Illustrated Souvenir of the Royal Visit.* Commending the firm's *'talented designer'* and the quality of its printed wares, the author, J. Child, went on to comment that:

'Being practical business men the firm have not made any ambitious attempt to produce anything in the way of showpieces; and this spirit characterises the whole of their productions... Their factory is one of the most up-to-date in the United Kingdom – complete in every detail, and perhaps the best evidence of the ability of the men who have guided, and are now guiding, the destinies of the business is the fact that wherever they have opened up trade they have always held it. Better testimony could not be borne to any firm. Their goods are all they are represented to be, and they are in great demand in America, as well as in the Colonies, on the Continent, and at home.'

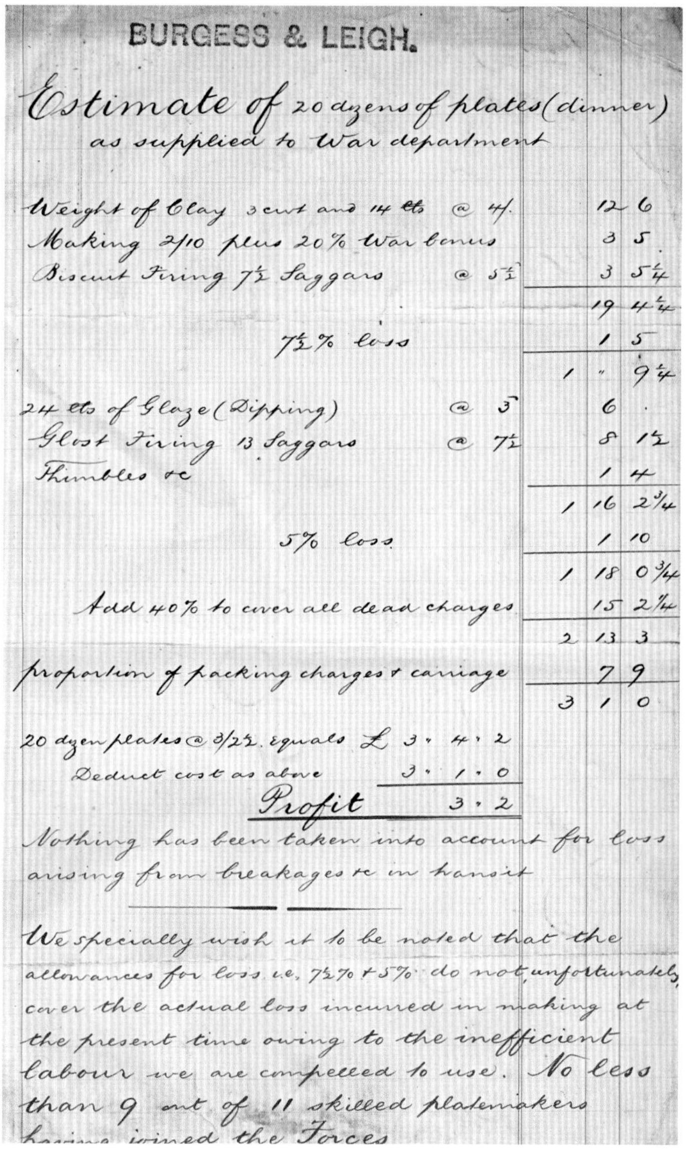

BURGESS & LEIGH.

Estimate of 20 dzens of plates (dinner) as supplied to War department

Weight of Clay 3 cwt and 14 lbs @ 4/.		12	6
Making 2/10 plus 20% War bonus		3	5
Biscuit Firing 7½ Saggars @ 5½		3	5¼
		19	4¼
7½% loss		1	5
	1	"	9¼
24 lbs of Glaze (Dipping) @ 3		6	
Glost Firing 13 Saggars @ 7½		8	1½
Thimbles &c		1	4
	1	16	2¾
5% loss		1	10
	1	18	0¾
Add 40% to cover all dead charges		15	2¼
	2	13	3
proportion of packing charges & carriage		7	9
	3	1	0
20 dzen plates @ 3/2½ equals £ 3 . 4 . 2			
Deduct cost as above 3 . 1 . 0			
Profit 3 . 2			

Nothing has been taken into account for loss arising from breakages &c in transit

We specially wish it to be noted that the allowances for loss i.e. 7½% + 5% do not, unfortunately, cover the actual loss incurred in making at the present time owing to the inefficient labour we are compelled to use. No less than 9 out of 11 skilled platemakers having joined the Forces

Costings for wares supplied during the First World War to the British War Office with a note indicating loss of labour to the forces.

The King's Hall pottery displays were subsequently displayed in *'Messrs Harrods establishment in London where the Queen made a special visit to inspect the collection again.'*

It seems that Edmund Leigh missed the royal visit, being away on business in America.[38] He returned in time to attend Kingsley's wedding on 29th April. It was to be the company's last overseas trip for several years as the following year Great Britain entered the *'war to end all wars'*.

The First World War 1914-1918

For the duration of the First World War Edmund Leigh took to heart the words of the young Winston Churchill (then a Liberal) at Guildhall in 1914: *'The maxim of the British people is "business as usual".'* The war had a mixed impact on pottery manufacture which was coordinated by the specially formed Pottery Trades and Standing Joint Committee. Demand for goods remained high and a number of potteries were to profit from an increase in trade gained from non-productive continental countries, particularly Germany. However, there were inevitable shortages of both raw materials and labour.

Many men from the Middleport Pottery were keen to fight for king and country and responded to Lord Kitchener's demand to join the forces in 1914. On the introduction of conscription in 1916, Burgess & Leigh wrote a letter to Major Walmsley, the Recruiting Officer in Stoke-on-Trent, appealing against further losses from their workforce:

> *'We have from the very first, at the outbreak of the war, done our very best to encourage recruiting amongst our hands, having right along paid allowances to the wives of all married men and rendered assistance to the dependents of single employees whenever necessary. More than sixty have joined the forces and several have been killed.'*

A list was duly compiled in May of some forty men of *'military age'* (between the ages of eighteen and forty-one years) in *'certified occupations'* whom Burgess & Leigh wished to retain. Amongst them was William H. Leigh, described as London and Shipping Agent; Denis Leigh, Commercial Manager; Harold Holdcroft and Robert J. Heath, Travellers; Sydney Hancock, Mouldmaker; Jack Smith, Head Biscuit Placer; J. Brereton, Biscuit Fireman; A.T. Downs and G. Smith, Printers; Thomas Edge, Packer; John Holmes, Head Carter; and L. Yates, Boilerman. Nonetheless, the following month a further list shows the names of fourteen men *'given up'* from all areas of production. While such men were away, women, as elsewhere, were called upon to do their work. When the father of retired packer Ben Ford went off to war, for instance, his wife took over his duties as a glost kiln placer, the heavy saggar being brought to and from her side for filling.[39] The number employed at the Middleport Pottery in 1914 was 442; by January 1917 this had dropped to 318 of which 140 were men and 178 were women.

It was not only Middleport Pottery employees who were eager to play their part in the Great War. When Thomas Wood wrote to Burgess & Leigh from Australia in 1917 requesting permission to enlist, Edmund, whilst admiring his patriotism, considered *'he would serve his country best by remaining at his post to earn 'silver bullets' by selling as much British merchandise as he could to help the country's finances bear the terrific costs of the war.'*[40] This view he extended to members of his own family, as well as other vital employees. William therefore remained at the London showroom for the duration of the war whilst Denis and Kingsley held the fort at the Middleport factory. Kingsley, when called up at the age of thirty-three, was discharged as *'unfit to serve in the army'* being *'permanently and totally disabled for military*

The *'Late Lord Roberts'*, the death of the Boer War General in 1914 prompted Burgess & Leigh to issue a commemorative plaque, probably designed by Swettenham, illustrated here in the Print Record Book.

Print for *Koson* Ware, illustrated in the Print Record Book.

Left: Print by Oharo Matao (1877-1945), a Japanese artist who, until 1912, signed his work 'Koson', which once belonged to modeller Charles Wilkes. *(Private Collection)*.

Chinese shaped vase decorated with *Koson* print with more muted, delicate colouring, c.1915.

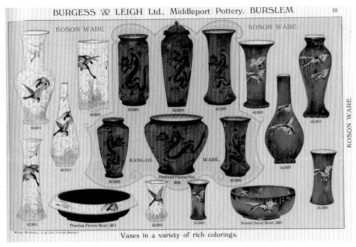

Koson Ware, shown left and right of *Kang-he*, catalogue page c.1920.

Burleigh Wares, an inexpensive line of printed patterns mixing florals and bright colours, catalogue of c.1920.

service'.[41] Although serious enough to exempt him from the forces, whatever disabilities Kingsley suffered fortunately did not prevent him from performing his key production duties at the Middleport Pottery. A large part of the company's output was for export and, in addition, the company had been awarded in 1916 a government contract to supply large quantities of goods (mainly pudding bowls!) for the War Office. Badged hospital wares were also produced for the Red Cross tending the many thousands of sick and wounded. Records show that the net values of goods invoiced by Burgess & Leigh that year was £33,500 for home orders, £16,000 for export, and £5,000 for Government contracts, totaling £54,500. In 1918 it was able to donate £1,350 to a fund raising event, *'Tank Week'*, which was part of industry's wider campaign in support of the war effort.[42]

Both 'Designer' Edwin Leigh and Charles Wilkes were too old for military service and continued to design new ranges which were shown throughout the First World War at the firm's London Showrooms. Indeed, towards the end of the war in 1918, *The Pottery Gazette* was advising that the London Showrooms' address *'should be noted by town and country customers as a useful rallying-point now that travellers' journeys are perforce restricted.'* One item possibly displayed there at the very beginning of the war was a wall plaque commemorating the death in 1914 of *'the late Lord Roberts'*, a hero of the Afghan and Boer Wars. Probably the work of Swettenham (who had designed the commemorative Gladstone plaque), *The Pottery Gazette* described it as *'a real work of art.... designed by an artist of real renown and engraved in faultless style.... It is not only topical but extremely artistic and it is to be hoped that the enterprise will be highly successful.'* More topical still was the collection of small, thrown and turned vases (pattern 1764), aerographed in black, green and salmon, featuring a lithographic transfer of another war 'hero' Lord Kitchener.

Also shown during the 1914-1918 years was the usual steady supply of toiletware, *'as washing has not yet been banned as a luxury'*, the trade press jibed.[43] Many new shapes were introduced, including the elegant *Belgigue, Française* and *Pallissy* all of which showed the enduring influence of the Empire style. Burgess & Leigh were also eager to promote new 'fancies' including flower and plant pots, already *'well known in the trade'* and ornamental vases and jars in the still popular oriental style. One such was *Koson Ware* which was made up until the 1920s. Its inspiration came from the work of Oharo Matao (1877-1945), the Japanese artist who until 1912 signed his works Koson. Prints by Koson of birds in flight are believed to have been acquired by Wilkes,[44] copied and then engraved for printing on to a range of ornamental shapes. The trade press

Damask, a chintz or sheet floral pattern applied to a range of suited tablewares and ornamental shapes, first issued in c.1914.

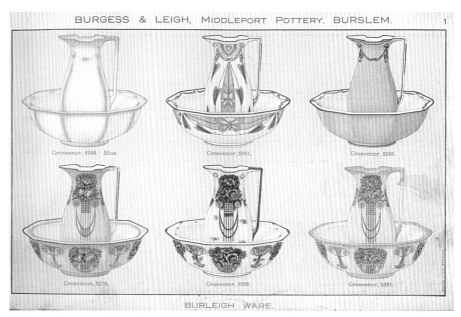

Toiletwares from around the time of the First World War showing *Kensington*, top centre, a butterfly pattern also illustrated, left, in the print Record Book.

An *avant-garde* 'flower power' pattern, top right and bottom centre, also shown in the print Record Book, left, c.1919.

Hot water jug and *Cranborne*-shaped teapot and stand in floral and striped pattern, c.1916. Height of jug 7ins (19cm).

Catalogue page showing the pattern on a *Portland*-shaped flowerpot, centre left.

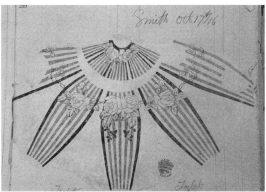

Print showing the pattern which was used for tablewares, toiletwares and ornamental wares.

This printed *trompe l'oeuil* design is often seen on unmarked mugs and jugs. Illustration from the Print Record Book.

commented on '*vases depicting a flight of wild ducks across the face of the moon, with mountain scenery below. The wild duck decoration was formerly supplied in soft toned blue and grey, but now some brighter colourings have been added…. which is sure to prove attractive in certain very busy markets.*'[45]

An equally successful, though very different series, was *Ye Ballades of Olde Englande* or *Old English Ballades*. Launched in 1914, this transfer printed series featured different traditional English scenes recalling well known songs, such as *Sally in Our Alley* and *Harvest Home*. Evoking '*the spirit of the time when England was younger, and possibly merrier*', the range reproduced '*at great cost*' original drawings made by an *eminent artist*'. Although not named, his choice of subject and style resembles that of the popular illustrator Cecil Aldin whose designs were to be used on a later Burleigh series.[46] '*Some sixty different useful and ornamental articles*'[47] were used including a Puzzle Jug (the puzzle being how to drink from it), again researched by Wilkes some years earlier. *The Manchester Guardian*, reviewing the Pottery and Glass Fair a year later, drew particular attention to both *Old English Ballades* and *Tapisserie*, one of Burleigh's 'new art pottery' series, whose decoration, as its name implied, gave an effective imitation of tapestry. Further designs in this series included *Faenza, Damask, Kyoto, Pruneau* and *Alexandra*, their names suggesting the source of their inspiration.

The *Guardian*'s reporter also noted that Burgess & Leigh did '*extensive trade in medium grade pottery. Within the limits of their class, their work is of the highest class*', a point reiterated by *The Pottery Gazette*'s report of 1st March, 1915:

'*Burgess & Leigh have a reputation extending over very many years for continually bringing out excellent schemes both in shape and designs. Their last year's spring samples were the talk of the trade, one of the best ranges that they had up to then brought out, but this year's efforts bids fair to eclipse that. For a really good middle-class trade Burgess & Leigh's lines, speaking generally will take a good deal of beating, and in those departments in which they clearly specialise, such as toiletware, dinner ware, flowerpots and suite ware – the last mentioned has been quite a strong point with them during the last few years – they have no difficulty securing special recognition*'.

Vase with printed design *Sally in our Alley* from *Ye Ballades of Olde Englande*, c.1914. The subject was to inspire a relief-moulded jug made by Burgess & Leigh in 1936.

Illustrated '*by an eminent artist*' so claimed a colour advertisement in a supplement to *The Pottery Gazette* in 1914.

Printed design for *The Bailiff's Daughter of Islington* in company archives.

The Bailiff's Daughter of Islington, a subject from *Ye Ballades of Olde Englande* printed on a moulded plate, c.1914, diameter 9ins (22.5cms).

During the period when many other manufacturers were unable to obtain the coloured lithographs from Germany used for cheaper wares, Burgess & Leigh were able to continue using the traditional printing techniques it had mastered over the last fifty years. *The Pottery Gazette* went on:

'*They do not go in for a slapdash bulk trade. It is their steady aim to uplift the commoner trade in pottery, and with that object ever before them they bestow infinite pains in the engraving of any new design, in order to get right away from anything in the nature of harshness. Moreover, nothing that is not right is good enough… It is this sort of thing which has given the firm a name in America and elsewhere, second to none for printed wares.*'

With such words of praise ringing in their ears, Burgess & Leigh would be striving to maintain their success throughout the war and beyond. Although they could not know it, the next two decades were to bring the company still more acclaim '*all over the globe*'.

CHAPTER FOUR

DESIGNED TO SUCCEED:
Burleigh Ware Between the Wars 1919-1939

Burgess & Leigh Limited

The guns of the First World War stopped firing in 1918, but negotiations for peace continued until the following year. Burgess & Leigh celebrated the occasion with the issue of a commemorative bowl; etched by Swettenham, it featured a Roman mosaic-style design and the lettering *Peace* and *Victory*. British hopes were indeed high during the immediate post-war period. Trade could not have looked better and order books were full throughout the Potteries. In 1919 Burgess & Leigh announced that it had become a limited company; it registered capital of £50,000 in £1 shares and named Edmund as its first Chairman, his three sons as the firm's first directors, and John Taylor Williamson as Company Secretary. 'Private Wages' books record their weekly salaries then as £15, £10 and £8 respectively. The company summed up the reason for their continuing success: '*We have maintained one policy – namely, that quality and originality must come first.*'[1]

That quality of ware was noted the same year by a group visiting the Middleport Pottery. Under the supervision of Senior Salesman Harold Holdcroft (a Blue Coats' orphanage boy nicknamed 'Lord Harry' on the factory for his proud bearing), the party saw a variety of processes, which showed that Burgess & Leigh combined the best of traditional and progressive methods of manufacture. *The Pottery Gazette and Glass Trade Review* reported:

'*In the decorating department the opportunity was taken of inspecting machine printing from roller engravings, which had not been seen at any of the other factories visited by this particular party, and particularly interesting was some work in process on the older hand-presses…. Burgess & Leigh rightly pride themselves upon the quality of their underglaze printing, in which both the printers and the transferrers seem to give of their very best. In the firm's showroom there was to be seen, in all departments of the domestic earthenware trade, a collection of samples of*

Printed mosaic-style design commemorating *Peace* and *Victory* in 1919.

'*Burleigh Ware*', *such as truly vindicate the firm's reputation in the potting world. On the conclusion of the tour of the works, a refreshing cup of tea was thoughtfully provided, and was accepted, we may say, with much appreciation, not only by the ladies.*'

In spite of such praise the company had to be alert to complacency, especially when, with sales to old export markets slow to return, the post-war economic boom proved to be all too brief. During the early years of the 1920s Britain found itself in the grip of a steep recession aggravated by worsening industrial relations. Edmund warned against potential rifts in the Potteries; at a luncheon that year to commemorate the war-time work of the Pottery Trades and Standing Joint Committee, he '*made a lengthy but captivating speech, in which he pleaded for frankness and unison between capital and labour, particularly in order that the export trade of the potters might be conserved.*'[2]

It was partially with the export trade in mind that William Leigh decided to return to South Africa in 1921 to act as the company's representative there. He had inherited his father's frail health and also felt that he would benefit from the warmer climate his wife's home country offered. However, only a few years later ill health forced him to hand over to the firm of Ross-Elliott and McKellar. From that time onwards William no longer took any active role in the family firm. Nonetheless, his talent for business remained and he amassed shares in numerous companies including South African gold mines.

With William in South Africa and their father, then aged sixty-five years, taking a less prominent role, Kingsley and Denis were effectively left in sole charge of Burgess & Leigh from 1921. Kinglsey continued as Works Manager leaving Denis to run the sales and commercial side. At around this time, the company's practice of hiring stock rooms in the south of England ceased and its sales representative, then Albert Aldersea, was rewarded with the first company car. However, rooms continued to be hired in the major northern towns of Lancashire and Yorkshire and in Scotland.

Middleport Pottery avoided the part time working which beset many firms during 1922. *The Pottery Gazette*, reporting a further visit there of trainee London sales staff attending a Benevolent Institutions Educational Tour, noted that manufacturing processes were '*carried out here on much more serious and competitive lines than at previously visited potteries.*' As ever, the occasion, hosted by Denis and John T. Williamson, was marked by Burgess & Leigh hospitality, with the '*provision of a dainty afternoon tea, served in the work's showroom*'!

The Death of Edmund Leigh

Such press reports must have proved gratifying to Edmund who, in his retirement, remained as interested as ever in the works. Unfortunately, the following year was to see a marked deterioration in his health. Despite the best medical care from '*an eminent physician*' collaborating with '*two well

Kingsley Leigh in his office. He bacame Chairman or Burgess & Leigh following the death of his father, Edmund, in 1924.

known local practitioners,'[3] he died on 1st January, 1924 of heart failure following long standing chronic bronchitis. He was sixty-nine years old and had completed fifty-six years with Burgess & Leigh. Like so many in the Potteries, Edmund Leigh had joined as an apprentice in what was then a small family concern in shared rented property. By his own endeavours, he left as a well-respected Chairman of a limited company, then employing over 300, producing and distributing world famous pottery from its own impressive premises, the Middleport Pottery.

Edmund was buried in Stone Cemetery. The Reverend Alan Stephens in his funeral address at Stone Congregational Church said: *'He gave to me a solemn charge….that if any memorial words were spoke of him, they should be free from all extravagance and be both true and modest….[He was] a man with a genuinely pitiful heart, especially pitiful to the poor.'*[4] Letters and telegrams of condolence were received from many people in Britain as well as overseas. Tom Heath, writing from Australia, spoke for them all when he said that Edmund's *'memory should live long in the Potteries. He had ability and vision far above that given to average man and above all he used those gifts for the betterment of his fellow creatures. No better employer was there in the district.'*[5]

Also sharing this sentiment at Edmund's funeral were over 150 employees from the Middleport Pottery. They included Messrs Smith, Hancock, Stevenson, Colclough, Clark and Edge, acting as coffin bearers; George Brett, the clay manager, and the Misses Lucie and S. Brett from the Decorating Department; William Howell, Assistant Manager; Harry Downes, Head Printer; Samuel Keeling representing the Glazing Department; Messrs J. Cartwright and J. Downes from the Biscuit and Glost Warehouses; and the longest serving man and woman, Mr J. Dono and Mrs E. Hart, who had each served fifty years with the company.[6] In his will,[7] Edmund left £45,000 gross, net £40,000. Of this, £100 was left to the Pottery and Glass Trades' Benevolent Institution (which he had championed since 1911 and of which he was a governor since 1917) and £100 to the Arts

and Library Committee of the National Liberal Club. A personal bequest of £250 was made to John Taylor Williamson as Burgess & Leigh's Company Secretary and Edmund's lifelong friend.

Edmund's obituary in *The Pottery Gazette* read: *'He was a man who by the force of his personality, inspired everyone with whom he came into contact, and had no difficulty in convincing his fellowman of his innate ability and worthiness to take his share as a leader.'*

When Edmund Leigh died, the company lost a strong and influential figurehead but his sons had by then shown themselves more than capable as directors of Burgess & Leigh Ltd. They were, in the decades that followed, not only to maintain Burgess & Leigh's worldwide reputation for 'quality and originality' but also to further enhance it by placing its products at the vanguard of modern ceramic design.

Post War Lifestyle and Design Changes

Edmund's sons had first assumed responsibility for the company at a time when the pottery industry was adjusting to major economic changes after the First World War. The ensuing recession had brought with it changes in lifestyle which caused a decrease in sales of many of the firm's staple items. The large, imposing Victorian villas, elaborately decorated and furnished by their wealthy owners, became increasingly difficult to run with the post-war shortage of household servants. New 'homes fit for heroes', built with government funding in Britain's expanding suburbs, provided smaller family units with more compact living spaces, their simple interiors uncluttered by large ornaments such as pots and pedestals. The luxury of their indoor toilets and bathrooms brought a fall in demand for the toiletwares in which potteries such as Burgess & Leigh had traded for so long. Middle-class households no longer aspired to the formal and frequently ostentatious meals enjoyed generations earlier in Britain's grand country houses. As people's dining habits became more relaxed and intimate, so the demand fell for the multitude of tableware and kitchen ware items.

As lifestyles changed, so, too, did popular taste and design became an issue which was much debated. Inspired by the successful promotion of links between art and industry by the Deutsche Werkbund (founded in Germany in 1907), the Design and Industries Association (DIA) had been established in London in 1915 *'to instill a new spirit of design into British Industry'*. The DIA became well known for its rather austere promotion of *'fitness for purpose'*, that design should be functional rather than fancy, plain rather than pretty, in fact, rather more like the products of the wartime enemy!

The DIA had warned pottery manufacturers in no uncertain terms that *'expert craftsmanship does not go hand in hand with good design'*,[8] prompting a continuing debate in the Potteries which, after the First World War, was led by Gordon Mitchell Forsyth, Superintendent of Art Instruction for Stoke-on-Trent City Art Schools. Forsyth, who had previously been Art Director for Minton, Hollins & Co. and Pilkington Tile & Pottery Co., provided a stimulating atmosphere for art students and ceramicists to discuss the wider design issues of the day. Under his leadership, Burslem School of Art (by then based in a building designed by A.R. Wood in c.1905) became a place where young designers were encouraged to be original and innovative rather than to

THE REAL ART OF THE POTTER is found in "BURLEIGH WARE," everything that is beautiful, tasteful, both in shape and design is embodied in the manufacture of this now world-famous Ware. The most discriminate Buyers stock it on its reputation alone, and Mrs. Willoughby Hodgson the well-known authority described some of the specimens of "BURLEIGH WARE" as the "sensation of the last British Industries Fair." "There's a reason."

OUR LONDON SHOWROOMS are always open, and all our latest productions are now on view.

**BURGESS & LEIGH,
BURSLEM, Staffs.**

LONDON—44, Farringdon Street, E.C. 4.
(One of the largest Showrooms in London.)
AUSTRALIA—T. W. Heath & Co., Ltd., Aberdeen House, 204, Clarence Street, Sydney, N.S.W
NEW ZEALAND—Thos. Webb & Co., Ltd., Ormiston Buildings, Albert St., Auckland.
SOUTH AFRICA—R. L. Hutty, Hulston's Buildings, Smith Street, Durban.

An advertisement from *The Pottery and Glass Record*, 1920.

Burgess & Leigh's display stand at the British Industries Fair in 1920 with the *Urbino* range of vases shown in the background.

mindlessly copy designs from the past. Forsyth's teaching was to draw many plaudits, including one from a visitor from New York's Metropolitan Museum who congratulated the Burslem School of Art on its approach to modern design.[9] However, Stoke-on-Trent's pottery manufacturers, battling the national recession, were initially resistant to art-school theorising; they were more concerned with economic survival than good design. In order to compensate for the decline in sales, many of them sacrificed quality for quantity by producing ever more ranges with the emphasis on 'novelty', the very antithesis, in fact, of the DIA's *'fitness for purpose'*.

New ceramic products were now exhibited at the British Industries Fairs, set up by the Board of Trade specifically to encourage British exports. In an advertisement placed by Burgess & Leigh in *The Pottery and Glass Record* of 1920 it was quoted that *'Mrs Willoughby Hodgson, the well-known authority, described some of the specimens of 'Burleigh Ware' as 'the sensation of the last British Industries Fair'.'* The company's tableware ranges were mostly, as before, printed underglaze with some banding and gilding. From 1921 patterns were also made available in china teaware from Salt & Nixon, a

Urbino vase with lustre decoration, c.1920.

Jardinière in the *Urbino* range whose bright colours, the trade press reported, *'bid fair appeal to the modern taste'*.

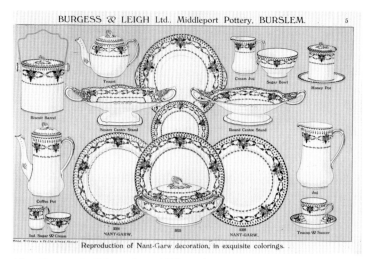

Nant-Garw on the *Belmont* shape, 1920s catalogue page.

The *Broseley* pattern illustrated in the Print Record Book.

small firm a few miles away in Longton, an option much *'appreciated by the dealer who is on the look-out for stock lines'*,[10] (popular patterns kept in large quantity by retailers).

One of the Burleigh tableware patterns that the now forgotten Mrs Willoughby Hodgson may well have seen at the BIF in 1919 was *Nant-Garw*. As its name implies, it purported to be reproduction of a pattern produced by the early nineteenth-century porcelain manufacturer Nantgarw at Swansea. Although traditional in style, this particular pattern was innovative in its use of underglaze tri-colour printing and enamelling and was available in three different colourways (3024-6).

Produced on the *Belmont* shape, *Nant-Garw*'s decoration was especially praised at a time when many tableware lines, for reasons of economy, were still decorated with poor-quality multicolored lithographs introduced during the First World War, *'those anaemic, vapid, insensate transfers'*,[11] as Gordon Forsyth had described them.

Burleigh Willow

'*Anaemic*' was not a description which could be applied to an engraved pattern Burgess & Leigh unveiled in 1924: *Ye Olde 'Dillwyn' Willow* (more commonly known as *Blue Willow*). The origin of the design is an interesting and intriguing story.

Burgess & Leigh had already manufactured numerous Chinese-inspired patterns for tableware, including some *Willow*-type designs. All are similar in style to the uninitiated but their subtle yet distinct differences are clear to *Willow* pattern cognoscenti. The first of the *Willow*-type patterns was *Broseley*, which the company produced during the 1860s at the Central Pottery. Thomas Minton had first engraved this pattern, a direct copy of Chinese landscape design, in the late eighteenth century at Caughley and numerous manufacturers went on to reproduce it, including Spode, Minton, Miles Mason, Coalport and to a lesser extent Davenport. It was known by a number of different names including *Pagoda* and is now commonly known to *Willow*-pattern aficionados as *Two Temples II Variation Broseley*.[12] The pattern comprises two buildings to the left, one in front of the other with a person standing in the doorway, a bridge to the centre right with two people on it, a fence to the lower right crossing a river and a willow tree. (The same pattern commonly appears in reverse on holloware items.) The border pattern incorporates a

butterfly, trellis and key motifs. How long Burgess & Leigh manufactured *Broseley* is not known but a sales catalogue of 1893 illustrates *Antique* and *Queen Anne* shaped teapots in the *Broseley* pattern, with pattern number 1837.

During the 1860s, Burgess & Leigh also manufactured what is known as the standard *Willow* pattern. Its essential design elements combine motifs from another of Thomas Minton's Caughley engravings, *Mandarin*, with others from an original Chinese pattern: a central willow tree hanging over a bridge on which are three figures crossing to an island, a tea house to the right with a large orange tree behind, a boat with a man in it, two birds flying towards each other in the top centre, and a zigzag fence across the foreground.[13] The pattern's border usually incorporates a distinctive key motif whilst a nankin (inner border) with cell or honeycomb design was sometimes used. Josiah Spode produced the earliest marked engravings of *Willow* in the early 1790s and many different manufacturers subsequently went on to make the pattern and variations of it. By the mid-nineteenth century it had become one of the most popular ceramic patterns produced, spawning an 'ancient Chinese' legend, in fact penned by an English author in c.1849!

A notebook entitled '*Pressers' Prices*' indicates that in November 1872 Burgess & Leigh were making the following variously sized table- and toiletware shapes in *Willow*: *Plates*; *Twifflers* [plates, variously described as between five and nine-inch in size]; *Muffins*; *Dishes*; *Gravies*; *Bakers*; *Drainers*; *Soup Tureen, Stands and Ladles*; *Sauce Tureens, Stands, Ladles and Boats*; *Covered Dishes*; *Salads*; *Root Dishes*; *Hash Dishes*; *Mustards*; *Salts*; *Eggcups*; *Toast Racks*; *Ewers*; *Basins*; *Chambers*; *Soaps*; *Brushes*; *Pressed Jugs*; *Thrown Jugs*; and three different shaped *Teapots*.

The standard *Willow* pattern printed on a moulded, footed vegetable dish, left, of 1883 and a plate made between c.1903-c.1920. (*Photograph courtesy of Scott Rogers.*)

1872 Nov 25	Willow Prescot Hawthn	Best Pattns	Printers Count	
			Willow	Nov
Plates	18	16	18	16
Tinflers	24	20	24	20
Muffns 7	30	24	30	24
" 6	36	30	36	30
" 5	36	36	36	36
Dishes 7 to 14	12	12	15 to 11	
" 16-20	6	6	12-12+14 6	6
Gravies 16.18.20	6	6	6	6
Bakers	12	12	12	12
Drainers 14	12	12	12	12
" 16	6	6	6	6
Soup Tureen	6	6	6	6
" Stand	6	6	6	6
" Ladles	12	12	12	12
Sauce Tureen	6	6	8	6
" Stand	12	12	18	12
" Ladles	12	12	18	12
" Boat	12	12	18	12
Covd Dishes	6	6	8	6

'Printers' Count' showing some of the items produced by Burgess & Leigh in *Willow* in 1872.

Examples of printed marks used on the *Willow* pattern in 1883, left, and between c.1903 and c.1924. (*Photograph courtesy of Scott Rogers.*)

An example of a Burgess & Leigh *Willow* plate, with an impressed datemark of 1883, has a printed backstamp cartouche featuring feathery bell motifs and the word STONEWARE with B & L. ('Stoneware' was in fact a misnomer as the body used was in fact a type of earthenware). The company continued to manufacture the standard *Willow* pattern after the move to Middleport Pottery in 1889 and into the 1900s. A *Descriptive Account of the Potteries* of 1893, which includes a report on the Middleport Pottery, mentions amongst Burgess & Leigh's warehouses one for '*Blue Willow*', confirming that it was produced in large quantities. Some time after 1903, when the Burleigh Ware brand was launched, the mark was re-engraved to include the words BURLEIGH WARE, WILLOW and ENGLAND and this mark was used, along with standard company marks, on Burgess & Leigh's *Willow*-type patterns until c.1924.

The company's production of both *Willow* and *Broseley* had probably dwindled around the time of the First World War, as much was made of the introduction in c.1924 of the new Ye Olde '*Dillwyn*' *Willow*.[14] First mention of it was made in *The Pottery Gazette* of 1st February that year which reviewed toiletware in: '*a smart new adaptation of the 'Willow' pattern, executed in enamel blue and orange.*' Essentially a Chinoiserie pattern, the design shares some elements with *Willow*, *Two Temples II* and other patterns in the Chinese manner such as *Long Bridge* and *Buddleia*: a tea house and smaller building to the right with an orange tree in front, a willow tree to the centre left over a bridge carrying three figures to an island, a fence to the lower left, a boat, two flying birds to the top left and a rock (sometimes with a figure behind) at the bottom centre. Borders usually feature either a bat or butterfly motif and a cell or honeycomb pattern, design elements repeated in the nankin when used.

Although the trade press reported that the '*Dillwyn*' *Willow* was reproduced from '*an actual old Chinese plate*' it seems that the source of the pattern was, in fact, a plate produced in the early 1800s by Dillwyn (at the Cambrian factory in Swansea). This was purchased by Edmund Leigh from an antique shop,[15] (Edmund was a collector of nineteenth-century blue printed plates and had some seventy pieces at the time of his death). The centre of the plate was copied by 'Designer' Leigh, a border designed to make up a new and unique pattern. It is intriguing that in spite of worldwide searching by Willow experts,[16] no example of the original '*Dillwyn*' or Swansea pattern has been found. What is absolutely certain is the fine quality of the engraving of '*Dillwyn*' *Willow*.

Engravings of the '*Dillwyn*' *Willow* were made for tableware, *Worcester*-shaped toiletware and ornamental shapes including flower pots and bulb bowls. Amongst the more interesting items from the '*Dillwyn*' *Willow* range are a teapot, and separate stand. They were originally produced as part of the *Cranborne* tableware shape, which was registered

The '*Dillwyn*' *Willow* pattern, left, and the standard *Willow* pattern, right. Diameter 9$\frac{1}{2}$ins (23.5cms).

'*Dillwyn*' *Willow*, as illustrated in the Print Record Book in 1923.

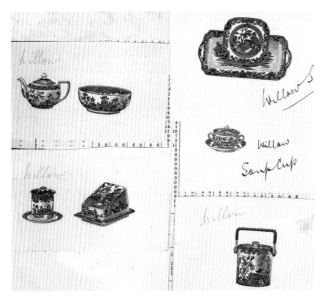

A scrapbook from the 1930s showing some of the shapes then made in the *'Dillwyn' Willow* pattern.

A loose page with a coloured print of pattern 1283, a version of *Broseley*, used on the *Cranborne*-shaped teapot stand, c.1910.

colours recorded are mulberry, dark blue, light blue and green dinner ware (patterns 3553-3556) and suite ware in green (3596). A more expensive variation also issued in 1924 was *'blue, richly traced and finished in scoured gold'* (3612). The trade press reviewed yet another version *'in that peculiar mixed colour which was in vogue a quarter of a century ago, and which was known at that time as "Unique". It is true to its name; the report went on, 'it is unique; and on that account the trade may quite likely be glad to have it.'* In fact, records confirm that the company was using the colour as early as the 1860s. (A colour jar labelled *Unique* still stands in the original colour room at the Middleport Pottery.) Further experimentation produced versions with flow blue printing, gold stippling, enamel painting and lustre applied to flower pots and bowls. During the 1920s, still more colour variations were added to tableware ranges, including *Imperial* (pale blue); *Canton* (pale blue/grey) and brown. Pattern 4176, which specified Wilkes' *Pekin* shape, was especially attractive, *'printed underglaze in pink and enamelled in rose and water green with the usual liquid finish'*.

'Dillwyn' Willow, most probably pattern 4176, *'in pink with underglaze enamels in rose and water green'*, late 1920s.

in 1910 and enjoyed much success with a variety of patterns during the years leading up the First World War. One of the patterns used for the teapot and stand in 1910 was *Broseley*. This has been identified[17] as the *Two Temples II* pattern, used in reverse, with additional elements taken from the standard *Willow* pattern: an extra willow tree near the teahouse and two birds. Interestingly, whilst the teapot has a *Two Temples II* butterfly border, the border used on the stand appears to be an original Burgess & Leigh design. The pattern was available in some seven different underglaze 'print and enamel' colour versions, all finished with a liquid gold edge. An illustration found in company archives shows one version, pattern 1283, which it names simply and misleadingly as *'Willow'*; beneath is noted: *'Printed underglaze golden brown, filled in Baker's green, crimson red, apple and 12's green. Traced and finished in liquid gold'*. It was decided to re-introduce the *Cranborne* teapot and stand, with its original *Broseley* pattern, as part of the *'Dillwyn' Willow* range. However, the old colour versions were abandoned and it was more commonly decorated with an underglaze blue print and gilded.

The *'Dillwyn' Willow* was itself produced in a very wide variety of different colourways. On first introduction in 1924 until c.1930, dinner ware, coffee- and early morning sets could be had in *'a still blue of very pleasing and quiet tint'* as well as *'print and enamel'* versions, with and without gilding;

Colour and glaze recipes for Burgess & Leigh's *Willow*-type wares from the nineteenth century, right, and twentieth century above.

Burleigh Willow

ITEMS AVAILABLE

1. Plate 8" Trade Size 24.0 cms. Actual Dia.
Plate 7" Trade Size 21.5 cms. Actual Dia.
Plate 6" Trade Size 19.0 cms. Actual Dia.
Plate 5" Trade Size 17.5 cms. Actual Dia.
Plate 4" Trade Size 15.0 cms. Actual Dia.
2. Soup Plate 7" Trade Size 21.5 cms. Actual Dia.
3. Coupe Soup Plate
4. Bread & Butter Plate
5. Dish 14" Trade Size 39.0 cms. Actual Dia.
Dish 12" Trade Size 34.0 cms. Actual Dia.
Dish 10" Trade Size 28.5 cms. Actual Dia.
Dish 9" Trade Size 25.5 cms. Actual Dia.
6. Teacup and Saucer
7. Coffee Cup and Saucer
8. Oatmeal Bowl
9. Rimmed Fruit Saucer
10. Fruit Saucer 4" Trade Size
11. Vegetable Dish
12. Covered Scollop

13. Fruit Bowl 8" Trade Size
Fruit Bowl 7" Trade Size
14. Sauce Boat and Stand
15. Cream Soup Cup and Stand
16. Teapot 1½ pint & ¾ pint (0.80 ℓ., 0.40 ℓ.)
17. Coffee Pot 1½ pint (0.80 ℓ.)
18/19. Sugar & Cream, Tea Size
18/20. Sugar & Cream, Coffee Size
21. Covered Sugar Bowl
22. Jug 1½ pint, 1 pint, ¾ pint
(0.80 ℓ., 0.60 ℓ., 0.40 ℓ.)
23. Sandwich Tray
24. Cheese Stand
25. Pepper & Salt
26. Footless Egg Cup
27. Jumbo Cup & Saucer
Round Dish
Soup Tureen

The above sizes and capacities are approximate

Printed in England

A leaflet from the 1960s-70s period.

All versions were well received at home and overseas, especially in the Australian, New Zealand and Canadian markets. However, it was the very first colour, a deep cobalt blue, described in advertising literature as a *'still Swansea blue'*, with gilding, which quickly established itself as the most popular and indeed after 1940 it was the only version to remain in production by Burgess & Leigh.[18] The company continued to produce it on a limited number of tableware and ornamental shapes until the late 1990s, on an ivory body until the 1960s and afterwards on a white body.

Today, the many collectors of Burleigh *'Dillwyn' Willow* continue to find *Swansea blue* appealing but also delight in seeking out more unusual colour versions and shapes. Amongst these variations might be more recent Burgess, Dorling & Leigh productions. For instance, for a short period of time in c.1999, the company produced ungilded versions in both pale blue and black. In 2002, basing their design on an earlier one produced for the Twinings tea

An unusual pre-war black printed and enamelled version of *'Dillwyn' Willow*.
(*Photograph courtesy of Scott Rogers.*)

A selection of post-war Burleigh *'Dillwyn' Willow* shapes.

company, elements of the *'Dillwyn' Willow* pattern were used on a small, lidded ginger jar-shaped tea canister for the London store Fortnum & Mason, whose trademark it bears. This continues a tradition of the Middleport Pottery supplying commissioned 'badged' wares for a variety of different institutions whose names were either prominently displayed on the front of items or were included more discretely on the bases.

Early 1920s: New Lines

'Badged' wares formed just a small part of the factory's vast and diverse output. By the mid-1920s, *The Pottery Gazette* was writing: *'We doubt very much whether we should be overstating the case if we were to put on record that, in proportion to its size, the Middleport Pottery maintains as big an assortment of moulds, engravings, and lithographs as any factory operating in the Staffordshire Potteries. And still new lines continue to make their appearance!'*

The predominant design influences during the 1920s were French, Egyptian and oriental. Burgess & Leigh produced several 'print and enamel' series on a variety of different shapes, featuring such designs as *Camels* (3125-9) and oriental figures from the *Mikado* (3513-4). Traditionally English subjects also remained popular; characters from the works of Dickens and Shakespeare decorated *Sunderland-, Alma-* and *Nelson*-shaped jugs (3476-3483) whilst *Hunting* scenes (3540) were used on a variety of ornamental and useful shapes.

A series introduced in 1925, optimistically entitled *'Merrie England'* (3513), featured village scenes by the well-known illustrator Cecil Aldin.[19] It comprised a total of six humorous designs – *Old English Revels, Off to Gretna Green, An Old English Village, The Roisterers, Dick Turpin's Ride to York* and *Sighting the Armada* – translated into lithographic transfers by the British Transfer Company of the Wedgwood Works in Burslem. In spite of its fairly heavy promotion in the trade press, it seems that it was not as popular as *Ye Olde English Ballades*, a similar series produced a decade earlier. (Interestingly, the following year Royal Doulton also issued a Series Ware range featuring Aldin's designs. Perhaps owing to Doulton's higher profile, its collection was rather more successful and remained in production until the mid-1940s.)

Traditional patterns usually called for traditional shapes

A leaflet advertisng *Merrie England* designed by Cecil Aldin and first issued by Burgess & Leigh in 1925.

Page from a catalogue of c.1927 showing items in *Merrie England*, bottom left, with more modern design, shapes and decorations including an Adams lustre design, shown centre.

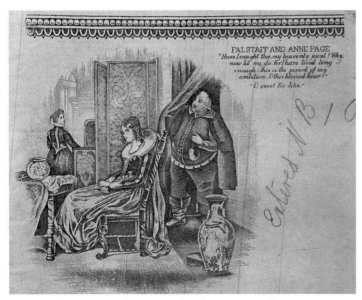

A print of Shakespearean characters used to decorate jugs in the 1920s.

From *Aberteifi Tabernacle* in Wales to *Waipukurau R.R. Rooms* in New Zealand, Burgess & Leigh supplied badged wares 'all over the globe'. These examples of engraved logos are compiled from 'badged books' dating from the late ninteenth century to the 1930s.

A lithographic transfer sheet made by the British Transfer Company, Burslem, for Burgess & Leigh showing Cecil Aldin's designs for *Merrie England: Dick Turpin's Ride to York*; *The Roisterers*; *An Old English Village*; *Off to Gretna Green*; *Old English Revels* and *Sighting the Armada*. Additional motifs were designed for printing on the base of items in this 1925 series.

but Wilkes also modelled more fashionable items, such as square spill jars, trinket-sets, powder-bowls and floating-bowls (to be filled with water and sprinkled with flower petals). Many suite ware items were registered in c.1928 including an hors d'oeuvre tray and a '*tennis tray.*' Wilkes also modelled then popular sandwich sets, comprising trays with spaces to store small plates. The *Windsor*, with a central handle, was one of two oblong-shaped trays with square plates. Those with triangular plates were the *Richmond*, a rhomboid-shaped tray again with a central handle, and the *Crescent*, which had a fan-shaped tray. Fruit sets, such as the *Avon*, the *Rex* and *Regina*, were made up of large sized 'scollops' or bowls with six small 'oatmeal' dishes. The *Burleigh Art Ware* range covered both useful and ornamental shapes, with vases and bowls for flowers, fruit and salad; *Kew*- and *Regent*-shaped 'floating' bowls; *Palissy* (named after the sixteenth- century potter), *Jacobean* and *Chinese* bowls; *Beverley* and *Avon* fruit bowls; *Dutch, Warwick, Sydney, Cairo* and *Adelphi* flower pots; and *Kato* and *Balmoral* bulb bowls.

'Designer' Leigh selected popular motifs for printing on to the new shapes:[20] oriental birds, exotic fish and fruit, mermaids and dolphins, butterflies, insects and dragons. These and other more abstract designs, such as *Satsuma* (3326) and the late 1920s 'print and enamel' sheet pattern *Paisley*, capitalised on the vogue for bright colours and glazes. Vivid reds, oranges, yellows, blues and mauves, were favourites, often used with a contrasting black. Such colours

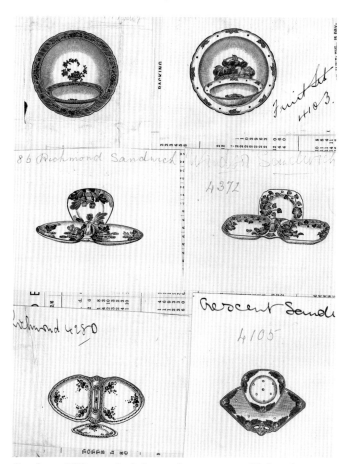

Page from a 1930s scrap-book showing fruit sets, top, and *Richmond*-, *Windsor*- and *Crescent*-shaped sandwich sets.

Avon-shaped fruit bowl in pattern 4000 and matching oblong sandwich tray and square sandwich plate, c.1927. Bowl diameter 9¹/₄ins (23.5cms).

Triangular-shaped sandwich plates with lithographic printed patterns 4148, left, and 4280, right, used with *Crescent*- and *Richmond*-shaped sandwich sets, c.1928.

Page from a Burgess & Leigh catalogue of c.1927.

might be painted underglaze or hand-enamelled. Increasingly, they were also aerographed (sprayed) or mottled by a decorator specifically named in the Pattern Books, William Adams. Amongst his earlier 'artistic' decorations were *Rouge-et-Noir* vases (similar to Doulton's *Flambé* range) and later the mottled blue pattern *Pomegranate* (3318). Together with his son, George, Adams was also responsible for decorating ranges of vases and bowls featuring lustre, a metallic, often iridescent glaze popularised by Daisy Makeig-Jones' *Fairyland Lustre* series for Wedgwood. Amongst the lustre ranges was a number with boldly outlined fruit, such as the *Lilium* (4190), and freer, more nebulous decoration, like *Sunflower*, which was available with either a blue or pink aerographed ground (4495, 4496). The distinctive style of decoration of *Riverside* (3693), issued in 1925, prompted *The Pottery Gazette* to report that Burgess & Leigh were '*not afraid of producing treatments which are quite different in type from anything which has previously been offered.*'

One of the more unusual of the Burleigh decorative lines was an impressive collection of wall plaques designed by Swettenham in an Arts and Crafts style. Launched at the BIF in 1921, *The Pottery Gazette and Glass Trade Review* for 1st April, 1921 enthused:

'*One of the chief features of the "Burleigh" display, and one upon which, if one had the time and space at one's disposal much might be written, was a series of magnificent*

Avon fruit bowl, left, pattern 4289, with lustre glaze, freehand painted by William Adams, c.1928; *Kew*-shaped floating bowl, right, with printed butterfly decoration, pattern 3660, c.1925. Bowl diameter 9¼ins (23.5cms).

"Burleigh" Ware. "The Paisley" No. 4223.

Range of Suite Ware items available in the *The Paisley* pattern, illustrated in a late 1920s catalogue.

underglaze paintings on large plaques by a talented artist who signs himself "L. T. Swetnam". [sic] The subjects are splendidly drawn, wonderfully free in their conception and execution, and worthy of finding a place of honour amongst the ceramic relics of the present age. Amongst the subjects depicted must be mentioned "St George and the Dragon", "Here's health to thee, my trustee friend" and "The Standard Bearer". Given sufficient latitude, the artist producing these pieces should have a good time in front of him and contribute in no small measure to the enhancement of the reputation to the firm by whom he is retained. That the "Burleigh" exhibit gave general satisfaction we think can be put on record with conviction.'

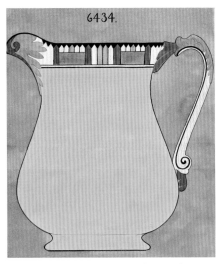

6434.

Bright and bold, a watercolour drawing showing pattern 6434 on the *Beverley*-shape ewer, also illustrated on a catalogue page, below, with a selection of other 1920s Burleigh toilet sets.

BURGESS & LEIGH, LTD., Middleport Pottery, BURSLEM.

"Ceeil" Shape. 6428. "Ceeil" Shape 6449. "Ceeil" Shape. 6424. "Georgian" Shape. 6349. "Beverley" Shape. 6434. "Ceeil" Shape. 6414B. "Empire" Shape. 6403. "Ceeil" Shape 6453.

"Burleigh" Toilet Ware.

Lavish and lustrous patterns with aerographed underglaze decoration by William or George Adams: left, vase 75 and Octagon salad bowl, pattern 4354, c.1928; right, *Beverley* fruit bowl and vase 69, pattern 4190, *Lilium*, c.1928. Largest bowl, diameter 10¼ins (26cms).

More lustres, left to right: vase 48, pattern 4479, blue ground aerographed underglaze by George Adams; handled vase, mottled brown and green glaze, 1930s; small vase and vase 48, *Sunflower* pattern, 4495, pink ground, aerographed underglaze by George Adams, c.1929. Tallest 10¼ins (26cms).

Dutch flower pot, pattern 4494, aerographed and underglaze painted in blue by William Adams, gilded, c.1929. Height 8ins (20cms).

Here's Health to Thee My Trusty Friend, left and *St George and the Dragon*, right, underglaze painted wall plaques designed and signed by Louis Thomas Swettenham, launched by Burgess & Leigh at the British Industries Fair in 1921.

These plaques appear not to have been produced in great numbers and as a result are highly sought after by collectors today, especially that showing a young woman with grapes (a version of which was later to be tube-lined by Charlotte Rhead at the Middleport Pottery).

The Art Deco Style

In 1925 a hugely influential exhibition was held in Paris: the *Exposition Internationale des Arts Décoratifs et Industriels Modernes* provided the first showcase – and the name – for Art Deco. Although this new decorative style was to diversify in Europe and America throughout the late 1920s and 1930s, its common characteristics in ceramics were an emphasis on individuality and hand-craftsmanship, and a preference for brightly coloured dynamic patterns on streamlined, geometric shapes. Nearly six million people attended the Paris Exhibition including Gordon Forsyth. He had to admit that the British pottery section, represented mainly by the larger north American focused manufacturers, displayed '*a real lack of spirit of adventure on the artistic side.*'[21] Appointed Art Advisor to the British Pottery Manufacturers' Federation in c.1921, Forsyth was determined to remedy this by actively promoting links between art and industry. Students from the Burslem School of Art, he maintained, would make ideal ceramic designers, decorators and modellers; not only would they have a good grounding in basic manufacturing traditions but they would also bring much needed innovation and creativity to the industry. Forsyth may have been surprised by a more ready acceptance of his ideas by the usually cautious pottery manufacturers. The truth was that the burgeoning dynamism in ceramic design owed less to art theory than to economic necessity.

From Recession to Depression

As the national recession continued, many companies were bankrupted and retailers went into liquidation. Kingsley and Denis Leigh, with the aid of their employees, showed a tenacity and determination which undoubtedly put them ahead of many of their competitors during the industrial difficulties. When in 1926 the Trades Union Congress called on all British workers to stop work in support of the miners' campaign to resist wage cuts, the National Society of Pottery Workers (not then affiliated to the TUC) advised their members not to join the General Strike. Production in the Potteries was not therefore significantly affected by the nine-day long national strike. However, some union activists mounted a small demonstration outside the Middleport Pottery in protest at what they saw as the misplaced loyalty of the Burgess & Leigh workforce.[22]

More damaging to pottery manufacture was the miners' strike, which continued for a further six months. During this time, a number of north Staffordshire miners elected to unofficially mine open cast outcrops of coal. Kingsley took it upon himself to locate these sites and bought in small quantities of coal to keep production at the Middleport Pottery going.[23] The firm's efforts did not go unnoticed and on 1st October, 1926 *The Pottery Gazette and Glass Trade Review* reported:

'*Middleport Pottery are able to pride themselves upon the somewhat remarkable achievement that they have been able to keep their factory going normally throughout the coal strike. In some respects, it might have been more convenient for them to have closed down for a period, particularly during the early stages of the strike, but the principals evidently had in their minds a dual ambition, viz., to keep faith with their customers and to provide employment for their workpeople. From this it will be seen that the Middleport Pottery has been one of the few bright spots in the Potteries from a trade point of view during the five months of comparative gloom that the strike has been successful in throwing over the North Staffordshire district.*'

Kingsley made a business trip to north America the following year. There, he possibly visited overseas agents, Reimer MacKenzie Corporation in New York, and George Phillips in Montreal, Canada (replaced in 1931 by John C. Boyle and in 1934 by Oakley, Jackson & Farewell, both of Toronto).[24] In 1928, the company also set up its first agency in Europe with the appointment of J. B. De Boeve in Soesterberg, Holland.

Any hopes for an increase in international trade were, however, to be dashed with the Wall Street Crash of 1929. This was a further blow to the 400 or so potteries in Stoke-on-Trent, already battling against the threat of imports, such as peasant pots from Czechoslovakia. To compensate for its depressed overseas market, Burgess & Leigh had to become even more competitive in the home market.

By that time the company had developed a new strategy for survival. Assessing the local competition, the company directors would have noted that those similar sized earthenware manufacturers doing comparatively well were firms like A. J. Wilkinson, Myott & Sons and Meakin, all of whom had responded to Forsyth's recommendations. Their bold new Art Deco wares, inspired by trailblazing companies such as Wedgwood, William Adams & Sons, A E. Gray and Poole in Dorset, did not require expensive investment in large quantities of sub-standard lithographic sheets. They were hand-painted by easily trained (and lowly paid) females and could be quickly changed or adapted for a novelty-hungry public. This made sound economic sense to the cost-conscious and canny Leighs!

But a problem existed: who was going to design the new patterns? By the mid-1920s the Middleport Pottery Design Studio was not at the very 'cutting edge' of design. It could not boast an influential and individualistic art designer, a Susie Cooper, Millicent Taplin or Clarice Cliff, an Eric Slater or Keith Murray. 'Designer' Edwin Leigh was nearing retirement age and Charles Wilkes had been modeller for the company for over thirty-five years. Although both men were experienced and skilled, neither could claim to have the freshness of vision to respond to a new generation's demand for innovative design. What was needed was new blood! And the company directors chose wisely with the appointment of three designers who were to change the face and fortune of Burgess & Leigh – Charlotte Rhead, Ernest Bailey and Harold Bennett. Although it is perhaps only Charlotte Rhead who is well known to the public today, the names of Bailey, Bennett – and the adaptable Wilkes – are also due some recognition. Together, their Burleigh Art Deco designs were to make the late 1920s and 1930s arguably the Middleport Pottery's most successful production period and certainly its most artistically innovative.

BURLEIGH ART DECO

Charlotte Rhead (1885-1947) by Bernard Bumpus

Charlotte Rhead joined Burgess & Leigh towards the end of 1926. Charles Wilkes may have suggested her appointment to the firm.[25] He was then working in his spare time with Charlotte's father, Frederick, on a small ceramic business project. The Wilkes and Rheads were also neighbours, both living in Marsh Avenue, Wolstanton, where they regularly played bridge together. (Indeed, cards seem to have been an important part in their relationship as Wilkes and Charlotte were known to sometimes have a game or two during the lunch break at Burgess & Leigh.)

The Rheads were also already well known to the Leighs as Frederick was a prominent figure in the Potteries. A founder member of the Pottery Managers' Association and its first President, he was also a prolific writer and the art director of Wood & Sons, a large and prosperous firm which owned several potteries in Burslem. Frederick's personal connection with the Leighs went back some fifty years, to the 1880s when the Burslem Liberals decided to make a presentation to the Liberal statesman, and sometime Prime Minister, William Gladstone. They had turned to Frederick Rhead, who was also a Liberal, and commissioned him to design and decorate a large vase in *pâte-sur-pâte* on the Gladstonian theme of Home Rule for Ireland.[26] Frederick had learned this difficult technique at Minton's where he had been apprenticed, aged fourteen, to the celebrated *pâte-sur-pâte* artist Louis Solon. When Gladstone excused himself from coming to Burslem to receive the gift, Frederick Rhead and Edmund Leigh went to Gladstone's North Wales home, Hawarden Castle, to make the presentation.

Charlotte was born in 1885. Her paternal grandfather, an art educationalist, came from an old Potteries family and had been one of Minton's best gilders. Two uncles had won scholarships to the South Kensington School (now the Royal College) of Art in the 1870s and her maternal grandfather was Charles Hürten, Copeland's leading flower painter. Hürten, a German from Cologne, had worked at Sèvres where he had married a local girl. He and his wife had come to England in the 1850s at the pressing invitation of

Charlotte Rhead with her dog, centre.

Alderman Copeland. So Charlotte had English, German and French blood in her.

Frederick Rhead, an experienced art instructor himself, had taught Charlotte drawing and the elements of designing. When he was the art director at Wileman's, around the turn of the century, he had kept the pattern books at his home, where his children had become thoroughly familiar with them. Among these patterns were those for a popular novelty line named *Intarsio*. The printed and painted designs were often humorous, an original departure from the usual designs of the time. Charlotte would have known these books well. In December 1905 the American arts and crafts magazine *Keramic Studio* published a light-hearted design for a tobacco jar by her, undoubtedly influenced by the *Intarsio* style.

By 1905 she had also become very competent tube-liner. Tube-lining, a method of decorating pottery with a thin line of clay squeezed through a fine glass tube, had been introduced in the Potteries by Frederick Barnard.

Barnard had come from Doulton's in Lambeth to join the Cobridge firm of James Macintyre in February 1895. There, in his own words, he introduced '*a new type of design, and a process which I had invented*'. Barnard named this process Gesso, though it soon became known as tube-lining and quickly became very popular. The technique was enthusiastically taken up by several members of the Rhead family.

By 1920 *Charlotte*'s wide and varied experience of tube-lining established her as one of the top designers of this type of ware. She had cut her teeth on the technique in the 1900s when she joined the small art pottery, Wardle's, where her brother was art director, many of Wardle's productions at that time being tube-lined. She had then worked as a designer and tube-liner of decorative tiles. This was at a period when many butchers' and fishmongers' shops were decorated with tile panels relating to their trades – cattle in a field, perhaps, or fishermen unloading a catch. Latterly she had assisted her fathers at *Wood*'s. He had been appointed art director there in 1913, and with her help, had set about improving the art wares. Charlotte had again concentrated on the tube-lined ranges and had been responsible for a whole raft of new and popular designs, mainly for Bursley Ltd, the Wood's subsidiary which specialised in art wares. She had even been permitted to market one tubed range for the Ellgreave Pottery, another Wood subsidiary, under the name Lottie Rhead Ware, an early instance of a woman designer being identified in England on a backstamp.

So when Charlotte joined Burgess & Leigh she had a thoroughly established reputation. This was reflected in a full-page advertisement the company placed in *The Pottery Gazette* on 1st March, 1927 announcing that they had '*secured the services of the accomplished lady artist Charlotte Rhead who has produced for us a number of original decorations, all pure handcraft. Combining grace and dignity of design with the most beautiful under the glaze colourings. Special display of these goods is now on view at our London Showrooms.*'

Burgess & Leigh had not made tube-lined productions before, so she would have had to train the decorators in this skill. There were usually three or four tube-liners working for Charlotte at any one time, though the composition of the team varied as girls came and went. Hilda Machin and Mary Rock (Mary née Jackson) seem to have been the earliest members of the original team, with perhaps Lily Marshall. By March, 1927, when the advertisement appeared, around fourteen designs were being produced. Each of these would

Burgess & Leigh proudly announce the appointment of Charlotte Rhead, March 1927.

Page from a catalogue illustrating Rhead's patterns 3973, 4001, 4002 and 4016, c.1927.

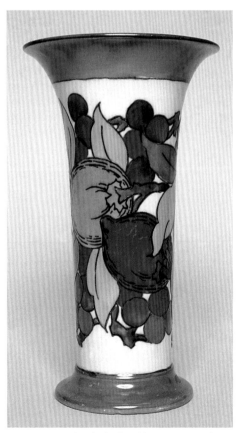

Vase with anemone border tube-lined in black, pattern 3973, believed to be Rhead's first Burleigh pattern, c.1927.

Vase 50, printed and tube-lined fruit pattern with matt and lustre glazes, pattern 4016, c.1927.

Vase 68, stylised tube-lined pattern 4001, *Gouda*, c.1927.

have been adapted by Charlotte to fit a variety of shapes, bowls of different sizes, flowerpots and a range of vases. Her designs were identified by a tubed signature, *'Lottie Rhead'*, on the base of each article which she probably added herself, at least at the start. Surprisingly, tube-lining may still not have been properly understood at the time by the trade press. A *Pottery Gazette* report of June, 1927 on a Burgess & Leigh display commented somewhat patronisingly: *'There are some quite original designs for fruit sets, hand-painted by Charlotte Rhead, under the glaze. Some of the fruit decorations are moulded as well as richly coloured.....'.* The reference to 'moulded' in conjunction with 'fruit decorations' seems to suggest that the reporter thought that the tubed designs had in fact been moulded.

The earliest of Charlotte's patterns was probably number 3973. It comprised a band of tube-lined anemones, in various colours, on a plain blue ground, the vases in this pattern having a broad black band above the anemones. Unsurprisingly, these first designs for Burgess & Leigh have a strong family resemblance to those she had made for Wood's. One of the most popular of these was the Bursley *Pomona* pattern, which featured pomegranates, black grapes and flower heads. The anemones on pattern 3973 are very similar to the *Pomona* flower heads, while the pomegranates and grapes reappear on another early Burgess & Leigh pattern (4000). In a few cases Charlotte even re-used designs that she had made for Wood's. Among them was a plaque featuring a seated Japanese girl (4011), Charlotte merely reversing the image of the girl, seating her on a mat and giving her new colourings for the Burgess & Leigh version. She had earlier used this same design, together with a pendant, a Japanese girl playing a shamisen, for a pair of tube-lined plaques for Wood's. They were probably taken from Japanese prints, or copied from one of the source books in the Rhead's extensive reference library.

Two other elaborate plaques also appeared about this time, a 'Persian' design of stylised flower-head and elongated leaves, and a pheasant and pomegranate design. They were

Plaque, pheasant and pomegranate design, pattern 4012, tubed by Rhead, c.1927.

Plaque, elaborate Persian design, pattern 4103, tube-lined by Rhead, c.1927.

Pomegranates were a favourite Rhead subject, here tube-lined with grapes on a plaque, pattern 4000, c.1927.

Pages from a Burgess & Leigh Pattern book showing patterns tube-lined by 'Miss Rhead', listing shapes and decorating costs.

Manificent underglaze painted plaque tube-lined by Charlotte Rhead, pattern 4111, inspired by a 1921 plaque with a similar design by Swettenham.

expensive to make, the pattern book giving the cost of tubing the pheasant and pomegranate design as twenty four shillings. These plaques are hard to find and it is likely that only very small numbers, perhaps no more than a dozen of each design, were made. The tube-lining, too, would have been difficult and it is likely that Charlotte herself would have undertaken it.

Wilkes (and later his assistant Bailey) were responsible for most of the shapes that Charlotte was required to decorate. These included about twenty different vases, various round and octagonal bowls, flowerpots, jardinières, bulb bowls and wall plaques. Charlotte must have had problems with a few of these shapes, particularly the *Palissy* bowls. These were embossed with an overlapping circle of vine leaves and her tube-lined designs had to be squeezed between the tips of the outwardly pointing leaves. The effects, as Charlotte certainly realised, were not always entirely successful. The bases of the vases were marked with a two-digit shape number while the bowls were not marked but known by their names, *Avon, Rex, Jacobean* and *Palissy*. Most of these shapes were moulded but at the time Burgess

& Leigh still employed two throwers [one known as 'young Enoch'][27] who worked with a wheel. Among the thrown pieces were a bowl, shape number 16, and a squat ovoid vase, number 76. Charlotte's designs can sometimes be found on these bowls and vases.

Charlotte, like her father Frederick, was a prolific designer and made many more patterns than could possibly be commercially produced. Some of these would never have got off the drawing board, while others would be initially produced in small quantities, so that they could be costed or tried out on the market by the firm's salesmen. Designs that did go into production were given a four-figure pattern number and entered in the general (unillustrated and undated) pattern book. As these entries were made by several different hands, the descriptions vary from the helpful to the minimal.

It is remembered[28] that Charlotte had been provided with a large room where she could work and at the same time supervise the tube-liners. She wore a clean smock which she had designed and embroidered herself, and she usually brought her little dog to work with her, a practice that was

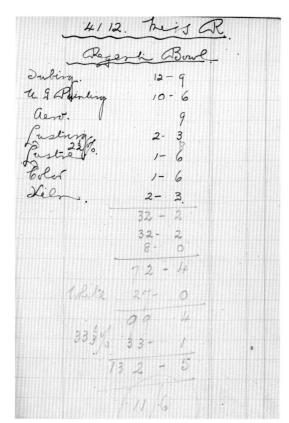

AMENDED
Price list of No's 4416 RED.   (Rhead)
4422. BLUE   "

Teas & Saucers		13/6d doz.
Coffee Cans & Saucers		13/6d "
Breakfast & Saucers		18/9d "
Teasets 21 pieces		15/2d set
Teapots 24s	4/9d	each
" 30s		4/3d "
" 36s		4/- "
" 42s		3/6d "
Teapot Stands		1/3d "
Coffee Pots 12's		5/6d "
" " 24's		5/- "
" " 30's		4/6d "
Greek Jugs No.1		3/3d "
" " " 2		2/9d "
" " " 3		2/6d "
" " " 4		2/3d "
Hot Water Jugs 24's Tofts		4/- "
" " " 30's "		3/9d "
Honey Pot		3/- "
Biscuit Jar		5/- "
Cheese Stand No.4		4/9d "
" " " 3		5/3d "
Triple Tray		5/- "
Sandwich Set Windsor		7/9d set
" " Oblong		6/9d "
Fruit Set Avon		7/9d "
Cheese Stand Diploma		3/- each
E.M. Set		8/6d set
Coffee Set		13/6d set
Chinese Bowl L/S		5/6d each
Ind. Sugars & Creams 1 per.		2/- pair
" & " 2 "		2/6d "
Regent Bowl S/S		7/6d each

'Amended' trade price list for Rhead's pattern depicting 'buds', produced in red, 4416, and blue, 4417, in c.1930.

Page from a factory notebook reckoning decorating and selling costs for *Regent*-shaped bowl with a tube-lined pattern, 4112, by 'Miss R'.

not always appreciated by her staff. It is also recalled that she went to the United States to visit her two brothers, Frederick Hürten and Harry. Both had emigrated in the 1900s, had become American citizens, and enjoyed successful careers in the American pottery industry. While Charlotte was away her younger sister Dollie took her place. Dollie was also a very competent tube-liner, but in 1911 had abandoned a career in the Potteries to become a midwife. She may not

Bowl, *Vine* pattern, 4113, with grapes tube-lined in black, c.1928. William and George Adams also decorated the *Vine* patterns which featured *Old Davenport* sprigged leaf motifs.

Embossed *Palissy*-shaped bowl, with vine leaves and tube-lined and enamelled poppy heads, pattern 4070, designed 1927.

Bowl, *New Vine* pattern with underglaze blue grapes and matt and lustre glazes, c.1930.

Avon fruit bowl with orange lustre interior and anemone border tube-lined in black as pattern 3973, c.1927. Diameter 9¼ins (23.5cms).

have done much designing in Charlotte's absence, but she seems to have had no trouble in keeping things going and had obviously not lost her tube-lining skills.

In 1928 the seventeen-year-old Edith Fullwood joined the tube-lining team. As the junior member, she had to make the tea and do the washing up.

Although Charlotte, a shy person, seems to have kept her distance and expected to be addressed as *'Miss Rhead'*, she was considerate to her staff. For instance, she once took Edith Fullwood home in her car when Edith was ill, evidently a rare occurrence at the time. The male employees too treated Charlotte with respect, putting her 'on a pedestal', as one of them expressed it. But conversation for the most part seems to have been restricted to polite but formal greetings such as *'Good morning'* or *'Good evening, Miss Rhead'*.

Charlotte was careful about the way her designs were applied and how they were coloured. She herself always adapted the designs to fit each different shape. At first much of the decoration was applied underglaze – a speciality of Burgess & Leigh which the company had emphasised in its advertisement announcing Charlotte's arrival. Later, however, she began to favour on-glaze enamels and the new broken glazes which gave a mottled effect. She often used lustres, a preference she had no doubt acquired at Wood's from her father. Lustres, though, do not wear well as can be seen today from some of the pieces she designed for Burgess & Leigh. One of the first lustred patterns she produced for the company was number 4016. It is an attractive design with lustred bands, top and bottom, over a tubed pattern consisting of large round red and yellow fruits, perhaps apples, on leafy stems, surrounded by small round fruits in red, green, blue and gold. It first appeared sometime in 1927 and sold well.

Charlotte was a versatile designer who could turn her hand to the utilitarian bread-and-butter lines, the suite ware, as well as the more expensive decorative 'fancies'. Some suite ware items were tube-lined, though the tubed motif could be small and simple to keep down the cost. Pattern number 4471 is an example. A small central stylised tulip panel was applied to some thirty different suite ware pieces, ranging from teapots in three sizes, to, rather oddly, spoons and forks. The *Sunshine* pattern (4609) is another; an even simpler design, it consisted of groups of three short

tubed dashes, the rims of the plates also being decorated with tubed dashes. *Sunshine* was applied to an even bigger range of wares, including a fifty-four-piece dinner service and various suite ware items: teapots in four sizes, three different cheese dishes, egg sets, beakers, mugs, teapot stands, trays, oatmeal bowls, scollops, large and small honey pots, cruets, covered butter dishes and what were described as *'toast racks, five bars'*, designed to take four slices of toast. Another suite ware pattern, number 4567, featured a floral

An advertisement in *The Pottery Gazette*, April 1928, showing Rhead's tube-lined pattern *Garland* on a *Crescent*-shaped sandwich set. Also shown, left, is the printed pattern *Sylvan* 3961 which inspired Rhead's later tube-lined pattern of the same name.

Page from Burgess & Leigh's Pattern Book listing *Windsor* sandwich sets with Rhead's tube-lined patterns, c.1930.

Bowl with stylised *'tulip panel'*, pattern 4471, used on a wide range of shapes, c.1930.

Crescent sandwich tray and plate with delicately tube-lined floral basket pattern.

Windsor sandwich tray and plate with stylised floral pattern tube-lined and enamelled, c.1930.

Windsor sandwich tray and plate; and coffee can and saucer, with *'Buds'* pattern 4416 in bright red, c.1930.

Bowl with *Sylvan* pattern 4100, c.1928.

Vase 48 with *Sylvan* pattern 4100 and, right, vase 52 with *Garland* pattern 4101, c.1928.

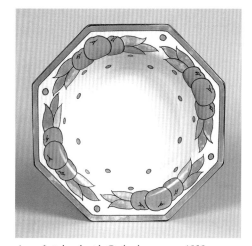

Avon fruit bowl with *Garland* pattern, c.1928.

design in coral, blue, turquoise and pink with cross sticks in orange. The tea- and dinner- sets were printed, while the other items in this pattern, *Greek*-shaped jugs, the teapots themselves, biscuit jars and trays, were tubed.

Tube-lining was very suitable for decorating the sandwich sets which, as a result of the crazes for various games, especially auction bridge and Mah Jongg, had become so popular during the late 1920s. Charlotte made many patterns especially for the purpose. One of these was

Garland, bands of overlapping leaves interspersed at intervals with round apples. The pattern was available in three different colour arrangements (4101, 4104 and 4105). It was attractive and easy to tube, economical to work and reasonably priced. In September 1928 *The Pottery Gazette* drew the attention of shopkeepers to this pattern in its three variations as *'lines which one might safely put before a customer who desires to make a respectable gift without embarking on more than a modest outlay'*. In the same article *The Pottery Gazette*

Rhead's *Florentine* pattern, 4752, of c.1930 used simple tube-lined designs, mottled browns and subdued lustre glazes on robust shapes.

Florentine wall plaque and bulbous jug, c.1930.

Avon fruit bowl with the *Carnival* pattern, 4120, tube-lined and enamelled, c.1929.

Carnival pattern 4120, as it appears on a vase, c.1929.

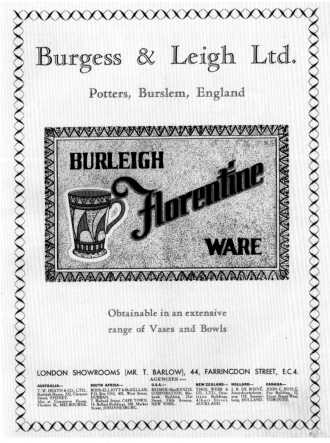

An advertisement placed in *The Pottery Gazette*, 1st June, 1932.

showed, rather belatedly, that it had caught up with the tube-lining technique which it named and, briefly and not inaccurately, described. It went on to say that '*Burgess & Leigh Ltd., have certainly done their best to keep the demand for sandwich sets going by providing the trade with something that is really original in shape and style*', adding '*…it is quite apparent that good business is being done in this department*'. Many of these sandwich sets were sold through the chain of Lawley's china shops, as *some are marked with a special backstamp*

Hot water jug (minus lid) and *Willow 'Pekin'* teapot in Rhead's popular *Rutland* pattern. Also called *Trellis*, it was available in buff, pattern 4356, and in blue, pattern 4367.

Later variation of the *Florentine* pattern, 4816, c.1932.

Earlier pattern, 4108, also called *Florentine* with delicate and expensive fruit and leaf pattern on a dark blue ground. This jardiniére was displayed at Burgess & Leigh's London showroom throughout the 1930s.

BURGESS & LEIGH. LTD.	CONTINUATION SHEET No.		
Prices of "RHEAD" decoration No.4356 (Trellis) Finished in BUFF			
ALSO " " " " 4367 (") " " BLUE			
Dinner-ware		9/-	scale
Teas & Saucers		13/6d	doz.
Teaset 21 pieces		15/2d	set
Coffee Cans & Saucers		13/6d	doz.
Breakfast & Saucers		18/9d	"
Teapot 24's		5/3d	ea
" 30's		4/9d	"
" 36's		4/6d	"
" 42's		4/-	"
Teapot Stands		1/6d	"
Coffee Pot 24's		5/3d	"
" " 30's		4/9d	"
" " 12's		5/9d	"
Greek Jugs No.1		3/6d	"
" " " 2		3/-	"
" " " 3		2/9d	"
" " " 4		2/6d	"
Hot Water Jug 24's Tofts		4/3d	"
" " " 30's		4/-	"
Honey Pot		3/6d	"
Biscuit Jar W/Hdle		5/9d	"
Cheese Stand No.4		5/-	"
" " 3		5/6d	"
Triple Tray		5/9d	"
Sandwich Set Windsor & Richmond		9/-	set
" " Oblong		7/9d	"
Fruit Set Avon		9/-	"
Cheese Dish Diploma		3/3d	each
E.M.Set		8/9d	set
Individual Sugars & Creams 1 person		2/1d	pair.2 person- 3x2/xxxxxx
Coffee Set		14/-	set
Chinese Bowl L/S		5/9d	each
Covered Butter			
Palissy Bowl		8/9d	each

Wholesale price list showing items produced in the *Trellis* pattern, also known as *Rutland*.

'Lawleys Norfolk Pottery Stoke'. This backstamp is, of course, misleading as they were all made at the Middleport Pottery, but its existence does seem to confirm *The Pottery Gazette* report that '*good business is being done in this department*'.

As time went on Charlotte's patterns tended to become simpler, though they continued to feature her favourite motifs, fruit and flowers. She made less use of lustres, too, preferring the new broken glazes, which gave a mottled effect. Fruits in particular, with their rounded forms, were still a satisfying decoration, and at the same time, easy to tube-line. Wares thus ornamented were consequently economical to make: Charlotte was a practical potter who appreciated as much as anyone the need to keep down production costs and yet to design attractive products.

Clarice Cliff's brightly coloured *Bizarre* designs had been introduced in 1928 and rapidly gained in popularity. Perhaps in order to compete, Charlotte also produced some highly coloured patterns at the time. The yellow and coral *Carnival* (4120) is a case in point. This is a particularly interesting design as it seems to resemble a giant flower when seen on the inside of a bowl and yet is more like a sunburst when viewed vertically on the side of a vase. Other bright patterns were *Harlequin* (4132), a design with small triangular shapes resembling harlequins' caps and enamelled in red, blue and green, and '*New Jazz*' (4133). Despite its name, this was a more conventional flower design, though the central stylised flower head was enamelled in a bright red. Both patterns are now found comparatively rarely.

By c.1930 Charlotte was producing designs in which more sombre colours and subdued lustres predominated combined with the mottled glazes. The most popular of these was *Florentine* (4752), which featured a repeating series of curved triangular shapes enamelled in various dark colours and set between mottled glazes. These changes may have been due to the depressed economic climate, though the tensions caused by the arrival of a new designer, Harold Bennett, could have been a contributory factor. At the end of 1931 or early in 1932 matters seem to have come to a head and either Charlotte felt that she had to leave or she was asked to do so, though it was later contended that Burgess & Leigh had only parted with her very reluctantly. This could well be true, as A.G. Richardson, the firm she joined at the end of 1932, prospered greatly under her guidance, at a time when many potteries were in deep trouble. That Charlotte herself was very sorry to leave is evident and her marked distress was noted at the time she left Burgess & Leigh. **(Bernard Bumpus, 2003.)**

For a list of Charlotte Rhead's patterns see page 239.

Ernest Bailey, Modeller (1911-1987)

In August 1927, when Charlotte Rhead had been at the factory just a year, fourteen-year-old Ernest Tansley Bailey was taken on in the Design Studio. The son of a farmer in Rode Heath, Cheshire, Bailey's home must have been artistic as he and two brothers were to enter the pottery industry in design related areas: Joe worked as a pattern designer for companies including Aynsley, Wedgwood and Crown Staffs whilst Kenneth ran his own Longton lithography firm, K. H. Bailey (still trading with Burgess, Dorling & Leigh). Prizes awarded to Ernest Bailey from both Newcastle-under-Lyme and later Burslem Art Schools reveal him to have been an accomplished and sensitive designer and painter.

Past employees remember Bailey as rather reserved, serious and clever minded, who was proud, and justifiably so, of his designs for the company. A devoted family man, his three children recall that he was always working on a ceramic project at home in the Westlands area of Newcastle-under-Lyme. When Saturday morning work was still compulsory, they accompanied him to the Middleport Pottery and made small models at his bench which were later fired in the kilns.

A fine bust which Bailey executed of his wife and son reveals wider artistic capabilities than those required of him by Burgess & Leigh. In the competitive pottery industry, designs had to be commercially viable and Bailey, like most ceramic artists and modellers, adapted his style for a mass market. A travel bursary awarded to him by the British Pottery Manufacturers Federation whilst still a part-time student at the Burslem School of Art during the 1930s allowed Bailey to travel to Paris and Italy. There he saw not only great works of art in their national museums but also contemporary commercial pottery production, for example, at the Richard Ginori Ceramics Company in Milan, whose modernistic tableware shape designs undoubtedly influenced Bailey's own work for Burgess & Leigh.

As well as an appreciation of modern art, Bailey also had a love of history, of which he was a fastidious recorder and preserver. He was to save many items discarded by others as junk. His greatest passion other than modelling was architecture, doubtless encouraged by the picturesque, industrialised character which the once proudly modern Middleport Pottery had assumed over the years. In his fifties, he restored two Shropshire cottages and some years later he and his son successfully petitioned to save a Tudor farmhouse, the oldest half-timbered building in Stoke-on-Trent, from demolition. The two men carefully dismantled the house, including its thirteenth-century stone foundations from Hulton Abbey, which they then rebuilt on land in Shropshire.

Even as a young man Bailey possessed a sense of history and tradition which paradoxically informed his modern designs for Burgess & Leigh. At first it was thought that he might work on pattern design but, in a change of direction which says much for his all-round artistic ability, he became instead an apprentice modeller to Wilkes. Nonetheless, he maintained an interest in sketching and watercolour painting at home and, initially, in pattern design at work. The factory Pattern Book records under number 4377 'Suite

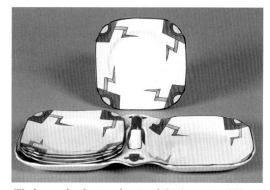

Windsor sandwich set with printed '*Jazz*' pattern, 4377, designed by Bailey in c.1930.

Ernest Tansley Bailey, 1911-1987, photographed in his studio at the Middleport Pottery during the 1950s.

Relief-moulded beaker modelled privately by Bailey of the Tudor farmhouse he saved from demolition. Height 4ins (10cms).

Bailey as a young man during the 1930s.

Apprentice pieces? Majolica-style jug and teapot modelled in fish-form, inscribed on the base with Bailey's name and the date, 3rd December, 1930.

ware etc, ivory glaze, printed Ernest Bailey pattern in black enamel, blue, pink, yellow, green, scarlet. Blue finish.' It was put into production in c.1930, with the Pattern Book listing the range of items manufactured, under the description *'Ernest Bailey pattern Jazz for Suite Ware, Vases etc'*. ('*Jazz*' was a commonly used description then for bright and bold Art Deco designs.) It seems that this was Bailey's only foray into pattern design and, forsaking paint for clay, modelling became his lifelong vocation.

During the fourteen or so years they spent together at the Middleport Pottery, Bailey and Wilkes enjoyed a good working relationship (which developed into an enduring friendship). Bailey, as an apprentice, initially followed Wilkes' instructions, modelling from his sketched designs. However, during the 1930s when Wilkes was coming into the factory for just a few days a week, there developed a more equal partnership with Bailey both designing and modelling. Unfortunately, the lack of records makes attribution of the two men's work difficult: their modelling styles were similar, as one might expect of master and pupil, although Bailey's tended towards the more robust. It has been suggested that Bailey, as the younger man, was solely responsible for Burleigh's more modern wares and Wilkes the traditional shapes. However, contemporary sketches by Wilkes suggest that the division was not so clear-cut.[29] Correspondence[30] and jottings written by Bailey in the early 1980s offer some clues as to who was responsible for individual ornamental pieces but

doubts remain. What is certain is that the collaboration between Wilkes and Bailey gave birth to the distinctive models which were to define the Burleigh Art Deco style.

New from Old: the Davenport and Alcock Moulds

Ironically, during Bailey's early years with the company, Burgess & Leigh's new ornamental shapes were not the result of fresh, original modelling but were reproductions from its vast stock of nineteenth-century Davenport and Alcock moulds, then stored in various dusty areas of the Middleport Pottery. Although Burgess & Leigh had dipped into them occasionally before, the directors, searching for a new and original (not to say inexpensive) product to boost sales in a time of economic depression, realised that it would be foolish of them not to capitalise on such a wealth of original 'archive' material. After all, Clarice Cliff was taking a similar route, by applying modern new designs to old shapes inherited from the Newport Pottery.

Old Davenport

In 1928, the same year that Cliff launched her '*Bizarre*' range, Burgess & Leigh reproduced a collection of suited tewares, *Old Davenport*, embossed with a vine or strawberry pattern, from Davenport's sprig moulds. (A few other potteries had produced the same or similar ware, including Thomas Hughes of Top Bridge Pottery in Longport who had also acquired moulds from their purchase of the Davenport works in 1887). Shapes included round and oval dishes; square plates; dessert dishes; teapot and stand; jugs; honey pot and stand; sandwich tray with plates; biscuit jar; cruet; and cheese plate. Like Cliff's wares, a wide variety of new decorative finishes were applied, usually by decorator William Adams to give the old shapes a new contemporary 'twist': these included on-glaze and underglaze enamel painting and printing, lustring and gilding and tube-lining. Although these late 1920s and 1930s colour versions were popular at the time, it was a plain white or ivory glaze, imitating the original Parian or stoneware body, which was to prove more enduring. When, in the 1960s one of Burgess & Leigh's retailers thought that such a range would do well in the London area, Bailey modelled additional dinner ware shapes to which Davenport leaf and flower sprigs were added. This revival proved so popular that *Old Davenport* remained in continuous production until 2002.

Old Davenport, Bailey's initials, ETB, can sometimes be found on dinnerware items he modelled during the 1960s.

Left: *The Arms of All Nations* jug. Plain glazed, left, c.1920, and decorated and gilded, 2001. Height 13¹/₂ins (34.5cms).

Above: Relief-moulded jug, nineteenth-century photograph found amongst a number in company archives.

The Arms of All Nations Jug

Amongst other moulds stored at the Middleport Pottery was *The Arms of All Nations* jug. This was one of a number of relief-moulded serving or ornamental jugs made by Samuel Alcock between 1842 and 1859, acquired by Burgess & Leigh from the Hill Pottery Auction in 1867, and reproduced during the 1930s. Such jugs had been made in plain glazed stoneware, earthenware or Parian from c.1835 with large quantities being shipped out for the North American market. Major producers were Ridgway, Minton, Copeland, Meigh and Dudson. Although Burgess & Leigh registered a few original designs, including the *Giraffe* in 1864, and acquired the Alcock moulds a few years later, relief-moulded jugs never became a major area of production for them in the nineteenth century.

The Arms of All Nations jug, sometimes called the *Jug of All Nations*, was the work of Henry Baggaley. He produced similar Parian and stoneware commemorative items in partnership with Richard Moore in Hanley until 1861, after which time he worked freelance. The jug's elaborate, quintessentially Victorian design featured the coats of arms of numerous nations or their heads of state: Great Britain, France, Belgium, Denmark, Portugal, Sweden, Sardinia, Savoy, Italy, Spain, Greece, Bavaria, Prussia, Russia, Austria, Brazil, the Papal States, Switzerland and Turkey as well as the flag of the United States. It was thought that Samuel Alcock & Co. originally produced *The Arms of All Nations* Jug to commemorate, as its name suggests, the Great Exhibition of Works of Industry of All Nations at the Crystal Palace in London in 1851. In fact, it was made for the Universal Exhibition held in Paris in 1855.[31] The *Staffordshire Advertiser* alludes to it in February 1860 in its description of '*the Volunteer Jug by H. Baggaley of Market*

Street, Hanley, designer of the Jug of all Nations, which attracted a good deal of attention at the Paris Exhibition.' Several moulds for the jug were later listed in the Hill Pottery Auction Catalogue in 1867 and it is probable that Burgess & Leigh acquired one at that time.

It is not known when the company first reproduced *The Arms of All Nations* jug. During Bailey's early years with the company, it was produced intermittently, in ones or twos only, as orders came in. Although it was then decorated with a dry plain glazed finish in imitation of the original Alcock parchment-coloured saltglaze stoneware, painted versions were made at other times. Bailey was to recall that Frederick Rhead was called in to research the true colours of the heraldic Arms and painted a special 'pattern' jug which was kept for safety in the Middleport Pottery's Modellers' Shop. During the 1950s, small numbers of the jug were produced with on-glaze enamel colours and gilding. In 2001, Burgess, Dorling & Leigh issued a similar version, in a limited edition of 150,[32] to celebrate two 'centenaries': the Great Exhibition and the 'founding' of the firm.

Reproduction Period Jugs

The reproduction of the Alcock relief-moulded jugs really came about by chance. In c.1930 retiring clay presser George Chapman was clearing out a drying stove when he came across a jug. This proved to be *Old Feeding Time*, which depicted a young décolleté 'wench' feeding several large dogs one of which forms the handle. The jug was successfully retrieved and taken to the modelling studio where Bailey immediately recognised its potential, as did the Leighs who consented to its reproduction. As the original block mould had been destroyed, Bailey remodelled the *Old Feeding Time* jug and it was reproduced from c.1933 until the late 1940s.

Gypsy Encampment, co-registered by Alcock & Co. in 1842. This Burleigh reproduction was made between c.1948 and c.1960. Height 7ins (17.5cms).

Watercolour design, attributed to Wilkes, for relief-moulded jug which was not produced.

Top row: Two of Bailey's models from the 1930s *Sally in Our Alley* and *The Village Blacksmith*. Bottom row, left and right, *Nell Gwynn* and *Tally Ho* modelled by Bailey in 1954 and, centre, *Old Feeding Time* reproduced from an Alcock & Co. model. Tallest, top left, 10 ins (25cms).

Perhaps to compete with other firms (such as Royal Doulton who had introduced a similar series of relief-moulded, underglaze painted, limited edition jugs in 1930), four more jugs were modelled between 1936 and 1938 in a similar 'traditional' style. Although original, the figurative composition and narrative subject matter of the jugs were inspired by two earlier printed Burleigh series: *Ye Olde English Ballades* issued in 1914 and *Merrie England* of 1925 (whose designs by Cecil Aldin also provided the subject matter for wall plaques issued at the same time). Modelled by Bailey, the first in 1936 was *Sally in our Alley*. The subject of the jug was taken from Henry Carey's eighteenth-century poem of the same name, which had featured in *Ye Olde English Ballades*.[33] The remaining three jugs were taken from the *Merrie England* series: *The Stocks*, and, from the traditional story of romantic elopement to Scotland, *The Runaway Marriage* (sometimes called *Gretna Green*) and *The Village Blacksmith*.

Combinations of Bailey's 'traditional' and Alcock & Co. original relief-moulded jugs were to remain in production for many years. Notes Bailey made in 1982 indicate that in 1948 a further three original Alcock jugs were 'blocked' (working moulds were made for their reproduction). They were *Bulrush*, which was first registered in 1858, *Babes in the Wood* and *Gypsy Encampment*. *Babes in the Wood* was based on J. H. Benwell's *The Children in the Wood* with landscape by W. Westall, which was engraved by W. Greatbach for the Art Union in 1847. Protât, who also worked for Minton, might have modelled the jug for Alcock which was subsequently also produced by Cork & Edge and shown at the Paris

The Runaway Marriage or *Gretna Green*, left, and *The Stocks*, right, modelled by Bailey during the 1930s.

Universal Exhibition in 1855. It is not known who originally modelled the *Gypsy Encampment* jug, sometimes known simply as *Gypsy*, but Alcock & Co. and Jones & Whalley registered its design jointly in 1842. It was then made in various sizes and colours, including Alcock's distinctive lavender ground.

In the early 1950s it was decided to revive Bailey's jugs *The Village Blacksmith*, *The Runaway Marriage* and *Sally in Our Alley* together with an original Alcock model, *Old Feeding Time*, for a series advertised in 1953 as *Reproduction Period Jugs*. In c.1954 Bailey contributed a similarly styled jug, *Nell Gwynn*, which commemorated the life of the mistress of Charles II, and *Tally Ho*, depicting fox and hounds. From the mid-1960s until c.1980 Burgess & Leigh reproduced *Babes in the Wood* and *Gypsy Encampment* together with *Sally in Our Alley*, *Old Feeding Time* and *Bulrush* decorated with an aerographed blue shading, a smaller quantity also being available in a pink matt colour. Up until that time, like the *Old Davenport* Wares, the 'traditional' jugs had been decorated with colourful underglaze paints in a variety of colourways, some of which were specially commissioned.

Burgess & Leigh Decorators

As was customary in the pottery industry, it was men who undertook the time-consuming 'prestige' underglaze painting, whose rich colours demanded more subtle and skillful shading than the rapid on-glaze enamel painting more usually carried out by women. However, during the 1920s and 1930s, the boundaries blurred a little; rather than face the 'dole' queue of the Depression, men were *'prepared to do women's work.'*[34] Names which are remembered from the Middleport Pottery are William Morris, *'an out of work violinist'*, Fred Salmon, who had trained at Newcastle-under-Lyme School of Art, and a Mr Walters.[35]

Many talented designers, when made redundant from struggling companies, also had to take a drop in salary and status by becoming decorators. This was the case when Fred Ridgway joined William and George Adams as one of Burgess & Leigh's small élite team of underglaze painters. Ridgway had joined the Middleport Pottery in c.1931, probably coming from A. J. Wilkinson's Newport Pottery. There he trained Clarice Cliff during the early 1920s, her name appearing in records alongside his design of a plaque featuring a bird and dragon motif.[36] These were amongst Ridgway's favourite subjects and featured in a number of his paintings on silk which he produced outside work. (He was indirectly related to Ernest Bailey, one of his sisters having married Ernest's brother, Kenneth.) It seems that neither the Newport nor the Middleport Pottery took full advantage of Ridgway's talents as a designer. He had previously worked as a *pâte-sur-pâte* artist for the china manufacturer, Birks, Rawlins & Co., owned by Frederick Rhead's close friend, Lawrence Birks. Ridgway's work for them was included at the International Exhibitions at Turin and at Ghent in 1913

where a *pâte-sur-pâte* cylinder vase, *Peacocks and Flowers*, was singled out for praise by the trade press.[37] At their King's Hall display the same year, reviewer, J. Child commented that *'Mr Ridgway has also quite a different and original method of applying coloured pastes in porcelain and his quaint marine and Dutch landscapes, treatments of birds in the Japanese manner, as well as decorative little Japanese figures, are quite distinctive in colour and method.'*

Post 1930s, when the male decorators had retired or left, some of the 'traditional' jugs were painted underglaze by women. Mary Harper was one of those entrusted with carrying out and instructing others in this superior work. A highly skilled and versatile paintress she had worked with Charlotte Rhead at T. & R. Boote's tile firm before coming to Burgess & Leigh. Her talents continued to be used by the factory until her retirement in the 1970s. In 1985, then in her nineties, she took part in a documentary television programme, *The Pottery Ladies*,[38] in which she talked about Charlotte Rhead, simultaneously revealing her own engaging personality and love of decorating pottery.

Burleigh Ware Art Deco Jugs and Vases
The Yellow Glazed Flower Jugs

When first re-introduced in the early 1930s, the original relief-moulded Alcock jugs were to have a major impact on the future design development at the Middleport Pottery, inspiring the most commercially successful of the company's series of jugs: the primrose-yellow glazed Flower Jugs. For many collectors today, the Flower Jugs typify Burleigh Art Deco. Jugs had always constituted a major part of Burgess & Leigh's output and its workforce and factory were well equipped for their manufacture. Most of these jugs had been utilitarian, belonging to its ranges of kitchen-, table- and toiletware. As production of the latter gradually decreased, this new decorative range of jugs provided the ideal replacement.

The idea for the series grew out of regular discussions between the directors, designers and the travelling salesmen who were ever alert to current trends in the market place. The basic shapes of the jugs were traditional but, like the original Alcock models, were enlivened by their relief-moulded form and detail. Individually, the Flower Jugs were quite distinctive in subject matter and design but as a collection they shared certain decorative characteristics: low relief modelling to the body of the jug; a 'feature' handle more usually modelled as an animal or a bird; a distinctive, usually primrose yellow, glaze applied, usually by dipping, to the exterior; a contrasting colour aerographed to the interior; and bright on-glaze hand-painted decoration, sometimes including a rim of black painted dashes (or a 'sunshine' edge, as it was called). Senior salesman, Harold Holdcroft is credited with the idea of producing a jug with a yellow glaze. Works Manager and glaze technician, Harold Lowe, successfully developed this by adding the metallic element antimony into the glaze to achieve the primrose or yellow colour so characteristic of the Burleigh Ware Flower Jugs. Although playful in subject matter, the jugs were cleverly designed and skillfully modelled, features which can sometimes be overshadowed by their bright, simple painting.

Although Pattern Books and Bailey's notes indicate approximate modelling dates, it is sometimes difficult to ascertain the exact year of introduction and withdrawal of the Flower Jugs, some of which were produced

Decorating jugs, Mary Harper, centre, Stella Kerry, left, with trainee James Docherty looking on.

intermittently over many years. There is no doubt that the first Flower Jug, *Squirrel*, (4801) was entered in the Pattern Book in 1931, although it was not launched until the following year. It was designed and modelled by Bailey, then just nineteen years old. Later in life he remembered that he initially gave the squirrel a smooth tail, an effect which unfortunately prompted the company's London agent to liken it to a 'drowned rat'. His artistic pride understandably wounded, Bailey, a perfectionist, remodelled the handle the following year to give it a more characteristic furry tail!

A further four jugs were modelled in that first year. The *Parrot* jug, another Bailey model, was also available with four matching beakers as part of a Lemonade Set. A variation was the now sought-after two-handled vase or loving cup. Parrot designs were suitable subjects for Australia and another jug featuring an indigenous creature, the *Kangaroo*, was modelled in 1931, specifically for that market. This was most probably the work of Wilkes as was the moulded and ribbed *Dragon* jug, which, featuring a fiery, scaly monster, was reminiscent of late nineteenth century oriental-inspired designs. His *Kingfisher* jug was especially popular and was extended to a range of embossed tewares.

Similar in design was Wilkes' vivid *Flamingo* jug of 1932. He followed this with a more traditionally English subject, *Harvest*, modelled as a small rabbit in a wheat field. This wavy-rimmed jug was available in three versions: with poppies, cornflowers or daisies. Bailey modelled a further three jugs in 1932, all of which featured human figures, unusual for the Flower Jug series. Two were perhaps closer to the *Reproduction Period Jugs* in style and subject matter: *Dick Turpin* (sometimes known as *Highwayman*) and *Pied Piper*. The cleverly designed and brightly coloured handles were modelled in the form of legendary characters with low-relief

Rhead's *Sunshine* pattern whose rim of black dashes was also a distinctive feature of the Burleigh Flower Jugs, 1931 scrap-book in company archives.

background scenes, painted in more subdued and shady tones, on the bodies of the jugs. The variously titled *Soldier*, *Guards* or *Guardsman* jug provided a bold contrast, being more geometric, less realistic and more typically Art Deco in style. With its brightly painted toy-like soldiers forward marching around the body (sometimes with a sentry box to the reverse), its more complex shape meant that it was not made in large numbers.

A return to animals as subjects came in 1933 with the modelling of two 'fox' jugs, both of which were most probably inspired by Aesop's *Fables*. The first, described in the Pattern Book as '*Fox Handle….in wheat*' (but also called *Fox in the Cornfield* and *Stoat* by collectors) is probably derived from the story of '*The Fox and the Farmer*' in which a fox retreats to a farmer's wheat field. The outer rim and body of the jug features a band of wheat or corn ears whilst the fox was modelled in handle form, similar to Minton's nineteenth-century relief-moulded jug *Hunting Game*.[39] Although resembling Bailey's *Squirrel* jug, sketches by Wilkes suggest that this is the elder man's design. *The Stork and the Fox* jug, taken from the tale of the same name, has a closed handle modelled as the stork with a sly and slavering fox modelled in low-relief on the ribbed body of the jug. Based on another lesser-known Aesop's *Fable*, was *The Monkey and the Cat* jug, modelled in 1934 for the South African market.

Yet another jug featuring a fox was also modelled at some time. Squatter and more ovoid in shape, the handle is shaped by the tail of a fox which creeps stealthily through an embossed field with flowers. Hollyhock flowers form the handle of Wilkes' *Rock Garden* of 1933, which depicts a tranquil and typically English cottage garden. In contrast, his *Galleon*, or *Old Ship* jug as it is described in the Pattern Book, is vigorously modelled as a ship in full sail. Not produced in great numbers, this latter jug is a comparatively rare model today.

A jug called *Palm* in factory records (and *Bird of Paradise* by collectors) was issued in 1935. The former name is perhaps more descriptive, as the jug has luxuriant palm leaves covering its flared body with a tiny bird nestling timorously on the uppermost part of the handle. A change in style was shown that year in *Honeycomb*, a simply shaped and initially naturalistically coloured jug, modelled to resemble a honeycomb with wasps or bees crawling at random over its surface. A matching preserve jar and small, lidded square butter dish were also modelled in the same style.

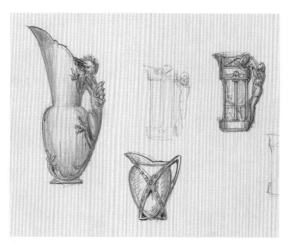
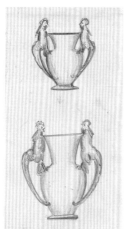

Pencil sketches attributed to Wilkes illustrating ideas for the *Dragon, Parrot* and *Kangaroo* Flower Jugs.

Watercolour design of the *Fox in the Cornfield* Jug in naturalistic colouring. As it more usually appears below right.

Watercolour design of the *Galleon* Jug, shown second row below, right, as it appeared on production.

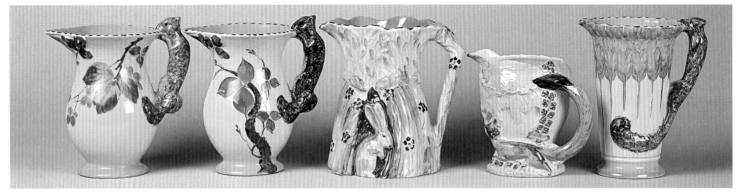

Countryside creatures, left to right: *Squirrel* with printed leaf pattern (5059); *Squirrel* with freehand tree and blue leaves (5247); *Harvest* with cornflowers, pattern 5076; 'Fox and Flowers'; and *Fox in the Cornfield* (5151). Tallest 10ins (25.4cms).

Ship Ahoy, left to right: three different colour versions of *Argosy* (that in centre shown back view) 5164, 5250 and 5256 embossed and painted on-glaze, registered 1934; *Galleon* in two of its three recorded colourways modelled in c.1933. Tallest approximately 8ins (20cms).

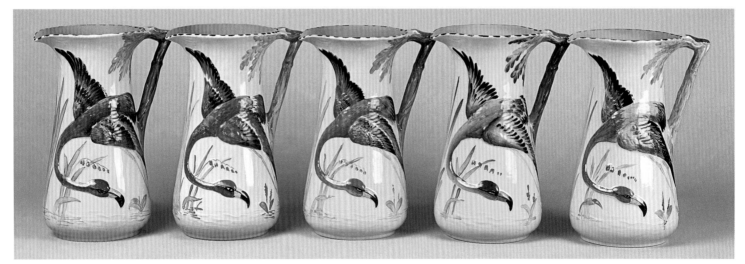

Five *Flamingo* jugs. The Pattern Book records nine colourways, each of which was allocated a separate four-digit pattern number which sometimes appears hand-painted on the jug's base, left to right: 5002, 5003, 4999, 5095 and 5904, modelled c.1932. Height 10ins (25.4cms).

Jugs with figurative handles, left to right: *Pied Piper*, black hat (5058), and *Pied Piper*, orange hat (5492), modelled in c.1932; *Pixie* (6347), modelled in c.1938; *Dick Turpin*, orange hat (5549), and *Dick Turpin*, green hat (5065), modelled in c.1932. Tallest approximately 8ins (20cms).

An English country garden, left to right: *Honeycomb* (5418), and *Honeycomb* with aerographed green interior (5484), modelled in c.1935; *Rock Garden* (5125), modelled in c.1933; *Butterfly* (7019), and *Butterfly*, orange tips (6054), modelled in c.1938. Tallest 8¹/₂ins (21.5cms).

Parrot, one of the most popular Burleigh Flower Jugs, shown here in four different colour versions (left to right, 7016, 5483, 5482 and 6935) with two parrot-handled loving cup to the centre, modelled c.1931. Height approximately 8ins (20cms).

Stylised Art Deco Jugs, left to right, three *Regent* jugs with printed leaf pattern (6640) and two abstract freehand-painted designs (5265 and 5051), c.1933-1935; ribbed spouted jug and ribbed conical jug, both with *Bizarre*-inspired patterns (4992 and 4995), c.1933.

Designed with 'foreign' markers in mind: Small, height 7¹/₂ins (19cms) and large-sized, height 10ins (25.4cms) *Kangaroo* Flower Jugs (4929 and 4911), c.1931 and the *Monkey and Cat* (5271) of c.1934, based on one of Aesop's *Fables*.

Hunters and prey, left and far right the *Stork and Fox* (5161 and 5162), based on Aesop's *Fables*, modelled in c.1934; centre, small and large sized *Kingfisher* Flower Jugs (4982, 5102 and 5480) modelled in c. 1931. Tallest 10ins (25.4cms).

Fruit and flowers. Left to right: Moulded Flower Jug, name un-recorded, enamelled flower border (4806); two un-numbered *Lupin* jugs, modelled in 1954; and *Vine* (6375) modelled in c.1938. Tallest approximately 8ins (20cms).

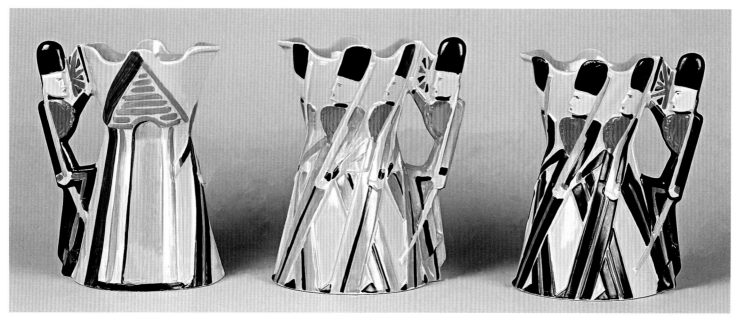

A patriotic *Guardsman* from 1932, showing the reverse and two colourways. Four colourways are recorded in the Pattern Book; '*black trousers, orange inside*' (5061) is shown here on the right and 5119 in the centre. Height approximately 8ins (20cms).

The *Dragon* Flower Jug was produced in two sizes. Its many different colour versions vary in detail and quality. Shown here left to right 4845, 4892 and 4893, modelled in c.1931. Tallest 10ins (25.4cms).

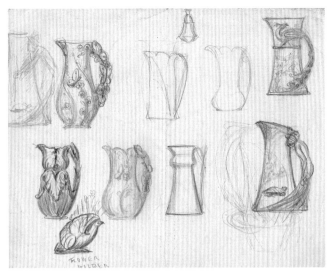

Further ideas from Wilkes including a butterfly-handled jug, top left.

List and doodles by Bailey, late 1930s.

Relief-moulded ferns applied to the ribbed body of the *Pheasant* jug of 1936 were equally naturalistic, in contrast, it must be said, to the rather crude modelling of the pheasant forming its handle. More pleasing perhaps was *Butterfly*, blocked in 1938, whose handle was moulded as an arc of butterflies and flowers. Also from 1938 was Bailey's *Budgerigar* jug, which, with one bird leaning into the handle and another in flight on the conical shaped body, is typically Art Deco in design. In contrast, his *Vine* jug of 1939, modelled as a bunch of grapes (and also known as *Grapes*), was perhaps inspired by a nineteenth-century Minton design. Although the more usual colour versions of *Vine* were either aerographed purple

or green, it was also produced with enamel colours and a primrose glaze and gilded with a white matt glaze. *Pixie*, a less commonly found jug, also from 1939, features a handle fashioned as a rather sinister green hobgoblin crouching on one of a number of relief-moulded toadstools which form a band around the centre of the jug. The design inspired a series of *Pixie* embossed teawares (also known as *Mushroom*); issued in 1939 in underglaze brown and orange or shades of green (6458, 6459) it was revived in 1955.

In common with most Burleigh ranges, the Flower Jugs were available in several colour and glaze versions, some specially commissioned, which were devised by Art Director, Harold Bennett. The most common colourways usually incorporated the distinctive primrose yellow glaze with variations of an aerographed interior and the bright on-glaze enamel colours which now typify Burleigh Art Deco – bright green, coral, red, blue and black. The *Kingfisher* range was made in over twenty different colour variations, followed by the *Parrot* and *Squirrel* jugs, whilst the Pattern Book records

Pixie biscuit barrel with wicker handle, c.1955. Height 7ins (18cms).

From an advertisement in *The Pottery Gazette*, July 1955.

Relief-modelled teapot, Anemone, 1950s. Height approximately 7ins (18cms).

just one for the *Monkey and the Cat*. Later colour versions noted in Pattern Books describe stippled grounds and lustrings as well as plain matt or gloss glazes, including ivory, green, mushroom and white. As might be expected in a decade when the bright and bold ruled, those jugs featuring the brightest yellow glaze and most vivid colours were (and remain) most popular. Each colour variation was allocated a four-digit pattern number, which may be found hand-painted on the jug's base, sometimes with the painter's mark or initials.

Whilst the Burleigh Flower Jugs were usually painted on-glaze by women, the men decorated some specially commissioned versions with more expensive underglaze colours. This has resulted, as collectors will testify, in a great variation in quality from the excellent with subtle shading and colour variation, most usually the work of William Adams or Fred Ridgway, to the rather crude, perhaps the work of a recently trained young paintress. On occasions in the past, employees were permitted in their lunch breaks to decorate jugs (and other items) in colours of their own choosing, perhaps for a friend or relative. Special 'employee sales' were also held from time to time; at one such during the 1970s surplus undecorated biscuit stock of Flower Jugs and other wares were backstamped (with a later Burleigh mark), glazed and sold off.[40]

The variety of shapes and individual modelling of the Flower Jugs meant that there were no standard sizes or heights but the largest was around 10ins (25.4cm) tall and the smallest approximately 6ins (15.2cm). A few jugs were available in two sizes, these being *Dragon* and *Kingfisher*, both 10ins and 8ins (25.4cm and 20cm); *Harvest* 7¹/₂ins and 5¹/₂ins (19.5cm and 14cm); and *Kangaroo*, 10ins and 7¹/₂ins (25.4cm and 14cm).

Any Flower Jugs smaller than about 10cm (4ins) are likely to be milk jugs from a range of associated embossed tewares. These sets, comprising milk jugs and sugar bowls, were first modelled in c.1932 and are listed in the Pattern Book as *Fox* (*in the Cornfield*), *Kingfisher* and *Parrot*. Soon after, a series of attractive embossed floral patterns were introduced to the range, namely *Thistle*, *Forget-me-Not*, *Strawberry* and *Poppy*. From the late 1940s, an embossed *Anemone* teaset was issued which in addition to the sugar and milk jug also had a teapot. Both the *Kingfisher* and *Parrot* patterns were produced as Early Morning Sets complete with

teapot, sugar bowl, milk jug, tea cups and saucers and tea plates. Other relief-modelled teapots included the *Dragon* and the *Fox in the Cornfield*.

Sporting Jugs

Amongst the 1930s Burleigh Flower Jugs was a collection of three 'Sporting Jugs'. Modelled by Bailey in 1934, each featured a sporting figure as a handle. Although most probably purely decorative, they were ideal for serving lemonade or beer in the clubhouse. With an eye to the export market again, the *Cricketer* jug was based on the then popular Australian batsman Don Bradman who, amongst his many batting records, made the greatest number of centuries in England v Australia test matches. The *Cricketer* jug must have provided a good topic of conversation when Denis Leigh made a tour of Australia and New Zealand in 1936. It was an ideal presentation gift, too, for the Australian cricket team manager when he visited Stoke-on-Trent in 1938 during the Australian Cricket Centenary celebrations. It is said that the cap of the cricketer had been painted in the wrong colour, a mistake initially blamed on the painters but finally traced back to the Art Director[41] (whose game was definitely football)! Two of the *Cricketer* Jugs are displayed in the Long Room trophy case at Lords Cricket Ground in London.[42]

Also on display today, this time in the Golfing Museum at St Andrew's in Scotland, is an example of the *Golfer* Jug. Produced in large and standard sizes in 1934 and 1935, this clever design features a golfer ready to take a swing down the fairway. Nattily attired in a flat cap and baggy plus-fours (or, as Bailey described them, '*Oxford bags*'), the golfer is thought by some to be based on the American champion, Henry Cotton, who first won the British Open golf competition in 1934. However, Bailey did not confirm this in writing nor did he suggest that his final Sporting Jug in the series, the *Tennis Player*, featured the famous French-born 1920s champion, Suzanne Lenglen. With her bobbed hair and beret, she nonetheless typified the stylish and liberated sportswoman, racket outstretched, which Bailey modelled in the form of the

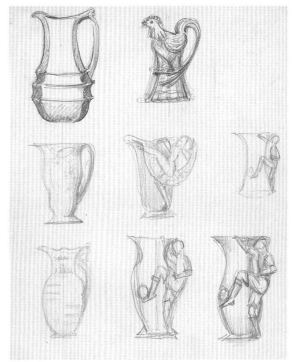

A sketch by Bailey, c.1936 swith various jug designs including a 'Footballer'.

Sporting Jugs, left to right, large- and small-sized *Golfer*; *Cricketer* (5333) based on Australian batsman Don Bradman; and *Tennis Player* (5329), all modelled in c.1934. Tallest approximately 8ins (20cms).

Flower Jugs with 'bird' handles, left to right: Two colour versions of *Pheasant* (5624 and 5623), c.1936; *Budgerigar*, modelled in c.1938; and two colour versions of *Palm* (5486 and 5429) from c.1935. Tallest 10ins (25.4cms).

Infinite variety: *Alma* (shown far left and right) and *Elers* shape jugs with freehand painted floral patterns, contrasting aerographed interiors and bases, sunshine edges or plain coloured rims, all with a primrose yellow glaze, c.1931. Tallest 10ins (25.4cms).

Embossed teawares, left to right: *Parrot* sugar bowl and milk jug (5071); *Strawberry* sugar bowl and milk jug (5390); *Kingfisher* sugar bowl, teapot and milk jug (5069); *Fox in the Cornfield* sugar bowl and milk jug (5025), c.1932-1935. Tallest 6ins (15cms).

Embossed *Parrot* teaset (5071) with sugar bowl, teapot and milk jug, ivory glaze and enamelled. Tallest 6ins (15cms).

Unusual Flower Holders, far left and right 'Garden' vase with 'crazy paving' base (5140 and 5159); second left, fish-shaped posy trough (6244); centre *Sundial and Kingfisher* vase (5193) painted by Ridgway; second right, 'Poplar trees and Cottage' (5976) mid-1930s. Tallest 10ins (25.4cms).

Typical source material from the archive: an advertisement for perfume inspires the design of the *Lovebirds* Flower Centre, shown right.

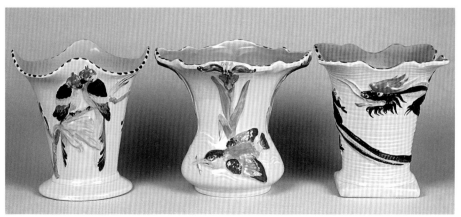

Wavy-rimmed Flower centres, left to right: *Lovebirds* (4939); *Kingfisher* (4896); and *Dragon* (4892), c.1933. Height 7½ins (19cms).

Simply designed Flower Jugs from c.1936-1937, left to right: *Eton* (5625); *Oxford*; *Cambridge* (5794) and two colour versions of *Venice* (5620 and 5621). Tallest 8¹/₂ins (21cms).

Stylised Flower Jugs and vases, left to right: *'Ovoid'* (5214); *Troy* (5170); *Meridian* (5176) painted by William Adams; *Luxor* (5166); and *'Ovoid'* (5205), c.1933-1934. Tallest approximately 8ins (20cms).

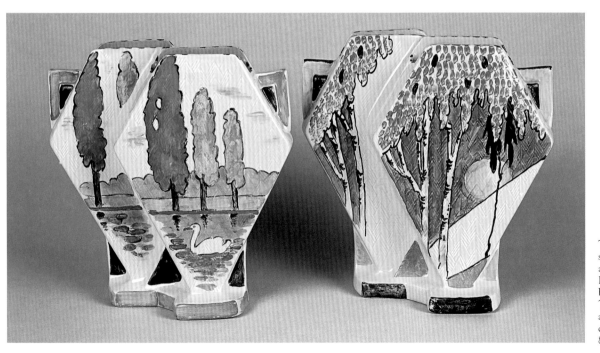

The *Zenith* 'double lozenge' shaped flower vase with arboreal patterns designed by Bennett and freehand painted by William Adams: *'Green Trees and Swan'* (5156) left, and *'Silver Birch'* (5155), right, c.1933. Height approximately 8ins (20cms).

handle of the jug. It is rumoured that a *Footballer* jug was produced, based on the Potteries-born England team player, Sir Stanley Matthews, who began his career with Stoke City in the 1930s. Whilst, Sir Stanley refuted this claim,[43] the existence in company archives of a sketch of a jug modelled as a footballer suggests that such a design was certainly considered.

As with the Flower Jugs, the Sporting Jugs were available in many different colour variations with either a plain or white glazed finish. After the Second World War, they were produced in plain matt glazes in blue, green and brown. Differing backstamp details readily identify production periods. With their popular subjects, superbly imaginative and skillful modelling, they are amongst the most sought after of the Burleigh Jugs.

Stylised Flower Jugs and Vases

Burgess & Leigh produced many other varieties of Flower Jugs and vases. Unfortunately, the frequently vague descriptions given in the unillustrated Pattern Books can make identification difficult. Amongst the more readily recognisable ranges were those relief-modelled jugs, vases and bowls, perhaps inspired by Alcock's *Bulrush: Carnation, Iris* and *Sunflower*. Of these the *Carnation* range was especially popular and was made in a number of colour versions.

Other jugs and vases were modelled in a more typically Art Deco stylised form like the *Regent* jug from c.1933. The relevant entry in the Pattern Book gives no indication of its distinctive shape. Its incised horizontal ridges owe much to Keith Murray's contemporaneous designs for Wedgwood. But whereas Wedgwood's pots were simply matt glazed, Burgess & Leigh chose to give their *Regent* jugs and matching beakers a brighter, more commercial appeal; usually they were decorated with the familiar primrose yellow gloss finish and stylised floral subjects, either 'print and tint' or freehand painted around their tops. The *Regent* jugs are sometimes called *Odeon* jugs by collectors; certainly their stepped shapes are reminiscent of 1930s Art Deco cinema design.

Burgess & Leigh adopted this more angular high Art Deco style with their issue of a further series of jugs, vases and flower holders with names evoking either ancient civilisations, *Troy, Argosy* and *Luxor*, or celestial spheres, *Zenith* and *Meridian*. Like the previous series of Flower Jugs, they were brightly coloured and yellow-glazed but were either triangular, diamond, double-diamond or ovoid in form. In this respect, they were similar to other products on the market at the same time, such as Myott & Son's pyramid-shaped vases; both companies probably acknowledged the influence of Clarice Cliff's earlier brightly coloured, geometric wares at the Newport Pottery.

The flat double diamond shaped *Zenith* vase or flower holder was first modelled in c.1933. Named after Bailey's tableware shape of the previous year, it has become known to collectors as a *Double Lozenge* vase. The hard angularity of its shape contrasts with the vase's freehand painted stylised English landscape scenes; the Pattern Book records that '*William Adams etc.*' painted the Art Director's designs: '*Silver birch trees and moon*' and '*Green trees and swan*'. The palette of these first two patterns was limited to the primrose yellow glaze, bold greens and black with an aerographed orange to the interior. Similar in style was a flat oval shaped vase; sketched and described as a '*single vase*' in the Pattern Book, it is now more commonly called *Ovoid*. Again, it was decorated with a tree, but in orange and black, the arc of its trunk echoing the curvilinear shape of the vase. Both the

Relief-moulded flower vase and shallow two-handled bowl, *Carnation* pattern 5603, c.1935.

Relief-moulded Daffodil jug, primrose yellow glaze, incomplete, 1930s.

Relief-moulded bowl, sponged and tube-lined floral pattern 5718, c.1936. Diameter approximately 12³/₄ins (35cms).

Jug, also pattern 5718, c.1936.

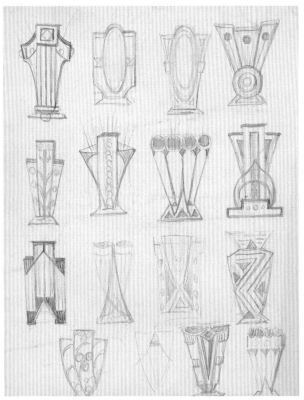

Pencil sketches of stylised Art Deco flower holders, early 1930s.

The *Meridian* vase, c.1933, and *Seagull* posy trough, c.1935, here with an oatmeal glaze. Vase height approximately 8ins (20cms).

Burleigh *Zenith* and the *Ovoid* shape were relatively complicated to make and time consuming to paint. Their high fashion design also had a narrower appeal and as such they were less commercially viable than the Flower Jugs.

The same was also true of the *Meridian* vase, a wonderful Art Deco construction of flat geometric shapes. Known to collectors in recent years as *Totem*, its original name *Meridian* more literally describes its abstract design of the sun over the equator, its semi-circular sunburst 'handles' and incised straight and zigzag lines highlighted in bold orange, green and black enamel colours.

Burgess & Leigh took care to take out patents in September 1934 on two distinctive and similarly styled relief-moulded jugs. The lozenge shaped *Argosy* jug (now commonly known by its design of *Galleon and Fishes*) was registered with shape number 796169, whilst the ovoid

shaped *Luxor* jug (frequently called *Leaping Gazelles* because of its Egyptian-inspired motifs) was numbered 796170. Each jug is archetypically Art Deco in style and again has the distinctive Burleigh palette of a primrose yellow glaze and a choice of bright on-glaze colours: green, brown, orange, grey and black. The Pattern Book records additional colour versions as being stippled brown under the glaze and lustred.

A further jug combining a modern design with an ancient name was *Troy*. With a triangular shaped body and handle, it was available in a wide variety of different patterns. These were usually freehand painted by William Adams and his son George and included designs of flowers such as iris, as well as more abstract patterns, like that featuring zigzags, dots and bold stylised flowers against stripes.

Alongside the introduction of new flat geometric designs in the mid-1930s, the company continued to produce further

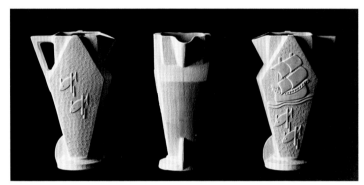

Photograph of the *Argosy* jug from its registration papers, 1934.

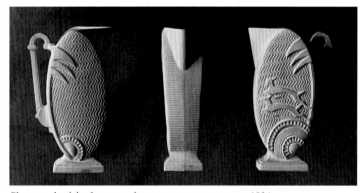

Photograph of the *Luxor* jug from its registration papers, 1934.

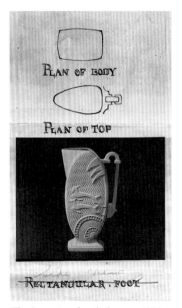

The *Luxor* jug, details from its 1934 registration papers.

The triangular *Troy* jug illustrated in factory 'scrap-book' with pattern 5179, c.1933.

varieties of and variations on its more popular yellow-glazed Flower Jugs. Flared, wavy-rimmed, relief-modelled vases, or 'flower centres' as they are called in factory records, were produced with different shaped bodies, one straight-sided and conical, others bulbous or square. Embossed patterns included *Kingfisher, Love-Birds* and *Dragon*. The Pattern Books list very many unidentifiable 'vases, bowls, etc', some of which may have been produced for only short periods of time. One such rarity is the distinctive *Sundial and Kingfisher* vase; it is not recorded how many were manufactured but only one colour version is recorded in c.1933 painted by Fred Ridgway.

In 1936-1937, the company produced a series of smaller sized, less stridently modelled jugs named after the cities of *Eton, Oxford, Cambridge, Stanley* and *Venice*. These were available in plain coloured glazes or in a variety of skillfully hand-painted and subtly-coloured floral patterns featuring, for instance, lilac blossom, crocuses or snowdrops, with white matt, oatmeal, green or primrose glazes. The neat, tubular *Eton* is particularly popular amongst collectors today. *The Pottery Gazette* reported on the series favourably, stating that '*their purpose, evidently, is to appeal to customers who are on the look-out for something of merit, but on a less expensive scale.*'[44] In a rare critical note, the same review described Burgess & Leigh's '*older series*' of Flower Jugs as '*pretentious.... with their ambitiously modelled handles and imposing decorations.*'[45] By this time, the exuberant excesses of Art Deco, pejoratively dubbed the '*Jazz Moderne*' style, were beginning to offend critical taste.

Reasonably priced on introduction, the original style of the Burleigh Flower Jugs brought the range instant popularity. It was said that every window in the terraced houses near the Middleport Pottery on Port Street boasted a Burleigh yellow Fower Jug, often with only one side of the jug painted to save on decorating costs! Success brought numerous imitations by other manufacturers, including

Clarice Cliff at the Newport Pottery who produced a relief-modelled jug depicting a flamingo (in uncharacteristic muted tones) and Arthur Wood whose *Dick Whittington* jug owed much to Bailey's *Dic Turpin* and *Pied Piper* jugs. Wade Heath also produced Flower Jugs as well as now fashionably kitsch Disney-inspired musical jugs.[46]

The high demand for the Burleigh Flower Jugs continued and by the early 1950s sales had exceeded 250,000. In 1953 Burgess & Leigh re-issued a pared down range comprising six of the most popular Flower Jugs: *Parrot, Kingfisher, Dragon, Squirrel, Butterflies* and *Pied Piper*. A further range of original designs may possibly have been planned but in the event Bailey modelled just one, *Lupin*, which was issued in 1954.

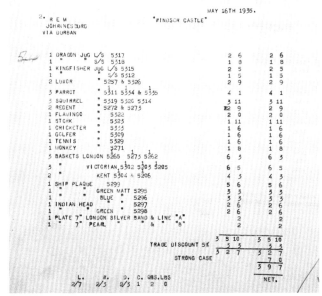

An order for 1930s Burleigh Wares from South Africa.

The *Eton* and *Venice* Jugs from an advertisement in *The Pottery Gazette*, 1st October, 1936.

The range of Flower Jugs re-issued in 1953, from *The Pottery Gazette* of July that year.

Some of the jugs continued to be produced in plain matt or gloss glazes up until c.1980. Today, the popularity of the earlier colourful versions has not waned and Burgess, Dorling & Leigh reproduced a selection from 1999. Many collectors, however, remain faithful to those made in the 1930s and are prepared to pay considerably more than the half a crown (50 pence) then charged to employees!

Wall Plaques

Equally sought after by collectors are Burleigh wall plaques. The earliest of the Art Deco period are those produced by Charlotte Rhead. The relevant Pattern Book ascribes some eight to her: 'Japanese Lady; Pheasant and Fruits; Persian Design; Lady and Parrot [inspired by an earlier Swettenham design];[47] Lady's Head (facing left); Lady's Head (facing right); Jazz;' and 'Ship in Centre'. Following her departure, her team worked on a further four tube-tooled designs introduced in the mid-1930s; one depicting 'trees and bridge' belonged to a range which also included 'vases etc', whilst a further three, all 'tubed and stippled', had as subjects 'Tulips'; 'Windmill'; and 'Windsor Castle', this last design perhaps inspired by the 1936 or 1937 Coronation.

At around this time, a number of relief-modelled wall plaques were introduced to complement or match the *Reproduction Period Jugs*. Like those, they were modelled by Bailey (and usually bear his moulded name) and were painted underglaze, mostly by Fred Ridgway. The subjects were *Sally in Our Alley* (from the *Ye Olde English Ballades* series of c.1914); *The Stocks* and *Gretna Green* (from Cecil Aldin's *Merrie England* of 1925); *Dick Turpin* (showing the *Highwayman* riding Black Bess); and *Sighting the Armada* (depicting Sir Francis Drake playing bowls). *The Pottery Gazette and Glass Trade Review* described them in 1937 as 'well conceived and uncommonly well handled' adding, somewhat ambiguously, 'besides which, there is nothing like them on the market'! In c.1939 the Pattern Book has two entries for a further plaque, described as a 'Hunting Scene', which may have been intended for this series. Bailey remembered that the plaque was never put into full production, possibly owing to the onset of the Second World War, but it seems some samples were made.

At around the same time, the Pattern Book records three ten-inch plaques, all decorated with a white matt glaze and

Decorative bowl, printed and hand-painted in black, lustre colours, pattern 3690, c.1925.

Design for a plaque from the Print Record Book Swettenham's name appearing above.

Plaque, tube-lined pattern 4118, by Charlotte Rhead, c.1928.

featuring freehand painted flowers on mottled backgrounds. Not specifically recorded as plaques are more abstract relief-moulded designs, which belonged to ranges of vases, bowls and other decorative items. For example, a distinctive and attractive plaque with a deer and foliage moulded in sharp relief against a striated background, although not mentioned in the Pattern Book, belongs to the *Verona* series of vases, jugs and bowls. Originally produced in c.1939 with a brown ground aerographed with a green or blue matt glaze, the *Verona* range could also had painted underglaze in fawn, grey and yellow with an oatmeal glaze. A lamp issued in this range in c.1952, in shades of browns, green and copper, was modelled or adapted by Bailey. However, it is thought that Wilkes was responsible for the original design.[48]

Ships, a popular Art Deco motif, appeared on a number of plaques, with one relief-modelled design featuring a sailing ship in a similar style to the Burleigh *Galleon* Flower Jug. Particularly appealing is a series of either round or scallop shell-shaped plaques featuring not only sailing ships but also seagulls or swallows against a setting sun. A relief-moulded circular bowl with birds flying above a choppy sea was also produced. Like most of the Burleigh Art Deco wares, the plaques were available either aerographed in plain green, old ivory and other matt coloured glazes or superbly hand-painted under the glaze, usually by William Adams. Judging by the comparative rarity of these plaques on the secondary market today, the series cannot have been produced for any length of time.

A similar high standard of painting can also be found on two different sized plaques, each of which Bailey modelled in c.1934 as the head of a Native American Indian. According to the Pattern Book, these arresting designs were either aerographed in blue or green, or painted in two different colourways with a white matt or primrose glaze. The same book records a relief-modelled plaque which it names as *Horse and Chariot* painted by Adams in three different matt colourways. Unusually, the plaque was not circular but took the outline of its subject. Very few seem to be in collections today, perhaps as a result of production problems or possibly due to its release so close to the outbreak of the Second World War.

Decorative bowl, mottled glazes, freehand painted design, pattern 5384, unsigned, c.1935.

Relief-moulded plaque, *Dick Turpin*, modelled by Bailey, painted and signed by William Adams. The plaque was available in 'sunrise' or 'sunset' colours, c.1936. Diameter 16ins (40cms).

Relief-moulded plaque, *Sighting the Armada*, modelled by Bailey, painted and signed by Ridgway, c.1936. Diameter 16ins (40cms).

Relief-moulded plaque, *Gretna Green*, modelled by Bailey, painted and signed by Ridgway, date impressed 1939. Diameter 16ins (40cms).

127

Above and below, pencil and watercolour sketches for plaques proposed for the *Verona* series, late 1930s.

The *Verona* range, post-war advertising leaflet.

Left to right: *Verona* vase with deer, shape 204, pattern 6451; *'Laurel Tray'*, pattern 6316; and 'elephant' jug, shape 202, c.1940-1960. Jug height 9ins 23cms).

Verona vase shape 201 with oatmeal glaze, post-war.

Unusual cornucopia-shaped jug from the *Verona Ware* range.

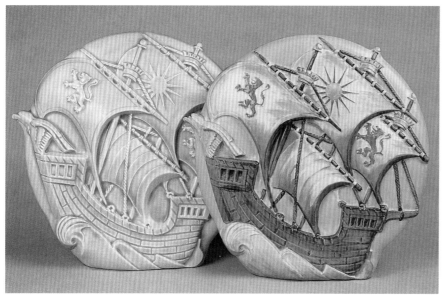

Galleon wall plaque, modelled by Bailey, c.1934, aerographed in oatmeal glaze, left, and painted, right. Diameter 13ins (33cms).

More sketches from Bailey showing the *Galleon* plaque.

Relief-modelled wall plaque with sailing ships at sunset, pattern 5945, hand-painted by William Adams, c.1936. It was also produced in plain matt glazes. Diameter 13ins (33cms).

Pencil design showing the sailing ships wall plaque, un-signed, c.1936.

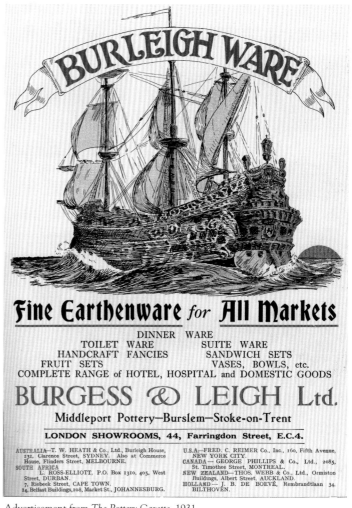

Advertisement from *The Pottery Gazette*, 1931.

Relief-modelled wall plaque with swallows, pattern 5943, modelled by Bailey, painted by William Adams, c.1936. Diameter 13ins (33cms).

'The Age of Speed'

Displaying the wide range of Bailey's modelling skills were two plain glazed, highly stylised, modernist models from 1935 of a jockey on a racing horse and a rider on a motorbike. Intended as a series on the theme of speed and putatively titled *The Age of Speed*,[49] it is said that a further model was made of a sprinter on the blocks, preparing to race. Unfortunately, Burgess & Leigh decided not to go ahead with manufacture of the Speed figures, their complex design, particularly of the horse and rider, presenting too many production problems. Any 1930s examples surviving today are prototypes only. These superb streamlined sculpted pieces bring to mind the work of the Italian futurist artists, whose work Bailey perhaps saw during his travels. Closer to home, Bailey was more than likely influenced by Skeaping, who worked for Wedgwood in the 1920s, and Olsen, Spode's artist-in-residence during the 1930s. The motorbike model also had something of the style of the fanciful teapots of Sadlers. The well known teapot manufacturer was one of many potteries whose 1930s products could be described today as 'kitsch', a defining characteristic of the Art Deco style.

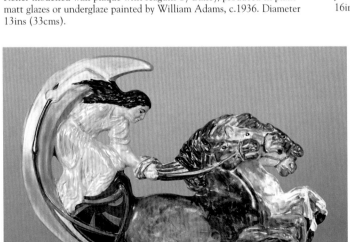

Relief-modelled wall plaque with seagulls by Bailey, produced in plain matt glazes or underglaze painted by William Adams, c.1936. Diameter 13ins (33cms).

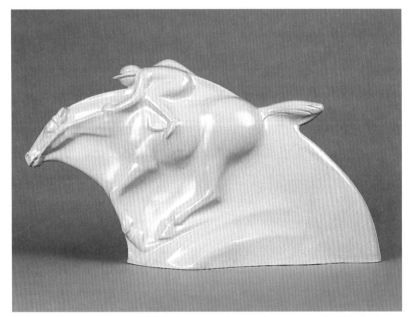

Jockey and horse prototype model for the proposed series *The Age of Speed*, 1935. Height 16ins (40.5cms).

Motorbike rider, prototype for *The Age of Speed*, 1935. A blue glazed model also survives. Length 13ins (33cms).

'Horses and Chariot' plaque (6307) modelled by Bailey and painted by William Adams, c.1939.

Pagoda Ware

With its history of teapot production, it is perhaps surprising that Burgess & Leigh did not venture into the 'novelty' teapot territory. Bailey is known to have modelled one in c.1934 in the shape of a *Cheltenham* caravan, although it is not thought to have been put into production at the time. It was reproduced by Burgess, Dorling & Leigh in 2001 with a new-shaped milk jug and sugar box. The *Pagoda* model of 1931, designed by Charles Wilkes,[50] and featuring another *Willow*-type pattern, came close. This range of tewares, decorated with a Japanese-style printed pattern, comprised different sized jugs, a teapot, sugar boxes and a preserve pot. Like the *Cube* teapots and jugs of the 1920s and 1930s (also produced by Burgess & Leigh), the items could be stacked, in this case, to form a pagoda. The whimsical element of this design should not obscure the care and precision which Wilkes put into its design. The pattern was subsequently revived in the 1980s for Mottahedeh, a New York based American company specialising in the reproduction of traditional and antique ceramic designs.

Further 'Fancies'

For many, part of the appeal of Art Deco, even at the time of production, was its manifestations of dubious taste in certain novelty items. Many of the Potteries' earthenware manufacturers unwittingly veered towards excess by producing gift ranges with garish colours, crude modelling, vulgarised misinterpretation of styles and fake exclusivity. Those Burleigh Ware items which come closest to the kitsch borderline are the mid-'thirties 'fancies'. Many of these miscellaneous novelty items conform to a defining quality of kitsch as *'the disguising of an object's function'*.[51] Although they might purport to have a useful purpose (usually as flower containers), essentially these fancies were just for fun!

Firmly in this category were oblong posy troughs modelled as a Native American Indian in a canoe, a fish or a gondolier; others were relief-moulded with popular Art Deco motifs such as the seagull, sailing ship and polar bear. Amongst a wide variety of 'posy holders' was one masquerading as a tree trunk and another as an upturned wide-brimmed hat! The latter was available in large and small sizes, and in a variety of patterns, either printed or freehand painted with bands or flowers. A series of ingenious

A *Pagoda Ware* teaset produced for the American company Mottahedeh in the 1980s. Teapot height 6¾ins (17cms).

'Quaint and beautiful' Pagoda Ware advertised in *The Pottery Gazette*, 1st June, 1931.

Large-sized posy bowl *Primroses* pattern 5439, freehand painted with 'sunshine' edge, c.1935. Diameter 6ins (15cms).

Pow-wow: A favourite subject for Bailey, the Native American Indian here modelled as a wall pocket, right, and wall plaques and variously coloured posy troughs, c.1935.

Pencil sketches for posy troughs, 1930s.

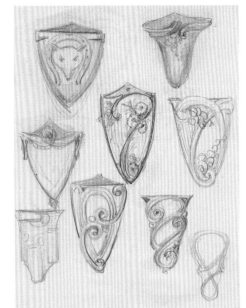

Pencil sketches for wall pockets include one with a fox and horseshoe, 1930s.

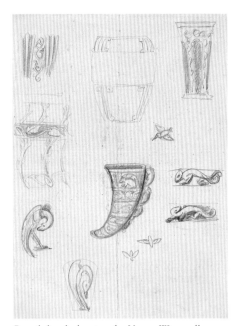

Pencil sketch showing the *Verona Ware* wall pocket as shown below.

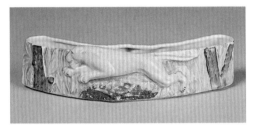

Relief-moulded posy trough, c.1937. Others featured seagull, sailing ship and polar bear motifs.

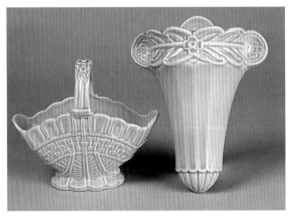

Relief-moulded plain glazed fruit basket and wall pocket, c.1935.

Verona Ware wall pocket, c.1939.

ring shapes decorated with a relief-modelled bird, squirrel, butterfly or leaves, on closer inspection prove to be flower holders with separate holes at the top for stems. Other models from the late 1930s include a bird and nest; a windmill; and a cottage with poplar trees.

It is thought that Bailey modelled most of the amusing novelties, which were usually either hand-painted in the bright Burleigh palette or glazed in matt green, oatmeal or ivory. His wall pockets covered a motley selection of subjects including: a budgerigar; Tudor cottages; a windmill; the head of a Native American Indian; an impressive bouquet of gladioli; and a fish! Wilkes was probably responsible for the more restrained designs, such as *Roman*, *Grecian*, *Bow* and *Flora* wall brackets, also produced with a variety of different decorations.

An unusual cornucopia-shaped wall pocket featuring relief-moulded squirrels was produced as part of the 1939 *Verona*

A selection of items produced in the *Acorn Ware* range, first issued in c.1939 and revived in 1953 in a choice of spring (6181), and autumnal (6180) colouring on a primrose glaze. Teapot height approximately 7ins (18cms).

Vases in the *Caluliflower Ware* range, pattern 6264, painted and sponged underglaze by William Adams, c.1939. These examples are post-war. Tallest 9ins (22.5cms).

Pencil sketch by Bailey of *Cauliflower Ware* shapes.

Cauliflower Ware vases and bowls were re-issued in the 1960s in a plain white glaze or aerographed in blue or pink.

Ware range. That which the Pattern Book identifies as an acorn may have belonged to a series initially called *Oakleigh* and later known as *Acorn*. Embossed with a relief moulded acorn and oak leaf decoration, this range of suite ware items included many different shapes, not all of which are listed in factory records. It was available in a choice of brown or green autumnal colouring and a primrose glaze. On its revival in the early 1950s, the range was advertised showing a teapot, water jug, sugar bowl, small milk jug and tray.

Also with a fruit and vegetable theme were embossed ranges of *Tomato* and *Cauliflower Ware*. *Tomato Ware* was similar to the leaf-moulded salad wares produced by other companies, such as Beswick and Wiltshaw & Robinson in their Carlton Ware range. Factory records from the mid-1930s show Burleigh *Tomato Ware* included such shapes as a salad bowl and servers, a cruet set, egg set and honey jar. In contrast, Bailey's 1939 *Cauliflower* range was more ornamental, comprising vases and bowls. Based on eighteenth-century Whieldon and Wedgwood ware, it was originally either aerographed or painted and sponged underglaze in naturalistic colours. From the 1960s, it

enjoyed a revival, being produced in a rather unsuccessful aerographed blue or pink. Also drawing inspiration from the past was a range of vases and bowls whose moulded, ribbed form and asymmetric handles imitated hand-thrown pottery from ancient Egypt. Examples from c.1936 were patterns, with a mottled fawn surface and sparse but bright freehand tulip decoration.

Studio-style pottery from Burleigh. Left to right: Jug, pattern 6456, oatmeal glaze, decorated by George Adams, c.1938; vase, possible trial piece 1930s; and vase, pattern 5618 'spattled' in fawn with freehand tulips traced in brown, c.1936. Tallest 9ins (22.5cms).

Diaper pattern, 5904, decorated by William Adams on three assymetric-handled vases, c.1938. Tallest 8ins (20cms).

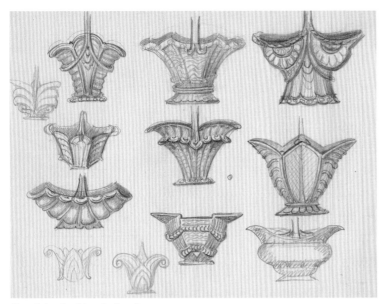

Pencil sketch of fruit basket shapes.

Fruit basket with wicker handle, enamelled flowers, pattern 5772, c.1938.

Fruit basket (minus handle) freehand painted pattern, c.1935.

One of a series of shell shapes, aerographed in oatmeal glaze, late 1930s. Length approximately 8ins (20cms).

Fruit basket (minus handle), primrose yellow glaze, freehand 'silver birch' pattern 5153, c.1933.

Fruit basket, with handle, and one of a number of alternative patterns 5154. Illustration from the 1930s scrap-book of patterns compiled by Burgess & Leigh.

Especially popular during the 1930s was a series of handled fruit baskets. These were available in different shapes, such as the *Victorian*, *London* and *Kent*, and various patterns, either embossed, hand-painted or printed. Some baskets, like cake plates, matched popular tableware patterns whilst others were decorated in the style of ornamental ranges, such as the ribbed *Regent* range of jugs and beakers. Of one, *The Pottery Gazette and Glass Trade Review* of 1936 enthused: '*A new fruit basket, so made as to receive a wicker handle with end clips, is offered in two sizes. This is called the Flora. Of true basket shape, it bears a modelled embossment in the floral style, which is picked-in by brush-work in colours. The base colour of the basket is variable.*' Later in the 1930s a fruit basket was available with the ubiquitous relief-modelled budgerigar, in some ten different colourways.

Less functional fancies included a series of modelled shells, variously decorated, either plain glazed or with stippling, aerographing, lustring and hand-painting. A 'clown's head' (presumably a wall plaque) was made in four different colour versions. Such novelties might not be 'in the best possible taste' but in the dark days of the Depression, they were a 'cheap and cheerful' pick-me-up for both manufacturer and consumer.

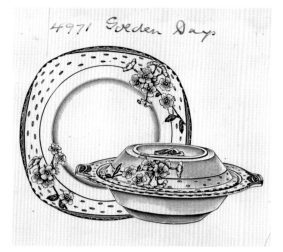
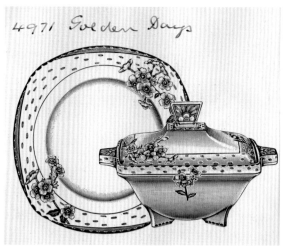

Zenith-shaped tureen and plate.   Zenith-shaped covered scollop with London plate.   London-shaped tureen and plate.

'Completely Modern': Burleigh Tableware Shapes of the 1930s

Arguably more vital to the company's long-term future than its fancies was the development of its tablewares. The *Sheraton* shape of 1930, with its square outline and practical curved interior, provided a first tentative break from the more traditional shapes of the 1920s. However, it was not until the following year that Bailey produced for Burgess & Leigh a tableware shape which was unquestionably up-to-the-minute in design: *Zenith*. Registered with number 766416 in 1931, *Zenith* was produced as tea-, suite- and dinner ware.[52] With plain circular, rimmed flat ware, its holloware was round and gently conical as seen in a footed vegetable tureen and discretely handled scollop or dish. A distinctive feature of the shape was the design of its triangular shaped handles the bases of which, like the knobs to lids, were modelled with a stylised leaf decoration. This naturalistic feature (which was complemented by the choice of surface patterns) had the effect of softening, even Anglicising, the angularity of the design. Described approvingly in the trade press as *'completely modern without reaching extremes'*,[53] *Zenith*'s design had immediate appeal to those who wished to be fashionable rather than *outré*.

Unlike *Zenith*, *London*, a new shape registered by Burgess & Leigh (772000) in 1932, was available as dinner ware only, with square shaped plates with rounded edges and a tureen with small flat relief-moulded lozenge as a knob or handle. *London* 'flat' shapes quickly came to be used in conjunction with *Zenith* tea- and suite ware shapes to make up complete dinner services.

Burgess & Leigh offered the customer further options with the introduction of another shape, *Imperial*, which it registered (791585) in 1934. Modelled by Bailey, it was similar in style to *Zenith* but with squarer, more ovoid holloware, oblong handles, and a moulded geometric 'cottage'-shaped detail to knobs and the tops of its handles. The overall impression was of a less extreme, more conventional design, more acceptable to the overseas market implied by its name. Available as dinner-, tea- and suite ware, the *Imperial* shape was almost always used in conjunction with *London* flat ware shapes.

Whilst *Zenith* and *Imperial* were the most popular and distinctive of the Burleigh Art Deco tableware shapes, and indeed remain so for collectors today, the company continued to release other shapes. Of these, only two made

any real impact: *Belvedere*, introduced in 1936, with an embossed ribbed effect, and the 1937 shape *Balmoral*. Although its streamlined curvilinear design suggests the influence of Bailey's exposure to contemporary Italian ceramic design, Wilkes is reported to have produced this shape.[54] In 1938-1939, when tableware shape design began to return to more traditional English forms, the company introduced shapes such as *Tudor*.

To complement its Art Deco *Zenith* and *Imperial* dinner wares, Burgess & Leigh introduced matching 'en-suite' ranges. These included tea- and coffee ware items; honey pots; biscuit jars, with and without bamboo or metal handles; and cheese dishes. Wilkes continued to contribute new shapes but many of his older designs, such as the triple or *hors d'oeuvre* tray, *Richmond* and *Crescent* sandwich sets, and *Avon* and *Rex* shaped fruit sets, also stayed in production. These took on a fresh new look when decorated with modern tableware patterns and were indispensable items for English afternoon or Sunday teatime.

Pride of place on such occasions was of course reserved for the teaset itself. In the 1930s home this was more usually displayed in the china cabinet, a tradition which many collectors of the *Zenith* and *Imperial* shapes continue today. Teawares, like all suite ware lines, could be purchased

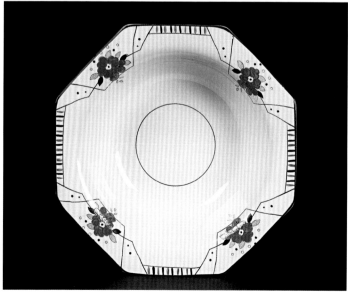

Avon fruit bowl with *Biarritz* pattern in red, 5013, c.1934. Diameter 9¼ins (23.5cms).

The *Zenith* shape registered in 1932.

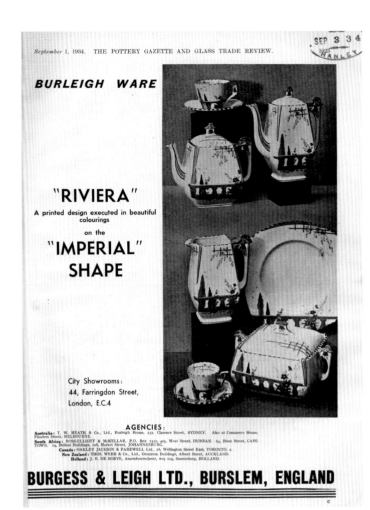

The *Imperial* shape registered in 1934.

The *Belvedere* shape registered in 1936.

The *Balmoral* shape regisered in 1937.

separately. They included a choice of three sizes of teapot (30s, 36s and 42s); a teapot stand; cups and saucers; a milk jug and sugar bowl; bread and butter plate; tea plates; and a cake plate (sometimes with a metal fitting). Coffee sets were made up of six coffee cans and saucers, a cream jug and sugar bowl and a coffee pot, usually large although a smaller size was occasionally made.

For breakfast, Early Morning teasets were available, comprising a teapot, two teacups and saucers, a milk jug and sugar bowl. The design of Burleigh egg-sets was nothing short of ingenious with egg cups – for two-, four-, five- or six persons – fitting into small trays with an optional cruet and additional three-bar toast rack. There were also individual footed egg cups; divided jam and butter dishes; three- and five-bar toast racks with separate or solid stands; oblong cruets; and cruets-cum-toast racks. 1930s Pattern Books listed such items under individual patterns which might also include lidded hot water jugs; large and small sized, handled

Afternoon tea Art Deco style. Teapot, milk jug, sugar bowl, teacups and saucers, side plates and bread and butter plate in *Pan*.

Oval sweet dishes or trays, that on the right with metal and bakelite handle, c.1935.

A description of *Dawn* as it first appears in the Pattern Book, c.1932.

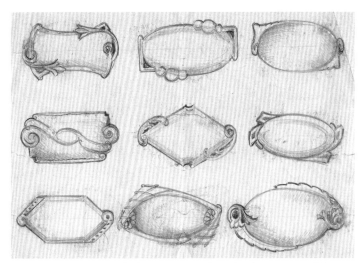

Sketches for 'fancy trays' which Burgess & Leigh produced in a variety of shapes with printed and freehand painted patterns.

The range of dinner-, tea- and suite ware items produced in *Dawn* on the *Zenith* shape, page from the Pattern Book.

Salad bowls and servers were made in several patterns during the 1930s, illustrated here, *Fragrance* pattern 4972.

Cecil shape toilet set comprising ewer and basin, vase and soap box, pattern 6638, c.1933.

Zenith shape toilet set comprising ewer, basin, chamber pot and soap box in *Tranquil*, pattern 6610, c.1933. Jug height 10¹/₄ins (26cms).

Zenith shape toilet set in the *Lilypond* pattern 6709, c.1933. Jug height 10¹/₄ins (26cms).

Empire shape toilet set comprising ewer and basin, two chamber pots, vase and soap box, print and enamel pattern 6375, c.1930.

and unhandled beakers; *St Ivel, Chedlet, Diploma* and *Zenith* shaped cheese stands; *bon bon* and triple trays; cress trays and stands; salad bowls with matching servers; covered muffins; and diamond-, square-, oblong- and oval trays.

Although post First World War, there had been a considerable reduction in the manufacture of Burgess & Leigh's toiletwares, production did not cease altogether. Indeed, *The Pottery Gazette and Glass Trade Review* of 2nd June, 1930 was reporting that *'Toiletware in the Burleigh range is certainly by no means dead, or even asleep'*, a comment which surely tempted fate as the next few years saw its fairly rapid decline! Amongst the smaller quantities still being produced during that decade (most of which were exported to Newfoundland and Malta), around sixty patterns were produced on the *Zenith* shape.

In all ranges both Wilkes and Bailey proved themselves to be innovative shape designers who always sought to maintain a balance between form and function. The two men's different ages and influences coupled with their common energy and imagination enabled the company to produce a wide range of both traditional and modern wares suitable for Burgess & Leigh's middle market. However, it is arguable whether either man's modelling could have achieved the success it did during the 1930s without the contribution of the person responsible for the design of Burleigh's decorative patterns, Harold Bennett.

Harold Bennett RI, NRD, Designer (1893-1976)

Harold Lawrence Bennett had joined the 'triumvirate' of new appointees to the Design Studio in 1929 in order to replace 'Designer' Edwin Leigh as surface pattern designer. Born on 20th January, 1893 in Congleton, Cheshire, he was the son of a local earthenware manufacturer, Charles Howson Bennett, and his wife Eleanor Ann née Stephenson. His paternal grandfather was a former mayor of Hanley in Stoke-on-Trent who had the unenviable task of reading the Riot Act on the steps of Hanley Town Hall during the Chartist Riots! In common with the Leigh family, Bennett was also a distant relative of the novelist Arnold Bennett, his great-grandfather being a brother of Bennett's grandfather, John.

Educated at Cauldon Road Senior School in Stoke-on-Trent, where he showed an *'unusual aptitude'*[55] for art, Bennett enrolled, aged fourteen, at Hanley School of Art. There he remained for seven years before taking up, in the first year of the First World War, a temporary appointment at Leek School of Art. Although a letter of reference from a teacher described Harold as having *'retained his ideals and his enthusiasm in the work and is particularly happy when giving instruction, in the work he loves so well, to young people'*,[56] he decided to forego teaching to seek employment in the pottery industry, first joining Gater Hall & Co. of Tunstall (which traded between 1895-1945) before coming to Burgess & Leigh in 1929.

Employees at the Middleport Pottery remember Bennett

Harold Bennett RI, NRD (1893-1976), Art Designer for Burgess & Leigh, 1929-1963.

Vase with Bennett's favourite subject, the tree; tube-lined design signed Bennett, early 1930s.

Ribbed vase, shape 93, and bowl, tube-lined patterns designed and signed by Bennett, c.1936. Tallest 10ins (25.4cms).

Left to right: Vase, shape 93, and bowl, pattern 5200, tube-lined design signed Bennett on base, c.1934; jug in *Lilypond* pattern 4897 tube-lined in black, enamelled and lustred, c.1932. Tallest 10ins (25.4cms).

Watercolour paintings from a scrap-book of Bennett's art-work, 1920s. (*Private collection.*)

Many of Bennett's small paintings were made into greeting cards for his wife. (*Scrap-book private collection.*)

Bright poppies. Stylised flowers and trees featured in most of Bennett's Burleigh designs. (*Private collection.*)

as something of a bohemian. Certainly, his style of dress was that of the aspiring artist; he always sported a bow tie with a boldly coloured shirt, tweed jacket and corduroy trousers. An enthusiastic rather than accomplished violinist, he and his wife, Clarice (née Gillman), a cellist, were members of the 'Centenary Amateurs', a musical group who put on lively renditions of Gilbert & Sullivan operettas at Burslem's Hilltop Methodist Church Hall. Bennett was well known in north Staffordshire as a make-up artist for a variety of amateur dramatic productions and local press reports describe '*the man with the box of grease paints*' as '*a one-hundred-per-cent enthusiast*'.[57] His colouring skills were put to good use with his own appearance in later years when the grey in his Brilliantined hair was cleverly disguised and his pencil moustache was dyed black by the liberal application of boot polish!

Most of Bennett's spare time, however, was spent not with greasepaints but with oils and watercolours and the painting of landscapes remained his lifetime love. Fellow workers at Burgess & Leigh remember him painting the canal-side scenery around the Middleport Pottery, smoking his pipe to keep away the flies! On cold days he would retreat to the warmth of his car, an Austin 10. (He was allegedly a terrible driver, his tortoise-pace prompting early examples of road rage.) At his then home, 4 St George's Avenue, Wolstanton, he worked in the more comfortable environment of his studio-cum-garage. Such commitment to art brought Bennett some measure of local, national and international recognition. His first solo exhibition had been held in 1926, before he joined the company, at the Grand Hotel, Hanley. There, amongst watercolour paintings of the surrounding and Welsh countryside, subjects such as '*Bluebells*' and '*Sunlight and Shadow*' reveal the inspiration for his subsequent tableware patterns for Burgess & Leigh.

In 1933 an exhibition at the Assembly Hall, Newcastle-under-Lyme, included several oil painting studies of St Ives in Cornwall where he had studied under John A. Park, ROI, and many of the local area, particularly Leek and the Staffordshire Moorlands, and the industrial Potteries. Local reviews were complementary, one astutely commenting that he '*eliminates the unessential, and selects with an eye to good composition.*' Another read:

'…. *the display was definite evidence of Mr Bennett's enthusiasm. The word enthusiasm is used advisedly; for while it is true that many pottery designers cannot leave the aniseed-and-turps atmosphere of the designing and decorating shop at a certain hour in the afternoon and say "Goodbye to all that" until tomorrow (the perfume would still be with them, if they could), only a few of their own choice deliberately and assiduously devote their leisure hours, and even their scanty holidays, to the cult of brush, paint and canvas. Mr Bennett is one of the few.*'

That Bennett's painting not only gave him pleasure but also acted as a stimulus for his commercial designs was never more evident than in the Assembly Hall Exhibition. Entitled '*Britain Beautiful*', it provided both the inspiration and the name for a Burgess & Leigh pattern, a fact noted by another reviewer who wrote that '*As the Art Director of a Middleport Pottery works he has introduced many of his 'Britain Beautiful' subjects as designs for brighter pottery, and the Queen recently purchased some of his works.*'[58]

Watercolour design for a fan by Bennett, c.1920. *(Private collection.)* Publishers Raphael Tuck & Sons purchased one of his paintings from the Royal Academy summer exhibition, 1945.

Page from a 'Private Wages Book' dated April 1930, shows that Harold Bennett then earned £7 per week.

By 1934 Bennett's weekly salary had increased to £10 while young Ernest Baily received £2 18s 5d.

Bennett's love of the countryside was reflected in his choice of home; he lived in the rural areas of all four counties within commuting distance of the Middleport Pottery: Staffordshire, Derbyshire, Cheshire and Shropshire.[59] He remained a lifelong member of the Staffordshire Society of Artists, participating in numerous local art exhibitions alongside his friend and rival Reginald Haggar (Art Director at Minton from 1929-1935). He was a frequent exhibitor at the Manchester Academy of Fine Arts of which he was a member (becoming friendly with the Mancunian artist Helen Bradley). Sretford and Stoke-on-Trent councils purchased examples of his work for their museum collections and other municipal galleries to show his paintings included the Walker Art Gallery in Liverpool.

A member of the National Society of Artists, Bennett was elected to the Royal Institute of Painters in Watercolour in 1956. A frequent exhibitor at the Royal Academy's Burlington House in London, he achieved notable success in 1945, when from a record wartime submission of over 10,000 works (of which 9,000 were rejected), two of his paintings were selected. Each sold for twelve guineas, *A Moorland Road* being purchased by Lord Woolton and *Longsdon, Staffordshire* by the publishers Raphael Tuck & Sons. A letter of congratulations came from Kinglsey Leigh who later commissioned Bennett to paint the Middleport Pottery bottle ovens prior to their demolition, the painting hanging for many years in the Directors' Board Room. Another London gallery showing his work was that of the Royal Society of British Artists. In spite of such acclaim, Bennett always remained very self-critical, putting his name only to the works which pleased him, the rest being signed *NBG: No Bloody Good!* Following his retirement from Burgess & Leigh in 1963, Bennett devoted himself to painting full-time, showing at the Paris Salon where he earned a silver medal and, closer to home, at the Stafford Art Gallery in 1972. Following his death in 1976, a memorial exhibition was held at the Mall Galleries in London.

Bennett had been at the Middleport Pottery for only two years when Charlotte Rhead left and he was appointed Art Director. As indicated earlier, there continues to be speculation about the circumstances leading to these events. In first appointing and promoting Charlotte Rhead as designer, the company had shown itself to be a progressive employer at a time when women designers, such as Susie Cooper and Clarice Cliff, were gaining recognition and prominence, not only by producing their own individualistic, signed wares but also by becoming Art Directors in their own right. As the elder and more commercially experienced ceramic designer who had been with Burgess & Leigh for three years longer than Bennett, she might have reasonably expected to have become Art Director rather than Bennett. Bernard Bumpus' research indicates that *'staff at the time felt that Harold's arrival was accompanied by a tension which grew up between him and the other design staff, of whom, of course, Charlotte was one'.* Certainly, it is known that the two did not enjoy a good working relationship, perhaps due to their very different characters: she, extremely shy, serious and retiring, with quiet, home-based interests, and Bennett, an extrovert with appropriate passions for amateur dramatics and football. (He was a lifelong Stoke City supporter in spite of his maternal grandfather's being a director of local arch rival Port Vale Football Club!) Perhaps Charlotte Rhead, a person of evident dignity and refinement, was offended by Bennett's notoriety as a 'ladies' man'; he allegedly had an eye for the prettier paintresses whom he would encourage to sit outside his studio,[60] those less favoured being banished to a place outside Bailey's modelling studio. As Bailey was quite a dashing and handsome young man, this was not quite the hardship Bennett envisaged!

It has been suggested that Bennett actively sought the position of Art Director, but his son recalls that Bennett was not an ambitious man and had no head for business, his wife acting as the driving force in his career. If this was the case, then she must be credited with Bennett's continuing salary increases! *'Private Wages'* books for staff record his weekly salary for January 1930 as £7, one pound less than 'Designer' Leigh's and nearly one pound more than Charles Wilkes'. Charlotte Rhead's name is inexplicably not listed throughout her time with the company whilst that of Ernest Bailey is first recorded in March 1934; then, aged twenty-two, he earned just £2 18s 5d. By that time, the weekly salary of forty one year old Bennett had risen to £10, with Wilkes'

remaining at £6 10s. Whilst these payments showed no increase for the rest of the 1930s, Bailey's wages did rise slightly; nonetheless they remained under half of Bennett's. This was perhaps less a reflection of the individual's value or contribution to the company than an adherence to the pottery industry's traditional hierarchy, which placed those working on decoration, such as the designer, well above those at the 'clay end', like the shape modeller.

Bennett was by all accounts a conscientious worker, rarely taking a day off. He remained loyal to the firm throughout his years there, during which he had more than one job offer from rival potteries.[61] Whilst the loss to Burgess & Leigh of Charlotte Rhead's talents cannot be gauged, there can be no doubt that Bennett's tenure as Art Director and Chief Designer for Burgess & Leigh was highly successful. He remained in the Design Studio for some thirty years where he produced the surface pattern designs for some of the company's and indeed the country's most collectable Art Deco tableware patterns.

'Resolutely English': Burleigh Tableware Patterns of the 1930s

Although Bennett's first love may have been painting for pleasure, his commitment to his commercial designs for Burgess & Leigh cannot be disputed. In 1939 he became a member of the National Register of Industrial Designers, formed in 1936 on the recommendation of the Board of Trade to raise the standard of design in the manufacturing industries. This he had undoubtedly achieved throughout the 1930s at the Middleport Pottery where he enjoyed much freedom to research his designs. He frequently visited museums as well as commercial outlets, such as wallpaper and fabric manufacturers, to keep aware of trends in interior decoration and gain inspiration for his patterns. On such days, he would arrive back at the Middleport Pottery in the late afternoon in an agitated state demanding the immediate firing of his design samples in the Climax kiln for the next day!

Bennett was by all accounts a prolific artist who would come up with half a dozen designs in an afternoon. It is remembered that Bennett, certainly in latter years, would eschew preparatory sketches, usually outlining his design directly on to a biscuit ware plate, sometimes initially with a pencil but more often in underglaze blue ceramic paint. When he had a selection of designs ready, he would call for Stan Johnson, the glost kilnman, who would carry the items on a board to the most talented paintress, Mary Harper. With the instruction, *'Let your fancy run'*, Mary would paint his designs in the colours of her choice before Bennett selected those he preferred. The plates would then be laid out in a line on the wooden factory floor for inspection by the directors and salesmen. The selection process, usually made ahead of trade fairs, was not something Bennett enjoyed as the strengths and weaknesses of his designs and the feasibility of their production were picked over – or perhaps, more accurately, kicked over – as approved designs would be inched from line gently by foot. Regrettably, many of the beautiful painterly designs of this prolific designer were not selected, as they were deemed not to be commercially viable. Bennett, who did not take rejection lightly, reworked and resubmitted many designs in the hopes that eventually they would be approved![62] For someone who did not like to repeat work and, whose mind was always racing on to the next design, this must have been frustrating.

"BRITAIN BEAUTIFUL"

Printed under the Glaze in the famous Burleigh Ware

A promotional leaflet advertising *Britain Beautiful*, the tableware range named after an art exhibition of Harold Bennett and featuring his landscape scenes, c.1933.

Design for a fish dish from the Print Record Book with backstamp incorporating Bennett's name, c.1939.

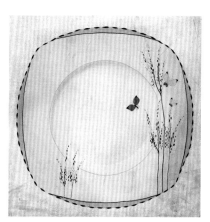

A rare example of Bennett's original design artwork showing *Butterfly*, pattern 5080, introduced in 1934.

Oval turkey dish, underglaze printed pattern. One of the few Burleigh designs whose printed backstamp incorporates the name of its designer, Harold Bennett, c.1939. Length 16¼ins (41cms).

Bennett's original artwork for *Daffodil*, pattern 4813, introduced in 1932.

Still 'All Over the Globe', from The Pottery Gazette, 1st March, 1933.

A home order from 1935.

Sometimes, as was normal practice in the potteries, Bennett's unique design samples, signed by him on the underside, would be sold off at special employees' sales for a matter of pence, each one a work of art! It seems that only a few printed backstamps incorporated his name, such as those used on late 1930s designs for turkey and fish dishes.

In spite of any misgivings Bennett may have had, the Leighs' high standards of selection paid off. The family had been in business for, at that time, some seventy years and knew what made a successful commercial tableware pattern. The Bennett designs they selected defined his apparently effortless style. In contrast with the more abstract patterns of other leading proponents of the Art Deco style in tableware, his designs were softer, more naturalistic, mostly depicting trees or favourite flowers of the 1930s, such as daffodils, bluebells, hollyhocks, pansies and tulips. Through simply drawn outlines and an economy of clear, bright colour, the best of Bennett's tableware patterns evoke the subtle nuances of place and mood, or a time of day or evening, which are quintessentially English. Even those patterns with more cosmopolitan aspirations, such as *Spa*, *Biarritz* or *Riviera*, evoke the safety and security of the south of England rather than the sophisticated pleasures of France. Today, the appeal of Bennett's patterns is nostalgic, bringing to mind memories or dreams of carefree days in idyllic countryside or taking tea in a cosy cottage garden. Judy Spours, writing in *Art Deco Tableware*, recognises the Burleigh tableware designs '*as amongst the most important British wares produced in the Art Deco style… [They] are examples of Art Deco ceramics in their most English realisation: stylised but not extreme, bright but not garish, the patterns simplified but still pretty…. resolutely English…*'[63]

The UK home market then accounted for about seventy-five per cent of company business, with successful sales from the local Co-op to the top London department stores, Harrods, Liberty and Selfridges. However, the '*resolutely English*' Burleigh wares were also eagerly sought overseas through agents in Australia, New Zealand, America, Canada, South Africa and Holland. From c.1936 the company also began a limited trade with South America, later to have its own agency operating from Buenos Aires in Argentina. Beeshy's, a china retailer in Ridgeway, Ontario in Canada, which stocked Burleigh wares from the mid-1930s, paid tribute in their centenary leaflet[64] to attempts made by English pottery manufacturers to design for specific markets. In a prose style from a now lost era, the author wrote:

'The Australian buyer calls for one thing, the South African another. That which intrigues the fancy of the Brazilian belle may arouse no thrill in the dusky bosom of her cousin in Chile or Peru. Milady of the United States has a yearning, as a rule, for less conservative patterns than the hostess of Old England. Curiously enough, however, the African Hottentot and the American matron may sometimes meet on common ground in their mutual admiration for some gaudily-painted decoration which is just the thing for camp or cottage use!… Some of the most charming and cultured gentlemen we know are to be found in the designer's sanctum at the work-shops of the world-famed potters whose productions we are privileged to market, and they are not too proud to burn the mutual midnight oil to create what one desires.'

Bennett would surely have agreed!

It is frustrating that there is so little original artwork for Bennett's designs. Pattern Books do contain a few illustrations and very brief descriptions of the decoration of his Burleigh Art Deco tableware designs. Unfortunately, although numbered, few are named. Indeed, some patterns were never given names and were known and ordered by their pattern numbers only. This can present problems with identification today.

What is clear is that Bennett's patterns were decorated in a variety of techniques by Burgess & Leigh's paintresses. Most often, as in the case of *Summertime*, for instance, (called by its factory name *'Windows'* in the Pattern Book) they were lightly printed in grey on an ivory glaze before being painted in clear, bright on-glaze enamel colours of greens, blues, yellows and oranges. Sometimes, they were freely hand-painted, perhaps first of all using a 'pounce', which transferred the pattern outline on to the ware using charcoal rubbed into pin-pricked tracing paper. *Shirley*, featuring poppies, is a good example of this decorative style.

Bennett also produced a few tube-lined designs. Pattern

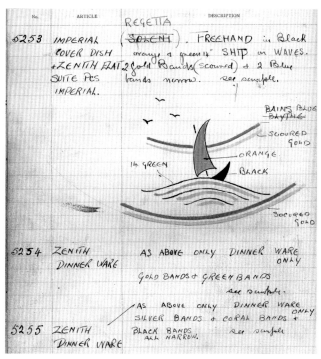

One of the few illustrations from Burgess & Leigh's un-dated Pattern Book showing pattern 5253, *Regatta*, 1935.

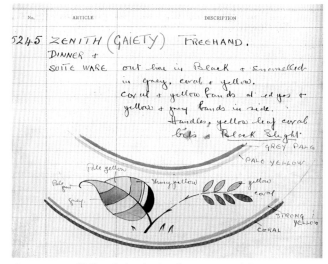

Gaiety, pattern 5245, with details of its shape, range and decoration, 1935.

Books record one of his patterns (5509) produced in the mid-1930s as *Zenith* dinner and suite ware. However, this fails to match the two colour versions of Charlotte Rhead's tube-lined pattern, *Orchard*, issued as *Zenith* suite ware in 1932 (after her departure). Of Bennett's tube-lined patterns, Bernard Bumpus writes:

> '...his tube-lined patterns are rather simplified when compared to hers. Bennett's name sometimes appears [handwritten] on the base of Charlotte's designs too – most notably her popular 'Florentine' pattern (4752). This pattern continued in production for some time after her departure while another of her patterns, 'New Florentine', (4908) was not even put on the market until after she had left. Tube-lining was relatively expensive, and the fact that Burgess & Leigh went on making and selling productions of this type and for the rest of the decade is a tribute to the standards Charlotte had set when she worked for the company.[65]

If the directors were regretting the loss of Rhead's tube-lining skills, they did not have to wait long for confirmation of Bennett's superior talents as a pattern designer. This came in 1932, with the introduction of *Dawn*, the tableware pattern which, undoubtedly, helped change the fortunes of Burgess & Leigh during the 1930s. Originally named *Sun Dawn* in the Pattern Book, its asymmetric design is typical of Bennett's restraint and economy: a simple, stylised tree silhouetted in grey against a yellow sun, and edging bands of yellow and green hinting at sunshine and green fields.

The effect of this individualistic and painterly pattern on Bailey's equally arresting *Zenith* shaped tableware proved irresistible to the buying public when it was first launched that year. It was viewed then, as now, as one of the most pioneering and astute designs produced by any manufacturer of the Art Deco period. Reporting on *Dawn* the year after its introduction, *The Pottery Gazette* commented at some length:

> 'Pottery dealers the world over will hardly need reminding that one of the most striking breakaways in designs for earthenware dinner ware was that which was undertaken

Tube-lined vase by Bennett with leaf motif as used on the *Gaiety* pattern, left, c.1936.

Dawn teapot (4760) on the *Zenith* shape. Height 7ins (18cms).

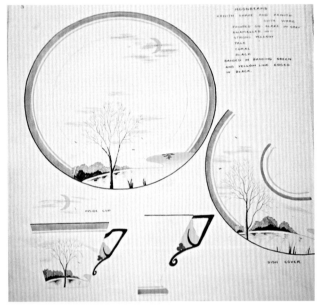

A page from a now lost Pattern Book showing *Moonbeams* on *Zenith*, 1934.

From *The Pottery Gazette*, 1st April, 1932.

by Burgess & Leigh Ltd when they decided to put upon the market their famous 'Dawn' pattern, for it was so unlike anything they had previously attempted, and yet so obviously sympathetic towards the changing outlook of ordinary folk contemplating the purchase of a new suite of tableware. Undoubtedly, however, this was a pattern which took the markets by storm. Although in some respects an innovation, the "Dawn" pattern was one which revealed an intelligent appreciation of what the public was demanding, or was likely to demand. We saw this pattern almost immediately the preliminary samples were in the hands of the travellers and agents, and we can look back with satisfaction to what we wrote of it at the time of its appearance, for we described it as a pattern portraying a very effective modern style of treatment, striking a note of real distinction, yet setting, as it were, a new fashion. We added, however, that it was no mere experiment, seeing that it was based on the surest of foundations – the ruling trend of refined public taste.'

If one story is to be believed, the reviews of Burgess & Leigh products during the 1930s might have been very different. The directors had already selected *Dawn*, but, before it was put into full production, asked for the opinions of their travellers who were in daily contact with customers. Albert Andersea, a usually perceptive salesman, considered the pattern to be too *avant-garde* for public taste and initially

refused to offer it. Tom Edge, a packer in the warehouse, allegedly included a sample cup and saucer of *Dawn* in the usual crated consignments to retailers and dealers – apparently this resulted in a flood of orders! In any event, *Dawn* became the best-selling pattern throughout the 1930s, a full dinner service costing 35s 4d.[66] It is interesting to note that when an attempt was made in 1934 to replicate its success with the similar design *Moonbeams*, also on *Zenith*, the fickle public could not be tempted in large numbers! Today, both patterns are amongst the most sought after of Burleigh Art Deco tableware patterns.

Equally desirable is *Pan*, Bennett's only figurative pattern, which depicts in silhouette the Greek god of pastures playing his pipes. First issued in 1933 with the same original grey, green and yellow palette as *Dawn* (4760), its idyllic and restful pattern was one of the first to combine *London* flat ware with *Zenith*. Others combining the shapes included *Britain Beautiful*, an underglaze printed pattern inspired by Bennett's earlier watercolour paintings. It was advertised in 1933 as 'A Charming Design in Chinese Blue, depicting various beauty spots in the British Isles... Balmoral Castle; Ludlow; Haddon Hall; Loch Lomond; Killarney; Beddgelert; Dovedale; Ben Lomond; Cockington Village, Devon; Norfolk Broads; and others in course of preparation'. The company, targeting both an overseas and home market, boasted that they 'confidently anticipate as great a success as that of our famous 'Dillwyn Willow' but in the event sales were disappointing. Three further print and enamel colour versions are recorded in Pattern Books although these were not made in great quantity. More plentiful are, for example, the popular floral patterns *Daffodil* and *Meadowland*, strong sellers on the *Zenith* shape from 1932.

As indicated, the naming – or not naming – of Burleigh

From *The Pottery Gazette*, 1st June, 1933.

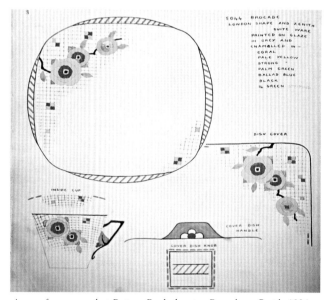

A page from a now lost Pattern Book showing *Brocade* on *Zenith*, 1934.

tableware patterns has given rise to some confusion. Some names, it must be said, are more descriptive than others, such as *Lilypond*, which depicts exactly what its name implies, and *Brocade* whose name suggests the tapestry-like effect of the design. A less apt name might be *Fragrance*, decorated with stylised tulips, or *Kew*, issued in 1933, which features red hot pokers! Other misleading or little known pattern names include the *Zenith* designs *Tranquil*, issued in 1933 and more commonly known to collectors by its subject *Windmill*; from 1934 *Evesham*, whose usual yellow colouring has earned it the name *Lemon Tree*; *Seville* also issued in 1934 and showing *Grapes*; and *Rushmere*, a more subdued

pattern introduced in 1935 which is more usually called *Bulrush*. With the lack of comprehensive factory records, the scarcity of advertising material and the frequent absence of a pattern name from printed backstamps, it is not surprising that collectors have come up with such creative inventions!

A readily recognisable pattern is *Butterfly*, the first to be listed in the Pattern Book on the *Imperial* shape and one of many patterns complementing the designs of Flower Jugs. Featuring freehand painted butterflies and delicate grasses, this pretty pattern has the lightly moulded corner panels of the *Imperial* shaped holloware and the straight edges of the *London* flat ware accentuated in bold green. Other 'print and enamel' patterns produced on the shapes, such as *Evergreen*, with its trailing diagonal of yellow belled flowers, and *Maytime*, a vivid spray of blue May flowers, have corner panels and edges highlighted in stripes.

Sometimes, agents, retailers or mail order catalogues such as Benthalls, might request their own special patterns or exclusive colour versions from Burgess & Leigh. *Tulip Time*, on

Tranquil, frequently called '*Windmill*', from the Print Record Book.

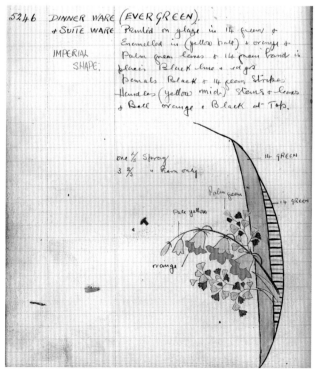

A rare illustration from the Pattern Book showing *Evergreen* introduced in 1935 on the *Imperial* shape.

147

Variations of the *Maytime* pattern on *Imperial* shape jugs. Lidded cocoa jug, third left, pattern 5252, introduced in 1935.

Maytime on *Imperial* teapots. left, with milk jug, pattern 5090; centre, in green, pattern 5089; right in the most popular colour, blue, pattern 5252, c.1935.

Zenith shape jugs, left to right: *Evesham* (5196); *Dawn* (4772); *Lupins* (4968) and *Meadowland* (4807). Jugs were available in 3ins, 4ins, 5¹/₂ins, 6ins and 7ins (7.5cms, 10cms, 14cms, 15cms and 18cms) heights.

Gravy boats. Back row, left to right: *Primrose* (5138) on *Zenith*; *Dawn* (4760) on *Zenith*. Far left: *Fragrance* (4972) on *Zenith*. Far right *Dawn* in orange (4772) on *Zenith*. Front left to right: print and enamel blue and yellow floral pattern on *Imperial*; *Pan* (4828) on *London*.

Tea for Two: *Brocade* (5044) on the *Zenith* shape, *London* shape plate.

Tea for Two: *Pan* (4827) on the *Zenith* shape, *London* shape plates.

Left to right: *London* shape gravy boat, plate and *Zenith* soup cup and stand, 'Grasses' pattern; *London* shape plate, *Golden Days* pattern (4971) and *Zenith* covered soup tureen and stand with *Meadowland* pattern (4807).

Zenith shape teapots, left to right: *Evesham* (5196); *Tranquil* (4900) and, with milk jug, *Pan* (4827).

Left to right: *Seville* (5021) on *Zenith* shape teapot and jug; *Riviera* (5088) on *Imperial* shape teapot and jug; and pattern 4823 on *Zenith* shape teapot.

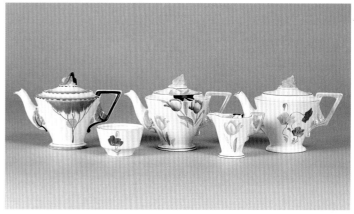

Left, to right, *Dawn* (4760) on *Zenith* teapot; pattern 5060 on *Zenith* sugar bowl; *Tulip* (4811) on *Zenith* shape teapot and jug; and pattern 5060 on *Zenith* teapot.

Zenith shape teapots: left, with jug, *Rushmere* (5354); centre, *Meadowland* (4807); right, *Primrose* (5138).

Balmoral shape teapot, *Rhapsody* pattern 5665, c.1937.

In the Art Deco style, this print and enamel pattern with sunshine edge (8128) in fact dates from the 1950s.

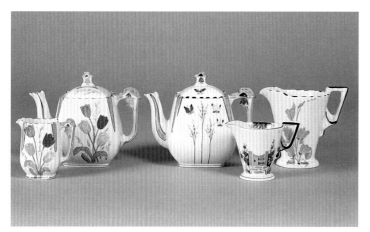

Produced especially for Lawleys, left to right: *Tulip Time* (5081) and *Butterfly* (5080) on the *Imperial* shape; and printed 'Garden Gate' pattern on small *Zenith* shape jug. Yellow tulip pattern on large size *Zenith* jug.

Zenith shape teapots, left to right: with jug, *Lilypond* (4927); *Bluebell* (4829); and pattern 5032, nicknamed 'crows' nests' by paintresses.

Teapots were produced in three sizes 30s, 36s and 42s measuring 6ins, 7ins and 8ins (15cms, 18cms and approx 20cms). Here the middle size on the *Zenith* shape, right, *Daffodil* (4813) and left *Rushmere* (5353).

Teapots on the *Zenith* shape, left to right: *Fragrance* (4972); with milk jug, *Pansy* (5136); and *Sweet Pea* (4814).

More toast? Toast racks with jam and butter: Back row, left to right: *Dawn* 4760; pattern 5579; *Bouquet* 4719. Centre, left to right: pattern 4824; *Pan* (4827); *Sunshine* (4609). Front, left to right: *Riviera* (5088); *Meadowland* (4807) and, toast rack with salt and pepper, *Golden Days* (4971).

Seven-piece egg sets, left, *Meadowland* (4807) back, black and yellow 'zigzag' pattern and front *Roseland* (4837) comprising plate, four eggcups and salt and pepper; with five-piece egg set, right, in *Meadowland* (4807).

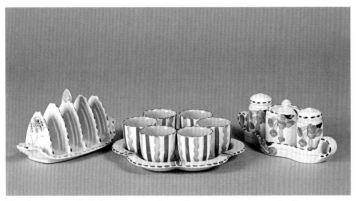

Five bar toast rack, left; cruet set right; and six-person eggset in the *Pageant* pattern (4689).

Wicker-handled biscuit jars, left to right, *Rushmere* (5354) on *Zenith*; *Maytime* (5089) on *Imperial*; and pattern 5579 on *Belvedere*. Front row: mustard pot and footed egg-cup in *Dawn* (4760) and muffin dish and *Zenith* beaker in *Fragrance* (4972).

The *London* shape: plates, left to right, in stylised leaf pattern in blue and *Laburnum* (4708); gravy boat 'Barley' pattern; tureen, pattern 5039.

Front, left to right: *Imperial* tureen, pattern 5506; *Imperial* gravy boat and tureen, pattern 5194. Back, *Zenith* oval meat dish pattern 5031; *Zenith* plate pattern 5040.

Unusual shapes in familiar patterns. left to right: footed tray, *Dawn* (4772); *Greek* jug *Bouquet* (4719); triple tray, *Rushmere* (5354); front, *Elite* bacon dish, *Meadowland* (4807); and footed dish and stand, *Pan* (4827).

Left to right: *Zenith* covered muffin dish *Meadowland* (4807); handled basket *Evesham* (5196); back, oval tray *Tulip Time* (5081); front, small dish *Fragrance* (4972); and *Zenith* cheese dish *Fir* (5350); and *Zenith* honey pot *Rushmere* (5354).

Left to right: *London* shape tureen 'Barley' pattern; and back *Avon* fruit set; front *London* meat dish; and right *London* tureen, all in *Pan* (4827).

Left and right, *Zenith* tureens in *Florette* (5468) and *Bluebell* (4829). Back, *Imperial* shape tureen in *Spa* (5276); and, front, *London* plate in *Butterfly* (5080).

Imperial tureen, left, and *London* plate back left, in *Briar* (5202). *London* gravy boat, centre; plate, back right; and tureen, right, in pattern 5350.

Left, *London* shape tureen and gravy boat in *Seville* pattern (5021); centre back *London* meat dish and *Imperial* small size tureen and stand in *Riviera* (5088); right *Imperial* tureen in *Geranium* (5349).

Left to right: *Zenith* tureen and lidded soup tureen, stand and ladle in pattern 5226; *Zenith* tureen, gravy boat and, centre, *Belmont* shape tureen in *Bouquet* (4719).

London shape oval meat dishes; *Imperial* shape gravy boat and tureen; and *Zenith* soup dish and stand with *Maytime* in blue (5252) and green (5089). Largest length 18ins (46cms).

Zenith dinner ware items, left to right: sauce boat and stand; dinner plate; tureen and large size soup tureen and stand, all with the *Moonbeams* pattern (5045), c.1934.

Plate and tureen in the *Balmoral* shape, printed and enamelled pattern 6163, c.1938.

Stylish patterns on *Zenith*. Left, coffee pot, cup and saucer, pattern 4836; teacup and saucer with green leaf pattern; coffee pot *Sunray* (4924) and milk jug *Kew* (4977).

Pattern 5040 on the *Zenith* shape, c.1934. The same printed tree was used on the *Lilypond* pattern.

Primrose (5138) on the *Zenith* shape, introduced in 1935 and purchased by Queen Mary.

An un-named, un-numbered pattern, on a *Zenith* plate and cup and saucer. Probably in production for only a short period.

Zenith shaped jug with pink enamelled flowers; and *Zenith* teapot, pattern 5035.

Milk jug, coffee cup and saucer, coffee pot, sugar bowl and large size jug, all *Bluebell* (4829) on the *Zenith* shape, c.1933.

Coffee for two: *Meadowland* (4807) on *Zenith*, print and enamel, sunshine edges, c.1932.

Coffee pots: left, *Zenith* with sugar bowl in *Spring Blossom* (5508); centre, *Imperial* with milk jug in *Golden Gleam* (5275); and, right, *Zenith*, *Golden Days* (4971A).

Coffee pots: left with jug, *Roseland* (4837); centre, simple grey and yellow banded pattern (5579) on the *Belvedere* shape; right, with jug, *Florette* (5468) on the *Imperial* shape.

Gilders and banders in the *'Top Gilding Shop'* right to left: Lizzie Matthias, Olivia Johnson, Ethel Kettle, Joyce Johnson and Agnes Pointon.

the *Imperial* shape, for example, was one of numerous designs to be supplied to Lawleys. (Whilst some patterns supplied to them might have the Burleigh backstamp alongside that of the retailer, others, as in the case of some of Charlotte Rhead's designs, might just show the Lawleys mark.)

Many of the Burleigh Art Deco tableware patterns, as well as the ornamental ranges such as Flower Jugs (whose surface patterns Bennett also designed) have a characteristic black enamelled edge painted in small dashes. This line decoration was sometimes called a *'dottle'* or *'stitch'* edge by paintresses at the Middleport Pottery. (This was possibly a contraction of the word *'dontil'* used to describe a similar style of gilded decoration or, possibly, after the method of supporting flat ware face upwards with a pin point beneath its rim, which is described as *'dottled'*.) However, Bennett (and the Pattern Books) referred to it simply as a *'sunshine'* edge. This was in recognition of the first pattern which used the decorative technique, Rhead's *Sunshine*, a simple and very effective design with a *'blown'* (aerographed) yellow band and three short black tube-lined dashes. As a result, collectors sometimes call those patterns featuring it *Sunshine Ware*.

The sunshine edges featured largely on the *Zenith* shape and to a lesser extent on *Imperial*. The technique was rarely used on the 1936 textured *Belvedere* shape which had a variety of decorative patterns. Of these, *The Pottery Gazette* favoured that with a *'rather unconventional rendering of the tulip in colourings of red, yellow and grey…. neither so bright as to be aggressive nor so restrained as to be cheerless'*. A number of patterns on the *Belvedere* and *Balmoral* shapes of the later 1930s utilised the technique of either underglaze or overglaze 'banding'. Usually used on borders, varying degrees of colour depth could be obtained by wash-shaded banding or solid-banding. For the 1937 pastel-coloured *Balmoral* pattern *Harmony*, a 'bander' first of all applied an underglaze wash band of colour to an item which was then passed to a freehand paintress. Using the handle end of her paintbrush dipped in turpentine, she would outline the design, a crocus,

in the colour band. This would then be filled in with enamel paints so that the painted design sat in the wash-banded border rather than being applied on top of it, giving a much smoother surface to the decoration.[67]

A wash band was also used on top of an on-glaze printed border design on the *Balmoral* pattern *Moiré*, this giving the effect of the watery silk fabric which gave it its name. Introduced in 1937, it was available in pale green, yellow,

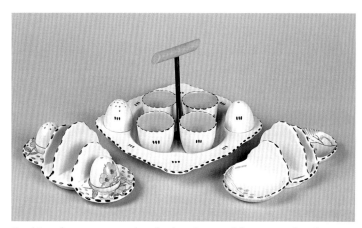

Sunshine edges on a toast rack with salt and pepper, left, a toast rack with jam and butter, right; and a 'seven-piece egg set' in Rhead's *Sunshine* pattern.

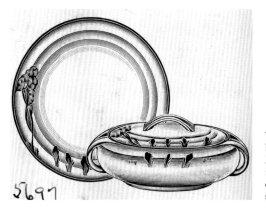

The freehand and banded pattern *Harmony* 5697, introduced in 1937 on the *Balmoral* shape.

153

Moiré on the *Balmoral* shape, introduced in 1937 and produced until c.1963.

peach or powder blue and finished with gold lines and gold 'dottled' edging. This subtle, restrained pattern satisfied a new demand from the public, now tired of novelty, for simpler, more reliable tableware patterns with longer production runs. Although one of the more expensive Burleigh patterns at the time, *Moiré* proved hugely successful and remained in production until c.1963. *Paisley*,[68] also produced on *Balmoral*, featured a rather bold and dominant floral pattern to the border and centre, the trade press helpfully pointing out that the border alone might be sufficient for some customers' tastes. Burgess & Leigh did not make the same mistake with *Bramble*, a wild rose spray also on *Balmoral*: it was offered in a choice of more muted, naturalistic tones as well as brighter, bolder colourings. (It was one of two tableware designs selected by the Duchess of Gloucester on visiting the Burgess & Leigh stand at the 1939 British Industries Fair.)

The new conservative taste was also reflected in formal table settings, such as dessert services and fish-, game- and turkey-sets. Tableware shapes, like *Tudor*, were developed for use with *Rex* flat ware and *Longport* teaware, their conventional style more appropriate for traditional patterns. *Minton* first produced in 1937 on an ivory body on the *Balmoral* shape, was a gold printed pattern imitating the acid gold technique of the famous firm after which it was named. Fortunately, Burgess & Leigh customers did not have to pay that manufacturer's high prices; the trade press then remarked on *Minton's 'very china-like appearance'*, noting '*yet it is moderately priced withal.*'

Leaflet advertising Losol Ware, the brand name of Keeling & Co. Ltd whose dinner ware patterns and shapes Burgess & Leigh purchased in 1937.

'*The New London Showroom of Burgess & Leigh Ltd*' from *The Pottery Gazette*, 2nd September, 1935.

Keeling & Co. Ltd: the Purchase of Losol Ware

Since 1935, Burgess & Leigh had been able to display its '*compelling range of "Burleigh Ware"*' in a new '*spacious and noble*'[69] showroom on the ground floor of Ely House at 13 Charterhouse Street, London EC1. In 1937 the company elected to hold an exhibition of its wares there rather than at the British Industries Fair. This was probably for reasons of economy which were made clear when Burgess & Leigh's announced to the trade that they had '*concluded an agreement with Messrs Keeling & Co. Ltd, manufacturers of Losol Ware, to take over their running dinner ware shapes and patterns*'. Keeling & Co., an old established earthenware manufacturer founded in 1886, produced dinner-, tea- and hotelware from the Dale Hall Works close to the Middleport Pottery. (Coincidentally, Charlotte Rhead had worked there for a short time in c.1906 as an enameller.)[70] On the works' sale in 1937 Dunn Bennett took over the works and manufacture of their hotelware whilst Burgess & Leigh bought most of their dinner ware patterns and shapes to manufacture, replacing the Losol trademark with its own Burleigh Ware mark. Although Keeling & Co. was costly to purchase, its customers included Harrods (already retailing Burleigh Ware), Thomas Goode and John Lewis, all valuable connections at the top end of the earthenware trade.[71] Burgess & Leigh lost no time in advertising a selection of Keeling's more popular and traditional patterns, such as *Indian Tree*, on their original shapes, *Woodland*, *Rita*, *Regent* and *Doris*.

Burleigh Nursery Wares

Whilst doting parents' could dine off a variety of Burleigh Art Deco tablewares, their offspring were also offered a choice of nursery ware patterns, which have since become equally popular with collectors.

As indicated earlier, the company had, since the 1860s manufactured wares for children. These were mainly transfer printed straight-sided mugs or 'toy cans' featuring transfer-printed designs of a typically Victorian self-improving character.[72] In c.1925, a range of nursery wares was introduced featuring a lithographic pattern, which the Pattern Book describes simply as *Rhymes*, bought in from J. H. Butcher & Co. Ltd of Hanley. This was applied with a liquid gold edge to quite an extensive range comprising a baby plate; bowl; muffin; soup; fruit; oatmeal; mug; beaker; teapot; teacup and saucer; and cream jug.

From the late 1920s and early 1930s Burgess & Leigh were eager to produce their own original patterns on nursery wares. The trend then was for females to design such wares, people like Barbara Vernon for Royal Doulton, Susie Cooper for A. E. Gray and even twelve year old Joan Shorter, daughter of the publicity-hungry Colley Shorter, for A. J. Wilkinson. Burgess & Leigh followed suit by initially requesting designs from Charlotte Rhead, who went on to produce tube-lined children's wares for her subsequent employers, notably A. G. Richardson's Crown Ducal range.

The unillustrated and undated Pattern Book shows the name 'Miss Rhead' against three nursery ware patterns: *Children's ware Dogs* (4419); *Children's ware Frogs* (later amended to read) *Cats* (4420); and *Children's ware Chickens* (4421). Lists detail those items to be produced in the ranges: a soup bowl, mug, teacup and saucer, fruit dish, baby plate and handled beaker. Further descriptions indicate that they were decorated with an ivory glaze, printed in black, (not tube-lined) with additional enamel colouring to the pattern and edge. A Print Record Book recording designs from copper plate engravings shows a border design of racing chickens beneath a date of 1929 and the name, *Miss Rheade* (sic). This pattern, which must be *Chickens* (4421), very closely resembles her tube-lined nursery ware pattern *Who Said Dinner?* produced for Crown Ducal in 1932. The copperplate engraving still exists amongst those held by Burgess, Dorling & Leigh. A further copper engraving shows a design featuring a dog (perhaps 4419 *Dogs*), which is very similar to the portrait of the family dog which Rhead tube-lined on a tile.[73]

The scarcity today of these nursery ware patterns suggests that they were only made for a very short period of time.

Three further nursery ware designs attributed to Charlotte Rhead are *Jack and Jill Went Up the Hill*, *Mary Mary Quite Contrary* and *Cinderella*. These patterns also feature on copper engravings and are illustrated in factory records, dated between December 1930 and January 1931, decorating a cup and saucer, a mug and a plate. Although the name 'Rhead' above the illustrations has been scribbled through, the distinctive matchstick characters are stylistically exactly the same as those the artist designed and tube-lined on Crown Ducal nursery wares. The omission of the patterns from the Pattern Book indicates that they perhaps only ever reached the trial stage.

After Rhead left in 1931, the company issued a number of nursery ware designs, assumed to be by her as the pattern numbers fall into the sequence allocated during her latter months with Burgess & Leigh.[74] However, they might be the work of Bennett, then working in the Design Studio. Unfortunately the Pattern Book is unhelpful; while it initially always indicated a Rhead design, later entries are less precise and fail to record any designer's name. The first of the relevant nursery ware is *Bunny* (4764). Depicting the silhouetted forms of bob-tailed rabbits against a setting sun, this could conceivably be the work of Bennett so closely does it resemble an earlier watercolour sketch in his private scrapbook. Likewise, *Quack Quack* (produced in two colourways, 4765 and 4766), with its four ducks outlined against the horizon, brings to mind the simply outlined designs of Bennett's tableware patterns, such as *Dawn* (4760), issued at the same time. This same quirky style may be seen in three further designs, *Bow-Wow* (4898), a dog howling at the moon; *Baa-Baa* (4899), two lambs gambolling in the moonlight; and a later pattern of c.1932, *Chick-Chick* (5098), a chicken and a broken egg shell. Confusingly, original unsigned artwork, now in a private collection, shows preliminary sketches for some of the patterns together with one which factory records definitely confirm as Rhead's *Chickens*.

All these and subsequent Burleigh nursery ware ranges comprised a simple cup and saucer; beaker; mug; eight-inch plates; six-inch soup dish; and heavy deep-rimmed baby plate. All designs were printed on-glaze in black and enamelled in bright colours. Like the Flower Jugs, items were aerographed in contrasting colours, either all over or just at the edges, and given a black sunshine edge.

From Harold Bennett's scrap-book, c.1920s.
(Private collection.)

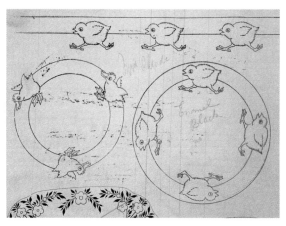

Nursery Ware patterns by Charlotte Rhead, left to right, *Cinderella*, c.1930-1931; *Mary Mary Quite Contrary*, c.1930-1931; and *Chickens*, c.1929, all illustrated in the Print Record Book.

Original un-signed and un-dated artwork with design ideas for Burleigh Nursery Wares. (*Private collection.*)

Mug and cup and saucer in the *Quack Quack* pattern from a scrap-book of designs compiled by Burgess & Leigh in the 1930s.

One of a number of 1930s woodblocks, these illustrating Nursery Ware patterns.

Above: Bunny by Bennett, from a scrap-book of his paintings, 1920s. (*Private collection.*)
Right: *Bunny*, the Burleigh Nursery Ware pattern, 4764, of 1932, from the print Record Book

Items of named Nursery Ware patterns, all printed on-glaze in black and enamelled, aerographed colours, black sunshine edges, 1930s. Largest plate diameter 8³/₄ins (22cms).

Pussy, pattern 5292, c.1935.

Bow-wow, pattern 4898, showing lettering to be applied to items in the range

From Burgess & Leigh's Print Record Book, a print of *Chick-Chick*, pattern 5098, which was purchased by Queen Mary.

Puff-Puff, pattern 5293, as illustrated in the Print Record Book.

Colour variations were available in some patterns. The amusing title of each pattern was often printed on the rim of flat ware. In 1933 *The Pottery Gazette and Glass Trade Review* enthused: '*The designs in this series throughout are such as will react instantaneously to the child mind, which, after all, is what one must allow for in connection with nursery wares, if they are to be successful sellers.*'

The same decoratation and range of items were applied to all subsequent patterns issued up until 1940. Taking into account both their style of design and pattern numbering sequence, it seems probably that these are all the work of

Artwork for *Teddy*, pattern 6219, late 1930s.

Artwork for *Wake Up*, pattern 5937-8, c.1936.

Artwork with proposed idea for Nursery Ware, 1930s.

Patriotic Nursery Ware pattern from the time of the Second World War, Print Record Book.

Original artwork for *School Time*.

Bennett. *Gee-Gee* (4973, 4974), a wooden play horse on wheels; *Pussy* (5292), showing a cat with a ball; *Puff-Puff* (5293), a steam train; *Neddy* (5515), a seaside donkey; *Punch* (5540), the stick-wielding puppet; *Jack in a Box* (5712), a springed toy; *Good Morning* (5939-40), a mother hen and chick lying in bed; *Wake Up* (5937-8),[75] and *Bedtime* (6218), two *Bunnykins*-inspired designs; *Teddy* (6219), a teddy bear sledging; and *See-Saw* (6492), toy animals playing on a plank and tree trunk see-saw. As ever, Burgess & Leigh kept costs down for customers with *The Pottery Gazette* reporting in 1940 that '*….there are some excellent printed and enamelled patterns in nursery ware. These strike one at once as being well worth all that is asked for them.*'

No new designs were issued during the war years although the Print Record Book and a copper engraving record a design entitled *Music Lesson* showing a group of rabbits singing the patriotic song *There'll Always be an England!* During the 1950s the Pattern Book lists a bought-in lithographic '*Baby Ware*' pattern (6997); the reintroduction of *Puff-Puff* (8184), distinguished from its pre-war version by the absence of any lettering; and *Noah's Ark* (8605), a lithographic pattern produced for the Fondeville agency in the USA. In the early 1960s it records a print and enamelled pattern described as *Bunnies* (8772), possibly another re-issue, which was produced on unspecified '*Baby Ware*' items and a jug.

Bunnies (8772) was the last nursery ware range to be

Publicity photograph for *School Time*, a Burleigh Nursery Ware pattern launched in 1962.

Noddy, Enid Blyton's comic character, lithographic transfer-printed, post-1970s. Bowl diamter 6¹/₂ins (16cms).

Original artwork by David Copeland (Art Director 1963-1981) for *At the Zoo*, 1970s.

listed in factory Pattern Books. Not included were the final patterns to be produced by Bennett, featuring black cats and kittens. Original artwork depicts a variety of anthropomorphic scenes but just two classroom settings were selected when this design was launched, with the name *School Time*, at the French Tableware Exhibition in 1962. '*They will have instant appeal*' ran the advertisement placed in *The Pottery Gazette* the following year. The company must have had some success with the range as the same cat subjects were depicted in a further series entitled *Bedtime* issued shortly afterwards.[76]

From the 1970s and 1980s onwards, occasional series were decorated with bought-in lithographic prints. They featured comic or television characters like *Rupert Bear* (produced as

a boxed set) and *Andy Pandy*, produced under license, or Victorian children in the style of illustrator Kate Greenaway. With the possible exception of the series, *At the Zoo*,[77] none can match the whimsical character of design and the vitality of colour of the Burleigh Art Deco nursery ware ranges.

One esteemed admirer of Burleigh nursery wares during the 1930s was HM Queen Mary. Well known for her love of pottery, she made purchases of various Burgess & Leigh products at British Industries Fairs. *The Pottery Gazette*, reporting her visit to the Burleigh stand in 1933, commented that:

'*on noticing a range of gaily coloured flower-jugs, with interesting relief-modelled handles, she recalled that she had purchased some of these from the firm a year ago. The Chick-Chick nursery wares were caught sight of by Her Majesty, and she promptly ordered an assortment of pieces in this series, as well as a morning set in the Kingfisher pattern which is the result of a mould embossment suitably hand-painted.*'[78]

She also ordered a dinner service featuring the aptly named *Balmoral* pattern[79] from Bennett's *Britain Beautiful* series.

In 1935 Queen Mary again visited the Burgess & Leigh stand. There, she purchased a dinner service in the *Primrose* design, several more Flower Jugs in the *Sporting* series, and half a dozen porridge bowls commemorating the Silver Jubilee. The desirability of the company's modern Art Deco designs could have no better endorsement and indeed the Burleigh Flower Jugs were advertised in the trade press with the proud boast '*as purchased by Her Majesty The Queen.*'

From *The Pottery Gazette*, 1st May, 1933.

Pottery Queen 1935 with her six 'attendant Princesses', one of whom, representing Burslem, is Burgess & Leigh's Lucy Johnson, *The Potterty Gazette*, 1st August, 1935.

The 1930s Middleport Pottery Remembered[80]

It was a 'Pottery Queen' of a different kind who was occupying the thoughts of some in Stoke-on-Trent during 1935 when thirty candidates from local pottery works entered a competition to win the annual title. Burgess & Leigh's entrant, Miss Lucy Johnson, was successful in being chosen as one of six 'Princesses' each representing one of the Potteries towns.[81]

Lucy was then one of some 450 people who made up the workforce at the Middleport Pottery. Like most family-run potteries in Stoke-on-Trent, it had always been a place where generations of loyal, long-serving families had worked together in largely good-natured harmony. However, the decade leading up to the Second World War, in spite of – or perhaps because of – its political and economic highs and lows, was especially enjoyable with previous employees remembering a genuine spirit of camaraderie.

The Decorating Shops

A visitor to the Middleport Pottery then would have found it crammed with employees, mainly female decorators. To accommodate their increased numbers, the factory was expanded in the early 1930s: a third storey was added above the Potters Shop for those working on Flower Jugs, and a new two-storey extension was built to the right of the factory's archway. Nicknamed the '*Town Hall*' owing to its size, the ground floor of the extension housed on-glaze paintresses working on 'print and enamel' tableware patterns, whilst its first floor became an export warehouse. Further freehand paintresses, banders, enamellers, aerographers and gilders were also accommodated on the third storey of the biscuit and glost warehouses. About fourteen female lithographers,[82] the poor relations of 1930s pottery decorators, found themselves working in more humble but apparently much-loved premises, known as '*the hut*'. This was, in fact, an old wooden army building from the First World War bought by the thrifty Kingsley Leigh! Erected next to the Packing House initially for use as a canteen, it was eventually demolished in c.1990 and now has been grassed over to make a flower garden.

During the 1930s, the only flowers to be seen at the Middleport Pottery were likely to be those painted on pots, by young girls such as Elsie.[83] She was just fourteen in 1936 when she started her seven-year apprenticeship as a freehand paintress. Out of a weekly wage of 5s 10d (in today's terms, about twenty-five pence), a few pence were deducted as

payment for training. In common with the 100 or so other paintresses who painted on-glaze patterns, Elsie began by learning how to mix her paints ready for use. Most colours and glazes, still then containing harmful lead, were made and prepared at the Middleport Pottery under the supervision of Harold Lowe. The very elderly Mrs Tomkinson is remembered as grinding the colours, which would then be mixed with the distinctively aromatic turpentine and oils to the right consistency. After the Second World War, when it became too expensive to frit glaze, all glazes and colours were bought in, mostly from the Harrisons company in Stoke-on-Trent.

Once she was competent with her colours, Elsie went on to learn how to use different brushes, usually called 'pencils', which, together with palette knives, she was required to buy herself. Some eighteen months to two years after she first started, she was ready for a simple pattern, her first job being to enamel the beaks on the *Chick-Chick* nursery wares! At this stage Elsie was paid piecework rates, whereby her weekly payment would be assessed for every 'dozen' pieces painted. Elsie's wages were paid every Friday with those of the other paintresses who after training might earn between £1 and £1 5s 0d; each cash payment was put into a small pewter 'wage can' and placed on a wooden tray before being brought on its hazardous journey from the office by the forewoman or '*Missus*'.

The wage cans were not alone in having a hazardous journey as the size of the Middleport Pottery meant that there was much fetching and carrying of ware by decorators. In fact, Burleigh Ware was described as '*giddy*' it was carried around so much! It might take three girls (and a good-natured passing man) to carry a huge basket stacked full of 'flat' (plates or saucers) to the warehouse whilst those gilders working on the top floor had to form a relay to transport pottery up and down two staircases. It certainly took some practice to carry a board of some twenty coffee pots up and down stairs without a breakage. Those men carrying boards of ware on their heads had a secret device to help them, namely their wives' stocking – silk before the war, nylon afterwards – which, when rolled up inside their flat caps, provided a nice firm base!

There were compensations for the hard and heavy work. On cold mornings, Mr Edge, the Lodge Man, would bring over a scuttle of coal and make up a fire in the iron fireplace in the Decorating Shop on which the women and girls might cook up a dinner of 'lobby', the tasty meat and potato stew still enjoyed in the Potteries. Added to this comfort, the decorators also enjoyed a certain degree of freedom; unlike other potteries, they were not required to 'clock on' but were entrusted to come and go freely. In this period of high unemployment, this contributed to Burgess & Leigh's rarely, if ever, having to advertise vacancies at the Middleport Pottery; new employees were usually appointed on recommendation or followed in the footsteps of their families.

The Print Shop

In common with most of the fashionable Art Deco designs, Burleigh wares of the late 1920s and early 1930s favoured freehand painted decoration or simple outline prints and on-glaze freehand painting and enamelling. This inevitably caused the engraver's art to suffer to some extent. However, unlike many potteries, Burgess & Leigh always maintained its production of traditional underglaze-printed tableware patterns and retained engravers, George Bateman and Mr Nicholls, who worked in close proximity to Bennett. In the busy upper

Aerographers spraying *Bunnies* Nursery Ware and *Parrot* Flower Jugs: Mrs Richards, far left, Mary Bosworth, Alice Tomkinson and unknown.

Pretty pottery ladies decorating *Dawn* and Flower Jugs during the 1930s. Mary Harper is seated, far right, others identified being Norah Bosworth, Agnes Pointon and Lucy Stockton.

Lithographers outisde their 'hut'. Left to right: Ada Kerry; Mabel Frost (back); Marlene Wright (front); Mary? (in shadow); Joan Pace; Kitty Sharmen (the Forewoman); Elsie?; and Margaret James, undated.

Fred Boulton demonstrates the art of ware carrying. (*Photograph courtesy of Donald Morris.*)

Printing Shop, Head Printer Harry Downs (who had played inside left for Port Vale) supervised teams of transferrers and cutters. Amongst the transferrers (or 'printesses' as they were nicknamed by the young paintresses) were the elderly Mrs McCue and Mrs Woodall, who are remembered presided over the Print Shop in their long white pinnies!

The Bottle Ovens

Many of these names are remembered today by Stan Johnson, the man who wooed and won paintress Elsie. Stan was the third generation of the Johnson family to work for Burgess & Leigh. His great uncle, grandfather, uncle and father had all fired the Middleport Pottery bottle ovens, occasionally on a freelance basis, simultaneously being hired by other firms, such as Weatherby's and Doultons. Stan remembers joining the company as a glost fireman on the day the Spanish Civil War broke out in 1936 and he was to remain in permanent employment there for sixty years. Although Stan's grandfather, a glost fireman nearing retirement, was paid a staff grade of £3 per week at that time, Stan's starting wage was just 11s 0d. Of this, he paid some nine pence to a shilling 'stamp' towards his pension. Prior to the introduction of the National Health Service after the Second World War, he also made a further contribution of one penny 'health insurance' to the Ceramic and Allied Trade Union; these funds covered any costs incurred at the Haywood Hospital in Burslem which treated potters with work-related injuries or illness. Less these stoppages, he handed over about ten shillings to his mother who gave him back one shilling pocket money to spend as he wished!

The skills required for Stan's job, and those of his co-workers on the ovens, had changed very little since the days of his forebears and were passed down from father to son. Stan remembers learning from his father how to recognise the distinctive smells of different types of coal – Coxhead, hard mine, hard bore, lump, slack, washed nuts, washed cobbles and so on – which he ordered from various mines in the area, the Sneyd in Burslem or Hanley Deep Pit, for example: *'Some smelt damp, some was mossy, some smelt of stale beer'*! (Stan's nose stood him in good stead with pottery ladies, too, whose occupation he could identify in the dark of the cinema stalls by their individual perfume; he could detect a gilder through the scent of aniseed; a paintress from the aroma of turpentine; and a lithographer by the smell of size!) Each type of coal produced a different heat and was thus used for a different purpose in the firing process, the quality of coal playing a significant role in its success or otherwise. One ton of coal would then cost some 30s 0d a ton. By 1941, Stan was paid marginally more than that for his labour, £1 18s 6d to be precise, standard wages for a fifty-six-hour week which included twelve-hour shifts. During the 1930s, a total of 100 tons of good coal was used (as opposed to thirty-five tons of clay). At the peak of the factory's production, there were five or six glost and two biscuit oven firings each week. During the same period as many as eighteen enamel kilns might be fired, each finishing nearly 5,000 pieces of ware, whilst the Climax produced two twelve-hour kilns a day.[84] Hot, heavy and exhausting work, particularly on the biscuit ovens, the team slaked their thirst with frequent brews of tea or cold drinks. Beer, sometimes permitted during the drawing of ovens on other potteries, was strictly forbidden at the Middleport Pottery with one ex-employee noting *'There was plenty of time for supping at the end of the shift without supping through it as well'*![85]

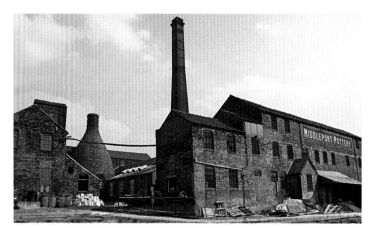

The Evening Sentinel celebrates Stan Johnson's retirement in 1997. Left, is his wife Elsie, a freehand paintress from the 1930s, and right Burgess & Leigh director, Barry leigh.

The Burleigh biscuit oven today. Generations of the Johnson family fired Burgess & Leigh bottle ovens.

The Middleport Pottery was very much a 'home from home' for Stan. It provided employment not only for the male members of his family but also the females: his mother, who had been an enamel placer during the First World War before resuming her job as a glost warehouse selector; his sister, Joyce, a freehand paintress; and an aunt, Olivia. It was thus an ideal place for lonely hearts: on his retirement in 1997, Stan told Stoke-on-Trent's local newspaper, *The Evening Sentinel*, *'In my opinion, what you should do is to work at Burgess & Leigh to get a good wife as my grandfather met my grandmother, my father met my mother and I met my wife here. I had a wonderful sixty years at the company. It was my life.'*

Stan took his responsibilities with Burgess & Leigh very seriously. He recognised that a disastrous firing could still cost the company dear in lost materials, ware and wages (for those at the clay end who were still paid 'good' from the biscuit oven until the 1940s).[86] Eager to learn more about the science of ceramics, he was able, unlike his ancestors, to take advantage of the Potteries' technical education centres, which Edmund Leigh had championed so vociferously. With this additional knowledge, he was determined to keep losses to a minimum; he was permitted just two per cent in his latter years. Stan's pride in his own job and his dislike of slipshod work from others made him an ideal fireman.

The Packing House

Although Ben Ford joined the firm, aged fourteen, in 1939, his memories of the Middleport Pottery began earlier in the 'thirties when, as a child, he frequently accompanied his father into work. Mr Ford, senior, had been taken on a decade or so earlier as a temporary cod placer; he was to stay for forty-two years, a record Ben beat by ten years! The Ford family was a large one with nine children, many of whom also worked for the company. They were amongst the many employees whose small terraced houses did not have a bathroom in the 1930s, and who visited the factory each Friday afternoon to make use of the 'Wad Cellar' washing facilities. Ben has never forgotten the harsh antiseptic soap, which, as a boy, he believed was more painful than any exposure to lead! During the 1930s, he remembers the bathroom was used by those working on the bottle ovens or, in emergencies, by those exposed to a harmful glaze. Following the Second World War, it eventually fell into disuse.

Ben was to serve a seven-year apprentice in the Packing House, starting on a wage of 6s 8d, under the Head Packer Isiah Brett. Other packers included Fred Addersley, Tom Edge and Les Green. Albert Shufflebotham was responsible for Export Packing, which had specific requirements; Australian and New Zealand agents, for example, preferred their ware to be packed in water-tanks, of which there was a shortage! They also requested that packing straw, bought in from Alsager, be especially disinfected to reduce infestation by insects. 'Reckett's Blue', a disinfectant, was also applied to the Packing House walls for the same purpose.

Ben had learnt the traditional method of packing in straw. Bales would be dropped from the top floor of the Packing House and doused with a bucket of water to keep the dust down. (Occasionally wood wool was used, before being banned for health reasons.) Sitting on a block on the floor, Ben would quickly and deftly place straw between layers of ware, more delicate patterns first being 'papered' in graphite tissue paper. Then came the careful and well-worked out system of filling the willow crates. Following the war, some metal mesh crates with sealed lids, which reduced the rate of pilferage, were introduced. Straw remained the preferred packing material for the home market; indeed, Burgess & Leigh was one of the last companies in the Potteries to use this traditional method of packing. However, in the late 1970s, and early 1980s, when retail agents complained of dust in their shops and losses in consignments (usually later found hiding in the straw!), the company abandoned straw in favour of paper, cardboard boxes and, latterly, cartons. Utilising his many years' experience of packing crates, Ben was responsible for the design of some of Burgess & Leigh cartons, to carry, for

example, twelve cups and saucers; forty cups; twenty-four eight-inch plates; jumbo cups and saucers; and special items.

Once packed and weighed, the large crane, one of the best in the Potteries, Ben remembers, lifted the ware on to a canal barge, twenty-four crates per barge and forty-eight per barge and 'butty' (its trailer). Ben did not experience canal transportation for long as delivery of incoming clay by sea coaster to the canal at Runcorn was deemed too hazardous to insure during the war years. This forced a change to rail and latterly, when the railway ceased carrying freight from Longport Station in the 1970s, to road transport. Prior to that Ben remembers that the smaller crane by the Packing House was used to load crates, five at a time, on to a horse drawn cart, and later a small truck, which made continuous journeys to and from Longport Station. Until the 1950s stabling for the Middleport Pottery's horses was still on the factory site, near Albion Street (prior to its demolition). There, the carter, Jack Hough, lived in one of the pottery's four terraced cottages,[87] looking after the factory horses as well as dray and dumping carts. Ginger, a huge Clydesdale, was the last of the horses, regularly making trips transporting non-recyclable factory rubbish to Burgess & Leigh's 'shraff' tips across the canal. It was said that Ginger knew when his seven daily trips were done and stubbornly refused to make an eighth journey!

During a day spent packing some forty crates, the packing team were glad of their breaks for refreshment. Following a 7.30am start, breakfast was from 9am until 9.30am. Ben remembers with particular affection the cook, Minnie Hilton, who, in the days before the provision of a canteen, used the 'Cook House' at the Port Street end of the glost warehouse to cook food brought in by employees. Those bringing in an egg would mark it with their own name to ensure they had no-one else's whilst rashers of sizzling bacon would be deftly flipped in the frying pan with Minnie's hairpin! Her hard work, if not her hygiene, was commendable; when not cooking she would be busy washing work clothes (and later cars) from a tap in the yard. Lunch-time was, in fine weather, spent by the canal-side and very occasionally workers were known to break factory rules by using the large crane to swing across the water. On one such occasion, a young man failed to make it across and took a dunking. Taken to dry off by the Climax kiln, he was, to his regret, found out and paid the price with his job!

The canal was later to be used to hide a stash of pottery stolen from the Middleport Pottery. It was discovered by chance by the 'rat catcher' during one of his visits to rid the factory of unwanted pests. The guilty employee was duly sacked. As in any workplace, pilferage sometimes occurred. It is remembered that one worker always wore a bowler hat when he left each evening, a cup and saucer just fitting neatly inside and another was found out when raising his arm to bid good evening to his employer, the crockery contents of his overcoat came crashing to the ground![88]

Ben still laughs about such events and has fond memories of those he worked with: Ernest Amos, the clay manager; Louie Pace, a bander and 'Bible thumper'!: Vernon Maskrey, the saggar maker; Ernest Bailey, 'a very nice chap and a superb modeller'; and Harold Bennett, with whom he would share a joke as he helped pack his paintings for London exhibitions. All and many more contributed to a happy working life for Ben who when interviewed in 2000 said: 'I would not have changed working at Burgess & Leigh for a minute.'[89]

Ben Ford packs his last Burleigh, photographed on his retirement in 1991.

'Mr Kingsley' and 'Mr Denis'

Kingsley and Denis Leigh undoubtedly valued such loyalty and hard work from their employees. In return, they were much respected by their workforce as 'firm but fair' bosses. Employees acknowledged their wider contribution to the pottery industry as a whole: Kingsley, as a founder member in 1937 of the British Pottery Research Association (now the British Ceramic Research Association), and Denis as Chairman of the United Commercial Travellers Association in 1933 and founder member in 1935 of the Earthenware Association which, in the few years it operated, did much to address the problem of low selling prices of earthenwares.

'Mr Denis', Elsie Johnson remembers, would walk around the factory each day with a 'Good morning, ladies' whilst 'Mr Kingsley', smartly dressed in his astrakhan collared coat, would finish his morning tour by sharing a cigarette with Stan's father, saying to him on more than one occasion, 'You know the secret of potting, Tom, is to get good firemen'! 'All gentlemen,' Stan describes the Leigh directors who each, to a greater or lesser degree, demonstrated the old-fashioned and near-vanished paternalism of the family pottery.

Following the death of their brother William, aged fifty-seven, in South Africa in 1937, Kingsley and Denis were left sole directors and joint managing directors. An obituary in *The Pottery Gazette* reported that William '*had a most attractive personality, and his death will be keenly felt by friends both here and in South Africa. He is survived by a wife and one son.*'[90] Whilst William's son did not take part in company activities, Kingsley's two sons, Edmund and Barry both began work at the Middleport Pottery in 1933 and 1938 respectively, becoming the fourth generation to work for the family firm. A keen cricketer and rugby player, 'Mr Barry' is remembered as regularly vaulting over the railings outside the lodge! The Johnsons remember him with much affection for his quiet acts of personal kindness, such as the £3 he tucked into an envelope for Stan before he went off to join the Air Force during the war, and his continuing visits during their retirement.

Social Activities

A characteristic evident in Burgess & Leigh employees and fostered by their employers was a social conscience. The company had always made regular donations to charities and good causes; an account book of the late 1890s records individual payments to a hospital, a 'holiday home', Ragged Schools, and St Paul's Old People, as well as to those institutions close to Edmund Leigh's heart, the Bible Society and the National Liberal Club. During the 1930s, Middleport Pottery workers, like those of other pottery manufacturers, liked to combine charitable fund raising with an enjoyable social activity. Typical events were a whist drive and dance, held as part of the Pottery Wakes Charity Effort in 1935. Sums raised then were £60 for the Haywood Hospital in Burslem, £40 for the North Staffordshire Royal Infirmary and £10 for the North Staffordshire Cripples Aid Society. Miss Lucy Johnson, in her capacity as Pottery Princess, was given the honour of presenting the cheques whose recipients '*all agreed that it had been a splendid example of how the workforce of the Potteries strove to maintain the voluntary institutions in their midst.*' Kingsley reportedly pointed out that the effort was organised entirely by the workpeople, paying tribute to the main organisers, Mr Bootherstone, Mr Tom Stevenson (Secretary) and Mr W. S. Hope (Treasurer).[91] Mr W. S. Hope, better known as Wilfie,

was the son of a holloware jiggerer at Burgess & Leigh, and later became a salesman. A keen cricketer, he organised the firm's team in their matches against rival sides, such as that from the Dunn Bennett pottery.

Another particularly popular social activity shared by employees was the Burleigh Concert Party. This fund-raising event typically combined a magic show and comedy sketches with a musical recital from a tenor, baritone, contralto and soprano. Such amateur singing groups, fictionalised in Bennett's *Clayhanger* as the '*Bursley Glee Party*', continued a strong musical tradition in the Potteries, born out of the old Wesleyan chapel choirs. The Burleigh Concert Parties would be held from time to time at local church or community halls, such as the nearby Wycliffe Hall, (another of A. R. Wood's designs). An old piano standing outside the modellers' shop at the Middleport Pottery would be much in use for rehearsals in any free time on the factory! Music certainly seems to have played a large part in the lives of employees with the women singing all morning as they worked; popular musicals such as *The Desert Song* quickly became a part of their repertoire whilst in the '*Town Hall*' hymns were more the order of the day. '*There was a real feeling of belonging*', Elsie reflects.

The names of all those involved in the manufacture of Burleigh Wares during the 1930s are too many to mention but their contribution is acknowledged. Indeed, the success of Burgess & Leigh during this important period was not due to one or another individual, but to the communal efforts of all those working at the Middleport Pottery: the business and manufacturing expertise of the company directors; the commercial and marketing acumen of sales staff; the combined talents and versatility of Charlotte Rhead, Charles Wilkes, Ernest Bailey and Harold Bennett in the Design Studio; the skills of the teams of mouldmakers, clay makers, printers, decorators, kiln operatives, packers, fetchers and carriers and the many others involved in the complex manufacture and distribution of pottery. All contributed to a greater or lesser degree to the production of what were undoubtedly the company's most original, innovative, '*resolutely English*' wares.

But not one of those working at the Middleport Pottery during the 1930s could have predicted the tremendous changes ahead for Burgess & Leigh, and indeed the whole of the pottery industry, when in September 1939 the announcement came of the outbreak of the Second World War.

A Christmas party at the Middleport Pottery during the 1930s.

CHAPTER FIVE

THE SECOND WORLD WAR:
Austerity and Prosperity 1939-1959

'It was with particular pleasure that we were able, a week or two ago, to revisit the Middleport Pottery… At the factory, one sees and comes into contact with those leading members of staff who are not to be frequently encountered elsewhere, and there is experienced, in consequence of that, something of a family reunion, a talk over a cup of tea and an exchange of reminiscences and experiences galore. But was it not ever thus in the Potteries?'

It is evident from *The Pottery Gazette*'s report of July 1940 that the early months of the Second World War had not altered the polite and unhurried way in which Burgess & Leigh conducted its business. But beneath the surface, changes had already been made, with still more to come.

On the outbreak of the war in 1939 pottery manufacture had been identified as a key industry and granted an Essential Work Order by the government. Kingsley was fifty-five years old at that time and not in good health but continued as Chairman and General Works Manager with Denis remaining as co-director in charge of sales. Kingsley's younger son, twenty-year-old Barry, enlisted shortly after the war started but his elder brother, Edmund, was to be rejected three times on medical grounds having had a mastoid operation.[1] Ironically, in 1940, the company had applied for a deferment.[2] He had then worked for the company for six and a half years, since the age of eighteen, simultaneously taking Management and Technical courses at the North Staffordshire Technical College in Stoke (now Staffordshire University). Since 1938, he had been responsible for controlling all exports within the factory, overseeing their production through the ovens and decorating shops to the warehouses. Acting as a deputy to his father *'whose health is uncertain'*, Edmund's particular knowledge, skill and experience was irreplaceable, it was argued, and the company was *'in a good position to increase exports if we are allowed to retain a limited number of key men. This is the only claim to reservation so far made though men of all registered age groups have left us to join the forces.'* It seems that the claim was a successful one and Edmund remained at the Middleport Pottery, where his responsibilities were arguably as onerous as those endured by some in the services.

In spite of its Essential Work Order, the pottery industry lost many employees to the war. Initially only young men were conscripted but over the next few years a number of managers in their early thirties were also called up to serve in the armed forces. Other potters went to work in local munitions factories in Radway Green, near Alsager, and Swynnerton in Staffordshire. By 1941 the total number of Burgess & Leigh's production staff had already fallen from some 450 to 324,[3] between a third and a quarter of its labour force. Of those remaining, females and those under eighteen years numbered roughly twice the men.

The 'Dads' Army' left behind also contributed to the wartime effort and there exists in company archives comprehensive and detailed records of the various government instructions implemented, regarding training to

War-time store cupboard at the Middleport Pottery.

Quick to respond, instructions on Air Raid Precautions, dated September, 1939.

detect and prevent possible attacks, and organisation of such things as air raid shelters. Some potteries, such as Wade's, went to the expense of building specific shelters, but after costing, it was decided that several different areas of the Middleport Pottery would be adequate. Amongst them were two disused 'reserve' bottle ovens (biscuit and glost) and various basement areas, including the 'wad, wash and glaze cellar'. A plan of each area was drawn up and calculations made as to how many and which employees might take shelter there. Under the direction of Edmund, who was ARP (Air Raids Precautions) warden, a number of personnel, including Bennett and initially Bailey, were given responsibility for different areas. A small rota of firewatchers or spotters was employed on 'night duty' to look out for possible gas and fire bomb attacks on the factory, an ideal lookout post being provided by the Dippers' Hot House tower. When not patrolling, each man had a camp bed in the 'Town Hall'; he was paid three shillings, it is remembered, and given as much tea as he could drink! Fortunately, the factory suffered no air raids but the speedy, efficient and voluntary co-operation of management and workers at this time provides a microcosm of the wider sense of communal responsibility.

BURLEIGH WARTIME WARES

Wartime Regulations in the Pottery Industry: Concentration of Production

In 1941 the Government Board of Trade issued special regulations to concentrate production in the pottery industry. With many smaller factories closing and others being amalgamated, this resulted in the severe contraction of the industry. Burgess & Leigh, as a successful manufacturer with a healthy export trade, was identified as a 'nucleus' manufacturer and amalgamated two smaller potteries less than two miles away from the Middleport Pottery: Kirkland & Co., which, like itself, manufactured utility and hospital goods, and Parrott & Co., of Albert Street Pottery which also manufactured earthenwares under the brand name Coronet Ware.[4] Both companies continued to produce their wares from the Middleport Pottery during 1939 to 1945 but, like many small companies, neither was to survive after the war.

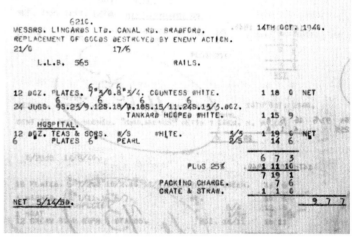

PARTICULARS OF AGREEMENT MADE BETWEEN "NUCLEUS" FIRM AND FIRM(S) FROM WHICH PRODUCTION IS TO BE TRANSFERRED

FOR MESSRS. KIRKLAND & CO. LTD:- We have agreed to make the whole of their White and Plain Ware. In some cases, we shall adopt their Shapes and, in others, they will take ours. Another Firm will do what Decorated Trade they have, although we shall make all Ware. They make almost entirely White Goods such as Mugs, Jugs, Pudding Bowls etc. and, especially, Hospital Goods. The Hospital Goods are very vital, at the present time, and can be supplied mainly outside the "Quota". Their Decorated Trade is very small and they estimate that what we shall make for them will amount to about 90% of their invoice figures. We invoice to them and they re-invoice.

FOR MESSRS. PARROTT & CO. LTD:- We have agreed to supply them with our own goods, invoicing to them and they re-invoicing. The amount we shall supply will obviously be governed - first, by the amount with which they can supply us with orders, and our own manufacturing power. We are both hopeful that it will be, at least, a minimum of £12,000 per year and probably more. We have also agreed to do our utmost to make a few lines in which they have specialized and also to try and protect any special customers they may wish us to do.

Burgess & Leigh's agreement with Kirkland & Co. Ltd and Parrott & Co. Ltd whose products they made at the Middleport Pottery during the second World War.

Utility and Export

As the labour force decreased during the war, so too did design and production. The months leading up to the announcement of the Second World War in September 1939 had been good ones for Burgess & Leigh. Their annual show at the British Industries Fair that spring received its customary favourable review from *The Pottery Gazette and Glass Trade Review* whose *Buyers' Notes* columnist wrote:

'One of the chief characteristics of 'Burleigh Ware' seems to consist in the soundness of the lines upon which the shapes and designs are built.... There is nothing outlandish about either the shapes or the decorations, the final product, in practically every instance, being a well-balanced compromise between freshness of treatment and unimpaired utility on the other.'[5]

'Utility' was an aspect of design that all potteries were forced to address in 1941 when the Government Board of Trade published its regulations governing wartime production of ceramics. Abandoning its earlier concessions for coloured glazes and bodies and simple line decorations, the Board of Trade ruled that only a limited number of simple tableware and toiletware shapes, in plain white or ivory, could be produced for the home market. All such utility wares were to be subject to price control: the Board

Burgess & Leigh replace an order 'destroyed by enemy action', 1940.

White and ivory glazed Utility Ware, an order from the Co-op store in Longton, Stoke-on-Trent, in 1942.

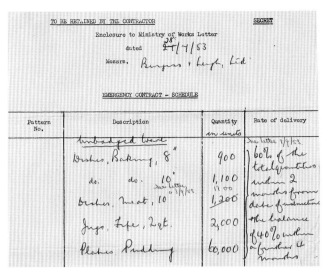

An army marches on its stomach! Burgess & Leigh make 60,000 pudding plates for the Ministry of Works.

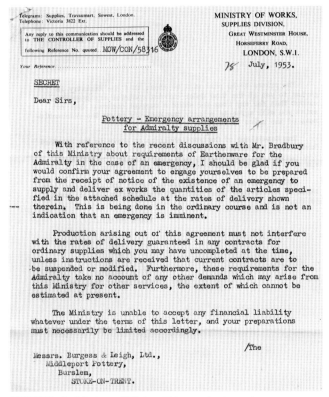

'SECRET', the Ministry of Works still instructing its earthenware supplier in July 1953.

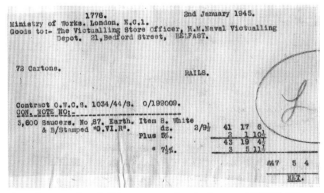

An order to produce 3,600 saucers in white backstamped 'GVIR' (King George VI).

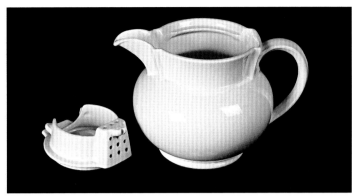

A Utility Ware white glazed teapot with 'strainer' lid patented by Burgess & Leigh during the war years.

placed each pottery manufacturer into one of three groups and allocated it a classification letter, A, B or C, to denote the maximum price which it could charge for goods. Burgess & Leigh, as good quality earthenware manufacturers, were placed in Group II and had to mark all their wares with the letter B.

It was ruled that decorated ware could only be sold in certain overseas markets in order to alleviate the national shortage of foreign currency. However, a small amount of decorated 'seconds', deemed unsuitable for export, was made available for the home market. Customers, particularly wartime brides, were desperate for such 'export rejects' and travellers vied with each other to secure them for their area. As it had been in the First World War, so, too, during the Second World War Burgess & Leigh were awarded government contracts to produce wares for the Ministry of Supply War Office and Ministry of Supply Works and Buildings.

These Government supplies, together with utility wares for the home market, essential hospital wares, and some decorated wares for export overseas, were thus to constitute the bulk of Burgess & Leigh's wartime production. Such regulations plus the loss of employees to the services meant that creative design, throughout the pottery industry, was to a large extent put 'on hold'.

Although in a reserved occupation, Bailey insisted on volunteering and left in 1942 to serve in the Royal Navy. With the retirement a year later of Charles Wilkes, then aged seventy-two years, the company was without a modeller for the remainder of the war. Bennett, who had not served during the First World War, was too old to serve in the Second and so remained at the Middleport Pottery. Restrictions meant that he was far from busy although he did design a few tableware patterns on existing shapes for export markets, in particular America and Canada: *Narcissus* on the *Tudor* shape and *Hollyhock* on the *Balmoral* (6659 and 6697) of 1942 were both pretty border patterns decorated in the usual grey print and enamel tint, '*a soundly-balanced range of decorations well-suited to the average requirements of a level-minded, middle-class public*'.[6]

Overseas markets' preference for more traditional patterns and typically English subject matter was also satisfied by the reproduction from original copper engravings of Davenport's *Hunting Scenes*, a range of items which also enjoyed lasting popularity with the home market after the war. The Pattern Book also records mugs featuring *British Sports* as well as a number of subjects from a series of print and enamel 'picture plates' produced for U.S. agents,

Two plates from Bennett's series *Ye Olde English Customs*, made for U.S. agents Fondeville. Diameter 6ins (15cms).

A publicity photograph for two typically English series, *Farmers Arms*, left, and Davenport's *Hunting Scenes*, right, 1940s.

Fondeville. Entitled *Ye Olde English Customs*, the series was designed by Bennett and depicted six '*scenes of Olde English Customs as recorded from the seventeenth century*'. Some subjects were taken directly from Cecil Aldin's *Merrie Englande* although most were inventions on a similar theme. Illustrated in a lightly drawn, lively and humorous style, the title of the series appears on the border of the plates together with that of the individual subject: *Roysterers and Nightwatchmen*; *The Maypole Dance*; *Cowcumbers to Pickle*; *The Drunkard's Cloak*; *Small Coale a Penny a Peake*; and *The Stocks*.

Patriotic Character and Toby Jugs

Wares intended to raise wartime morale at home were encouraged. Bailey, in the years before he enlisted, was kept busy modelling items of a patriotic nature, mostly toby jugs

(representing the full body) and character jugs (head only). Although samples were made either underglaze painted or with a plain ivory glaze it seems that few, if any, were put into production.[7] Neville Chamberlain was the first of these subjects to be modelled in character jug form in 1938, (Bailey had previously modelled him in profile as a wall plaque to commemorate his election in 1937.) Sir Stafford Cripps, a Labour statesman opposing Chamberlain's appeasement policy, followed soon after.

Perhaps to compete against similar products from other companies such as Royal Doulton, a series of character jugs of wartime allied leaders was then planned. Although the collection, to be entitled *The Grand Alliance*, never went into full production,[7] some jugs were produced as samples, with backstamps detailing their subject and their modeller's initials, ETB, on their reverse. All the jugs reveal Bailey's talent for accurate portraiture, which, as evidenced in models he produced in his own time, could develop into irreverent and humorous caricature. Photographs in his private papers indicate that Bailey might have been planning to model the president of the executive council in China, Chiang K'ai-shek, but this never reached the clay stage. First to be modelled instead, in 1941, were America's President Franklin Roosevelt and General McArthur. Although notes made by Bailey in 1982 state that this latter three-inch high jug was not produced, a small number may have been exported to the USA. A striking model of the Soviet Union's *Generalissimus* Joseph Stalin, with his hammer and sickle surreptitiously tucked behind his back, failed to be put into production. That of the South African Prime Minister, General Smutts, is believed to have run into copyright difficulties; a consignment of 500 had to be returned to the factory to be destroyed but not before a small sample distribution had begun in the home market. Prototype models were also produced of British Field Commander (later Field Marshall and Viscount) Montgomery (of Alamein).

Churchilliana

The distinctive characteristics of Great Britain's wartime Prime Minister, Winston Churchill, made him an ideal subject to portray but not all of Bailey's 1940-1941 models of him were produced. Of those which were, the most sought after depicts Churchill as a determined John Bull figure[8] standing astride an equally implacable bulldog. Emphasising the point, 'BULLDOGS' is written boldly across the front of the base. Fewer than 500 are thought to have been manufactured,

General Smutts, South Africa's War-time Prime Minister. Character jug, height 5ins (13cms).

Generalissimus Joseph Stalin, Soviet Union War-time leader. Character jug, height 5ins (13cms).

Franklin Roosevelt, president of the U.S.A. during the war. Character jug, height 5ins (13cms).

Sir Stafford Cripps, President of The Board of Trade from 1945. Toby jug, height 6ins (15cms).

Neville Chamberlain British Prime Minister, 1937-1940. Wall plaque, height 8¹/₂ins (21.5cms).

War-time photograph of Bailey's portraits of Churchill: in character jug form, left; as a toby jug, centre; and as a relief cameo on a loving cup with Roosevelt on the reverse.

Humorous designs from the print Record Book, above right, and above left original artwork from the archive. It is not know whether either design was produced.

From the Print Record Book, illustration of a patriotic War-time commemorative plate.

some with a detachable hat. A smaller version was also modelled in 1941 but did not go into production.

More commercially successful was Bailey's character jug portrayal of Churchill. Originally intended for the *Grand Alliance* series, it was produced, in both two-inch and three-inch sizes, for the duration of the war and for some time afterwards. Churchill is depicted in naval uniform, in his previous role as First Lord of the Admiralty. The backstamp

reads: '"WE SHALL DEFEND EVERY VILLAGE, EVERY TOWN AND EVERY CITY" CHURCHILL PREMIER 1940'. On the reissue of the character jug to commemorate Churchill's death, the backstamp was amended to include that date, 1965. (It is thought that a small bust of Churchill, modelled in 1941 in naval dress, failed to go into production.)

Bailey also modelled Churchill in toby jug form as a squat caricature, giving a thumbs up salute with his right hand and, with his left, his famous 'V' for Victory sign. 'Victory' is reproduced as a morse code message across the front of the base whilst the backstamp is impressed simply: CHURCHILL 'VICTORY'. This model was again reproduced on the death of Churchill 1965.

In 1941 a two-handled loving cup with relief-moulded heads of Churchill and Roosevelt was issued commemorating the Anglo-American wartime relationship; gilt and embossed lettering read 'Champion of Democracy' around its rim, whilst its backstamp quoted Churchill's entreaty: 'Give us the tools and we'll finish the job.'

It is not known whether Churchill, who notoriously disliked any portraits of himself, ever saw any of the Burleigh models he inspired. The nearest official approbation they received was in 1984 when Edmund Leigh, as Director of Burgess & Leigh, was invited to the opening of the Cabinet War Rooms. There, a small exhibition of Churchill 'memorabilia' was displayed including the three Burleigh Ware jugs whose *'extremely good likeness'* was commended by the organiser.[9] It is a view shared by author and expert on Churchill commemoratives, Ronald Smith.[10]

A measure of the public's enduring fascination with and respect for Churchill was the re-issue in 2000 by Burgess, Dorling & Leigh of several of the company's related wartime models: small- and miniature-sized character jugs of Churchill in naval uniform; the *Bulldogs* figure; the 'V' for *Victory toby*; the 'Champion of Democracy' loving cup; and a 'Churchill' cigar ashtray. It was also exciting to discover in store the mould for a relief-modelled plaque commemorating the Battle of Britain, its border reading: 'Never have so many owed so much to so few'. It seems that this design was not put into production in 1940 but was reproduced, hand-painted, in 2,000 in a proposed edition of 150 for Sewells, a London retailer. The plaque was subsequently made generally available with a revised backstamp.

In his spare time Bailey also modelled a number of small three-dimensional model wartime aeroplanes for presentation to his fellow firewatchers; packer Ben Ford is today the proud owner of a model Spitfire (the famous fighter aeroplane designed by Potteries-born Reginald Mitchell) which was painted for him in the factory by Mary Harper. (During the 1980s Bailey was to privately produce a plain glazed stylised model of a Spitfire with two German bombers; entitled *Spirit of the Battle of Britain*, an example is owned by the Potteries Museum in Stoke-on-Trent, which also has a small collection of Burleigh Ware.)

Dickens Toby Jugs

In the summer of 1941 Bailey began work on a series of toby jugs (not all of which went into full production)based on the illustrations by *Boz* of characters in Charles Dickens' novels, again a popular subject for many pottery manufacturers. The first five to be modelled in a suitably lively style were *Mr Pickwick, Mr Pecksniff, Mr Micawber, Sam Weller* and *Sairey*

Burleigh Dickens toby jugs. Above, left to right: *Tony Weller, Mr Pickwick, Fat Boy* and *Sairey Gamp*.

Right, top, left to right: *Mr Pecksnitff, Daniel Peggotty, Mr Micawber* and *Nicholas Nickleby*; Bottom, left to right: *Scrooge, Dickens, Oliver Twist* and *Sam Weller*.

Left, *Mrs Bardell*. Tallest *Dickens*, 7ins (180cms).

From *The Pottery Gazette*, January 1951.

Gamp. Produced in small sizes (between 13cm and 14.5cm) and originally underglaze painted, the range sold well overseas during the war through the firm's agency in the USA, Fondeville. A number of undecorated jugs was also made available for the home market.

Bailey was to add a further seven subjects to the series between 1946 and 1948: *Scrooge, Oliver Twist, Nicholas Nickleby, Daniel Peggoty, Tony Weller, Mrs Bardell* and *Fat Boy*, finally completing it in 1949 with a large size toby of *Dickens* himself. From that time the production range never exceeded eight. *Pickwick, Sam Weller, Tony Weller, Mr Pecksniff, Nickleby, Scrooge, Peggoty, Micawber* and *Dickens*. They were painted with on-glaze enamels, in varying quantities until 1985. During the 1960s, some plain aerographed pink matt and blue or brown gloss glazed versions were also made.

Records reveal that in 1941 average monthly sales

totalled £4,632 of which £2,530 was for home sales, £1,161 for export sales and £491 for government sales. Under the Limitation of Supplies Order, sales for the six months up to May 1941 were £6,665, nearly half of that for the previous six months. In spite of such a decrease, Burgess & Leigh were able to record that a normal working week was being worked with several departments doing overtime.[11] However, an announcement from Burgess & Leigh in the trade press in January 1943 showed that wartime production was not easy: *'We are endeavouring to give equitable distribution of supplies as they become available to our numerous clients.... the difficulties of manufacture in these troubled times are doubtlessly fully appreciated by the trade.'*

Post War Factory Refurbishment

Unfortunately, the hardships endured throughout the war years did not end with the cessation of hostilities in 1945. The war may have been won but the austerity of wartime Britain continued, certainly in Stoke-on-Trent where regulations governing pottery production were still in place. Many in the Potteries must have felt that they could as yet see little reward for the long hard years of the war.

Although Stoke-on-Trent had escaped the severe bomb damage to property inflicted on Britain's larger cities, several potteries (fortunately not Burgess & Leigh) had suffered some minor damage. As many were still waiting for skilled operatives to be demobilised from the Forces and for supplies of raw materials, including coal, to return to normal, it made sense for pottery manufacturers to begin repairs and long overdue improvements to their factory buildings. For some small family firms, the expense of this undertaking was just too much and, having survived the war, they then found themselves swallowed up in takeovers and mergers. Following a successful pre-war production period, Burgess & Leigh were able to avoid this. In 1947 appointing the factory's original firm of architects (now named Wood, Goldstraw & Yorath), the directors set about implementing changes to the Middleport Pottery.

Technological Changes in the Pottery Industry

Although Burgess & Leigh was to retain its traditional methods of manufacture, the Leighs, particularly Kingsley, as a member of the Council of the British Pottery Research Association, and his brother Denis, who participated in the Pottery Experimental Group during the late 1940s, were eager that the company should adapt to recent advances in technology. Therefore, whilst making improvements to the fabric of their factory buildings, they also took the opportunity to modernise production by the installation of new machinery.

Ironically, Burgess & Leigh's programme of 'modernisation' had begun earlier in c.1940 with an attempt in cost-saving DIY. The Leigh family, whilst holidaying in Wales, spied an abandoned boiler in a field. With commendable economy, they saw that, with a little repair, this now rusting piece of machinery still had a good few years' life in it. Indeed, it was just what was needed to replace the old Lancashire boiler, which had served Burgess & Leigh so well for the past fifty years or so! In the event, removal of the 'new' boiler from its frosty mountainside was too problematic. A second-hand boiler, also made in the early 1900s, was purchased instead and installed in the Middleport Pottery where it is working to this day.[12]

When necessary, however, the Leighs did not balk at financing alterations and enthusiastically implemented the most radical of the post-war changes to pottery manufacture by updating its firing methods. On visiting Stoke-on-Trent while on his 'English Journey', published in 1933, British author J. B. Priestley had written:

'I have seen few regions from which Nature has been more ruthlessly banished.....It resembles no other industrial area I know. I was at once repelled and fascinated by its odd appearance. ......although there was more smoke than I had ever seen before, so that if you looked down upon any one of these towns the drift of it was so thick that you searched for the outbreak of fire, there were no tall chimneys, no factory buildings frowning above the streets; but only a fantastic collection of narrow-necked jars or bottles peeping above the house-tops on every side.... These, of course, are the pottery kilns and ovens [which]....represent the very heart and soul of the district.'

At that time there had been around 2,000 bottle ovens in the Potteries, a number which was to decrease rapidly in the decade following the Second World War. Acting ahead of the 1956 Clean Air Act, Burgess & Leigh joined other progressive pottery manufacturers in replacing some of their bottle ovens with modern, continuous gas and electric firing tunnel kilns. The change over caused a major upheaval at the Middleport Pottery as the first of the glost ovens were demolished to make way for the erection of a building to accommodate the new tunnel kiln, together with a placing area and new glost warehousing. Space was limited but in the end there was just room – losing the old enamel placers' area and one end of the Dippers' Hot House – to install a 140-feet long Allied gas-fired tunnel oven between the 'number one' glost and biscuit bottle ovens (at the Port Street end). Throughout this six month building period in 1949, production was, amazingly, still maintained and the remaining glost ovens temporarily up and firing.

Two years later a Bricesco radiant tube enamel kiln was purchased, replacing the old Climax kiln. This time, it was the office staff who suffered as their ceiling was taken out in order to build a reinforced concrete floor to carry the weight of the new kiln above them. Fortunately, the huge expense and disruption were found to be worth it. Now pottery could be easily and cleanly placed, unprotected, on an open shelved truck made from refractory material. This then passed through each tunnel's central firing zone, emerging at the other end for cooling. The whole clean, labour-saving process took an average sixty hours to fire biscuit ware and thirty for glost. In 1951, the directors wrote proudly that *'already several of the bottle ovens have disappeared and very soon the remainder will become a memory and with them the smoke and dust inseparable from coal fired ovens.'*[13]

In fact, by 1957 the number of working ovens in the Potteries had been reduced to 550,[14] which had a dramatic effect on the landscape of the area. The city's other buildings, blackened by centuries of soot, were cleaned and the redundant slag heaps from Stoke-on-Trent's coal mines were buried, grassed over or made into lakes as part of the city's policy of land reclamation. Whilst romantics might have mourned the loss of the area's distinctive and unique character, potters welcomed the pleasanter environment which afforded them improved standards of health and working conditions.

For the directors at Burgess & Leigh this had long been a priority and their workforce was now able to take advantage of new automatic jolleying and jiggering machines to shape hollow- and flat ware. (Edmund Leigh had seen examples of similar machines in action at modern factories in California during his sales trip to America in 1952.) Although the company was never to abandon the traditional underglaze printing which had secured its reputation, it did update its machinery in the 1950s, replacing old steam heated printing machines with electrically heated ones. Later in the 1950s, a Murray-Curvex printing machine was introduced at the Middleport Pottery. First devised by Guy Murray at Spode in 1955, this machine still utilised an engraved copperplate but was fixed with a gelatine dome which transferred colour from the copperplate to unglazed biscuit flat ware. Operated by just one person instead of the team required in the traditional printing process, the machine revolutionised one-colour printing in the industry. Later in the 1960s,

Post war modernisation at the Middleport Pottery included the installation of semi-automatic machinery, here plate making in the Flat Shop.

A pristine Export Warehouse photographed in 1951.

Burgess & Leigh replaced their hand-operated model with two automatic Murray-Curvex printing machines, one of which was used for backstamps.[15] The quality of lithographs was much improved after the war and became more prevalent; new water-slide lithography, which had plastic-coated transfer-prints or 'decals', was increasingly used for multi-coloured printing, in preference to conventional 'stick down' lithography which used size or glue.

The drawbacks to the company's new cost-effective and labour-saving mechanisation were the inevitable losses of some jobs from a workforce already depleted by the war. Modern dryers, for instance, introduced in the Potters' Shops after the war, resulted in the redundancy of mould runners (and moulds!) whilst gas tunnel firing reduced the numbers of glost placers from sixteen to six and biscuit placers from seven to two.[16] Lithography marked a decline in the employment of freehand paintresses.

In certain areas of production, however, labour was still required. Ware carriers, for example, were taken on after the war specifically to relieve trained makers and decorators from a time-consuming and unskilled task. Prior to the introduction of their Murray-Curvex machines, Burgess & Leigh also recruited from Stoke-on-Trent's wartime immigrant population to relieve a shortage of skilled operatives in their underglaze printing department. The directors wrote in 1951: 'Foreign labour, Poles, Lithuanians and Germans, has been recruited and every effort is being made to add substantially to the labour force and the Firm will not rest satisfied until this department is at least as strong as before the War.'[17] The recruitment of 'foreign labour' was to cause some disquiet amongst some short-time employees later in 1952. Responding to workers' questions, Denis Leigh said 'that the firm felt that it owed a duty to the Foreign Operatives who had undertaken and were doing essential work, for which it had not been possible to obtain British Labour. Should serious unemployment arise, no doubt there would be some general agreement with the Union on the subject.'

'Mr Barry will look into the matter'

The issue of 'foreign labour' was one of many raised by the Works Production Committee, a group formed in March 1948 specifically for employers and employees to share information and concerns. Many of the committee's regular meetings were held in the new works' canteen. Together with a joiners' shop, stabling and garaging for the directors' cars, the canteen formed part of a new building erected on land adjacent to the Middleport Pottery near Harper Street. With rationing of food only finished in 1954, the post-war government was much preoccupied with nutritional matters. So it seems was Burgess & Leigh who produced a printed tableware pattern, possibly acquired from Booth's, entitled *The Healthy Vegetable Family*! If the minutes of the Works Production Committee are to be believed, employees, too, frequently had food on their minds; in February 1951, it was noted that 'a complaint had been sent in, concerning the increase of 1d on toasted cheese sandwiches. While Mr Barry offered to look into the matter when the sandwiches were next produced at the canteen, it was considered that "off-the-ration cheese" had been used, which was probably accountable for the increase.' Price increases, slow service, shortage of chairs and chipped cups were just a few of the repeated complaints regarding the canteen to be raised in meetings over the years, all of them met with the promise that 'Mr Barry will look into the matter'. In 1968, the management of the canteen, which had been carried out by an independent catering company, was taken back in-house. A Works

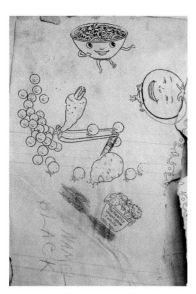

Burgess & Leigh took post-war governmental diet concerns to heart. Left, a canteen leaflet, and right, *The Healthy Vegetable Family* pattern from the Print Record Book.

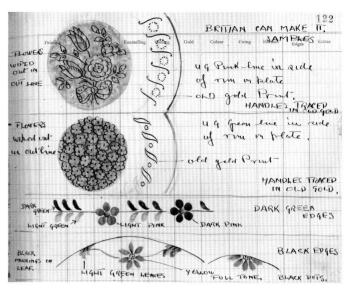

A page from the Pattern Book illustrating sample patterns produced for the 1946 *Britain Can Make It* exhibition held at the Victoria and Albert Museum.

Production Committee representative promptly enquired *'whether the Canteen Manageress could include fritters on the menu for Fridays? Everyone agreed that it was quite an extra amount of work for one person, but Mr Barry promised to look into the matter'*. In 1983 the canteen building and land was eventually sold, *'Mr Barry'* no longer had to *'look into the matter'*!

Although the concerns regarding the canteen might in retrospect seem trivial, the founding of the Works Production Committee was a progressive move by Burgess & Leigh and provided a genuinely useful forum for workers to air worries and management to give reassurances relating to issues of production, employment, training, safety and building repairs.

'Fancies' and Festivals
Production was uppermost in the directors' minds in the immediate post-war period. Signs of recovery had first come in 1945 when, under the *'Domestic Pottery Manufacture and Supply Order'*, certain manufacturers, Burgess & Leigh included, were granted licence by Sir Stafford Cripps, then President of the Board of Trade, to produce 'fancies' or ornamental decorative wares for the home trade.

Like all manufacturers, Burgess & Leigh were keen to start production for the home market again. However, without Bailey, who was not back at his bench until the following year (being hospitalised with a leg injury sustained during active service), the company was forced to resume manufacture of its pre-war wares. A limited number of Flower Jugs was made along with traditional *'Reproduction Period Jugs'* and toby jugs. It was also decided to reproduce the *'Giraffe'* jug in the style of the pre-war yellow glazed jugs, but in the event only a very small number were produced.

Under the instigation of Sir Stafford Cripps, the Council for Industrial Design (founded in 1944 to encourage good design) mounted an exhibition to boost trade at the Victoria and Albert Museum in 1946. Opened by King George VI, the exhibition was entitled *'Britain Can Make It'*, a pun on the wartime slogan *'Britain Can Take It'*. Burgess & Leigh were pleased to be amongst the pottery manufacturers selected as possible exhibitors. The exhibition received considerable coverage by the press, which dubbed it *'Britain*

Can't Have It' as many of the designs displayed there were still bound by government restrictions and available to export markets only. Photographs of Burgess & Leigh's selected tablewares featured on the front page of Staffordshire's *Evening Sentinel*.[18] With Bennett's floral patterns on Bailey's *Tudor* and *Balmoral* shapes, these contrasting designs exemplified both the pretty, traditional and the more linear, modern styles then in vogue. A Burleigh Ware coverdish and plate now in the reserve collection of the Victoria and Albert Museum and purchased by them in 1948 for 18s 0d and 2s 6d respectively were probably selected from those exhibited in 1946.[19] The exhibition did much to awaken a new interest in design, especially amongst the young. The marriage of HRH Princess Elizabeth (now HM the Queen) to HRH Prince Phillip in 1947 and the Ideal Home Exhibitions staged at Olympia in London in the late 1940s, also contributed to the new focus on home-making and consumerism.

'London' Toby Jugs
London was the inspiration for two toby jugs produced in 1949: *Ye Olde Yeoman of the Guard*, commonly called the *Beefeater*, and the *Chelsea Pensioner*. These wonderfully characterful models in their distinctive and colourful uniforms were painted both underglaze and, later and less

The Beefeater, left, and the *Chelsea Pensioner*. Height 7½ins (19cms).

effectively, on-glaze with gilding. *Beefeater* models produced prior to the coronation of Queen Elizabeth II in 1953 bear King George VI's cypher, GR, rather than that of the Queen, ER. An informative printed backstamp and an impressed '*ET Bailey*' are included on the base of the toby jugs. Designed with tourists, specifically Americans, very much in mind, they were stocked by outlets such as Harrods in London.

Shakespeare Toby Jugs

It was the company's American agents, Fondeville, who requested a *Shakespeare* collection in a similar style to Bailey's *Dickens* series of toby jugs. Bailey began the collection in 1950 with a large size *William Shakespeare* toby jug, complete with the bard's signature and dates, 1564-1616, incised on its base. Fifteen different small-sized Shakespearean characters followed, Bailey's notes from 1982 indicating that the modelling time for the whole collection was an impressive five weeks. The smaller tobies included *Macbeth, Touchstone, Shylock, Wolsey, Falstaff, Romeo, Portia* and *A Midsummer Night's Dream*. This latter subject was a

Shakespeare toby jugs. Top, left to right: *Othello, Romeo, Juliet* and *Julius Ceasar*; Bottom, left to right: *Ophelia, King Lear, Malvolio* and *A Midsummer Night's Dream*.

Top, left to right: *Wolsey, William Shakespeare* and *Portia*; bottom: *Shylock, Falstaff, Touchstone* and *Macbeth*. *Shakespeare* height, 6ins (15cms).

A selection of Shakespeare tobies were revived in the 1960s and produced with an aerographed blue glaze, here, photographed outside Ford Green Hall in Staffordshire.

slightly smaller and more complex model featuring *Bottom* as an ass with *Titania* and a playful *Puck* either side. Additional tobies made in smaller quantities were *Julius Caesar* and *Ophelia* whilst those not put into full production were *Malvolio, Othello, King Lear* and *Juliet*.[20] Unfortunately, sales failed to match the earlier *Dickens* series whose better-known subjects were perhaps better suited to Bailey's vigorous style. Nonetheless, the company continued their manufacture and from the 1960s produced some subjects from the series, like the *Dickens* toby jugs, aerographed in blue, pink or in gloss brown. More recently, Burgess, Dorling & Leigh produced samples of certain models from the series together with a number never before put into full production.

'Fifties Festivities: '*A Century of Progress*'

The success generated by the Ideal Home exhibitions of the late 1940s prompted the then Labour government to make plans to mark the centenary of the 1851 Great Exhibition; just as its predecessor had done 100 years ago, the new Festival of Britain, as it was called, would act as a showcase for everything that Britain had to offer in the Arts, Sciences, Architecture, Technology and Industrial Design. Built on a twenty-seven acre bombsite next to Waterloo Station in London, the Festival was opened by King George VI in the presence of Winston Churchill, by then re-elected as the country's Prime Minister. A total of 10,000 objects were displayed in specially designed pavilions, drumming up trade for some 3,500 firms.[21] The success of the Festival was summed up by one of Britain's promising playwrights, Michael Frayn, who wrote that it '*was a rainbow – a brilliant sign riding the tail of the storm and promising fairer weather. It marked the end of the hungry 'forties, and the beginning of an altogether easier decade.*'[22]

Hopes for an 'easier decade' were not bright, however, in Stoke-on-Trent as the pottery industry faced a new international competitiveness. To succeed against European, American and Japanese competitors, it had to make rapid and drastic changes in both manufacture and design. Burgess & Leigh showed a characteristic enthusiasm, even producing a tableware pattern called *Festival*. While the government had been organising the Festival of Britain, they too had been busy drawing up plans. The company had its own centenary to celebrate and designs to display in its smart new Showroom at the Middleport Pottery.

The decision to celebrate the centenary of Burgess & Leigh in 1951 continues to be a subject of some debate, as there is contention over the exact date of the firm's founding. There can be no doubt from company archives and trade gazettes that the founders of Burgess & Leigh first established their business partnership in 1862. 1851 was the first year of trading of Hulme & Booth, from whom Burgess & Leigh acquired moulds, coppers and the lease of the Central Pottery in 1862. At some stage, the company adopted Hulme & Booth's founding date as its own, having effectively taken over the firm as a going concern.

Both founding dates, 1851 and 1862, have been quoted in the press at various times over the years. A trade advertisement in *The Pottery Gazette* in 1898 was the first to give the founding date as 1851. However, on 1st August, 1911, *The Pottery Gazette* wrote: '*Edmund Leigh 'reported that early next year the business would celebrate its fiftieth anniversary. He thought it constituted a record in the Potteries that the present partners of a firm which was established in 1862 should be the sons of the founders'*. By 1913 *The Pottery Gazette* once more gave 1851 as the date of first establishment! '*Est.d 1851*' was also incorporated into the redesign of its 'beehive' backstamp in c.1929, thus permanently setting the questionable founding date in stone – or at least in print. Since then, 1851 has been used consistently in all backstamps and company literature. In keeping with the best of royal traditions, it seems that Burgess & Leigh can celebrate two birthdays – one actual and one official!

Thus, the company chose to celebrate its 100th birthday in 1951 and in some style. It was not the only pottery to do so; in June *The Pottery Gazette* reported: '*It seems that centenaries and jubilees are very fashionable this year of grace 1951 for not only is this Festival Year, but several pottery manufactories, appropriately enough, are celebrating bicentenaries, centenaries and jubilees*'; amongst those mentioned were Royal Worcester celebrating its bicentenary; Weatherby's its sixtieth anniversary; and both Meakin's and '*the famous firm*' of Burgess & Leigh, their centenaries.

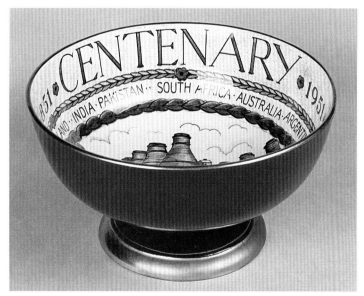

Bowl, underglaze decorated in blue and brown with Bennett's view of the Middleport Pottery (as plaque, shown above) and '*gilt in best gold*', 1951. Diameter 16ins (41cms).

The Middleport Pottery hand-painted in sepia by Harold Bennett on a wall plaque commemorating the company's centenary in 1951. Diameter 16ins (41cms).

Centenary wall plaque, hand-painted and gilded, with 'B&L' insignia and the names of the company's overseas markets, 1951. Diameter 16ins (41cms).

Burgess & Leigh made numerous commemorative items for the occasion, in small numbers, '*all richly decorated in accordance with traditional techniques and depicting various stages in the development of the firm.*'[23] Large wall plaques featured several attractive hand-painted designs by Harold Bennett. These included the Coat of Arms of Burslem within a border reading *BURGESS & LEIGH CENTENARY* and the names of the directors past and present; the famous Burleigh beehive mark; and a view of the Middleport Pottery (this also appearing on a bowl framed by a commemorative border listing the company's overseas markets). *The Pottery and Glass Record* reporting the '*Centenary of Burgess & Leigh*' in November 1951 described one bowl as *'decorated in underglaze blue and brown, and elaborately gilt in best gold. The inside of the bowl has a commemorative inscription, while on the outside are depicted the various processes of pottery manufacture – throwing, printing, placing, mould-making and packing.'*

Perhaps most ambitious in design was Bailey's relief-modelled wall plaque, which is literally a potted history of the company. This complex design shows an oak tree with shields in its branches inscribed with the names of members of the Burgess & Leigh families whilst ribbons winding around and spreading from the tree trunk name the company's home and export markets then: *Great Britain, Australia, New Zealand, South Africa, South America, Canada, the USA, Norway, Ceylon, Pakistan* and *India*. In the background are scenes of pottery manufacture with the names of Burgess & Leigh's potteries and dates: the *Central Pottery 1851-1868*, the *Hill Pottery 1868-1888* and the *Middleport Pottery 1889-1951*. The company's monogram B & L appears to the top of the plaque; the coats of arms of the county of Stafford and the city of Stoke-on-Trent are either side; and *To Commemorate the Centenary of Burgess & Leigh*

Prototype bust of Edmund Leigh, with glasses, left, and as it was produced, without glasses and enamelled, in 1951. Height 8³/₄ins (22cms).

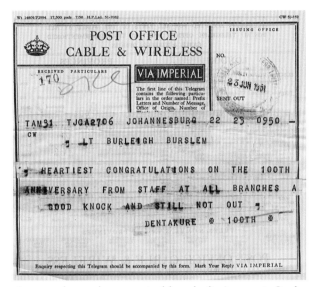

A congratulatory telegram received from the firm's agency in South Africa: *'Good Knock and Still Not Out'*.

Bailey's relief-modelled plaque commemorating the centenary of Burgess & Leigh, 1951. Diameter 16ins (41cms).

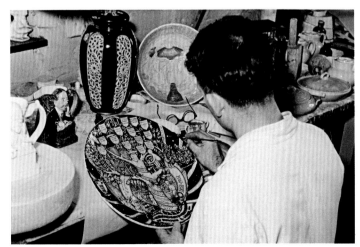

Bailey at work on the plaque in his studio, 1951.

Ltd is inscribed on a garland at its base. Further garlands are inscribed: *A Century of Progress* and the dates *1851-1951*. The relief modelling has a buff or sepia glaze against a coloured and gilded background.

Bailey also produced two portraits of the company's first chairman, Edmund Leigh: a finely modelled bust, only a few of which seem to have been made, and a jug, the front of which shows a relief-model of *'Edmund Leigh JP'*, sitting at his magistrate's bench, teapot in hand! Incised on the front of the jug at its base are the dates of the years the company spent at the Hill Pottery. Approximately twenty-four of this design were made for distribution to overseas agencies and dealers.

Further tribute to the firm's overseas representatives was made in a centenary pamphlet *'A Century of Progress 1851-1951'*. With a keen eye on further export opportunities, the pamphlet read:

'It is a coincidence that the Centenary year of Burgess & Leigh falls in the year of the Festival of Britain when no doubt many of the Firm's valued customers will be visiting this island. We hope that they will be able to visit our Factory, where we shall be very happy to show them Burleigh Ware in the making.'

Providing a brief history of the company, the pamphlet also acknowledged the loyal service of the company's employees at the Middleport Pottery many of whom were now close to retiring age; in 1940 over twenty men and women had served fifty years or more at the factory, the record being held by the Head Packer who had completed sixty-eight years on his retirement! As a mark of thanks to their workforce in the new Showroom, each employee was presented with a certificate and a small gilded mug, decorated with a sepia printed scene of the Middleport Pottery, again taken from an original watercolour design by Bennett.

A celebratory dinner held in June at Ash Hall Hotel was attended by overseas representatives from Australia, New Zealand, South Africa and America, members of the staff, manufacturers and officials from both the British Pottery Manufacturers' Federation and the National Society of Pottery Workers. Reported in the *Evening Sentinel* under the headline *'Value of Family Tradition'*, the dinner was followed by one in December for staff and their families at the George Hotel in Burslem. Again, the celebration paid tribute to the Burgess & Leigh employees with the presentation of a cheque to the newly appointed director, Mr A. H. Holdcroft.

Unfortunately, ill health prevented Kingsley (who had celebrated his sixty-seventh birthday on 1st April of that year) from attending this last event but Denis, replying to a speech from Mr G. Lloyd, then Sales Manager, said that:

'Mr Kingsley and himself had been associated in the business for nearly forty-six years, for thirty of which they had been in sole charge. Despite the harassing nature of their responsibilities, there had been many compensations, and he was very happy to state that at no time had there been anything in the nature of a quarrel, and he was pleased and proud that the relationship between directors, management and work people had always been a happy one…. The secret of their own success lay primarily in the sound foundations

Bennett's design used to decorate mugs presented to all the Middleport Pottery employees in 1951, from the Print Record Book.

14

OCTOBER/15/1951.

1851.   CENTENARY   1951.
                 of
           BURLEIGH WARE.

'To commemorate this occasion, a Mug has been specially Modelled and Designed, which the Directors have pleasure in presenting to you as a memento, with their compliments!

The certificate accompanying each presentation mug.

laid by the late William Leigh and the late Mr F. R. Burgess, whose motto had been "good products at a fair price".'

Sadly Kingsley continued to suffer from ill-health over the next few years and he died in December 1954 leaving his wife and two sons, Barry and Edmund, by then directors of the family firm. Kingsley had been Chairman of Dalehall Mills Ltd in Burslem; *'one of the staunchest supporters'*[24] of the British Ceramic Research Association; and a member of the Council of the Chamber of Commerce. As Chairman of Burgess & Leigh for over thirty years, Kingsley must take credit for the company's outstanding success during the late 1920s and 1930s. At the thirty-sixth Annual Meeting of the Shareholders of Burgess & Leigh, it was recorded that *'under his personal direction (often carried out under acute illness), the company prospered even at times of general trade depression. These results were mainly due to his inspiration and guidance.'* Kingsley would readily have acknowledged the parts played by other members of his family, particularly his brother, Denis, not to mention the company's workforce, in what had been perhaps the Middleport Pottery's greatest commercial and design success.

Burgess & Leigh's centenary celebrations in 1951 would not have been complete without a visit in June to the Festival of Britain. So it was that the directors, management and workpeople of Burgess & Leigh, who always enjoyed an annual outing to such places as Blackpool or north Wales, set off from Burslem railway station at five o'clock one fine morning to travel by steam train to London. The *'mammoth of a day'* is remembered[25] with great delight: breakfast served before arrival at Euston, a boat trip to Greenwich in the morning followed by a visit to the Festival during the afternoon and an evening at Battersea Fun Fair. There was a long walk back to catch the overnight train to Stoke, the Works Production Committee later noting that *'appreciation was expressed for the gesture of Mr and Mrs Edmund in being present at the departure of the party on the homeward journey.'* A late supper was enjoyed on the train before arriving back at 4.45am in Burslem, by then, it is remembered, deep under unseasonal snow!

Wartime Restrictions Lifted

It was in the following spring of 1952 that the first indications came that war instructions governing pottery manufacture were gradually being lifted. Then the Board of Trade announced that the home market could purchase 'frustrated exports', the name given to huge stocks of decorated wares which many potteries had accumulated following the reduction in imports imposed by British Commonwealth countries. In the summer of the same year came the news for which Burgess & Leigh and all potteries had been waiting: sales of decorated wares were to be permitted for the home market and price controls removed. Pottery manufacturers were at last given back the freedom to produce new wares for a home market which, for ten long years, had been starved of colour and innovation in design.

One would expect there to have been an outburst of creativity in ceramic design. However, public taste at home was something of an unknown quantity to manufacturers for a while and many potteries played safe, reproducing a selection of tried and tested pre-war wares alongside wartime export ranges. Gradually, however, as industrial confidence returned, existing ranges were expanded and new ones introduced.

Commemorative Wares

The production of commemorative wares for the Coronation of Queen Elizabeth II provided a more than welcome boost to the trade, making the years 1953-1954 extremely profitable for Burgess & Leigh. Although records are scant, the company had produced commemorative wares since the late nineteenth century, usually celebrating the achievements of national political and wartime figures, such as Gladstone, Lord Roberts, Kitchener, Churchill and others. Occasionally, they were asked to produce items commemorating specific events, like the 1929 Royal National Eisteddfod of Wales.

Like all pottery manufacturers, the company produced commemoratives for royal events, usually with officially approved designs. Occasionally, items were commissioned by specific retailers and incorporated their name. Queen Victoria's long reign provided potteries with many occasions to commemorate. Burgess & Leigh may have produced items at the Hill Pottery for her Golden Jubilee in 1887. Certainly, they commemorated her Diamond Jubilee in 1897 with the production of an elaborately shaped teapot featuring a blue

Oval plaque, with relief-moulded border, featuring underglaze blue printed portrait of Gladstone, designed by Swettenham. Issued in 1898 to commemorate The statesman's death. Length approximately 15¹/₂ins (39cms).

A page from the Print Record Book illustrating a design commemorating the English novelist, Charles Dickens.

A page from the Print Record Book showing prints used on the teapot below.

Moulded and gilded teapot with underglaze blue printed portrait of Queen Victoria, issued to commemorate her Diamond jubilee in 1897.

Underglaze printed plate of Caernarvon Castle in Wales. Issued to commemorate the Coronation of King Geroge V who had been made prince of Wales in 1901. Diameter 8³/₄ins (22cms).

A commissioned commemorative Coronation design illustrated in the Print Record Book.

printed portrait. (A tableware pattern was also produced with the name *Victoria* in recognition of the Queen.) The Coronations of King Edward VII and Queen Alexandra in 1902 and of King George V and Queen Mary in 1911 were also commemorated with items such as simple 'print and enamel' beakers and cups and saucers.

During the 1930s, the skills of Bailey and Bennett were utilised in the production of relief-moulded shapes and printed and hand-painted designs. An impressive round plaque was modelled by Bailey to commemorate the Jubilee of George V and Mary in 1935; it featured a double portrait of the King and Queen and was produced in plain, matt coloured glazes in green, oatmeal and pale blue. The Royal Standard flag was the inspiration for a tall relief-embossed and gilded jug with a distinctive 'GM' monogram to its neck.

Double portrait plaque of King George V and Queen Mary issued in 1935 to commemorate their Silver Jubilee. Diameter approximately 15³/₄ins (40cms).

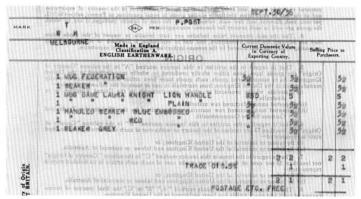

An order from Australia for a *'Dame Laura Knight'* commemorative mug, 1936.

Above, right, ivory glazed and gilded cup and saucer, with Union Jack handle. Coloured lithographic print features a portrait of King George V and Queen Mary whose Jubilee it commemorates, 1935.

Other 'Jubilee Ware' items from the print Record Book, left.

Mug with elaborately modelled handle and coloured lithographic print commemorating the 'Coronation' of King Edward VIII who abdicated in 1936.

A plainer mug with a revised print featuring the portrait of King George VI and Queen Elizabeth, 1937.

An original lithographic transfer print designed by Dame Laura Knight for the 'Coronation that never was'.

Relief-embossed Loving Cup, left, originally produced for the coronation of Queen Elizabeth II and an ivory glazed and gilt jug based on the Royal Standard, issued in 1935 for the Silver Jubilee of King George V and Queen Mary. Taller approximately 10ins (25.4cms).

Original artwork by Harold Bennett for items produced on the coronation of Queen Elizabeth II in 1953.

At the same time, tableware items were produced with a printed commemorative design, and Union Jack handles, some of which Queen Mary herself purchased from the Burgess & Leigh stand at the BIF.

Before King Edward VIII abdicated in 1936, the company had produced wares in preparation for what became known as 'the coronation that never was'. These included another finely modelled, plain glazed portrait plaque by Bailey and a small commemorative mug with a stylish and distinctive multi-coloured printed design by Dame Laura Knight, the British painter elected to the Royal Academy the same year. (Other companies also produced her official design.)[26] Instructions were given for the lithographic transfers to be destroyed and a revised print was made for a similar sized, different shaped mug for the Coronation in 1937 of King George VI and Queen Elizabeth. An official photograph by Marcus Adams was the likely source for Bailey's relief-moulded plaque featuring the King and Queen and their two young daughters, the Princesses Elizabeth and Margaret. To mark the Queen's Golden Jubilee in 2002, Burgess, Dorling & Leigh reproduced the plaque, with a selection of 1953 Coronation commemorative items, exclusively for Buckingham Palace's gift shop. All items were decorated with a blue wash and gilded. (A miniature *Guardsman* Flower Jug was also included in the range, in either the same decoration or in red and blue colours.)

The 1953 Coronation prompted a burst of activity in the Middleport Pottery. Cup machines were utilised for the production of many hundreds of cups, mugs and beakers. Some forty lithographers were then employed to apply lithographic prints; the Pattern Book records several, most featuring the Queen's portrait and one showing Windsor Castle and Westminster Abbey. Other mugs and a plate were embossed with double head 'cameo' portraits of Queen Elizabeth and Prince Phillip within an oval laurel frame. An embossed and gilded two-handled loving cup showed a single portrait of the Queen. The 1937 embossed 'Royal Standard' jug was also reproduced, with the 'GM' monogram adapted to 'ER'. Bailey modelled three, more elaborate, jugs which were produced for the occasion in small numbers. The first of these was decorated with an embossed and incised composition showing the Queen's Coronation in Westminster Abbey; it was available either hand-painted

underglaze or, less expensively, in a plain blue or red tinted 'wash' glaze. A second high-relief jug depicts the Queen seated on the *'Great Gothic Chair'* used in the Coronation ceremony. Its detailed backstamp[27] reveals the painstaking historical research which Bailey applied to these and all of his subsequent large commemorative pieces.

Occasionally, Bailey's more ornate designs brought problems and this was the case with the third jug commemorating the Queen's Coronation, a representation of the Queen on horseback during the Trooping of the Colour ceremony. Modelled without the horse's legs, it gave the rather unfortunate impression of horse and royal rider ploughing through a field! Press reaction was not favourable. As he had done with his very first *Parrot* Flower Jug, Bailey took the criticism on board and later remodelled the piece to show the whole body of the horse. Twenty-four of the jugs were subsequently issued, hand-painted and gilded, to commemorate the Queen's Silver Jubilee in 1977.

Another of Bailey's complex designs was A *Great Lineage* Jug whose relief-moulded and embossed composition,

Bailey's ornate relief-modelled jug, A *Great Lineage*, first issued in c.1959 and revived in 1970 to mark the 250th anniversary of the *Mayflower's* sailing from Plymouth to North America. Height 11ins (28cms).

Bailey at work on the 'Trooping of the Colour' Jug shown completed, right.

The 'Trooping of the Colour Jug' twenty-four of which were produced for the Queen's Silver Jubilee in 1977. Height 10³/₄ins (27.5cms).

Jugs, produced for the coronation of Queen Eizabeth II in 1953. Left 'the Great Gothic Chair; centre, 'The Trooping of the Colour' and right, 'The Coronation Ceremony'. Tallest approximately 10ins (25.4cms).

together with a lengthy inscribed backstamp, describes the American ancestry of Queen Elizabeth II. Distinctive features of the jug are the portrait of the Queen to the centre of the jug and a model of a Native American Indian to its handle. The Canadian China and Glass Company of Toronto distributed the jug to coincide with the Queen's tour of Canada in 1959. The jug was revived in 1970 to mark the 250th anniversary of the Pilgrim Fathers' sailing from Plymouth to North America, and from this time became known as the *Mayflower* Jug. An inexpensive sepia-wash glaze, highlighting its many details, imitated the Victorian Parian and stoneware relief-moulded jugs which inspired its design. (Simpler commemorative plates and trays, with

printed designs and occasional gilding, were also produced in 1970 to commemorate the sailing of the *Mayflower*).

Although Bailey had a tendency towards elaboration in the design of some decorative items, his tablewares were more simply shaped. His plain cylindrical half-pint mug, for instance, was selected as a commemorative item for Queen Elizabeth II's 1977 Jubilee. Decorated with a three colourful and stylish designs of the Queen's silhouette and Royal Cyphers (by David Copeland, Art Designer from 1963), it was amongst a number of products selected by a panel of judges, including HRH The Prince of Wales, for inclusion in a special Design Council exhibition of well-designed and tasteful souvenirs for the Queen's Silver Jubilee. Burgess &

Leigh endeavoured to apply the same design criterion to subsequent commemorative items, such as a mug with an '80' shaped handle produced for the birthday of Queen Elizabeth the Queen Mother in 1980, and a printed floral gift ware range for the marriage of Prince Charles and Lady Diana Spencer in 1981.

Exports in the Post-War Period

As it struggled to return to normality post-war, the pottery industry faced continuing competition from abroad and

Award winning mugs designed by Art Director David Copeland for the Queen's Silver Jubilee, 1977. Height 3¹/₄ins (8cms).

Items produced for the eightieth birthday of Queen Elizabeth the Queen Mother in 1980. Shapes by Bailey, printed designs bought in from Johnson Matthey.

Simply shaped mugs from Bailey and plain graphic designs from David Copeland for mugs issued for the marriage of Prince Charles and Lady Diana Spencer in 1981. Height 3¹/₄ins (8cms).

output fell, especially of earthenwares. Burgess & Leigh's export drive started in 1952 with Edmund Leigh's promotional tour to North America. Crossing the United States and Canada by rail, he stopped at each provincial capital to display Burgess & Leigh products in hired stock rooms. It was Barry's turn in 1954 when, with no sales experience whatsoever, he was sent to South Africa. He was by all accounts eased in gently: 'A fortnight's sea voyage in the 'Windsor Castle' with the weather becoming progressively warmer did not involve much work except for an hour or two each morning with a large scale map of South Africa and a list of customers. Deck games, two swims a day, sunbathing and dining each evening in dinner jacket played a large part'.[28] But a 'steep learning curve' began on shore; in five weeks he showed fourteen new patterns to a total of 117 customers in Cape Town, Port Elizabeth, East London, Dunbar and Pitermaritzberg, Johannesburg, Pretoria and Reef Towns, Salisbury and Bulawayo. A tortuous flight home took thirty-four hours with stops at Livingstone, Nairobi, Khartoum, Cairo, Athens, Rome and Frankfurt! It was a journey Barry must have eventually come to consider worth undertaking, at least by the following year when invoicing to South Africa had doubled, making it for a while Burgess & Leigh's largest export market.[29]

In 1957 Edmund was back on the road, this time in Australia and New Zealand where he spent four and a half months. Again, his visit gave satisfactory sales results in spite of increased competition from Germany and Japan in Australia and the tightness of bank credit in New Zealand. Eager to explore new export markets, particularly in Europe, in 1956 Burgess & Leigh appointed Ove Larsen as Scandinavian agent. Throughout the 1950s period, exports accounted for some thirty to forty per cent of the company's total sales.[30]

Back to the Future: *Fantasia* and other Burleigh Ware Designs of the 1950s

At home, in spite of reassurances from the Conservative Prime Minister, Harold Macmillan, that 'most of our people have never had it so good', there was considerable hardship in the pottery industry in the mid-1950s. A decrease in sales as a result of a raised purchase tax on domestic pottery led to redundancies and short term working in the Potteries. The Suez crisis brought petrol rationing although transport and other strikes fortunately had only a limited effect on Burgess & Leigh.[31]

A plain glazed and gilded bust, left, and painted figure of George Bernard Shaw, modelled privately by Bailey during the 1950s. Taller approximately 7ins (18cms).

Toby Philpott teaset comprising sugar bowl, teapot and milk jug, issued in the early 1950s. Tallest 6ins (15cms).

Sioux Indian character jug modelled by Bailey c.1954, originally produced for the Canadian market. Height 5¼ins (13cms).

Bird-shaped flower holders intoduced in 1955 with a primrose yellow glaze, naturalistically painted. Tallest approximately 6ins (15cms).

At the Middleport Pottery, Bailey must have felt a rather isolated figure without the companionship of Wilkes. Like many, he had been unsettled by the war and for a time in the early 1950s, he had even contemplated setting up his own business in partnership with his brothers. At this time, he modelled numerous character figures, in rough clay, whilst his brothers trialed small printed items in bone china, such as brooches, for possible production ranges. In the end as new challenges presented themselves within their existing jobs, the Bailey brothers decided to remain with their respective and reliable employers.

Following his 1951 company and 1953 royal commemoratives, Bailey returned to more familiar subjects. In 1954 he modelled two new jugs, *Lupin* and *Tally Ho*, to add to a pared down collection of the 1930s yellow glazed Flower Jugs which the company had advertised the previous year. His *Pixie* and *Acorn* teawares were revised slightly and the *Verona* range expanded and adapted. Bailey also continued to produce the occasional character jug. In 1954 he modelled a *Sioux Indian*, which was produced, with underglaze painting, for the Canadian market until c.1960. A small novelty teaset, depicting the traditional 'toper', *Toby Philpott*, was also issued, comprising an underglaze painted teapot, cream jug and lidded sugar bowl. Although the set failed to sell well, it was made intermittently, in small numbers until c.1980. More successful was Bailey's *Cactus* range of ornamental vases, jugs and bowls, which, like his earlier *Cauliflower* series, was inspired by natural forms. It was produced for several years in different decorations, one version being aerographed in 'elephant' grey and shaded crimson at the base.

A new range of small-sized, brightly coloured flower holders was introduced in 1955, each modelled as a bird. The collection numbered six: a wren, blue tit, bullfinch,

kingfisher and budgerigar were modelled in small sizes whilst a turkey was made in a larger size. Bailey also modelled a large sized owl and cockatoo at the same time but these failed to go into full production. The bird flower jugs were produced naturalistically painted and with a yellow glaze like the earlier Flower Jugs whose success they sought, and unfortunately failed, to replicate. A grey and crimson colouring is more rarely found. In 2000 Burgess, Dorling & Leigh revived the turkey jug, producing 100 for an American retailer.

A popular and detailed model of a bottle oven has also been recently revived. It was thought that Bailey modelled it during the 1950s, when it was reproduced, unmarked, as a lamp base with a parchment shade for Charles F. Bristol & Son Ltd of Regent Place Birmingham. However, factory

Model of a bottle oven by Bailey. Originally produced as a lamp base in the 1950s, c.2001. Height 8ins (20cms).

notebooks indicate that the model dates from the late 1930s when Bailey is believed to have included Stan Johnson's father, a glost fireman, in the low relief modelling. A trade advertisement for *'Dealers' Accessories'* made the suggestion: *'The attractive little lamp would add its own interest to a display of pottery, the base being in the form of a pottery kiln with tiny figures depicting operatives at work in the pottery.'*

Display and design had reasserted themselves as topics of discussion in post-war style-conscious Britain. In 1956 the Design Centre first opened in London as a showcase for 'Design Centre Approved' products. By then the 'New Look' or 'Contemporary' style showcased at the 1951 Festival of Britain was beginning to be more readily accepted by an increasingly affluent and independent public. Ceramic design reflected the interests of the new aspirational, atomic age: shapes were streamlined and curvilinear while patterns included delineated stars and dots, microscopically observed natural forms and consumer durables! Design and new technology had a reciprocal influence. The printing methods offered by the Murray-Curvex machine brought a predominance of single colour patterns, perhaps highlighted with contrastingly block-coloured holloware or enamelled details. Colours were either bright primaries or more muted pastels, pale turquoises and greys, more suited to the light open-plan Scandinavian-style interiors.

Burgess & Leigh produced new designs to tempt young homemakers. Post war, Bennett was encouraged to use less costly painting in his pattern designs and printed versions of his old Art Deco patterns, *Pan*, *Riviera* and *Maytime* were introduced on a new *London* shape. More successful was *Kensington* (8188), a design similar to that shown at the 1946 *'Britain Can Make It'* exhibition. Although advertised in 1956 as a *'contemporary design'*, its traditional *Tudor* shape and *'old gold line at the rim'* suggest something of a compromise in style. From 1956, Burgess & Leigh showcased their new products at the Blackpool Trade Fair. They used Rooms 249 and 251, one for tableware and the other for 'fancies', at the Imperial Hotel where, before the introduction of large purpose built exhibition centres, exhibitors would sometimes display their wares on makeshift stands set up in salesmens' bedrooms!

It was not until Bailey's *Viscount* shape made its appearance in 1956 that Burgess & Leigh showed a return to their pre-war form. The new shape's rimless coupe flat ware and sleek curvaceous holloware had something of Bailey's earlier – and then still current – *Balmoral* shape, but the sharper edges of *Viscount* gave it a more truly 'contemporary'

From *The Pottery Gazette*, March 1951.

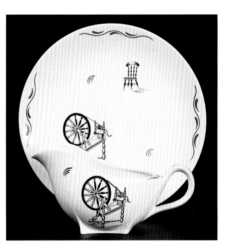

A less than successful mix of the traditional and modern, pattern 8541 on *Viscount* shape, late 1950s. Diameter 10ins (25cms).

style. *Thistledown* and *Starlight* were both produced on *Viscount*; the first, a wispy floral design with either a red, green or black shoulder band, and the second, a delicate border pattern of thin black lines broken by red stars, showed that Burgess & Leigh's design team could still keep pace with current styles.

One of the most effective patterns to be used on *Viscount*, and that which most typifies 1950s designs, is Bennett's *Fantasia*. Advertised in the trade press in 1959 as *'a fresh treatment of the fashionable black and white theme'*, the Pattern Book describes it simply as *'bottles'*! This refers to its random all-over design of overlapping flasks, pots, cups and bowls, which were simply outlined, stippled or block-coloured in black. Printed underglaze, its holloware shapes, excepting its coffeepot and teapot, together with small lids and bases were decorated with a solid black matt glaze. This style of decoration was typical of those patterns printed with the Murray-Curvex machine, such as Enid Seeney's *Homemaker*

A Harold Bennett design, in fashionable grey and red, on the *Viscount* shape, late 1950s.

'fantasia'
A fresh treatment
of the fashionable
black and white theme

Bennett's *Fantasia* on Bailey's *Viscount*, from *The Pottery Gazette*, 1959.

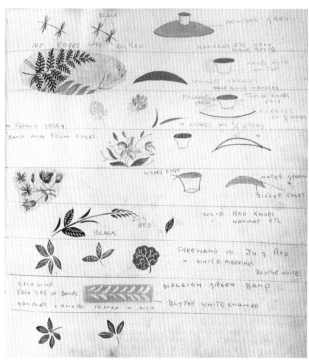

A page from the Pattern Book showing typical 1950s designs.

being displayed at the Design Centre in London and at the Council of Industrial Design exhibitions in Glasgow, Bristol and Southsea. The same year also saw the launch of a new white earthenware body, on the *Windsor* shape. New backstamps were engraved to incorporate the white body's new name, '*Ironstone*', chosen to suggest durability and strength. Gradually it replaced the old ivory-coloured body for all new patterns, such as *Hyde Park*, as well as older traditional ones, such as the '*Dillwyn*' *Willow* which was heavily promoted from this time.

Bailey modelled various vases, jugs and bowls for new ornamental series, whose decoration often matched that of tableware ranges. *Polperro*, for example, a black printed design by Bennett of sailing ships in the Cornish harbour town, was produced on both dinner ware and a range of vases with aerographed red interiors. The *Marlborough* ornamental collection, with embossed leaves and berries, was a particularly successful and long-lasting range. It was produced in a variety of colourways: with mottled beige or green grounds, and autumnal tints.

Other vases were modelled by Bailey in 'contemporary' curvilinear shapes and given fashion-conscious names like

"MARLBOROUGH" No. 8077
These popular shapes have a mottled beige ground and are decorated with a pleasing leaf design in autumnal tints with purple berries.

Also No. 8125—mottled green ground and green leaves.

BURLEIGH WARE

BURGESS & LEIGH LTD
Potters · Burslem · England

From *The Pottery Gazette*, January 1954.

for Ridgway, the archetypal 1950s tableware design, which had undoubtedly inspired Bennett's *Fantasia*. Jumbo cups and saucers and mugs and beakers were later added to the range which was re-issued for a time in the 1980s.

Also listed in the Pattern Book are hotelwares, which must only have been produced in small quantities, and '*kitchen wares*', robust utilitarian shapes whose handles and knobs were decorated in bold contrasting colours; colourways included stippled grey and red; yellow and red; or yellow and black. Less strident colours were seen in the lithographic pattern *Blue Mist*, a floral design available in a choice of blue, pink or shades of grey and green, with either solid blue or patterned holloware. Issued in 1959, its more subtle and traditional design earned both customer and critical acclaim,

Jugs and a bowl, pattern 8077, in the *Marlborough* range '*blown white matt, stippled underglaze colours*', 1954. Tallest 10ins (25.4cms).

185

Shapes from the *Flair, Vogue* and *Harmony* ranges with light printed designs and aerographed interiors, 1950s. Tallest, upright tray, approximately 12ins (30cms).

Shapes 47 and 38 from the *Harmony* range, pattern 8443, late 1950s.

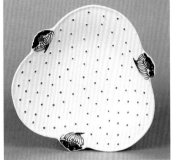

Tray, red polka dots and stylised flowers, pattern 8463, late 1950s. Diameter 11ins (28cms).

Fancies in popular black and white from the 1950s, streamlined irregular shapes by Bailey and distinctive designs from Bennett, 1958 publicity photograph.

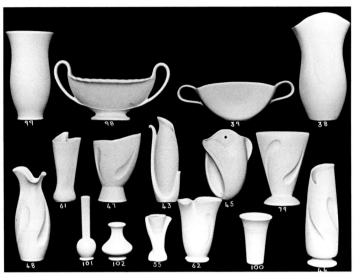

Shapes modelled by Bailey for the *Harmony* range, late 1950s.

the form of a stylised bird and fish, similar to those produced by Jo Ledger at Doulton. Sometimes, the combination of shape and pattern appeared incongruous; a 'contemporary' shaped vase, entitled *Top Hat*, was decorated with a black printed silhouette of a Victorian top-hatted character.

In spite of the occasional anachronistic design, Burgess & Leigh had survived and prospered during a difficult post-war decade. In 1956 its chairman, Denis, had celebrated fifty years' service. That half-century was nothing compared to the employment record of Harry Holdcroft who was then still working at eighty years of age. He had first joined the company as an office boy in 1890, subsequently acting as northern sales representative for fifty years (in spite of never learning to drive!) For thirty years, he had also held the position of Company Secretary before being made a director of the firm. On his death in 1958, he had served an incredible sixty-eight years with Burgess & Leigh. Harry Holdcroft was amongst the last, if not the last, of the company's employees who could remember back to Queen Victoria's 'land of hope and glory', during which the first generation Burgess & Leigh had striven for success. Would England's 'swinging sixties' and the ensuing 'seventies provide the same opportunities for achievement for the fourth- and fifth generations of the family firm?

Flair or *Vogue*. A variety of patterns were used, including, on the latter collection, a distinctly pre-war style decoration, lustred inside and painted with freehand flowers and a '*stitch edge.*' Bailey's irregular shaped trays followed the forms of Bennett's silhouetted designs, which included a penguin, rhinoceros, swallow, beehived ballroom dancers and a curvaceous reclining lady with flowing hair. These were printed in modish black on a white ground or vice versa. The Pattern Book records other subjects printed on vases '*blown red inside*': a jester, miscellaneous circus performers and a '*beach girl*' with a '*red sweater and turquoise ear-rings*'. Wavy-rimmed vases and bowls with aerographed interiors might also be decorated with hand-enamelled spots, stars and small amoebic shapes; colours were bright red, yellow or black against a stark white. Unusually, Bailey modelled new vases in

Harry Holdcroft, office boy in 1890, Company Director at the time of his death in 1958.

CHAPTER SIX

BURGESS & LEIGH, THE FINAL YEARS 1960-1999

Buying and Selling

1960 started well with the company's purchase of the goodwill, moulds and engravings of John Lockett & Co., a family firm, which had manufactured ceramic hospital wares since 1763. Lockett's wide range of bedpans, urinals, inhalers, sickfeeders, canisters, galley pots and other *'chemists' sundries'* complemented Burgess & Leigh's own hospital wares, which it had by then produced for nearly a century. Following the demolition of Lockett's factory in Longton, Stoke-on-Trent, Burgess & Leigh moved production to the Middleport Pottery where the Lockett & Co. name was advertised alongside their own. Some items continued to be made exclusively for sale through Boots the Chemist and were backstamped with their name. One of the more interesting articles made was *Dr Nelson's Improved Inhaler*, first mentioned in the medical journal *The Lancet* in 1865 when it was manufactured by S. Maw & Son as *'a simple and efficient apparatus… for the topical medication of the air-passages by the inhalation of the vapour of water impregnated with various substances.'*[1] Initially all went well with sales of Lockett & Co. wares contributing nine per cent of Burgess & Leigh sales in 1961. However, there was to be a gradual

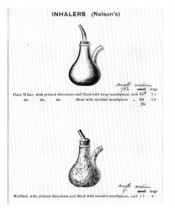

From a catalogue of John Lockett & Co., the company purchased by Burgess & Leigh in 1960.

Still in production, *Dr Nelson's Improved Inhaler*, a sick feeder, right, and an early twentieth-century catalogue page, left.

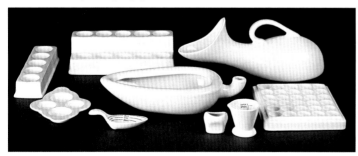

'Chemists' Sundries' and hospital wares remained in production a the Middleport Pottery until the 1980s.

decline in demand for hospital wares in the 1970s and 1980s, as plastic and stainless steel replaced breakable and less hygienic earthenware for larger items.

Demand for Burleigh table and ornamental wares remained satisfactory given that trade was fairly slow throughout the industry during the early 1960s. Sales staff were Wilfred Hope representing the Midlands, Southern England and Wales; the young and lively David Finn responsible for Northern England, Scotland and Ireland; and Arthur Glew, a brother-in-law of Edmund Leigh, who replaced Tom Barlow as agent for London and the South-East. Overseas, Europe was to become an increasingly important market, compensating for losses in old colonial markets, such as South Africa where the *'winds of change'* were then beginning to blow. In 1963, Glew and Edmund took a stand at a trade fair in Paris resulting in the appointment of an agent in France, to add to those in Holland and Scandanavia. Further agencies were set up, in Italy and Switzerland, and by the time Britain joined the EEC in 1973, the company's European sales amounted to eighteen per cent of the total sales.[2]

Successful sales, Burgess & Leigh had learnt, started with good innovative design. Although Bennett's freehand painted and 'print and enamel' patterns were ideal for their time, post-war it was agreed they were outmoded in style and costly to produce. By the early 1960s, when Britain celebrated youth as it never had before, Bennett was approaching seventy years of age. It was time once more for a young, fresh pair of eyes.

David Copeland, Art Director

David Copeland joined the Design Studio in 1963 having completed a Graphic Design and Ceramics course at Stoke-on-Trent College of Art (now Staffordshire University). Whilst there he had gained plaudits for his designs, having won first prize in the Graphic Design section of *The Pottery Gazette* Design Competition in 1960, sponsored by *The Pottery Gazette and Glass Trade Review* to encourage and identify young design talent. Required to produce a pattern for an earthenware tankard, Copeland's linear design of a train going over a viaduct was described as *'a beautifully drawn, carefully planned and nicely arranged design that was superb for its continuity, as well as its colour suitability. It was very clever and full of interest.'*[3] (It was uncannily similar to Burgess & Leigh's *'Railway Coloured Mugs'* produced at the Central Pottery in 1862!) The commercial potential of the design was recognised by one of the judges, Roy Midwinter, who purchased it and a later tableware pattern by Copeland for possible production by his Burslem company. He also went on to buy a design Copeland had completed for the cover of the Royal College of Art's prospectus.

In spite of his ceramic training and interest from ceramic style-leaders Midwinter, Copeland initially pursued a brief career with an advertising agency, Osborne Peacock, in Manchester. His experience there is evident, not only in the graphic style of his Burleigh patterns, but also in his design of

David Copeland, Art Designer 1963-1981. Pictured here during the 1970s.

Burgess & Leigh's 1860s design for a mug.

Mug with printed 'railway' design which Burgess & Leigh produced from 1862 until the late nineteenth century. This example marked 'B&L', c.1870.

David Copeland's 1960 design for a mug which won first prize in a design competition sponsored by *The Pottery Gazette*.

their accompanying publicity literature. As a young man, just twenty-one years old, employed to inject some 1960s pop culture and style into the company, Copeland found himself in surroundings far from Carnaby Street cool. However, the warmth of his welcome by the Middleport Pottery more than compensated and his memories are of a good family firm whose workers had much respect for their employers. Appointed as a surface pattern designer alongside Bennett, it was thought that Copeland might also provide a little assistance to Bailey as a modeller but in fact his input into shape design was confined to discussions only. He worked

with Bennett for just a few months before the latter's retirement to paint full-time. Copeland remembers him as a unique, larger-than-life personality. Indeed there were many 'characters' at the Middleport Pottery including paintress Mary Harper, by then a sprightly 60-something-year-old, who elected to act as his tea-maker! Mary, Copeland remembers, often enjoyed a 'flutter' with Joe, the dipper, who was something of a self-appointed expert on horse racing form. Putting sixpence on her favourite horse, Mary invariably won, much to Joe's annoyance!

Burleigh Goes Pop: 1960s Tableware Patterns and Shapes
Although there was lots of fun on the factory floor, the Leighs, as they always had done, ran a tight ship. Copeland quickly realised that, although he was given complete artistic freedom, his new designs not only had to generate sales but also save on production costs. As a young graduate, he had anticipated using all that modern technology could offer the commercial ceramicist. However, although Burgess & Leigh had made concessions to new techniques, it wished to maintain its traditional methods of manufacture. Faced with this challenge, Copeland came up with the ideal solution: modern, up-to-date designs using the copper-engraving skills employed by the Middleport Pottery.

From a 'Private Wages Book' of July 1963 showing the names of D. Copeland and, scored through, H. Bennett.

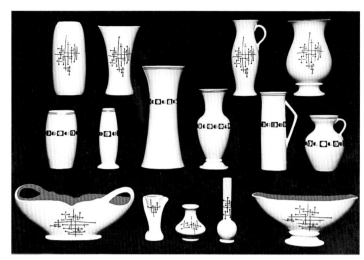

Copeland's 1963 designs on Bailey's shapes.

Up until the 1950s, Burgess & Leigh had continued to employ an engraver, a Mr Nicholls. (He is also remembered doing a little engraving work on jewellery for employees in his spare time, charging sixpence a letter. Packer Ben Ford's signet ring cost him 1s 6d!) By the 1960s, however, any work required was done externally by a highly skilled engraver called Tom Blaize. Operating from a workshop in Burslem, it was Blaize who interpreted Copeland's patterns, one of the first being *Cordon Bleu*. Designed in 1964 for Bailey's new and hitherto unsuccessful *Concord* shape, it used holloware aerographed in blue with a printed pattern on white narrow-rimmed *Edinburgh* flat ware. (The *Concord* shape used three flat ware shapes: *Coupe* with no rim, *Edinburgh* with a narrow rim and *Rex* with a broad rim.) The pattern was a simple linear one using a repetition of an 'OXO' pattern around the border. Edmund Leigh, with his customary talent for inventing appropriate pattern names, coined the witty title *Cordon Bleu* and the pattern's success was assured. Indeed sales at home and overseas, especially in Scandanavia (through Ove Larsen) and Canada, were so great that Burgess & Leigh's recently purchased automatic Murray-Curvex printing machine was put into operation to cope with extra production. The pattern was accepted for inclusion in the Design Centre's Design Index, showing that Burgess & Leigh were once again in the vanguard of modern design.

Together with *Random*, an engraved border pattern, printed in black and painted in arbitrary colours by paintresses, *Cordon Bleu* established Copeland's reputation at the Middleport Pottery and he confidently went on to produce other successful patterns in a similar graphic style.

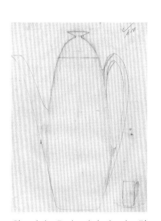

Sketch by Bailey, left, for the *Planet* shape which was produced briefly during the early 1960s. Shown right, with the *Sienna* pattern.

Cordon Bleu, Copeland's hugely successful design of 1964.

Random by Copeland, underglaze printed and painted pattern (8955), 1964.

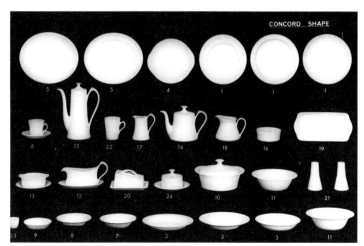

The *Concord* shape modelled by Bailey during the early 1960s.

Mosaic, Burgess & Leigh's 'proudly modern' design of 1966.

Those on the *Concord* and *Coupe* shapes included *Thatch*, a brown border design, and *Mosaic*. Advertised in 1966 as '*proudly modern*', Mosaic followed the successful format of blue holloware with white flat ware but this time was decorated with a distinctive central pattern. Again, it was immensely successful for the company, the *Birmingham Post* reporting in July 1966:

> '*While the emphasis is still on traditional patterns, particularly with allegiance to Victoriana, there is another school of design thought producing a more primitive styling with the sophisticated finish of the highly skilled professional but with the individual look of the craftsman potter.... One of the most exciting designs comes from David Copeland for Burleigh. It is a deliberate departure from border patterns which have predominated in the past few seasons. The pattern is in blue, green and peacock and looks like a mosaic play on a sunflower. A twenty-one piece tea set in this design costs £3 16s 6d.*'

'*Screenie Jean*' Jean Cawley, screen printing during the 1970s.

Carnaby, an on-glaze lithrographic pattern from Copeland on the *Concord* shape, c.1967.

When Princess Margaret showed an interest in Copeland's Burleigh patterns at the Carlton Tower Exhibition of new designs in London in 1966, he finally felt that he could relax a little, having proved his worth to his employers. By that time he had been experimenting with silkscreen printing. This complex process of multi-colour printing developed from the Murray-Curvex machine but no longer made use of the copperplate engraving. Instead, it used a stainless steel screen or mesh fitted with a photographic stencilled design, through which colour was transferred to special printing paper. The technique allowed the industry more scope and versatility in designing and enabled ideas to be quickly translated into finished products by either transfer printing, direct printing or themoprinting. The company eventually allocated Copeland the finance to set up a small silkscreen printing team which included George Ball and Jean Cawley or '*Screenie Jean*', so-called because she operated the silkscreen printer! Together, they successfully coped with production runs of transfer prints. *Medallion*, a 1964 pattern of large blue-grey medallions finished with a silver edge, and *Floret*, a simple Mary Quant-inspired floral pattern of 1967, were both successfully produced by the silkscreen method.

Other pop art inspired designs by Copeland were *Carnaby*, an on-glaze litho 'flower power' pattern printed by J. Matthey (the company's usual external lithographic print supplier),

Burleigh
present....

ORBIT

Fresh and scintillating as if from outer space!
This thrilling new idea in modern tableware is a bold exercise in spatial relationships. It combines a varying degree of depth from the startling whiteness of the body through to the carefully planned colour variations of the motif.
An attractive pattern with a difference!
ORBIT in two exciting colour schemes.

Pattern and leaflet designed by David Copeland.

A page from the Pattern Book showing *Orbit*, 1969.

Magyar, an on-glaze print on the *Anglia* shape, 1968.

Coniston, with reactive glaze and banding, on the *Anglia* shape, 1973.

Florenza, a silkscreen printed and banded pattern which remained popular in the 1970s.

Items produced on Bailey's *Anglia* shape of 1967.

Castile

An echo of the individualistic skills and qualities of the ancient craft potter. Castile, a permanent underglaze decoration designed on the 'Anglia' shape as oven-to-tableware, is available in two subtle colourways: olive and slate blue or olive and chocolate brown. Fitting into a long tradition of successful underglaze decorations this new design has already established itself as a firm favourite with the modern minded.

BLACKPOOL FAIR GOLDEN MILE CENTRE STAND E4

From *Tableware International*, May 1971.

The demands of the new 1960s consumer impacted not only on tableware pattern, but also on shape, as the young and fashionable shared communal meals inspired by travel to the Mediterranean. The stylised and more formal elegance of Bailey's *Concord* shape contrasted with the squatter, chunkier forms of *Anglia* which he modelled in 1967. This shape was used effectively with patterns like *Marrakesh*, *Minaret*, *Mistral* and *Magyar*, an on-glaze print based on Yugoslavian embroidery. *Castile* was Murray-printed underglaze and hand-banded (using the skills of paintresses Mabel and Rose, its designer remembers) with a deliberately streaky water-based colour. Like subsequent patterns of the 1970s, such as *Coniston* which used reactive glazes, it imitated rustic handmade studio pottery but satisfied new consumer demands for convenience and practicality, being both oven- and dishwasher proof. Originally designed for Scandanavia in 1969, *Castile* was also very successful in the home market.

The mould store still continued to provide inspiration for a number of embossed tableware ranges. In c.1968, Bailey was asked to model additional shapes for the *Old Davenport* series to form a tea and dinner ware range which was produced in a honey, green or white glaze. This last variation sold consistently well, only recently being withdrawn from production. Later, in 1980, the nineteenth-century *Bamboo* shape was also successfully revived for certain tableware shapes and produced with both a white glaze or with on-glaze enamel colours. Bailey modelled another original embossed, plain glazed tableware range; featuring a small all-over leaf

The *Bamboo* shape, first made by Burgess & Leigh in c.1880, and revived a century later.

and *Orbit* a more arresting design, which was inspired by patterns by the Swiss firm Longthal. Produced in 1969 on Bailey's *Anglia* shape, the company advertised *Orbit* as '*Fresh and scintillating as if from outer space! ... in sparkling tangerine and marigold or vivid green and midnight blue.... This thrilling new idea in modern tableware is a bold exercise in special relationships. It combines a varying degree of depth from the startling whiteness of the body through to the carefully planned colour variations of the motif.*' When Edmund visited recession-hit Australia in the 1970s, he introduced *Orbit* where it sold well, providing a huge contrast to the country's other favourite Burleigh pattern, the '*Dillwyn*' Willow.

An embossed coffee set from Bailey produced with a honey or green glaze, c.1970.

Coquille, shell-shaped tableware orginally made during the 1950s and revived in the 1980s.

The *English Inn Signs* series of mugs introduced in c.1967.

Watermarks, a boxed set of six mugs based on historical watermarks, 1969.

A 1970s leaflet showing Burleigh mugs in the traditional *Farmers Arms* pattern and contemporary designs like '*Love-Hate*'.

design, its style was reminiscent of Portmeirion's *Totem* and Wedgwood's *Pennine* ranges. In 1976, the *Marlborough* shape, with an embossed 'basket weave' border, was purchased from Simpsons, Potters of Cobridge, and subsequently produced with various bought-in floral lithographic patterns, such as *Moselle* from K. H. Bailey.

As the casserole replaced the covered tureen, the now ubiquitous mug was offered as an alternative to formal tea- and coffee-cups and saucers. Perhaps influenced by the work of his counterpart, John Clappison, at the Hornsea Pottery, Copeland designed in c.1967 a series of mugs which placed Burgess & Leigh in the forefront of the Staffordshire pottery mug explosion. Inspired by a visit to the Stafford Arms pub one summer's evening, his first collection of six mugs featured typically English inn signs with a carefully researched animal theme: *The Pig and Whistle; The Unicorn; The Spotted Dog; The Black Bull; The Nag's Head;* and *The Bear Inn*. Drawn in simple cartoon style, the pattern was printed by 'Screenie' Jean on to a plain cylindrical shape from Bailey. The collection was displayed in shops and stores with a miniature wooden inn sign reading *English Inn Signs By Burleigh*, also designed by Copeland and made onsite by the Middleport Pottery's joiner! The DIY advertising tactic worked well and the mugs were best sellers at home and overseas although a collection of large-sized tankards bearing the same designs was less popular.

Watermarks, a boxed set of six mugs was issued in 1969 but, surprisingly given its stylish and original design, it failed to match sales of the earlier series. Based on different historical watermarks, it was decorated with a silkscreen

pattern either printed in white on a black matt glaze, or in grey on a white glaze. Subsequent boxed sets included *The Sun*, '*motifs in bright orange, red and yellow*'; *Chintz*, '*a more delicate all-over floral design in attractive colours*'; and a set of chunky cups and saucers decorated with large, bold numbers in read and white or black and white colourways. '*Down On The Farm*', a series from 1970, was decorated with on-glaze transfer-printed designs of humorous farmyard animals. During the 1970s, some mugs were sold singly, such as those decorated with black printed hunting scenes or a Victorian steam engine in the style of both Copeland's earlier student design and Burgess & Leigh's '*col'd railway mug*'.

Calico and the Revival of the Underglaze Printed Patterns

With their store of nineteenth-century copperplate engravings Burgess & Leigh were well placed to capitalise on Britain's nostalgia for Victoriana. Ironically, it was production of a new design, *Calico*, sourced by American company, S.&S. Agencies, using the trade name Crownford China, which instigated the revival of the company's underglaze printed wares. Entered into the Pattern Book with number 9086 on 1st February, 1968, *Calico* was

Lidded jar with underglaze printed *Cracked Ice and Prunus* pattern and on-glaze enamelling, c.1910. Height 4ins (10cms).

Cracked Ice and Prunus pattern from the Print Record Book.

described simply as a *'solid floral print in blue'*. In fact, its design was based on the *Prunus* or plum blossom pattern, which was used, often against a 'cracked-ice' background, on seventeenth- and eighteenth-century blue and white Chinese porcelain. When the oriental style influenced British ceramic design during the late nineteenth century, Burgess & Leigh joined other pottery manufacturers in producing similar all-over or 'sheet' patterns. The company's *Daisy* pattern is just one of the forerunners of *Calico*. All-over floral ceramic patterns have sometimes been called 'chintz', as similar designs were used on fabric, including calico, the printed cotton cloth which gave the Burleigh pattern its name.

Although the the source is known, the name of the original designer of *Calico* has not been recorded. It has been suggested[4] that a representative from S&S Agencies brought a piece of American chintz fabric showing the design to the Middleport Pottery with the proposal that it be copied for translation on to pottery[5]. Peter Wild of the Hanley based firm, Grapha Print, is thought to have engraved the pattern from this same piece of fabric. (He and his colleagues John Humphrey and Brian Tomkinson, now retired, have been responsible for all Burleigh engraved patterns from this time onwards.) The quality of craftsmanship and manufacture of this instantly appealing pattern brought huge sales in all markets.

Originally some seventy to eighty per cent was exported

Burgess & Leigh's *Daisy*, a nineteenth-century 'sheet' or all-over pattern.

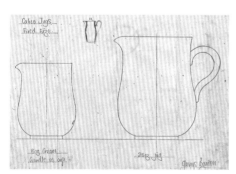

Drawing by Glenys Barton of shapes for Habitat's *Calico* range, 1974.

Calico tableware shapes from un-dated leaflet.

Un-dated *Calico* leaflet.

Decorative shapes with the *Calico* pattern, c.1980s.

Calico shapes, a publicity photograph from the 1970s.

to the USA when it was sold through Crownford and marked with their backstamp. Demand only dropped during America's recession in the 1970s, caused by the global oil crisis. At the same time, the pattern was available in England through the Habitat chain of stores. This UK version bore a different printed backstamp, incorporating the floral *Calico* name and pattern, which was especially designed by David Copeland and engraved by Tom Blaize. (A simple printed name was used on seconds earthenware.) Towards the end of the 1970s, *Calico* became generally available in the UK. It also found a popular market in Germany where it was sold in green and brown as well as its original blue colourway.

Initially produced on the *London* tableware shape, *Calico* has decorated all manner of tableware, kitchen ware and ornamental shapes. Unfortunately, there are no records at the factory listing them all, although (undated) publicity leaflets give some help. Terence Conran at Habitat commissioned a number of tableware shapes for the pattern from Glenys Barton, a Royal College of Art-trained ceramic sculptor although it is not known whether these were ever produced. There have been several imitations of *Calico* since its introduction but, for many, the Burleigh version remains the original and the best!

S & S Agencies brought further designs to Burgess & Leigh. Some of these were *Royal Staffordshire* branded patterns acquired from A.J. Wilkinson whom S & S Agencies as Crownford had represented in the USA until the mid-1960s.

Bennett's underglaze blue pattern *Britain Beautiful* was reworked by Copeland during the early 1970s, and produced briefly on a round, fluted shape.

Elegance, a bought-in pattern which remained popular during the 1960s.

Amongst them was *Charlotte*, a design of a floral basket 'engraved from original drawings by J. Cutts Designer c.1830', which was first introduced in the 1970s. It was, however, the huge popularity of *Calico* which led to the reintroduction and re-engraving of some of the company's own original nineteenth-century underglaze printed floral patterns. *Arden*, for example, was issued in 1972 in blue on *Windsor* holloware and *Rex* flat tableware shapes with other colour versions subsequently produced on Wilkes' old *Willow Pekin* shape: green in 1976 and a fashionable plum in 1980. The same shape was also used for *Victorian Chintz*, an all-over large rose design which was re-engraved from original nineteenth-century coppers and produced from 1977 in pink, blue, and, for some markets, black. *Felicity*, a tiny delicate floral pattern, introduced in 1980, was also offered in a choice of colours: blue, pink, plum and maize. These floral designs joined two other best-selling sheet patterns, *Bluebird*, which had remained in continuous production since its launch as *Chinese Peacock* before the First World War, and the *'Dillwyn' Willow* which had been first introduced in 1920. In 1975, Copeland up-dated the theme by designing *Chequers*, an all-over pattern of geometric shaded squares, for *Swansea* holloware and *Rex* flat tableware shapes. Nearly thirty years later, it remains one of the company's most popular patterns.

During the height of the underglaze printed pattern revival, the Printing Shop, employing some twenty printers and transferrers, was reorganised with a conveyor belt and 'washing-off' and 'vibro rubbing' machines. A part-time 'twilight' shift was also added, a flexible arrangement for working mothers who could come into the Middleport Pottery four evenings a week while their husbands cared for children at home.

Although printed wares constituted the bulk of the company's production from the late 1960s onwards, some

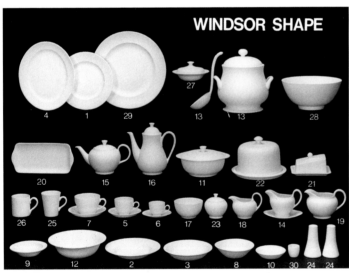

The *Windsor* shape used for Burgess & Leigh's *Arden* pattern of 1972.

Charlotte, in blue and pink, previously produced under A.J. Wilkinson's *Royal Staffordshire* brand, made by Burgess & Leigh from the 1970s. Largest 10ins (25.4cms).

tableware patterns utilised different decorative techniques. Lithographic transfers had improved in quality post-war but were often disappointingly unimaginative in design and could be expensive to purchase, particularly if the pattern did not sell well. Those on-glaze litho patterns that did included *Blue Mist, Elegance, Costa Brava, Aragon* and *Branksome* while one that did not was K.H. Bailey's 1980 design, *Staffordshire Rose*. During the years 1980 – 1986 Burgess & Leigh were pleased to take over production of the tableware and giftware pattern *Christmas Tree* for American importers Cuthbertson Ltd. (Its design which Cuthbertson assert dates from the 1920s is almost identical to Harold Holdway's 1950s pattern of the same name for Spode.) Although its manufacture prompted a temporary revival of on-glaze lithographing and banding at the Middleport Pottery, the emphasis on underglaze printed wares inevitably led to a reduction in the number of lithographers and decorators.

Teawares commissioned in 1973 by the London fashion store Biba were decorated with a smart high gloss black glaze and the store's gold logo of a silhouetted dancing couple,

Cuthbertson's Original Christmas Tree®

This popular range of products has sold well in the U.S.A. since circa 1928. For the first time in almost 53 years, this popular and distinctive pattern is available to other countries in the world. Over fifty items are in the range; indeed a comprehensive tableware and giftware group of products to enhance the Christmas festive season.

The ceramic items are all produced in Ironstone, to high quality standards, in Staffordshire, England. All customers can be assured that Cuthbertson's Original Christmas Tree® is tried and proven and will grace their tables for countless happy Christmases to come.

Leaflet produced by American importers Cuthbertson Ltd, 1980s.

Some of the shapes produced with Cuthbertson's 'Original' *Christmas Tree* pattern between 1980 and 1986. Tallest 6¼ins (16cms).

Mayfair, a 1980s aerographed pattern. Tallest 8¼ins (21cms).

Milk jug, from teaware produced for Biba, the London fashion store, in 1973. Height 4ins (10cms).

exemplifying the Art Deco revival in which Biba indulged. Ten years later variations of the design were made, without the logo, for export, mainly to Germany: then called *Mayfair*, it was produced in aerographed black with a red band; grey with a maroon band; yellow with a blue band; and blue with a yellow band. In 1981 the Swedish store Ikea also commissioned Burleigh tableware, with a simple underglaze band and line pattern.

The Fifth Generation

While Burgess & Leigh enjoyed considerable sales success during the 1970s, they were also testing times for the business. Denis Leigh had died in 1968 following sixty-two years' service for the company. He had been a director for forty-nine of those and chairman for thirteen. In addition, he had played a prominent role in the pottery industry as a whole, sitting on various committees and for two years acting as Vice Chairman of the British Pottery Manufacturers Federation. His death had left Edmund and Barry, as directors in charge of Burgess & Leigh, to confront drastic changes within the pottery industry and indeed the whole country as inflation and unemployment rose, wage payments increased and productivity declined.

Union calls for industrial action prompted a series of work stoppages, none more damaging to the pottery industry than the miners' strike. Just as the third generation Leighs had pre-empted the 1926 strike, so the fourth anticipated that of 1972, buying in fifty tons of coal, supplemented by wooden floor joists obtained from local building sites! As supplies ran out, three lorries brought back a further fifty tons from an open-cast mine shortly before the arrival of pickets. The efforts paid off again, with turnover and profits rising, giving the company its best results for many years![6] A second coal strike a year later was more serious for the Middleport Pottery resulting in reduced power- station output. Some kilns were not operated and others fired during the night and at weekends. Less successful solutions to the crisis included the installation of an electricity generator, running (erratically) off the steam engine, to provide power for essential work, and the purchase of a live oak tree (too green) to burn on the boiler! During a national three-day working week, the directors were grateful for the continuing co-operation and loyalty of their 150 or so employees, some of whom frequently worked weekends to keep the pottery productive.[7]

It was during this period of national industrial and economic decline (which saw Britain realise its worst trade deficit on record) that the fifth generation Leigh family joined the firm. In 1973 Edmund's son, Kingsley (the second), an engineer by training, joined the company together with his cousin, Alan, Barry's son, a mathematics graduate with a specialist interest in computer systems. By that time Burgess & Leigh was one of the few old independent family firms left in the Potteries; indeed, five years after it had co-founded an industrial training group in 1966 with four other family-run businesses, it found itself to be the only one remaining.[8] Like their forefathers, Alan and Kingsley were encouraged to gain experience of all aspects of company manufacture and business, including on occasions attending trade fairs. In the late 1970s, when the firm started exhibiting biannually at the international Frankfurt Trade Fair, exports accounted for sixty-nine per cent of the company's total sales. Displays continued at Birmingham's National Exhibition Centre, and later Harrogate, in an attempt to increase home sales. However, with two million unemployed by 1978, a level unknown since the 1930s, results were often disappointing. Burgess & Leigh reduced its sales staff to just one, covering England and Wales, and placed its employees on a shortened working week.[9]

By 1980, Edmund and Barry were in their early sixties and glad to share responsibilities with their children and co-directors, Kingsley and Alan. But there were some very difficult decisions to be made during the next twenty years.

The End of the Burleigh Design Studio
From the 1970s, Burgess & Leigh increasingly manufactured wares for customers such as commissioning agents S & S Agencies or china distributors ICTC (the Intercontinental Cooking and Tableware Company based in the south of England) who originated their own designs and surface patterns from freelance artists or other sources. In a belief that a saving could be made on its own in-house design and development, it was decided in 1981 to wind down the Design Studio. Ernest Bailey, then aged seventy, would work two days a week while sadly David Copeland was to be made redundant, together with his team including 'Screenie' Jean.

During his eighteen years with the company, Copeland had produced some hugely successful contemporary designs, a number of which were included in the prestigious *Design Index*. On leaving the Middleport Pottery, he initially thought that he might expand his teaching of design at evening classes at Cauldon College in Stoke, simultaneously working for Burgess & Leigh and other firms in a part-time freelance capacity. However, when G. B. Decor in Hanley, a print supplier to the pottery industry, offered him a job, he took it, enjoying a successful career before joining Decor Italia as a Sales Director. Like most of its past employees, he retains an interest in the future of the Middleport Pottery and regularly

Leaflet for *Elektra*, an underglaze printed pattern designed by freelance artist Chris Nunn, 1980s.

An open stock lithographic pattern on the embossed *Florentine* shape, late 1980s.

provides professional advice to Burgess, Dorling & Leigh.

Following Copeland's departure, all patterns were derived from Burgess & Leigh's own copperplates, sourced by agencies or commissioned by the company from freelance artists. The most frequently used artist was Chris Nunn, now combining freelance ceramic designing with teaching watercolour painting and antiques dealing. During the 1970s Nunn had acted as chief designer for pottery supplier, Johnson Matthey, before being introduced to Burgess & Leigh by Roy Midwinter.

Bailey eventually retired from the Middleport Pottery in 1983. His tableware and ornamental shape designs had made a tremendous contribution to the company's success over five decades, and, indeed, continue to do so. He produced numerous models during his retirement (including an

Plates commissioned by Mottahedeh for US customers in the 'heritage' market. Largest 10¹/₂ins (26cms).

Made for US importers John Roth and depicting scenes from American history. Largest 10ins (25cms).

Camilla, in blue, and *Cornelia*, in green; a Mottahedeh commission for Historic Charleston, 1980s. Largest 12¹/₄ins (31cms).

Blue and green versions of *Torquay*, a pattern produced for Mottahedeh for the Winterthur museum in the USA, 1980s, later sold in the UK. Diameter of plate 10ins (25cms).

individualistic figurative composition called *Spirit of Britain* commemorating Prime Minister Margaret Thatcher during the Falklands War.)[10] Without Bailey, new shapes were brought to Burgess & Leigh by retail customers, or produced from moulds acquired or as a result of pottery mergers and takeovers. *Florentine*, an embossed tableware range, was amongst a number of shapes purchased in 1987 on the closure of S. Fielding & Co. (better known by their trade name, Crown Devon), another company represented by S.&S. Agencies.[11]

Later Printed Ware

In common with other pottery manufacturers during the 1980s Burgess & Leigh developed overseas 'heritage' markets wishing to import genuine and traditionally made Staffordshire pottery. An important customer was Mottahedeh, a New York-based company, licensed to reproduce traditional and antique ceramics for American museum collections. Amongst tableware patterns commissioned from the Middleport Pottery was one for Historic Charleston; called *Camilla* in pale blue and *Cornelia* in green it was '*reproduced from an original Staffordshire pattern c.1820*'. Blue and green versions were made of *Torquay*, a bold shell pattern produced for the Winterthur Museum. Mottahedeh also commissioned plates for other clients, commemorating events in American history, such as the *Texian* [sic] *Campaign* or *Benjamin Franklin's Election*. Similar commemorative items were also made for John Roth, an American importing company, and the Canadian firm Haywood & Warwick, for whom Burgess & Leigh made the *Atlantic Canada* collection of twelve scenic plates. One of the more unusual items to be made at the Middleport Pottery for Mottahedeh was a large Passover plate modelled by Bailey; more familiar was *Pagoda*, Wilkes' Chinese-inspired teaware design of the 1930s which was amended slightly for reproduction in c.1980.

Pagoda was one of the few commissioned patterns to be marked Burleigh, most others bearing the customer's mark. This also applied to those wares made for more commercial retail outlets overseas, such as A Thing of Beauty Inc. which commissioned the *Garden Trellis* tableware pattern, and Stoneware Kitchen which took *Fruit Harvest* in pink. Although North America was to remain the company's largest anglophile export market, a successful trade with Japan was also developed, mainly through Sazaby. By 1992, the Japanese market constituted ten percent of the company's total sales.

At home, Habitat was to remain an important customer in the 1980s. From 1981 it sold *Scilla*, a pale blue/grey printed sheet pattern on the *Windsor* shape, by freelance designer Lillian Delevoryas, best known today as a watercolour artist specialising in flowers. In 1984, at the request of Terence Conran, *Asiatic Pheasant*, Burgess & Leigh's late nineteenth century pattern was also produced for Habitat; it was re-engraved for the *Windsor* shape from original copperplates by

The Passover plate modelled by Bailey and produced by Burgess & Leigh for Mottahedeh in the 1970s. Diameter approximately 14¹/₄ins (36cms).

Four of the twelve plates in the *Atlantic Canada* series produced for Haywood & Warwick. Diameter approximately 8ins (20cms).

The *Garden Trellis* pattern made for A Thing of Beauty Inc. Plate diameter 8¹/₄ins 21cms).

Highland Game, a 1990s Burleigh pattern in brown. Plate diameter 8¹/₄ins 21cms).

Scilla, a pattern by Lillian Delevoryas sold through Habitat from 1981 before becoming generally available. Tea canister height 6ins (15cms).

Blue Shell, designed and made for Moorland Pottery. Plate diameter 8¹/₂ins (21cms).

Chintzware for Laura Ashley, 1989. Tallest 6¹/₄ins (16cms).

Pictorial Britain by freelance designer Chris Nunn, early 1990s Burleigh pattern. Plate diameter 8¹/₂ins (21cms).

Poynter 'By Recollections' for the Victoria and Albert Museum, 1980s. Tray diameter 11¹/₂ins (29cms).

Homefarm designed by Chris Nunn, a later 1990s Burleigh pattern. Plate diameter 7ins (17cms).

Dovedale designed for Burgess & Leigh by Chris Nunn in the 1990s.

Promotional leaflet for *Renaissance*, a Burleigh pattern from the 1990s.

Ivy, one of the few green patterns, 1990s.

Leaflet for *Animal Farm*, an underglaze litho' pattern designed by Alice Cotterill, 1990s.

Chanticleer, an Alice Cotterill pattern produced for china distributer ICTC, 1990s.

Brian Tomkinson of Grapha Print. Some five years later, Burgess & Leigh produced *Chintz Ware* for Laura Ashley, its pretty floral pattern in green, pink or blue suiting perfectly the traditional English image of the shop.

The Victoria and Albert Museum Shop in London also commissioned table- and gift ware; named *Poynter*, its underglaze blue printed pattern was based on the blue and white tiles decorating the museum's original Grill Room which had been designed by Sir Edward Poynter, the Pre-Raphaelite artist and designer. In an unusual link-up, Burgess & Leigh also produced an underglaze blue printed pattern, *Blue Shell*, designed by the nearby Moorland Pottery.

The 1990s saw a continuation of all-over underglaze transfer printed patterns, such as the 'leaf' patterns *Burgess Chintz* and *Ivy*. *Pictorial Britain*, one of Chris Nunn's designs with random pottery shapes against a patterned background, was based on *China Cabinet*, a tableware range produced by A. J. Wilkinson in the mid-1960s. His more original interpretations of traditional subjects were *Dovedale*, featuring underwater fish, and *Homefarm*, depicting countryside scenes. Again a member of the Grapha Print

team interpreted both of these loosely painted designs.

Continuing the animal theme, china distributor ICTC commissioned the Middleport Pottery to produce *Chanticleer*, a tableware pattern featuring a red-plumed and beaked cockerel. Its decoration combined underglaze transfer printing in blue with a red on-glaze lithograph, imitating the stencilling and sponging technique used on French peasant-style pottery. Designed by freelance artist, Alice Cotterill, *Chanticleer* marked an attempt to embrace more fashionable decorative styles and techniques. Cotterill also designed *Animal Farm*, a simple underglaze lithographic design of farmyard animals. Both of Cotterill's patterns were ideal for display with other blue and white pottery on the farmhouse kitchen dresser.

Kitchen Wares

A new national interest in cookery in the 1960s had prompted Burgess & Leigh to embark on a more commercial interpretation of its domestic kitchen wares. Co-ordinated ranges, suitable for display in modern fitted kitchens, were produced in Bailey's simple cylindrical shapes, most often bearing David Copeland's printed graphic decoration. A Stilton cheese stand in a plain white glaze, hand-banded in

Kitchen storage jars decorated with a bought-in pattern, 1970s.

Open-stock ivy leaf pattern on simple hooped jugs, lidded canisters and oblong butter dish, 1970s.

199

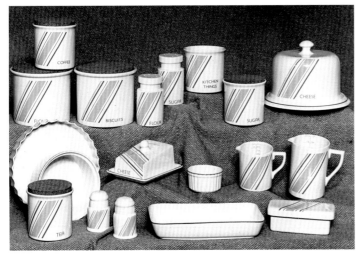

Designed to co-ordinate with popular kitchen colours, 1980s-1990s.

Ever-popular cow creamers produced from the 1980s in Burleigh printed patterns.

Victorian Chintz in blue, pink and black decorated tablewares, kitchenwares and toilet wares. Plate diameter 10ins (25cms).

blue and proclaiming CHEESE in stylised capitals, became a best seller through Habitat before being made generally available. Canister-shaped storage jars with ceramic or cork lids were decorated with printed 'labels' divulging their contents: SUGAR; TEA, COFFEE, SALT, RICE, FLOUR and so on. Glazes were plain or coloured; later, additional printed decoration might match tableware patterns or feature floral or stripey motifs. New items included quiche and soufflé dishes, pizza dishes and trays, ramekins and rolling pins, salt and pepper pots and measuring jugs. A cow creamer, believed to have been acquired from Crown Devon, was decorated with a variety of underglaze printed patterns and has remained a popular item.

Customers in the 1970s failed to be amused in large numbers by *Butcher's Apron*, a humorous cartoon character decorating a range of miscellaneous kitchen ware items. The 1980s saw the return to more serious design with the launch of a range of red-lettered kitchen ware, *Cuisine Rouge*, for display in popular red colour-coordinated kitchens. Storage

Mathilda's Kitchen in blue and *Bathroom Nostalgia* in pink, 1990s. Tallest 8¾ins (22cms).

Examples of lithographic printed items made in *The Sanderson Gallery* range made for the Sanderson Wallpaper Company briefly during the 1980s. Taller 5½ins (14cms).

Farmers Arms was recoloured and adapted for screen printing by David Copeland during the 1970s.

1970s designs, including Staffordshire poodles and spaniels remodelled by Bailey.

Butcher's Apron, sold for a short period in the 1970s.

jars were produced for many food companies, such as Tate & Lyle, whose printed brand name was incorporated into the design. Kitchen ware ranges from c.1990 revisited Victoriana, with decorations featuring printed tableware patterns *Burgess Chintz* and *Calico*, with white lozenge labels announcing their use or contents. Paying tribute to one of the co-founders and his daughter, they were entitled *Frederick Rathbone Burgess Traditional Kitchen Ware* and *Mathilda's Kitchen*, the latter pattern designed by Chris Nunn from an idea by Alan Leigh.

Toiletwares

Although toilet sets were no longer essential household items, Burgess & Leigh continued to manufacture what were now called 'bathroom accessories'. Again, the nostalgia for the Victorian era inspired 1980s ranges to complement Laura Ashley wallpapered bathrooms or bedrooms. The ewer and basin, display pieces for the dressing table, were produced with items such as a beaker, tumbler, toothbrush holder, soap box, 'apothecary jar', puff box, a soap tray shaped as a Victorian roll-top bath and a lotion bottle. Some of these shapes were taken from Crown Devon or A. J. Wilkinson's Newport Pottery moulds. Others were from Burgess & Leigh's own store: during the 1970s S & S Agencies commissioned the *Sweeney Todd* shaving mug as a novelty item, featuring a printed design telling the dark Victorian tale of the 'demon barber'!

Like the kitchen ware ranges, patterns for 'bathroom accessories' were underglaze printed, more often in blue but sometimes in pink in *Calico*, *Arden*, *Victorian Chintz*, *Ivy*, *Burgess Chintz* and *Celeste*. The on-glaze floral pattern *Staffordshire Rose* (also produced as tableware) proved less successful than the embossed *Davenport* sprigs, both of which were used to decorate new bathroom shapes and produced in a plain white glaze. Nunn's printed pictorial design *Bathroom Nostalgia*, was produced during the 1990s in pink or blue.

'*Bathroom Accessories*', leaflet from the 1990s.

Tahiti, a white matt glazed and freehand painted pattern (9112) decorating 1960s vases.

Silkscreen printed pattern 9012 with aerographed interiors in brown or black, 1965.

New Gift Ware Ranges: Vases, Jugs and 'Fancies' Revisited
Vases and jugs did not feature prominently from the 1960s. Copeland selected slender and elegant shapes modelled by Bailey in a style similar to those of Poole Pottery a decade earlier. He chose simple printed motifs as decoration, a number from tableware patterns, such as *Medallion*. Other series were hand-decorated to imitate studio pottery; *Sahara*, for example, produced on ten different shaped vases, was aerographed in three colours and washbanded inside in mustard, whilst *Tahiti* was freehand painted with bold flowers. Some vase shapes were used as lamp bases during the 1960s and 1970s and produced in plain coloured glazes or with printed patterns.

Character and toby jugs occupied less of Bailey's time from the 1960s onwards although, following the death in 1965 of Sir Winston Churchill, a number of his wartime jugs were re-issued. The *Shakespeare* and *Dickens* tobies also remained in production in bright blue or pink aerographed glazes. As character and toby jug manufacturers, such as Royal Doulton, expanded their ranges, Burgess & Leigh also considered more popular subjects. A toby jug depicting a fictional character from the popular television cowboy series, *Wagon Train*, was never produced although Bailey modelled a prototype of actor Robert Horton in his role as Flint McCullogh. Jimmy Edwards, a well-known radio star during the 1950s-1960s, also failed to be produced.

As it had done in the 1930s, so during the 1970s Burgess & Leigh continued to produce small, inexpensive novelty ornamental shapes, some of dubious taste: a miniature watering-can, poodle-shaped flower holder, Victorian style boot and more saucy stiletto could be had decorated with playing card motifs! Some of these shapes were modelled by Bailey, others produced from bought-in moulds. For instance, an unusual tray modelled as a pair of cupped hands (called 'gowpens' on the factory), is thought to have been acquired from the Newport Pottery. Burgess & Leigh subsequently produced it with a rather unattractive flesh-coloured glaze for sale through gift shops. A number of 'useful' items were given a humorous appeal; a canister-

Prototype model of the character 'Flint McCullogh' from the TV series *Wagon Train*. Height 6¼ins (16cms).

Small tray in cupped hands form, 1970s. Length, upright, approximately 6ins (15cms).

1970s and 1980s novelties: shapes were either bought-in or modelled by Bailey.

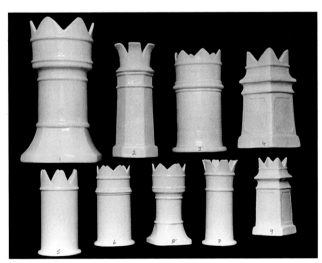

An ornamental range of Victorian style chimney pots, a decorative range modelled by Bailey in 1978.

Plates from *The Edmund Leigh Gallery* a collection instigated by Alan Leigh in c.1990. Selected designs are now produced for Fortnum & Mason as cheese stands.

shaped 'string and scissors holder' was screen-printed with Copeland's illustrations to indicate its use whilst a novelty storage jar disguised itself as a small dustbin.

An unusual range of nine different sized Victorian-style chimney pots were modelled by Bailey in 1978 and decorated in various styles: *Ullswater* had a bought-in floral lithograph; the more local *Longport* was decorated with an underglaze 'print and enamel' pattern; *Burslem* printed with an on-glaze silkscreen transfer; and *Bradwell* aerographed with a terracotta coloured glaze. A yet more distinctive range featured a printed Santa Claus, following the trend for collectors' plates the company produced in c.1990. The *Edmund Leigh Gallery*, individually boxed plates featuring underglaze blue printed designs '*from approximately 1820 to 1840 reproduced form the private collection of Edmund Leigh JP Master Potter: Chinoiserie, Nankeen, Vine, Zebra, Dromedary, Elephant* and *Beehive*.

Advertising Wares

A large part of Burgess & Leigh's production during the 1960s-1980s period was in advertising wares, mostly moulded ashtrays, whisky and water jugs, printed with the names or slogans of various tobacco companies, whisky distillers, breweries and other companies or institutions wishing to promote themselves. This business was operated largely through Hancock, Corfield & Waller Ltd of Surrey. Acting on behalf of their clients, HCW would dictate the form, decoration and quantity of the commissioned item; they would supply a drawing from their own designer, or, on the occasions when Burgess & Leigh took over another pottery's production, provide a sample article for reproduction. All this meant that interpretation rather than creativity was required from Burgess & Leigh's Design Studio. Only very occasionally would Copeland be asked to design an item, one being *Ogden's Vintage Tobacco* of 1970. More often he would advise on the feasibility of the printing; if gold were required, for example, then Burgess & Leigh would probably ask local firm, Johnson Matthey, to take it on.

Bailey also modelled to the customer's specification, jugs and ashtrays being the most requested items. (When an ashtray was designed with cigarette 'rests', it attracted higher purchase tax, making it more expensive for the customer.) Items were usually aerographed (by Ethel and her team) or dipped (by Joe, the dipper) and printed on-glaze. Honey, green and Rockingham, a treacly transparent brown, were popular choices.

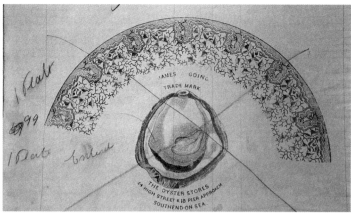

Pages from the Print Record Book showing prints for early advertising or promotional wares, c.1890.

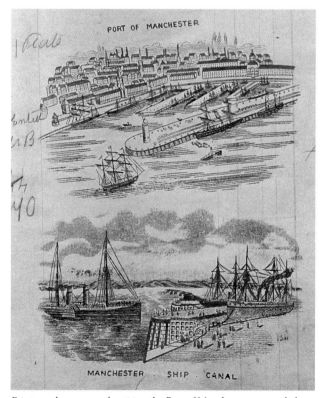

Prints used on wares advertising the Port of Manchester, top, and also commemorating the opening of the Manchester Ship Canal in 1894.

Occasionally Bailey was required to model more interesting shapes, such as *The Sherry Girl*, a small six-inch figure of a maid, suitably dressed in bonnet and apron, carrying a tray laden with a bottle and glasses of sherry. Produced for Williams & Hubert Ltd, it required a special cardboard packing carton which was designed by Head Packer Ben Ford. Bailey also modelled for HCW a small sized promotional model of Eduard Eriken's famous statue,

The Little Mermaid, which was presented to Copenhagen in 1913 by the Carlsberg Brewery. Burgess & Leigh produced 5,000 of the models for Carlsberg in a bronzed green colour.

In 1982 the Quaker Oats cereal company commissioned Burgess & Leigh to produce a promotional toby jug for them, depicting the traditional Quaker figure familiar to all porridge lovers. Issued in a limited edition of 3,500, the jug was modelled as a bust, with a detachable lid and handle,

'I'd love a Babycham', a design submitted by Hancock, Corfield & Waller for production by Burgess & Leigh in 1959.

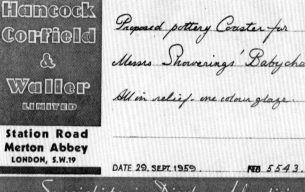

Design for Carlsberg's *Little Mermaid*.

A page from a 1968 factory notebook listing some of the advertising wares produced by the company then.

A sample of the many different shaped jugs used to advertise and promote drinks. A small square cruet, second right, does the job equally well. Tallest approximately 8ins (20cms).

For the bar. Most of Burgess & Leigh's advertising wares were not marked 'Burleigh', but had backstamps for the agent Hancock, Corfield & Waller. Tallest 8ins (20cms).

Aerographing and on-glaze printing were the usual methods of decoration for advertising wares. Tallest 7ins (17cms).

A selection of printed and moulded and glazed ashtrays which were made by Burgess & Leigh in large quantities during the 1960s-1980s. Largest diameter 6ins (15cms).

The Sherry Girl modelled by Bailey for William & Hubert Ltd. Honey glaze. Height 6ins (15cms).

Right: Photograph, with a real-life 'Sherry Girl', found at the Middleport Pottery.

The Burleigh *Quaker Oats* jug. Height approximately 8ins (20cms).

Self-advertisement, c.1989. Diameter 7ins (7.5cms).

'Delft' bricks, left, advertising and commemorating the fiftieth anniversary of *Readers' Digest* in 1988, and right, made for Mottahedeh for Winterthur Reproductions. Length 6¹/₂ins (16.5cms).

and painted in underglaze colours. A separate numbered edition of forty was also produced with the usual BURLEIGH IRONSTONE' backstamp.[12]

Some advertising or specially commissioned commemorative wares were more oblique in design. An unusual brick, in imitation of eighteenth century English Delft ware, was produced to commemorate the fiftieth anniversary of *Reader's Digest* in 1988. (A similar model was commissioned by Mottahedeh for Winterthur Reproductions.) Like many commissioned and advertising wares made at the Middleport Pottery, it does not bear a Burleigh backstamp.

After the 1980s this line of business petered out with Wades taking a lot of the contracts. Burgess & Leigh was to produce its own 'silent salesman', a plate featuring an underglaze blue printed design showing a view of the works' entrance. This may date from 1989 when the company also produced a small blue and white tray, printed with the nineteenth-century engraving of the factory, to mark 100 years of production at the Middleport Pottery.

The Middleport Pottery 1960-1999: Repairs, Recessions and Receivers

By the 1980s, the fabric of the Middleport Pottery was showing clear signs of its age. Alive to the new 'white-hot' world of technology, a programme of expensive modernisation had been resumed in the mid-1960s with the purchase of two gas-fired intermittent tunnel kilns to replace the biscuit bottle ovens. Originally it was thought that they might be accommodated in a building to the east of the factory site, acquired from Anderton & Co., canal carriers, who had used it for their boat repairs. However, in the end the plan was deemed impractical and the two kilns were installed in what had been the Green House and Biscuit Saggar House areas. This necessitated the demolition of two biscuit ovens, which were last fired during installation of the kilns in 1965. As it abutted the main working area of the factory, the 'number one' bottle oven (which had not been used since c.1950) was left untouched. From fourteen smoking chimneys in 1889, there now remained just one smokeless oven.[13]

But the new tunnel kilns did not disappoint and were fired every weekday night, excepting holidays. They were found to be especially useful for refiring 'crooked' plates upside down! On one memorable occasion shortly after their installation, it was decided to refire crooked holloware on Christmas Eve. When Barry Leigh visited to check proceedings on Christmas Day he found that the heat had ignited the roof two floors above, which had collapsed on to the new kiln. The fire brigade was promptly called out to make the area safe while the next day an architect from Wood, Goldstraw & Yorath, allegedly pleased to relieve the tedium of his Boxing Day, advised on the installation of fire-

Still smoking in 1964. The bottle ovens finally stopped firing in 1965. (*Photograph courtesy of Donald Morris.*)

proof doors to the Potting Shops and the building of a flat concrete roof. The tunnel kiln was firing eleven days later and the last of the crooked ware refired by Easter![14]

The works suffered only a few other minor fires. At around the time of the First World War an insurance claim was made, in good faith, for a quantity of ware smoke damaged by fire; duly compensated, the company found that the pots, once washed, were as good as new! A later fire occurred in the 1970s when attempts to thaw frozen pipes unfortunately destroyed the office door's original leaded glass which had had read '*Private Office*'. (That reading '*General Office*' remains.) It was perhaps symbolic as, around that time, office staff were getting to grips with new technology: telex and later fax machines to improve communications and the first computer to simplify sales and accounts.[15] It was a far cry from the old leather-bound ledgers with their careful copperplate entries. Those on the factory floor were also adjusting to further modernisation, such as the installation of a third kiln in 1973 and the electrification of the Slip House in 1977.

The ongoing repairs and improvements to the factory continued to present problems. When in 1982 the company requested permission from Stoke-on-Trent Council to demolish the remaining bottle oven in order to extend existing biscuit warehousing, it found itself at odds with current thinking on building preservation. The bottle oven, together with the works, had since 1979 been granted Grade II Listed Building status, being of '*special architectural or historic interest*'. The City Council, rejecting the company's request, declared the oven to be: '*one of the finest examples of the few potters' updraught bottle kilns remaining in the city; a striking townscape feature which is clearly visible from the principal road, rail and waterway approaches to the city; has considerable archaeological value as the most important component in a group of nineteenth-century industrial buildings.*'[16]

Accepting the council's decision, the company was to struggle under the financial burden of preserving the factory buildings and site. There were still few signs of a recovery in the pottery and wider national industry. In 1983, for the first time in its history, Great Britain, 'the workshop of the world', was declared a net importer of manufactured goods. While the nation blamed poor government, over-powerful unions, bad management, the ascendancy of the accountant and lawyer and the low status of the manufacturer, Burgess & Leigh, like all potteries, battled with a declining turnover, rising fuel and wage costs, and the doubling of interest rates. Some capital was raised from the sale in 1983 of the works' canteen, land and, later, a number of terraced houses, including that in Port Street in which the works' Lodge Man had conveniently lived. Directors also made additional investment and, with some recovery in the pottery industry during the mid-1980s, the company saw an increased turnover in 1988. This helped pay for new office equipment including the replacement of its telephone system, then a mere sixty-five years old! During that year, Mary Babb, Edmund's married daughter and sister of Kingsley, joined the company to work in an administrative capacity, eventually becoming Company Secretary. Although inflation was high, in 1989 the company saw an increase in sales, a return to profitability, and its best results for many years. In 1990 the directors were able to declare a dividend for the first time in ten years. However, it was to be a false dawn.

The same year the Middleport Pottery was designated a conservation area by Stoke-on-Trent City Council. But in spite of considerable expenditure – some £60,000 profits were spent on repairs and renewals in 1991 – the factory remained in a poor state and presented a real risk to employee safety. The increasing number of accidents was especially worrying to the Leighs, whose model pottery had once boasted exemplary conditions for its workforce. Kath Wilson, an aerographer who had followed her mother into the factory back in the 1960s, remembers that the works seemed 'to have stood still'.[17] While other potteries were fitted with modern machinery, such as electric mixers, she remembers having to break the ice on her glaze on freezing cold Monday mornings. On two occasions while mixing her glaze, she fell into the 'dolly tub', having to be dragged out by the ankles! In spite of the conditions, the extreme cold, the lack of investment in new technology, the constant 'fetching and carrying', the back-breaking hard work, Kath remained loyal, preferring the small close-knit community and the family-feeling absent from many more modern and impersonal factories.

While the perspective from the factory floor might suggest a lack of commitment from the directors, it was rather a lack of funds which prevented investment for modernisation. Certainly respect for the Leighs seems to have been sustained over the generations. Like their forebears, Edmund and Barry never entirely retired, continuing to come into the factory for a couple of days a week throughout the 1990s. While 'Mr Edmund' remained in the office attending to the business side, 'Mr Barry' was known to all those on the factory floor, on whom he exerted a quiet but caring discipline. On one occasion, Kath dared to test his authority by using a vegetable stain, like that routinely used in other potteries, as a marker to guide her aerographing (spray) gun. Barry was sceptical. On reassuring him that the stain would fire off in the kiln, he replied 'I hope, for your sake, it does, Kath'! Fortunately, it did and the technique was adopted. However, the incident may be seen as an example of an increasing insularity within the family firm, in spite of efforts to embrace new methods of production, training and marketing, all of which were identified as lacking by a 1990s consultancy firm.

That the Leighs valued their employees' old-fashioned hard work and gave due consideration to their personal circumstances is well attested. When Kath experienced housing problems, for instance, Barry offered her flexibility in wages to assist with financial repayments. Kath's husband,

Ken Wilson, and his brother Gus, also worked in the factory; Barry praised them as the best glost placers he had come across, though he still saw fit more than once to suggest that Ken might squeeze another eggcup on to the kiln truck! Later, when Kath had to give up her job, Alan reassured her that it would always be open to her should she decide to return. Ken's daughters were also to join the factory, Sue Goulding being appointed Home Order Supervisor in 1981. She became increasingly concerned for the future of the company during the 1990s when she witnessed a worrying lack of orders, inefficiency in production, a reluctance to embrace change and low staff morale, all of which, it is true to say, were prevalent throughout the industry.

Kath and Sue were amongst the seventy employees already working a four-day week who were asked in February 1998 to reduce their hours further to avoid redundancies. In the local press Company Secretary Mary Babb blamed the strength of the pound for hitting the company's seventy per cent export output, saying that 'Poor demand in Japan, because of the Far East situation was also a factor in the downturn of trade… We aim to overcome these difficulties and stay in business but it is just not possible in the present climate to predict when things will improve.'[18] Unfortunately, there was no improvement and by the following year, it was reported that, in 'the first move of its kind in the industry', Burgess & Leigh staff were working an average two days a week while simultaneously claiming the government's 'jobseekers' allowance.[19]

Circumstances took a yet more drastic turn for the worse when in June 1999 the Middleport Pottery bottle oven was put on English Heritage's 'buildings at risk' register, requiring a considerable outlay for its immediate repair. Payment was also due to employees, now down to fifty-five, for 'potters', the early summer holiday. Although the company had a healthy turnover of £1 million, its debts were such that these two coinciding financial demands finally brought about its collapse. On 23rd June, the directors, Edmund, Barry, Mary, Kingsley and Alan, made the difficult and decent decision that the firm should go into voluntary receivership, the minutes of their last meeting recording that 'having given full consideration to the company's overall financial position [they] conclude that the company will be unable to meet its liabilities'. Sending home its sad workers with emergency holiday pay and the promise of more to follow, the company's bank called in the receivers after 110 years. The Middleport Pottery gates were closed until further notice.

CHAPTER SEVEN

BURGESS, *DORLING* & LEIGH LTD:
Recovery and Rebirth of the Middleport Pottery

'....The death of Burgess & Leigh was indeed exaggerated.'[1]

For its owners, employees and customers, the collapse of Burgess & Leigh was devastating. For others, the news from Stoke-on-Trent was familiar: just one more bankrupt pottery with outstanding debts and dwindling sales – a crumbling, outmoded factory in the middle of a run-down area of declining industrial opportunity. Few would have predicted that some twenty bidders would soon be lining up to buy the company as a going concern.

In fact, Burgess & Leigh had considerable advantages over many larger, more high-profile and technically advanced potteries, then struggling with rationalisations and redundancies. An investor's check-list would have indicated that the company had a turnover of around £1 million and that the £180,000 debt precipitating the crisis was not overwhelming. (Unusually for a company in receivership, all the secured creditors were to be paid in full and trade creditors receive part payment.) Its healthy order book was testament to a good-quality, traditionally manufactured product, for which there was a potential increase in demand from important niche markets. The pottery employed a small, highly skilled and loyal workforce. A strong brand-name had been established through five generations of the same family. It boasted a well-established and varied manufacturing history and had preserved a wealth of original designs in copper engravings and moulds. Enthusiasm for its past products, particularly its Art Deco designs, had led to the writing of two collectors guides and the formation in August 1998 of the Burleigh Ware International Collectors' Club with its own newsletter, *The Beehive*.[2] The business operated from a Grade II listed Victorian working pottery in a developing area of 'heritage' tourism. Local business commentators agreed that all Burgess & Leigh lacked was sufficient vision and optimism – in short, new blood was needed.[3]

William and Rosemary Dorling
Amongst the potential buyers who offered that, and more, were husband and wife, William and Rosemary Dorling, owners of the China Box Company, a small ceramics retail and mail order company based in Hampshire in the south of England. The success of their business owed much to the couple's shared experiences, interests and goals. Both had spent their early years in South Africa, Will in Johannesburg and Rosemary (née Creasy) in Umtali in Southern Rhodesia and later Salisbury, before returning to England as teenagers. As a pupil at Abbotsholme School in Rocester, Staffordshire, Will had visited Wedgwood's factory after which he was inspired to make his own moulds, an early indicator of his future vocation! From his mother, a prolific artist whose works have been shown at the Royal Academy and other galleries in Europe, he inherited a love of art but Will chose to pursue a career in crafts. Having inherited his business acumen from his father, at the age of twenty he took up wood-carving and for eight years ran a craft gallery in County Kerry, southern Ireland. This led him to pursue a new career in Information Technology and he subsequently worked for several legal firms in London.

Before raising her two children, Rosemary had worked in a similar environment, as a Legal Executive in various solicitors' firms. She, too, had an interest in the arts, especially poetry, and in nature, which had been nurtured during her childhood in Africa and later led her to study wild flowers. Her father, an English architect, who acted as Assistant to Sir Louis de Soissons, Architect to the Imperial War Graves Commission in Rome, doubtless encouraged her appreciation of architecture. As a pen and ink artist specialising in Italian scenes, he also gave her a sense of colour and design. Although neither she nor Will had any direct experience of manufacturing, it was in their blood, both families having owned mills in Scotland: Rosemary's grandfather had a jute mill, the Buist Spinning Company at Stobwell Works in Dundee, and Will's great-grandfather a tweed mill, Henry Ballantyne & Sons, in Walkerburn, Peebleshire.

The China Box Company
The entrepreneurial genes met when Will and Rosemary founded The China Box Company in 1992. A recession in London in the early 1990s had resulted in both losing their jobs and they were desperate to find alternative employment. It was a friend and neighbour, Elizabeth Murray-John, who first suggested that they should consider setting up a business specialising in something in which they both had an interest: English earthenware. Their lack of funds – they had capital of just £250 – proved to be no deterrent and in January 1992 they made their first buying trip to the factory shops of Stoke-on-Trent. Heartened by a small profit made on their first sale of 'seconds' pottery, they began selling at charity events and lunch-time sales held by large companies. They were soon making regular buying trips to the Potteries; driving north at dawn, the couple would return late at night to unload and wash pot after pot, which were rapidly filling every available space of their Winchester home.

When their small front room began to resemble a china shop, the Dorlings decided they might as well open one. Granted temporary planning permission by the council, on the understanding that they could not display an outside sign, The China Box opened for business in June 1992. In the event, a small cardboard sign pinned to a lamppost and a nine-year-old, placard-bearing godson (now in marketing!) were all it took before word-of-mouth advertising began to bring a steady flow of customers. Beckoned inside by a tempting window display, they found themselves in a comfortable room dominated by a borrowed antique dresser whose busy display of blue and white pottery soon became the hallmark of The China Box Company. A family atmosphere prevailed and visitors regularly found themselves being served by the local retired vicar who had just called in, or enjoying a cup of tea while sitting next to a neighbour's dog, Bobby, snoozing on the fireside chair. For the Dorlings' first Christmas in 1992, customers queued

Rosemary and Will Dorling at The China Box.

The antique Burleigh *Bluebird* jug given to the Dorlings on their wedding in 1990 and now back at the Middleport Pottery where it was made. Height 8ins (20cms).

'Enquiries to be made at the Lodge'.

down the steps while inside home-made decorations and oranges and lemons adorned the stairs, a log fire burned, carols played and mince pies were served. A more traditionally English scene would have been hard to find.

But the customers did not only call for the welcoming atmosphere, they also came to buy and within their first year the Dorlings had sold more than £70,000 worth of pottery. Over the next few years a loyal customer-base was established which resulted in the company being featured in two influential magazines, *Country Homes and Interiors* in the UK and *Victoria* in the USA. A total of 4,000 worldwide enquiries were generated and the decision was made in 1996 to establish a mail order service, its postcards proudly advertising: *'English blue and white earthenware, china and porcelain, handcrafted in old, well-established potteries in Staffordshire and some unusual potteries around the country.'*[4]

When the increased business resulted in pottery being stored under the bed, on the stairs and in the bath, the Dorlings knew it was time to move to larger premises! In 1997 they rented a barn on Chilbolton Down Farm near Stockbridge, just a mile and a half across the fields from their new home in Crawley. The barn, which Will fitted with floorboards acquired from Tunstall High School, housed a studio where he decorated his own spongeware pottery, a pattern called *And The Garden Went Wild*, which was sold through The China Box Company. It was a very different environment from the industrial Potteries but the Dorlings remained champions of Staffordshire pottery, then saying, *'We believe fervently in the English Potteries and that the cheaper European pottery which is being sold widely is of inferior quality to our own traditional earthenware …there is an immense variety*

of high- quality, resilient and good value for money…. We are proud to be supporting the English Potteries in a tradition of trade that goes back 300 years.'[5] On attending a Country Living Fair in 1997, the couple were inspired to have a car sticker printed reading: *'Do you drink out of English clay? If not, start today. Support our English potteries'*.

In spite of its isolated position on top of the Hampshire Downs, customers still flocked to The China Box and sales days would see some £10,000 in the Victorian till. One of the best-selling lines, which accounted for seventy percent of their sales, was Burleigh Ware. A friend, Penny Bullivant, had given the Dorlings their first piece of Burleigh, a *Bluebird* jug found in an antique shop, on their marriage in 1990. It was to prove an auspicious gift, although it was only when Rosemary and Will visited the Middleport Pottery on a buying trip for The China Box Company that they realised where their *Bluebird* jug had been made.

In fact, it was to take the Dorlings several months' searching Stoke-on-Trent for 'Burleigh' before they were first able to locate 'Burgess & Leigh' in 1992. Having found the Middleport Pottery tucked away in the back streets, they went on to visit it every month during the 1990s; setting off before dawn from Hampshire, they rewarded themselves with a flask of hot chocolate in Birmingham and breakfast in a café in Burslem before arriving at the Middleport Pottery's lodge at 7.45a.m. Welcomed by staff, they would spend some three hours in the 'top seconds' warehouse selecting and packing items of *Bluebird, Calico, Asiatic Pheasant* and other traditional blue and white ranges for their customers. Over the years, their love of Burleigh Ware extended to the Middleport Pottery, which they viewed as a *'hidden treasure'*

The façade of the Middleport Pottery in Port Street and the sign which still greets visitors today.

of Victorian industrial buildings, its authentic 'Five Towns' atmosphere inadvertently preserved by the Leighs. But never during their many visits, did the Dorlings imagine that one day they would own the pottery, not even when they joined other customers concerned for the future of Burgess & Leigh.

The Saving of the Middleport Pottery

Rosemary and Will first heard that the Middleport Pottery was in the hands of the Receivers on 23rd June, 1999 while they were on holiday on the Isle of Wight. They were stunned to hear that thirty-seven of its fifty-five employees had already been made redundant as corporate recovery experts KPMG embarked on an attempt to restructure the business as a viable investment. But the couple's concern was not only for job losses. They could not believe that such a saleable product as Burleigh Ware might also disappear should new investors decide to break up the business by

selling off its valuable coppers and moulds. The Dorlings immediately decided to mount a campaign to save the Middleport Pottery. But time was short. They began writing letters to all the influential people and institutions they thought might be willing to help, including the National Trust, English Heritage and the Sainsbury Family Charitable Trusts. All organisations agreed that the Middleport Pottery was a valuable heritage site and should be saved but their legal conditions meant that they were unable to structure funding by the Receivers' deadline of 10th August, 1999. The couple also wrote to HRH the Prince of Wales, a champion of English architectural and manufacturing heritage, whose concerns and good wishes for the campaign were conveyed by letter.

As the weeks passed, the Dorlings began to despair. On Thursday, 5th August they spent £3,500 on what they feared could be their last ever order of Burleigh Ware. Booking into Manor House Farm, their usual Staffordshire bed and breakfast, they feared that the situation was hopeless. But with the dawn came the belief that they themselves had to act. As Will was later to recall: '*I had put the idea out of my mind at first because it seemed an impossible task. We had tried to get other people to do it, but then realised that we had the power ourselves.*'[6] Hurrying to the Middleport Pottery on Friday morning, the Dorlings faxed a bid to the Receivers KPMG (then unaware that the couple had just £400 in their bank account!) Over the weekend they made desperate attempts to raise funds, planning to sell their holiday home on the Isle of Wight and calling on their families, including Will's father, Mr Tony Dorling, and his ninety-nine year old great aunt,

Mrs Eve Bingham, to loan them money. At ten o'clock on Monday, 9th August they presented their business plan to the bank manager. Recognising that they had equity, as well as un un-quantifiable but vital entrepreneurial spirit, he agreed to a loan of twenty-five percent – but on the Burgess & Leigh business only, not the works. At that stage, the only feasible solution seemed to be to move the business to a modern manufacturing unit in Stoke-on-Trent, which would have left the Middleport Pottery's unique Victorian site at risk of inappropriate and possibly destructive development.

However, walking back from the bank a chance meeting with their old friends and neighbours, Peter and Judith Goldring, was to radically change the course of events. On hearing of their plans, the Goldrings convinced Will and Rosemary of what the couple knew in their hearts already – that the Burgess & Leigh business was inseparable from the Middleport Pottery. But how were they to raise funds to acquire the works as well? Acting on the Goldrings' advice, the Dorlings managed to obtain a meeting at 3p.m. that same afternoon with a broker who did not foresee any difficulty in raising a commercial mortgage on the Middleport Pottery and the remortgage of their Hampshire home. With just one hour to the deadline, the couple hurriedly called the Receivers – from a pay-phone in a local supermarket – and at five o'clock, faxed through their revised offer for the business and proposed purchase of the works. William Leigh's 1855 maxim 'A cat in gloves catches no mice' might have been written especially for them!

It was to be a long night waiting to hear if their offer was successful. The number of firm bidders had been whittled down to three, described in the press as: '… an out of area group with local interests, …a local pottery manufacturer and… a consortium, which is believed to have backing from the United States.'[7] The competition was arguably more powerful, with better financial backing, a longer business record and undoubtedly more manufacturing experience, but it did not take the Receivers long to decide that the Dorlings were the most convincing option. Three days after the exchange of contracts on the 27th August, the Dorlings' identity as purchasers was finally revealed under a seemingly incredulous press headline in *The Sentinel: 'Couple stake their future on a potbank.'* For better or worse, the Middleport Pottery was theirs!

Burgess, *Dorling* & Leigh: a Family Business

Living out of suitcases at Manor House Farm for six months, Rosemary and Will began to readjust to their new lives as owners of the Middleport Pottery. Fortunately, they had the support of their family, as Rosemary's children, Susannah and Simon, joined the firm which was renamed Burgess, *Dorling* & Leigh.

Susannah had been familiar with Burleigh Ware since she was a teenager helping to run The China Box Company at weekends. Following a course in Art and Design, she put her knowledge and love of pottery to use by starting her own sales and marketing business which had several small north Staffordshire potteries as clients. Although Susannah had been sad and shocked to hear of the collapse of Burgess & Leigh, she admits that she thought that Will and her mother had taken leave of their senses by buying the firm! Now she was doing all she could to support them by giving up her own business to take on the challenging and responsible job of sole Sales Manager. Her brother, Simon, who had a

The family firm in the early months. Left to right: Simon Baird, Will Dorling, Rosemary Dorling and Susannah Baird. Edmund Leigh, photographed, looks on.

Susannah Baird, Sales Manager.

Sue Goulding, Works Manager.

background unrelated to pottery in rural resource management, left his old friends and way of life to become Project Manager overseeing the maintenance, running and repair of the pottery. After making some inroads into this gargantuan task, Simon's greater love of the outdoors lured him away to pursue his own business interests outside the pottery industry. A legacy he leaves is the attractive rose and herb garden, which now welcomes visitors to the pottery.

One person the Dorlings knew they had to have as a member of their team was Sue Goulding, previously Burgess & Leigh's Glost Warehouse Manager and one of those made redundant in 1999. The Dorlings had become friends with Sue during the years they visited the pottery as customers and had always been impressed by her knowledge, experience and enthusiasm for the Burleigh product. She was more than happy to accept their offer of a new position as Works Manager. The early months of the Dorlings' tenure, Sue remembers, were particularly hard with Will and Rosemary working twelve hours a day, seven days a week. The most critical task they had to undertake at the outset was to maintain pottery production to fulfill orders. However, as Will got to grips with the company finances, he realised that there was no money even to purchase raw materials. Rosemary was forced to make telephone calls to Burgess & Leigh's worldwide customers to ask if they would be prepared to pay in advance in order to generate cash flow. Such was the customers' faith in Burleigh Ware, that every single one agreed.

With no experience of pottery manufacture, the Dorlings were indebted to members of the local pottery industry who came forward with offers of help on the production side. They were amused and delighted to receive a telephone call from two retired pottery directors, John Hanley and John Scott, who offered to act as self-appointed 'godfathers' to Burgess, Dorling & Leigh. While illness prevented Mr Hanley's continuing assistance, John Scott's experience and knowledge of man-management, manufacturing and production was simply a lifeline to the business. He remains a regular visitor, supporter and adviser. Gradual recruitment has increased the number of employees to fifty, including the hands-on roles of Will, as financial director; Rosemary, responsible for marketing; and Susannah in charge of sales. A recent recruit is Director of Operations, Mike Lomax, with fifteen years' experience at Spode. He joins Trevor McCarthy, who was appointed General Manager in 2001 after twenty-five years at Sadlers Pottery in Burslem.

Gradually, Burgess, Dorling & Leigh began to make improvements to the works. Two 'new' electric kilns were installed; a regulatory fire alarm system was fitted; electricity wiring renewed; and small general building repairs were made, taking care to preserve the original character of the building. Working conditions were also improved by, for example, bringing heating to especially cold areas. Royal Doulton also provided some equipment free of charge. Employees were particularly eager to help, offering Will and Rosemary accommodation in their own homes and providing them with lunches when they were too busy to take a break. 'We've been overwhelmed by the reaction of the people of Stoke-on-Trent,' Will has reflected, 'Nothing could have prepared us for the support we have received from the locals and the workforce at the pottery.'[8] The Dorlings are already earning the same loyalty and support which Middleport Pottery employees had showed to generations of the Leigh family. Sadly in December 1999, Edmund Leigh died but

Trevor McCarthy, General Manager, left, and Mike Lomax, Director of Operations.

Barry continues to visit the Middleport Pottery to meet old friends and to collect his order of Burleigh Ware.

Just as the Leighs had struggled with coal strikes, so the new regime found an ingenious and economical solution to its short supplies when building work uncovered a coal seam in Sue Goulding's father's garden! She and her step-mother, Kath, together bagged eighty-six sacks of top-quality coal which they brought in as fuel for the boiler.[9] A recent power cut has evoked pre-war days when the sudden breaking of a belt or pulley from the steam engine would shut down the DC generator it then drove to light the warehouses and decorating shops in the 'Town Hall'. Then, late in the afternoon everyone would be plunged into darkness![10] During the latest crisis, while hasty repairs were made to the fuse box, candles were lit around the pottery giving it a truly Victorian atmosphere.

Together with maintaining production, expanding markets and keeping the business' customer base happy, from the outset Will and Rosemary were eager to meet the challenge of repairing and restoring the long-neglected Middleport Pottery site, particularly the threatened bottle oven. In time, they propose to create a museum and visitor centre with factory tours and a tearoom, making the site an attractive addition to Stoke-on-Trent's developing tourism industry which, since the 1970s, had capitalised on the area's pottery manufacture and industrial history. The Middleport Pottery is a genuine Victorian working pottery ideally placed in a site already designated a regeneration area. That which had made it the 'model pottery of Staffordshire' in the nineteenth century – its advantageous canal-side position, 'high-tech' steam engine and transfer-printing presses, and

A view through the cobwebs of the old Export Manager's office.

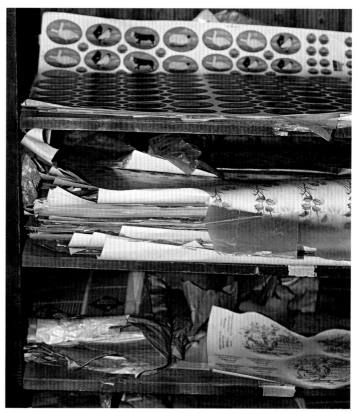

A cupboard in the Litho' Store.

Stacks of 'flat' in the biscuit warehouse.

Abandoned hospital wares including, far right, the 'Welsh hat' commode pan.

Edwardian biscuit ware under layers of soot and dust in the old 'Town Hall.'

modern bathroom facilities for its workers – could now make it a successful tourist destination in the twenty-first century heritage industry.

With full restoration estimated at between £2- and £4 million and no working capital, the Dorlings first embarked on the tortuous bureaucratic maze of grant funding on completion of their purchase of the Middleport Pottery works in March 2000. Not until December 2002 would they hear their first piece of good news, that £135,000 of European Community funding was to be released to them through the Middleport Townscape Heritage Initiative. Essential restoration work could at last begin including the repair of the insidious crack which had developed in the bottle oven. The steam engine, idle for nearly thirty years, is gradually being brought back to working life with help from a volunteer team of steam enthusiasts from the Etruria Industrial Museum. The Packing House, subject of a commissioned report by architectural historian Dr Malcolm Nixon, is earmarked for future conversion to a tearoom. The 'Wad House' bathroom, currently submerged under metres of muddy water, is shortly to be excavated by him in preparation for its restoration. Will and Rosemary continue to be grateful to such experts and supporters, including Jeremy Miln from the National Trust; advisers from English Heritage and the Phoenix Trust; Ken Barnes of Business Link in Staffordsire; and members of Stoke-on-Trent City Council. Local Member of Parliament Joan Whalley, who had provided invaluable support for Burgess & Leigh when the business was first under threat in the late 1990s, remains an especially enthusiastic supporter and lobbyist for grant funding for the Middleport Pottery.

The Burleigh Factory Shop

An immediate priority for Burgess, Dorling & Leigh was a retail outlet and within two months of the firm going into receivership, a Factory Shop was duly opened on the ground floor of the old 'Town Hall'. Just as the nineteenth-century warehouses had been fitted out to attract customers, so the new Factory Shop was furnished with a counter from the last working silk mill in the Staffordshire town of Leek to complement original wooden racking and a log fire. Additional tables and kitchen dressers were bought to show off Burleigh Ware ranges to their best advantage, Rosemary's design flair giving a distinctly feminine touch to the display. When the old Victorian elementary school in Middleport, designed by A. R. Wood, was sadly demolished, Rosemary was eager to preserve architectural features and fittings salvaged from the building; its tiny desks and chairs are now part of the Factory Shop for children to use while their parents shop or relax with free tea and coffee.

The homely atmosphere of The China Box in Winchester has been recreated in the Burleigh Factory Shop which gives a warm welcome to visitors from all over the world. The Dorlings are eager to encourage contact from their local community through inviting residents to events such as the Christmas party. Former Stoke-on-Trent City Councillor Ted Owen is one regular visitor and supporter, dropping by with tempting cream cakes, while confirmed Staffordshire oatcake enthusiast, Dr Malcolm Nixon, is another, frequently calling in with his family to offer advice and encouragement. Steve Davies is far more than a Factory Shop manager; the son of a paintress of Burleigh toby jugs during the 1940s and 1950s, his knowledge of the history of the company and its products is much appreciated by Burleigh Ware enthusiasts.

A year after the establishment of Burgess, Dorling & Leigh, Rosemary and Will were still reeling from the changes to their lives but their own enthusiasm was made clear in their first newsletter:

'As you can imagine our first year at the Middleport Pottery has been not only the most exciting year of our lives, but the most privileged and challenging.... Huge areas of exquisite industrial architecture, a steam engine, a disused Victorian bathroom, cobbled courtyards, a bottle oven, and a factory powered by coal. A directors' office totally intact, a Second World War helmet, glaze book recipes written in script... cough mixture unopened from 100 years, all preserved, nothing having been removed by the Leigh family... A mould room, where in we found around some 15,000 moulds, some

The Burleigh Factory Shop with its manager, Steve Davies.

covered in thick inches of ancient dust. A quiet sanctuary of creativity, some moulds dating back to the early nineteenth century. We have discovered daily the most beautiful pieces, some of which, especially those of the 1930s we have transformed into ceramics.'[11]

The Mould Store Revisited

An employee advising the Dorlings on the contents of the mould store is John Machin, mould maker at the Middleport Pottery since 1977. John was apprenticed for seven years at Staffordshire Potteries where his father was head modeller (having served his own apprenticeship at Burgess & Leigh during the 1930s). During his spare time, he had started cataloguing the moulds, some of which had never been used. Will and Rosemary could not wait to begin production and made an initial selection of 1930s Flower Jugs, which were launched in their original colourways at the NEC Spring Fair in Birmingham in 1999. Additional items from the mould store followed over the next couple of years, hand-painted by Carole and Phil Green, skilled ex-Royal Doulton painters. Some were produced in new colourways and made in limited editions for special markets.

A cupboard in the Directors' office spills its contents, including a Second World War helmet.

John Machin, mould maker, applying sprigged decoration to an *Davenport* comport.

The Middleport Pottery mould store.

Burgess, Dorling & Leigh Flower Jugs in new and original colourways, photographed in the Middleport Pottery showroom. Top, *Rock Garden* with *Kingfisher*; middle, *Butterfly* with *Flamingo*, third left; bottom, *Dragon*, *Turkey* and *Budgerigar*. Tallest 10¹/₂ins (26.5cms).

Top, large and small *Cricketer* jugs with yellow and white glazes; middle, *Tennis Player* and *Golfer* jugs; bottom, *Pied Piper* with trial piece, production piece, and special limited edition colourway, right. Tallest 7¹/₂ins (19cms).

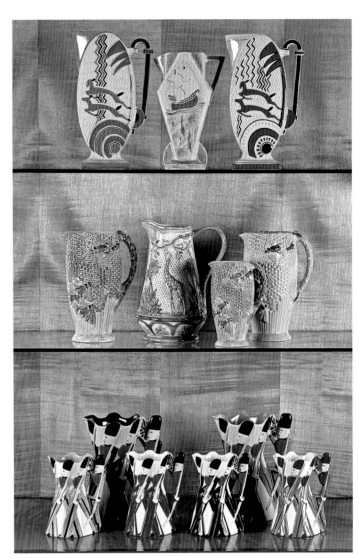

Top, '*Leaping Gazelles*' (*Luxor*) with trial piece of *Argosy*, centre; middle, large and small *Honeycomb* jugs with *Giraffe*; bottom, *Guardsman*, large and small in different colourways. Tallest 10ins (25.4cms).

Dragon jug, with 'crackle' lustre and platinum gilt decoration by young freelance ceramic artist, Dean Sherwin. Renamed the *Vesuvius*, it was produced in a limited edition in 2001. Height 7¹/₂ins (19cms).

Other items were completely new discoveries from the mould store and had never before been produced. Caster Roy Davies, for instance, who had worked with Ernest Bailey during the late 1970s, had found a mould for his 'Battle of Britain' plaque just three weeks before the sixtieth anniversary of the event, enabling Burgess, Dorling & Leigh to issue it as a commemorative. His wife, Alison, a fettler sponger, came across the mould for Bailey's novelty *Cheltenham* caravan teapot which was supplemented by a new shaped milk jug and sugar box modelled by John Machin. A small advertisement placed in *Caravan News* brought in 350 orders for the set, which continues to be a popular purchase.

The re-issue of Burgess & Leigh's 1930s' items[12] was contentious for some collectors and became part of a continuing debate within wider ceramic circles regarding modern day recreation of designs from the past.[13] A new Burgess, Dorling & Leigh backstamp had been designed to incorporate the initials *B,D&L* in the old Burgess & Leigh 'beehive' backstamp. However, some unscrupulous antiques dealers were able to mislead collectors and the company was compelled to include an impressed date mark in order to clearly distinguish current reproductions from original models. It was all part of the learning process for the new owners who were arguably only continuing a practice followed by most pottery firms over the centuries.

Burgess, Dorling & Leigh have remained true to the company's original ranges. New badged and advertising wares, for instance, have included a tea canister decorated with a pattern based on the *'Dillwyn' Willow*, and produced especially for the London department store Fortnum & Mason. A range of items

Battle of Britain plaque, modelled by Bailey in 1940 and first issued as a commemorative by Burgess, Dorling & Leigh sixty years later. Diameter 10ins (25.4cms).

Cube teapots, from left to right, *Burgess Chintz, Felicity*, a plain glazed white with a small jug in *Arden* in front, *Victorian Chintz* and *Asiatic Pheasant*.

Caravanserai: pink, blue and green versions of the *Cheltenham* caravan teaset from 2001. Height 3ins (7.5cms).

Roy Davies, caster, with a mould for a small size ewer.

Alison Davies, fettler sponger, ready to smooth the edges from biscuit ware canisters.

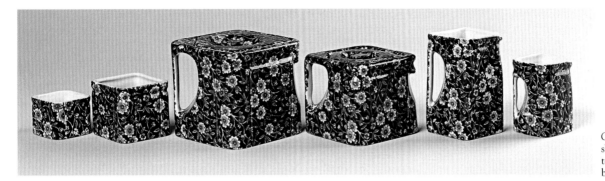

Calico cubes, revived in 2000, showing two sizes of teaset: teapots, milk jugs and sugar bowls. Tallest 6ins (15cms).

Royal Commemoratives, re-issued with a blue wash and gilded for the Queen's Golden Jubilee in 2002. A small *Guardsman* jug, in blue and red, was also part of the collection.

Sweet tray and jug, in the in-glaze *Naïve* pattern, part of the range produced especially for Crabtree & Evelyn. Diameter 6ins (15cms).

made for Crabtree & Evelyn, English toiletries manufacturers, features a design called *Naïve* which they brought to Burgess, Dorling & Leigh. Printed in-glaze, this successfully reproduces the soft blurred tones of the traditional flow blue glaze. The National Trust, which shares Burgess, Dorling & Leigh's aims to maintain and preserve English heritage, sells the company's kitchen wares through its Beatrix Potter Gallery in the Lake District. More recently it has commissioned an exclusive range of Burleigh patterns entitled *Birds, Fruit and Flowers*, which it will sell, with matching fabrics, through selected National Trust shops in the UK. Collections of commemorative wares[14] have been made from existing moulds, not only to mark events in the Second World War, but also to celebrate the Jubilee of Queen Elizabeth II. The company took particular pleasure in having certain items in the latter range selected for sale exclusively through the Buckingham Palace shop.

2001 'Centenary' Celebrations

The Dorlings have elected to continue the Leigh tradition of celebrating 1851 as the founding date of the company. To mark its 150th anniversary in 2001, Burgess, Dorling & Leigh reissued the *Jug of all Nations* in a limited edition,[15] while further celebrations included a special event on 12th July at the Middleport Pottery. Amongst the past employees attending was retired Head Packer Ben Ford who gave a display of traditional packing in straw, *'like a magpie making his nest'* as one visitor commented! Items packed by Ben formed part of a special consignment of pottery, which was delivered from Middleport Pottery wharf to Camden Lock in London by two original cargo carrying narrowboats, the *Sweden* and the *Buckden*.[16] It was believed to be the first such canal delivery of pottery since 1950. It took the narrowboats two weeks to travel to London where Burleigh products were delivered to customers Divertimenti

Original 1940s shapes recreated by Burgess, Dorling & Leigh as Second World War Commemoratives in 2000. Top, left to right, Churchill character jug in naval uniform; Churchill ashtray and cigar; Churchill 'V for Victory' toby jug, tallest 5ins (13cms). Bottom, left to right, miniature Churchill character jug in naval uniform; 'Bulldogs' toby jug; and Union Jack Churchill mug, tallest 11ins (28cms).

Cookshop. En route, the boats made publicised stops to sell Burleigh Wares, the £3,000 taken more than covering the cost of the trip. The event was followed by press, radio and television reports, which the Dorlings continue to attract. One documentary television programme to feature the works was *Trading Places*; offering an entertaining insight into different work experiences, Brigitte Dix, a transferrer in Middleport Pottery's Print Shop since 1989, swapped jobs with an employee at a highly automated ceramics manufacturer nearby. Brigitte was more than happy to stay at

the Middleport Pottery making Burleigh Ware the traditional and more unhurried way – becoming something of a local star in the process!

***'One feature of 'Burleigh Ware' is that it does what we all should do – it grows better as it grows older.' The Pottery Gazette,* 1st March, 1907**

Burgess, Dorling & Leigh have made a decision to concentrate production on underglaze transfer-printed kitchen- and table wares, thus returning to the company's

Burleigh Ware, en route from Middleport Wharf to Camden Lock in 2001.

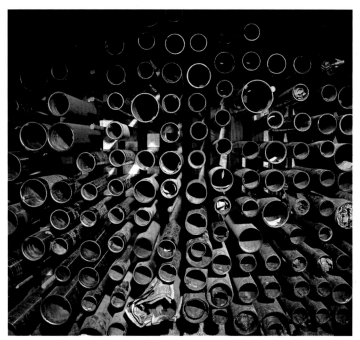

Copper 'rollers' at the Middleport Pottery. The engraved cylinders were first introduced by Burgess & Leigh in the early 1900s to use in conjunction with flat copper plates.

Brian Tompkinson, engraver, working on a Burleigh pattern.

A copperplate engraving showing the *Danish Fern* pattern selected by Martha Stewart for reproduction by Burgess, Dorling & Leigh.

Printer Paul Thomas guiding a sheet of tissue of the famous Burleigh *Calico* as it comes off the Roller Printing Machine.

Transferrer Ann Simmill (née Wilson) cutting prints for application on to biscuit ware.

Transferrers Sylvia Thomas, left, and Brigitte Dix, right, at work in the Print Shop, fitting the print tissue.

Sylvia Thomas rubbing the tissue paper on to ware using a stiff bristle brush and soft soap and water 'size' in the Print Shop.

Carole Stanyer 'washing off' prior to firing. Every piece of Burleigh transfer printed ware is washed by Carole.

Thelwell Campbell-Smith, also known as 'Kelly', making Burleigh bowls the traditional way.

Linda Davies, twenty-seven years at the Middleport Pottery, operating the Murray-Curvex printing machine whose gelatine 'bomb', centre right, applies print to biscuit flat ware shapes.

earliest trade when Frederick Rathbone Burgess and William Leigh first exported their wares to North America in the 1860s. Many of the kitchen ware shapes, produced in '*natural white glazed ironstone*' (high-fired earthenware), date from that time: *Etruscan, Tankard* and *Dutch* shaped jugs; banded pudding bowls and planters; hooped *Churn* and *Tankard* jugs; bread crocks and colanders; lipped mixing bowls; blancmange and jelly moulds; ewers and basins; storage jars; and Stilton cheese stands. Traditional 'Suite Wares' decorated in underglaze printed patterns include popular items from the 1930s like toast racks and four-person egg trays with more recent shapes like the tea bag holder. 2003 has seen the successful re-issue of miniature '*cream tot*' jugs, previously made in 1905 for the hotel trade, which are now produced in a variety of different patterns.

Discontinuing some patterns, such as *Home Farm* and *Scilla*, and reviving others, the company's general range of underglaze printed patterns now includes those produced by Burgess & Leigh in the nineteenth and early twentieth centuries: *Asiatic Pheasants; Arden;* and *Bluebird,* together with later best-sellers from the 1960s onwards: *Calico; Chequers; Felicity; Burgess Chintz;* and *Victorian Chintz.* Just as the company did in the past, Burgess, Dorling & Leigh have recently invested in nineteenth-century copperplate engravings acquired when local pottery (and former China Box Company supplier) Blakeney went into receivership in the late 1990s; their patterns *Claremont; Gentian; Provence* and *Pale Roses* (an exclusive China Box pattern) are now produced on Burgess, Dorling & Leigh shapes. A new pattern '*for kids and cats*' features a cut-out *Calico* cat decoration. Blue remains the predominant colour for all patterns but variations in depth are offered, from the very dark cobalt of *Calico* to the soft paleness of *Asiatic Pheasants.*

The Middleport Pottery Showroom, today, with glass and wood veneered shelving installed for the 1951 centenary celebration.

The Burgess, Dorling & Leigh stand at the Ambiente Trade Fair in Frankfurt, Germany, 2002.

A page from a catalogue of c.1928 showing kitchen wares of the kind Burgess & Leigh were making in 1862.

Jellies, jars and jugs displayed the Dorling way.

Nineteenth-century shapes for a twenty-first century lifestyle.

Continuing the tradition: Burgess, Dorling & Leigh jelly moulds made from original nineteenth-century moulds.

'Natural White' for the pantry. Beneath the stillage is a wooden-lidded bread crock; originally a foot bath, it also sells today, without a lid, as an oval planter.

A page from a Burleigh Catalogue of 2002-2003.

The *Bluebird* pattern, originally named *Chinese Peacock*, has often been in production during the last ninety years.

New additions for 2002. Nineteenth-century printed pattern originally produced by Blakeney Pottery in Stoke-on-Trent: *Claremont*, left and second right; *Pale Roses* (previously a China Box Co. exclusive pattern) second left and far right; and *Provence* third left.

Chequers, an underglaze printed pattern designed by David Copeland in 1975.

Pages from the Burleigh Catalogue, 2002-2003.

The English summer... a pink version of *Felicity* first introduced by Burgess & Leigh in blue in 1980.

BURGESS DORLING & LEIGH LTD
Manufacturers of

BURLEIGH WARE
Established 1851

Felicity   Arden

Arden a nineteenth-century pattern revived by Burgess & Leigh in 1972, shown on this 1999 leaflet with *Felicity* in blue.

GENTIAN
(no plates available)

These various archive patterns depicting hawthorn, roses, mosses and seedpods, in subtle shades of blue are perfect for mixing to make a patchwork of pattern on the kitchen dresser and the table.

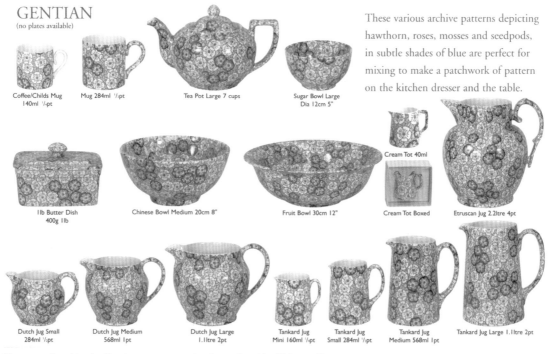

Coffee/Childs Mug
140ml ¼-pt

Mug 284ml ½pt

Tea Pot Large 7 cups

Sugar Bowl Large
Dia 12cm 5"

Cream Tot 40ml

1lb Butter Dish
400g 1lb

Chinese Bowl Medium 20cm 8"

Fruit Bowl 30cm 12"

Cream Tot Boxed

Etruscan Jug 2.2ltre 4pt

Dutch Jug Small
284ml ½pt

Dutch Jug Medium
568ml 1pt

Dutch Jug Large
1.1ltre 2pt

Tankard Jug
Mini 160ml ¼pt

Tankard Jug
Small 284ml ½pt

Tankard Jug
Medium 568ml 1pt

Tankard Jug Large 1.1ltre 2pt

Shapes produced in the *Gentian* pattern, previously produced by Blakeney Pottery.

ASIATIC PHEASANTS

Cream Tot Boxed

Cream Tot 40ml

Tankard Jug Mini 160ml ¼pt

Tankard Jug Small 284ml ½pt

Tankard Jug Medium 568ml 1pt

Tankard Jug Large 1.1ltre 2pt

Dutch Jug Small 284ml ½pt

Dutch Jug Medium 568ml 1pt

Dutch Jug Large 1.1ltre 2pt

Sandringham Jug 568ml 1pt

Etruscan Jug Large 2.2ltre 4pt Small 1.1ltre 2pt

Dutch Flower Jug 9ltre 16pt

Ewer Medium 1.6 ltre 3pt

Ewer Large 3.8ltre 7pt

Fruit Bowl Large 38.5cm 15½" Medium 30cm 12"

Storage Jar Tea Ht 14cm 5½"

Storage Jar Coffee Ht 14cm 5½"

Storage Jar Sugar Ht 14cm 5½"

Storage Jar Utensils Ht 14cm 5½"

Storage Jar Biscuits Ht 19.5cm 7½"

Storage Jar Flour Ht 19.5cm 7½"

Bread Crock 36 x 28 x 16.5cm 14" x 11" x 6½"

Stilton Cheese 17cm 7"

Churn Jug Milk 1ltre 1¾pt

Cow Creamer

Round Butter Tub Ht 9cm 3½"

Tea Bag Holder

Soap with Drainer 13 x 10.5cm 5" x 4"

Loving Cup 12.5cm x 10cm 5" x 4"

Oval Planter 36 x 28 x 16.5cm 14" x 11" x 6½"

Asiatic Pheasant and flowers. The pattern was first produced by Burgess & Leigh in 1862.

The pale blue of *Asiatic Pheasant* is a true reproduction of its original colour.

VICTORIAN CHINTZ
(no plates available)

Coffee/Childs Mug 140ml ¼pt

Mug 280ml ½pt

Tea Pot Large 7 cups

Sugar Bowl Large Dia 12cm 5"

Cream Tot 40ml

Butter Dish 400g 1lb

Chinese Bowl Medium 20cm 8"

Fruit Bowl 30cm 12"

Cream Tot Boxed

Etruscan Jug 2.2ltre 4pt

Dutch Jug Small 284ml ½pt

Dutch Jug Medium 568ml 1pt

Dutch Jug Large 1.1ltre 2pt

Tankard Jug Mini 160ml ¼pt

Tankard Jug Small 284ml ½pt

Tankard Jug Medium 568ml 1pt

Tankard Jug Large 1.1ltre 2pt

Victorian Chintz, a page from the 2002-2003 Burleigh Catalogue which shows, top left, the decorative backstamp used on the pattern today.

CALICO

Dutch Flower Jug 9ltre 16pt

Ewer Medium 1.6ltre 3pt

Ewer Large 3.8ltre 7pt

Fruit Bowl Large 38.5cm 15¹⁄₂" Medium 30cm 12"

Storage Jar Tea
Ht 14cm 5¹⁄₂"

Storage Jar Coffee
Ht 14cm 5¹⁄₂"

Storage Jar Sugar
Ht 14cm 5¹⁄₂"

Storage Jar Utensils
Ht 14cm 5¹⁄₂"

Storage Jar Biscuits
Ht 19.5cm 7¹⁄₂"

Storage Jar Flour
Ht 19.5cm 7¹⁄₂"

Soap and Drainer
13 x 10.5cm 5" x 4"

With label

Churn Jug Milk 1ltre 1³⁄₄pt

Round Butter Dish
Ht 9cm 3¹⁄₂"

Cow Creamer (no label)

Mug Tea
284ml ¹⁄₂pt

Mug Coffee
284ml ¹⁄₂pt

Tea Bag Holder

Bread Plate 28cm 11"

Bread Crock 36 x 28 x 16.5cm
14" x 11" x 6¹⁄₂"

Stilton Cheese
Ht 17cm 7"

Dish - 4 sizes available
25cm 10", 28cm 11", 34cm 13¹⁄₂", 39cm 15¹⁄₂"

Soup Tureen 2.2ltre 4pt

Sauce Tureen 568ml 1pt

Soup and Sauce Ladle

Oval Planter 36 x 28 x 16.5cm
14" x 11" x 6¹⁄₂"

FOR KIDS & CATS!

Baby Cat Plate 19cm 7¹⁄₂"

Baby Cat Bowl 15cm 6"

Baby Cat Mug
140ml ¹⁄₄pt

Cat Rimmed 15cm 6"

Cat Fruit 12cm 5"

The most popular *Burleigh* pattern, *Calico*. A 'Victorian' pattern from 1968, Burgess, Dorling & Leigh have introduced new shapes and a range entitled *Calico Cat* especially '*For Kids & Cats*'.

Calico, with fruit

...and flowers.

227

BURGESS CHINTZ

A delicate blue chintz flowered pattern dating from the early 1900's, derived from the wild geranium.

Plate 17.5cm 7"   Plate 19cm 7½"   Plate 21.5cm 8½"   Plate 26.5cm 10½"   Soup/Pudding 21.5cm 8½"

Cereal Bowl 16cm 6½"   Egg Tot   Egg Tot Tray 16cm 6½" sq   Fruit Dish 12cm 5"   Tea Cup & Saucer 250ml ½pt   Breakfast Cup & Saucer 420ml ¾pt

Coffee/Childs Mug 140ml ¼pt   Mug 284ml ½pt   Chocolate Mug 284ml ½pt   Tea Pot Large 7 cups   Tea Pot Small 3-4 cups   Hot Water Jug Lge/Sml Large 7 cups Small 3 cups

Tea Box 800g 2lb   Tea Cream Jug 290ml ½pt   Sugar Bowl Large Dia 12cm 5"   Sugar Bowl Small Dia 9.5cm 4"   Covered Sugar/Jam 200g ½lb   1lb Butter Dish 400g 1lb

Burgess Chintz. Introduced in the early 1990s, its name pays tribute to the company's nineteenth-century co-founder Frederick Rathbone Burgess.

Photographed here in twenty-first century 'life-style' fashion.

'Burleigh, from clay to cup… pure English'

The Dorlings' flair for marketing its products has been to a great extent the key to the successful revitalisation of the firm. Rosemary's claim that she knows what people want to buy is backed up by an appreciation of the importance of brand-image. The presentation of Burleigh Ware in a contemporary country 'lifestyle' setting has re-awakened the public to a brand which shows itself to be equally at home in the twenty-first century as it was in the nineteenth. Susannah, with sales assistant Jane Ratcliffe, regularly attend UK exhibitions, such as the NEC in Birmingham and Top Drawer in London, and international trade fairs, like Frankfurt and Maison et Objets in Paris. This has not only helped to reassert the global profile of the Burleigh brand but has also attracted new accounts, 150 in the UK and seventy overseas, simultaneously rebuilding the confidence lost by some old customers. Top stores, such as Harrods, Libertys, Chinacraft and Fortnum & Mason in London, as well as many small, discerning shops all over the country, all

The Burleigh 'mixed dresser' in large and miniature. Cream 'tots' and miniature plates with birds, fruit and flower patterns introduced for the National Trust in 2003.

Rosemary and William Dorling, Directors, Burgess, Dorling & Leigh Ltd.

stock Burleigh Ware. They are eager to recreate Rosemary's successful formula for display, a happily haphazard selection of patterns on painted country kitchen dressers supplied by Burgess, Dorling & Leigh. New Burleigh Ware ranges are also regularly featured in top 'glossy' magazines.

Some seventy-five percent of Burgess Dorling & Leigh's turnover is overseas. There are good accounts in Europe, particularly in France and Germany, and a distributor in Spain. The company is represented in its old colonial markets of New Zealand, through Parnell Agencies, and Australia, where Lindt Trading has the account. In the U.S.A., Burgess, Dorling & Leigh's largest export market, Staffordshire Imports in Maryland act as agents. Important American customers include lifestyle 'guru' Martha Stewart, design house Ralph Lauren and Stonewall Kitchens, Maine U.S.A. Business is also excellent in anglophile Japan; Mr Yoshi Iwatani is an especially loyal customer having knocked on the factory door during Burgess, Dorling & Leigh's first week. There are many more potential, non-traditional, export markets to be developed where customers appreciate a truly English-made earthenware product like Burleigh Ware.

'This building breathes....'
'This building breathes and I'm sure that is because over the years there have been so many people working here together.'[17]

If the Middleport Pottery 'breathes', it is, in part, due to the efforts of the Dorlings who have resuscitated this once ailing business. In the process, they have given some new life to the Potteries and to the pottery industry. As Rosemary says *'Our English ceramics are unequalled in the world and the magic is still in the hands of the people.'* Such a passionate view is, importantly, wedded to a level-headed business acumen. The Dorlings have set themselves an ambitious challenge but they agree that although their years at the Middleport Pottery have been

difficult at times, they have also been immensely exciting and rewarding. Their enthusiasm continues to grow and amongst plans for the future is the appointment of Royal College of Art trained ceramicist, Grahame Clarke, to act as design consultant to the firm.

The future is never certain in any business and the manufacture of non-essential products, such as ceramics, is especially susceptible to downturns in demand. However, the groundwork has been done, motivated by a love of Burleigh Ware, which celebrates its centenary in 2003, and for the Middleport Pottery, of which the Dorlings see themselves as custodians. There is every hope that if it maintains its emphasis on traditional manufacture, while simultaneously recreating the dynamism, innovation and flair for design which Burgess & Leigh showed in its heyday, then Burgess Dorling & Leigh will succeed. The story continues.

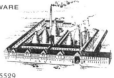

Company letterheads in chronological sequence.

NOTES TO CHAPTERS 1-7

CHAPTER ONE

1. Baker, Diane, *Potworks, The Industrial Architecture of the Staffordshire Potteries*, p.36 (Royal Commission on Historical Monuments 1991).
2. Bennett, Arnold, *The People of the Potteries*, first publ'd 1911 (Hepburn, James, ed. *Sketches for an Autobiography*, George Allen & Unwin Ltd 1979).
3. Cooper, Emmanuel, *Ten Thousand Years of Pottery*, p.227 (British Museum Press 2000).
4. Shaw, Simeon, *History of the Staffordshire Potteries 1829* (David & Charles, reprint 1970).
5. Leigh, Alan, draft article on company history, Burgess, Dorling & Leigh Ltd company archives.
6. Information from Chris Weatherby indicates a connection with a Samuel Mawdsley of Burslem whose daughter, Mary, married a J. E. Weatherby in 1864. This was possibly the same Samuel Mawdsley who worked as a traveller for Doulton & Co. during the 1880s period and is described in Desmond Eyles' book *The Doulton Burslem Wares* (Hutchinson 1980).
7. Obituary, *The Pottery Gazette and Glass Trade Review*, March 1889.
8. Later to merge with Enoch Wedgwood & Co.
9. *The Pottery Gazette and Glass Trade Review*, p.686, 1st April, 1924.
10. Record of his christening on 4th August, 1833 at Wolstanton.
11. Research by Rodney Hampson from local trade directories indicate that Richard Burgess lived in Beswick Street, Tunstall in c.1845 when Gibson & Burgess started trading from the George Street Pottery in the vicinity of Watergate Street, Tunstall, premises which were taken over in the mid- to late-1850s.
12. Wilson, A. N., *The Charter*, Ch.3, p.44, *The Victorians* (Hutchinson 2002).
13. Ward, J., *The Borough of Stoke-upon-Trent*, 1843.
14. Copeland, Robert, *Spode & Copeland Marks and Other Relevant Intelligence*, Appendix III, *Pottery Trade Sizes*, pp.142-144, (Studio Vista 1997). Copeland explains the complex issue of wage settlement thus: *'The method adopted was based on the 'dozen', for which one price was fixed for each object, so that a maker to obtain that price needed twelve articles. That 'price for dozen' held for all the other sizes made of the same design, but, in order to obtain that price either more small articles or less larger ones had to be made. The 'count to the dozen' was determined by the number of a given size that would fit on a standard size of work-board [6 feet x 9 inches], in the case of clay articles, or would fit in a warehouse basket, in the case of fired ware. These trade sizes were applied particularly to holloware objects; it was the number and not the capacity that decided the count to the dozen.'*
15. Graham, Rev. Malcolm, *Cup and Saucer Land*, p.28, originally publ'd 1908 (Staffordshire and Stoke-on-Trent City Archive Service 2000.) Some of the 1890s photographs by the Rev. Graham, *'Sometime Vicar of St Paul's, Burslem'*, have been identified as being taken at the Middleport Pottery.
16. *The Pottery Gazette and Glass Trade Review*, p.686, 1st April, 1924.
17. 1857 was the date given by Edmund Leigh in an interview with *The Pottery Gazette and Glass Trade Review* in 1906. Kelly's Post Office Directory of 1860 lists Hancock, Leigh & Co., Swan Square, Burslem, earthenware manufacturers, p.515; Harrison's directory of 1861 lists Hancock Leigh & Co., Swan Bank.
18. Haggar, R. G. and Mankowitz W., *Concise Encyclopaedia of English Pottery and Porcelain*, p27 (Deutsch, London 1957).
19. White's Trade Directory confirm Hulme & Booth's occupancy as 28th July, 1851.
20. White's Trade Directory of 1851.
21. Information in a letter signed *'Burgess & Leigh'* to Joseph Boulton, 28th July, 1863, in bound book of correspondence c.1863-1865, p.38, Burgess, Dorling & Leigh Ltd Company Archives.
22. Local trade directories, Kelly's (1860) and Harrison's (1861), list a Thos. Hulme, previously trading with a Mr Booth, as an earthenware manufacturer at the Central Pottery, Burslem. Burgess & Leigh appear in Slater's directory for the first time the following year, 1862, trading from the same address. Applications for the pottery's lease were to be addressed to a Mr Alcock, solicitor of Burslem, or John Alcock, a Cobridge banker and earthenware manufacturer, with whom Burgess & Leigh banked initially. An account book in Burgess, Dorling & Leigh company archives, dated 1862, is entitled *'Messrs Burgess & Leigh in account with J. Alcock & Co.'*
23. Ewins, Neil, *Supplying the Wants of Our Yankee Cousins… Staffordshire Ceramics and the American Market 1775-1880*, Journal of Ceramic History, Volume 15 (City Museum & Art Gallery 1997).
24. Hampson, Rodney, *Pottery References in The Staffordshire Advertiser, 1795-1865*, p.82 (The Northern Ceramic Society 2000).
25. Blake-Roberts, Gaye, ed. *True Blue, Transfer Printed Earthenware*, Copeland, Robert, *'The Marketing of Blue and White Wares'*, p.17, Exhibition Catalogue (Friends of Blue 1999).
26. Elliott, Gordon, *The Design Process in British Ceramic Manufacture 1750-1850*, Appendix C, (Staffordshire University Press, c.2000). Scriven's Report of 1843 records that Simpson's Earthenware Works in Longport employed *'30 or thereabouts'* whilst Davenport's had *'at a rough guess from 1200 to 1400, many of them children.'* In 1876, Minton's earthenware works employed 1514 workers in total (ref. Boxes 43-44, Minton Archives).
27. Wilkinson, Vega, *Spode Copeland Spode, The Works and its People*, p.214 (Antique Collectors' Club 2002).
28. Burgess, Dorling & Leigh Ltd company archives.
29. *'F. L. Goode'*, mentioned in Lidstone's poem was a partner in Burgess, Leigh & Co between c.1868 and 1878.
30. Blake-Roberts, Gaye, ed, *True Blue, Transfer Printed Earthenware*, Pulver, Rosalind *'Changing Styles 1840-1870'*, Exhibition Catalogue (Friends of Blue 1999).
31. Fuller, Lance, *Trade in Copperplate Engravings, An Investigation of the Second-Hand Market*, Staffordshire University MA Thesis, 2000, Spode Museum Trust Archives.
32. Letter dated 26th August, 1864 from Burgess & Leigh to Mr J. Latham reads *'We shall not pay for the Hawthorn engravings until the agreement has been carried out….'* Bound book of correspondence 1863-1865, p.311, Burgess, Dorling & Leigh Company Archives.
33. Kowalsky, Arnold A. & Dorothy E., *Encyclopaedia of Marks On American, English, European Earthenware, Ironstone and Stoneware 1780-1980*, Appendix pp.399-400, *Patterns by Potters* (Schiffer Publishing Ltd 2002).
34. Greenslade, M. W., *A History of Burslem*, p.135 (reprinted from the *Victoria County History of Staffordshire*, Staffordshire and Stoke-on-Trent Archive Service, 2000).
35. Wedgwood, H., *Staffordshire, Up and Down the Country*, (Hitchings, Hanley, 1880), photocopied extract Burgess, Dorling & Leigh Ltd Company Archives.
36. Joan Jones, Royal Doulton Curator, confirms that there is no mention of Lowndes-Goode in T. S. Goode & Co. material in the Minton archives index.
37. Hampson, Rodney, *Pottery References in the Staffordshire Advertiser 1795-1865* (The Northern Ceramic Society 2000).
38. Leigh, Alan, draft article on company history, Burgess, Dorling and Leigh Ltd Company Archives.
39. John Shorter, Edmund Leigh's friend and Burgess & Leigh's agent in Australia, in a lecture

given to the Connoisseur Club in Sydney, Australia in 1926, states that a second brother of Edmund, William Leigh junior, left the Potteries to live and work in Birkenhead.

CHAPTER TWO

1. *The Pottery Gazette and Glass Trade Review*, *'Some Familiar Faces in the Potting Trade, Mr Edmund Leigh, JP'*, p.920, 1st August, 1906.
2. *The Pottery Gazette and Glass Trade Review*, 1933, p.69, Edmund Denis Leigh quoted.
3. Letter of condolence from Edwin Kent, Burgess, Dorling & Leigh Ltd Company Archives.
4. Dudson, Audrey, *A Pottery Panorama*, p.144 (Dudson Publications Ltd 1999).
5. The earliest ledger, dated 1876, lists *'Matchings Ordered to Manufacture'* (these being other companies' products subcontracted to Burgess, Leigh & Co); *'Matchings Received from Other Manufacturers'* (wares produced by other potteries to be included in orders sent out from the Hill Pottery); and *'Matchings Ordered by Other Manufacturers'* (Burgess, Leigh & Co.'s own products to be sent out with other firms' shipments). Robert Copeland, in correspondence with the author, suggests that pages in the archival Day Book listing items *'Borrowed From'*; *'Returned To''*; and *'Lent To'*, most probably refers to moulds and copperplates.
6. Wright, Norma, *Wedgwood Finds in the Dudson Archaeological Dig*, Proceeds of the Wedgwood Society, No. 13, 1990 (Wedgwood Society). Courtesy of Rodney Hampson.
7. Burslem News Cuttings 1872-1907, p.52, Hanley Reference Library, Stoke-on-Trent City Archives.
8. Burslem News Cuttings 1872-1907, p.52, Hanley Reference Library, Stoke-on-Trent City Archives.
9. *The Pottery Gazette and Glass Trade Review*, 1878.
10. Building Society account books in Burgess, Dorling & Leigh Ltd Company Archives.
11. *The Staffordshire Sentinel*, *'Death of Mr Edmund Leigh JP, Manufacturer and Liberal Leader'*, Wednesday, 2nd January, 1924.
12. *The Pottery Gazette and Glass Trade Review*, 1st August, 1906, p.920-922, *'Some Familiar Faces in the Potting Trade, Mr Edmund Leigh, JP'*.
13. *The Staffordshire Sentinel*, *'Death of Mr Edmund Leigh JP, Manufacturer and Liberal Leader'*, Wednesday, 2nd January, 1924.
14. See Chapter Four, Charlotte Rhead by Bernard Bumpus.
15. From a lecture by Edmund Leigh's friend and Burgess & Leigh's agent in Australia, John Shorter, given to the Connoisseur Club in Sydney, Australia in 1926.
16. Obituary, *The Pottery Gazette and Glass Trade Review*, p.289, 1st February, 1924.
17. *The Staffordshire Sentinel*, *'Death of Mr Edmund Leigh JP, Manufacturer and Liberal Leader'*, Wednesday, 2nd January, 1924.
18. Morris, William, *Art and the Beauty of the Earth*, a lecture delivered at Burslem Town Hall, October 1881 (Hanley Reference Library, Stoke-on-Trent City Archives).
19. Anon, *A descriptive account of the Potteries (illustrated)*, Messrs Burgess & Leigh, Pottery Manufacturers, Middleport Pottery, Burslem, advertising and trade journal, p.57, 1893, bound with *Industries of Staffordshire*, British Industrial Publishing Co. Ref. S 805 Hanley Reference Library, Stoke-on-Trent City Archives.
20. *The Pottery Gazette and Glass Trade Review*, 1903.
21. Methodist Hymn Book, inscribed *'Presented to Mr Edmund Leigh by the Trustees of the Wolstanton Wesleyan Chapel on his leaving the district 18th March, 1908, J. A. Lowndes (Treasurer), Wm Walklate (Secretary)'*, Burgess, Dorling & Leigh Ltd Company Archives. Edmund went on to become a member of the Congregational Church in Stone, Staffordshire.
22. Potter, John, Chairman of the Arnold Bennett Society, in conversation with the author, July 2001.
23. Leigh, Alan, *Mostly Fact with a Little Help From Anna*, draft article, Burgess, Dorling & Leigh company archives. Alan Leigh suggests a number of theories as to which of Bennett's characters were based on members of the Leigh family and its immediate circle of friends. He also makes a case for Bennett's using the Hill and Middleport Potteries as inspiration for certain fictitious potteries, a view which receives some support from Rodney Hampson in their correspondence, 6th May 1997.
24. Flower, Norman, Ed, *The Journals of Arnold Bennett 1896-1910*, p.343 (first published by Cassell & Co Ltd 1932).
25. Potter, John, Chairman of the Arnold Bennett Society, in conversation with the author, July 2001.
26. The book was not published until 1902.
27. Lecture by Burgess & Leigh's agent in Australia, John Shorter, given to the Connoisseur Club in Sydney, Australia in 1926. Permission to quote granted by Shorter's grandson, John Shorter CBE.
28. Hopwood, Irene and Gordon, *The Shorter Connection, A Family Pottery 1874-1974* (Richard Dennis Publications 1992), gives much valuable information on the Shorter family and associated potteries.
29. By the late 1920s Arthur Shorter's son, Colley Shorter, co-managed A. J. Wilkinson Ltd (then Shorter & Son) employing his second wife, Clarice Cliff, at a new factory, the Newport Pottery in Burslem where the Royal Staffordshire brand-name was used. Midwinter took over the works in 1964 and following other mergers and takeovers, the works were eventually closed during the 1980s when Burgess & Leigh acquired moulds and copper plate engravings.
30. Letter from John Shorter's grandson, John Shorter CBE, to Audrey Dudson, March 2001.
31. *The Pottery Gazette and Glass Trade Review*, p.956, 1934 *'Half a Century as a Dominion's Agent'*, an interview with John Shorter aged 81, research by Alan Leigh, Burgess, Dorling & Leigh Ltd Company Archives.
32. *The Pottery Gazette and Glass Trade Review*, 1st April, 1910.
33. By 1883, sixty-eight pottery firms had showrooms in London of which the vast majority were operated by agents acting for one or more companies. *The Pottery Gazette and Glass Trade Review*, Supplement 1st December, 1883, quoted in *Potworks: The Industrial Architecture of the Staffordshire Potteries* (Royal Commission on Ancient Monuments of England, 1991).
34. According to advertisements in *The Pottery Gazette and Glass Trade Review* and other trade journals, Burgess & Leigh's London showroom moved premises several times. Over the years they had premises at: 16 Thavies Inn from 1881; Charterhouse Street from c.1897; 46 Farringdon Street from c1899 until 1903; 44 Farringdon Street until 1935; Ely House, 13 Charterhouse Street until 1969; and Room 38, 6 Holborn Viaduct during the 1970s.
35. Edmund and his wife, Jane, after a short stay with his parents in Newport Street, Burslem, spent the 1880s in Emberton Street, Wolstanton, and 203 Waterloo Road, Burslem, research by Alan Leigh in Burgess, Dorling & Leigh Ltd company archives.
36. Registered Oct 29 1880, Kowalsky, Arnold A & Dorothy E, *Encyclopaedia of Marks On American, English, European Earthenware, Ironstone and Stoneware 1780-1980*, Appendix pp399-400, *Patterns by Potters* (Schiffer Publishing Ltd 2002).

37. Burgess & Leigh were to produce a different pattern, also named *Kensington*, in c.1919 and again during the 1950s.

38. Lockett, T. A., *Davenport Pottery and Porcelain* (David and Charles 1972) states that the land was sold for £3,230. The buyer is not named.

39. Cooper, Betty, *A. R. Wood, The Sentinel*, 8th April, 2001.

40. Anon, *A descriptive account of the Potteries (illustrated)*, *Messrs Burgess & Leigh, Pottery Manufacturers, Middleport Pottery, Burslem*, advertising and trade journal, 1893, bound with *Industries of Staffordshire*, British Industrial Publishing Co. Ref. S 805 Hanley Reference Library, Stoke-on-Trent.

41. The first representation of the Middleport Pottery is the engraving in *The Pottery Gazette and Glass Trade Review*, 1st April, 1889. A different engraving is used in *A descriptive account of the Potteries (illustrated)*, *Messrs Burgess & Leigh, Pottery Manufacturers, Middleport Pottery, Burslem*, p.57, an advertising and trade journal of 1893. This was also used in the article *A Typical Staffordshire Industry, The Middleport Pottery, Burslem*, which appeared in the *British Journal of Commerce* in January 1898. It was subsequently used by the company in further advertising material and as a letterhead. The Middleport Pottery was not included on the 1890 OS Map for the area but was shown on the 1900 2nd Ed: 1:1250 OS for Middleport.

42. These documents, together with a survey of the Middleport Pottery made in October 1982, subsequent to an unsuccessful request by the firm to demolish the last remaining Grade II listed bottle oven, helped form the basis of the Stoke-on-Trent Historic Buildings Survey of the Middleport Pottery of October 1984, during which a complete photographic record was made with measurements and drawings of the front elevation. The results of this survey were written by Diane Baker and later published in Chapter 5, pp.90-94, in *Potworks, The Industrial Architecture of the Staffordshire Potteries* (Royal Commission on Ancient Monuments of England, 1991).

43. Later, the steam engine powered towing boxes (machinery for the smoothing and removal by tow, rough hemp, of imperfections from clay flatware); dust extractor fans; and in the 1930s a DC generator for lighting the warehouse and decorating shops. The steam engine operated until c.1977 when the Slip House was electrified. A second smaller steam engine was also installed at a later date, supplied with steam from the Lancashire boiler, and drove a variety of machinery including holloware jiggers, polishers and from c1920 the mangle used by dippers. Information from a draft article on company history written by Alan Leigh in Burgess, Dorling & Leigh company archives.

44. Anon, *A descriptive account of the Potteries (illustrated)*, *Messrs Burgess & Leigh, Pottery Manufacturers, Middleport Pottery, Burslem*, advertising and trade journal, 1893, bound with *Industries of Staffordshire*, British Industrial Publishing Co. Ref. S 805 Hanley Reference Library, Stoke-on-Trent.

45. *The Pottery Gazette and Glass Trade Review*, 1st April, 1889 report of the Middleport Pottery.

46. Stan and Elsie Johnson in conversation with the author, 2001.

47. Correspondence from A. R. Wood dated 28th September, 1897 in Burgess, Dorling & Leigh Ltd Company Archives.

48. Graham, Rev. Malcolm, *Cup and Saucer Land*, p.24, originally publ'd 1908 (Staffordshire and Stoke-on-Trent City Archive Service 2000). Some of Graham's photographs were taken in the 1890s at the Middleport Pottery.

49. Johnson, Stan, retired glost fireman, Burgess & Leigh, interviewed 31st January, 2001 by the Potteries Museum.

50. *The Pottery Gazette and Glass Trade Review*, 1st April, 1889, report of the Middleport Pottery.

51. Leigh, Alan, draft article on company history, Burgess, Dorling & Leigh Ltd Company Archives, states that by the 1930s this was still used to power the holloware jiggerers, dippers' mangle and polishers' lathes.

52. Baker, Diane, Recorder, Dobraszczyc, Andrew, Supervisor, *City of Stoke-on-Trent Historic Buildings Survey, Middleport Pottery* (Potteries Museum and Art Gallery, 1984) states that there were ventilations holes in the top parts of window frames and from c1900 ventilation chimneys.

53. Daniel Heath (father of Thomas, the founder of T. W. Heath & Co., Burgess & Leigh's Australian agency) was responsible for the installation of the casting process in c.1919. He retired from his position as Casting Shop Manager in the early 1920s.

54. Graham, Rev. Malcolm, *Cup and Saucer Land*, p.39 (originally publ'd 1908, republished Staffordshire and Stoke-on-Trent City Archive Service 2000). Some of Graham's photographs were taken at the Middleport Pottery during the 1890s.

55. Graham, Rev. Malcolm, *Cup and Saucer Land*, p.40 (originally published in 1908, re-published Staffordshire and Stoke-on-Trent City Archive Service 2000).

56. Baker, Diane, Recorder, Dobraszczyc, Andrew, Supervisor, *City of Stoke-on-Trent Historic Buildings Survey, Middleport Pottery* (Potteries Museum and Art Gallery, 1984).

57. Bennett, Arnold, *Anna of the Five Towns*, Chapter *On the Bank*, (London Chatto and Windus, 1902).

58. Copeland, Robert, *Words of the Potter*, p.21, (Spode 1978, revised 1980) Spode Museum Trust archives.

59. Ford, Ben, in conversation with the author, August 2002, reported that the bay window was knocked down so frequently by delivery lorries that it was eventually rebuilt (post Second World War)!

60. Information from and question posed by Rosemary Dorling, March 2002.

61. Birks, Steve, www.thepotteries.org

62. Baker, D., *Potworks, The Industrial Architecture of the Staffordshire Potteries*, Chapter 5, p.90 (Royal Commission on the Historical Monuments of England 1991) reports that Thomas Twyford had introduced washing facilities into the Dipping Room of his sanitary ware factory in Cliffe Vale built in 1879.

63. To be the subject of a 2003 archaeological survey by Dr Malcolm Nixon.

64. Bill from contractor dated 28th September, 1897 in Burgess, Dorling & Leigh Ltd company archives lists '*six hovels*' (bottle ovens); also *Burgess, Dorling & Leigh, Middleport Pottery, Burslem, Packing Warehouse* by Dr Malcom Nixon details OS Survey Middleport: 2nd Edition, dated 1900, 1/1250 Sheet XII which shows six bottle ovens. However, engravings used from 1889 onwards show seven ovens.

65. Johnson, Stan, transcript of interview for the Potteries Museum, 13th January, 2000, stated that Simpsons of Waterloo Road was the only other firm to have such a kiln.

66. Bennett, Arnold, *Anna of the Five Towns*, Chapter *On the Bank*, (London Chatto and Windus, 1902).

67. Readers are referred to *Burgess, Dorling & Leigh, Middleport Pottery, Burslem, Packing Warehouse* by Dr Malcom Nixon, '*An archaeological appraisal and recording in support of the Middleport Waterfront, Trent & Mersey Canal, Townscape Heritage Initiative 2002*', copies in Burgess, Dorling & Leigh Ltd company archives and Hanley Reference Library, Stoke-on-Trent City Archives.

68. For a time, after the late 1930s, tanks were used as packing cases for South Africa, and were later sold on by Burgess & Leigh's agents to farmers! This and other relevant information on packing from Ben Ford, Head Packer, who worked for Burgess & Leigh in the Packing House for 52 years. Ben gave a taped interview to John Ecclestone and Will Dorling in 1999 for the

National Trust Sound Archive and was interviewed by the author in 2001-2002.

69. Two Building Account Books from 1888-1889 record monthly payments of approximately £500 to W. Cooke amounting to £7637, Burgess, Dorling & Leigh Ltd company archives.

70. '*Workshop over the Slip House; Six Hovels; New Storey Biscuit Warehouse; Straw Shed, Bridge of Room Over; New Lead House; Arched Floor over Boilers; Extra Height of Chimney; Blue Plinth to Front; Rendering Roofs; Floor over Archway; Extra Stone Sett; and Brick Paving to Clay Bank etc.*'

71. Information from Rodney Hampson.

72. Leigh, Alan, reference made to an *In Memoriam* card in '*Mostly Fact with a Little Help From Anna*', a draft article in Burgess, Dorling & Leigh Ltd company archives.

73. Leigh, Alan, '*Mostly Fact with a Little Help From Anna*', draft article in Burgess, Dorling & Leigh Ltd company archives.

74. Burslem News Cuttings 1872-1907 p.158, Hanley Reference Library, Stoke-on-Trent City Archives.

75. Leigh, Alan, draft article '*Mostly Fact with a Little Help From Anna*', Burgess, Dorling & Leigh Ltd company archives.

76. Obituary, *The Pottery Gazette and Glass Trade Review*, p.246, March 1889.

77. Obituary, *The Pottery Gazette and Glass Trade Review*, p.513, 1st May, 1912.

78. Obituary, *The Pottery Gazette and Glass Trade Review*, p.513, 1st May, 1912.

79. Leigh, Alan, draft article on company history, Burgess, Dorling & Leigh Ltd Company Archives.

80. Ben Ford, retired Head Packer at Burgess & Leigh, in conversation with the author January 2002. Ben's father, also employed at the Middleport Pottery, spoke of Richard Burgess arriving at the Middleport Pottery by horse.

81. Leigh, Alan, draft article on company history, Burgess, Dorling & Leigh Ltd Company Archives.

82. Johnson, Stan, retired Glost Fireman at Burgess & Leigh in conversation with the author, 2002. Information from Stan's father, Tom, also a kiln fireman. A draft article on company history, Burgess, Dorling & Leigh Ltd Company Archives states that Tom remembers Richard as being highly regarded at the Middleport Pottery.

83. A '*Private Wages*' book dated from c.1914, Burgess, Dorling & Leigh company archives, indicates regular payments until 1919 to a 'Miss B'. These payments may have been made to Mathilda Burgess as a result of the partnership agreement after Richard S. Burgess' death in 1912. Edmund Leigh bought out the Burgess' interest in the company in 1919.

84. Notebook dated 1901 in private collection.

85. Atterbury, P. and Batkin, M., ed. *The Minton Dictionary of Art*, p.300 (Antique Collectors' Club 1990) records a Joseph Slater who had worked at Samuel Alcock's Hill Pottery as a designer, gilder and armorial crest painter, and his sons, John Slater, Art Director for Doulton & Co from 1867-1914 and James Billington Slater, who served his apprenticeship at Mintons from 1880-1888.

86. Barnes Dr G. and Mrs A., *The Samuel Alcock Porcelains 1822-1859* in Staffordshire Porcelain, ed G. A. Godden (London: Granada Publishing 1983).

87. Eyles, Desmond *The Doulton Burslem Wares* (Hutchinson 1975) refers to a Louis Thomas Swettenham. Ed Atterbury, P. and Batkin, M. *The Dictionary of Minton* (Antique Collectors' Club) note his name as Lewis Thomas Swetnam.

88. Eyles, Desmond *The Doulton Burslem Wares*, Appendices, p.182 (Hutchinson 1980).

89. Bumpus, Bernard, *Collecting Rhead Pottery, Charlotte, Frederick, Frederick Hurten* (Francis Joseph 1999).

90. Correspondence between Wilkes' successor, Ernest Bailey, and Bernard Bumpus, 25th May, 1981.

91. In one of numerous sketch books in company archives and a private collection; other addresses given include 47 South Street, Mount Pleasant, Stoke-on-Trent; The Grove, Bradwell Lane, Wolstanton; and Blythe Bridge, Staffordshire.

92. Dudson, Audrey, *A Pottery Panorama, Dudson Bicentenary 1800-2000* (Dudson Publications Ltd., 2000).

93. Burgess & Leigh company promotional leaflet 1991.

94. Coysh, A. & Henrywood R., *Dictionary of Blue and White Printed Pottery 1780-1880* (Antique Collectors' Club, Vol 1 1982, Vol 11 1989).

95. In another Bennett connection, Thomas Hurd may have been the partner of Arnold Bennett's father, Enoch, at the Eagle Pottery in Nile Street, Burslem, now home to Royal Doulton. Drabble, Margaret, *Arnold Bennett, A Biography* (Publ'd 1974), p.25, research by Rodney Hampson.

96. The Mayer Pottery name might possibly have originated from a Samuel Mayer who had a works in Waterloo Road in c1839-1840 or, alternatively, from Mayer's Bank, both areas just off Nile Street. Coincidentally, a pottery owned by a Henry Burgess traded from Kilncroft Works not far from Mayers Bank from 1863 to 1892 whilst a William Rathbone & Co. manufactured Jet and Rockingham at Sylvester Street from c.1880-1892. Information from Rodney Hampson.

97. Two bank books for F. R. Burgess & Co. of Mayer Pottery, c1891 to c.1900; correspondence and a further bank book for F. M. Hurd & Co. Burslem, c.1890-91, Burgess, Dorling & Leigh Ltd Company Archives.

98. Anon, *A descriptive account of the Potteries (illustrated)*, *Messrs Burgess & Leigh, Pottery Manufacturers, Middleport Pottery, Burslem, p.57*, an advertising and trade journal of 1893, records that '*a second pottery known as the Crown Works, Burslem, deals with the manufacture of Rockingham Ware*'.

99. *The Pottery Gazette and Glass Trade Review*, p.1245, 1st October, 1898.

100. Winch, Diane, *The British Galleries 1500-1900, A Guide Book*, p.52 (V&A Publications 2001) records the registered shape 281721, registered number 285771, Applied registered number 281720; Lid registered shape 281721, patent 688082, information from the Victoria and Albert Museum catalogue.

101. The Victoria and Albert Museum catalogue records two versions of the Huntley & Palmer biscuit tin teapot in the M. J. Franklin Collection, C277-83, displayed in Gallery 123, brown printed, and C278-83, pink printed; and two items modelled by E. T. Bailey, 496-1948, an earthenware plate, and 496-1948, a dish and cover designed by Harold Bennett (496-1948) acquired in 1948. These later acquisitions were possibly chosen from items selected, though not necessarily displayed, in the Council of Industrial Design's '*Britain Can Make It*' exhibition of 1946.

CHAPTER THREE

1. Subsequent New York agencies of Burgess & Leigh were: from c.1927-1931 Frederick Reimer of 49-51 W. 23rd Street and from c.1931 of 160 5th Ave; from c.1931 Reimer-MacKenzie at the same address; from c.1940-c.1960s Fondeville & Co. 149/151 5th Ave.

2. Hopwood, Irene and Gordon, *The Shorter Connection, A Family Pottery 1874-1974* (Richard Dennis Publications 1992).

3. Letter of condolence on the death of Edmund Leigh, Burgess, Dorling & Leigh Company Archives.

4. Records in Burgess, Dorling & Leigh Ltd Company Archives.

5. Edmund had one daughter, Mabelle, who married a Mr Parkhill in 1930.

6. Fowler, Norman, ed. *The Journals of Arnold Bennett 1896-1910*, p.112 (Cassell & Co., first publ'd 1932).

7. *The Pottery Gazette and Glass Trade Review*, p.114, January 1952, Denis *'was very happy to be able to state that at no time had there been anything in the nature of a quarrel, and he was pleased and proud that the relationship between directors, management and work people had always been a happy one.'*

8. *The Pottery Gazette and Glass Trade Review*, p.1166, 1st October, 1908.

9. *The Pottery Gazette and Glass Trade Review*, p.173, 2nd February, 1903.

10. *The Pottery Gazette and Glass Trade Review*, 1905.

11. *The Pottery Gazette and Glass Trade Review* of 1903 reported Edmund's resignation from Burslem Town Council but just two years later in 1905 it reported his becoming a member of Staffordshire County Authority.

12. Burgess & Leigh promotional leaflet, 1991, Burgess, Dorling & Leigh Ltd Company Archives.

13. *The Pottery Gazette and Glass Trade Review*, p.93, 1st January, 1906.

14. HM Inspector's report showed that between 1896-98, the number of persons 'working in the lead' in the Potteries was 4703 with 1085 suffering from lead-poisoning. Figures quoted by Millicent, the Duchess of Sutherland in *'On the Dangerous Processes of the Potting Industry'* in *The Staffordshire Potter* by Harold Owen, publ'd 1901.

15. Letter from Bernard Moore, 1915, Burgess, Dorling & Leigh Ltd company archives.

16. Obituary, *The Pottery Gazette and Glass Trade Review*, p.289, 1st February, 1924.

17. *The Pottery Gazette and Glass Trade Review*, p.1905, 1st September, 1905.

18. *Art Nouveau 1890-1914*, Greenhalgh, Paul, ed. Chapter 8 *'Le Style Anglais: English Roots of the New Art' The Observer*, 5th July, 1969, Sir Lawrence Gowing, quoted (V&A Publications 2000).

19. Hawkins-Opie, Jennifer, *Art Nouveau 1890-1914*, Chapter 12, *'The New Ceramics'* (V&A Publications 2000).

20. *The Pottery Gazette and Glass Trade Review*, p.385, 1st April, 1912.

21. *The Pottery Gazette and Glass Trade Review*, p.1023, 1st April, 1912.

22. *The Pottery Gazette and Glass Trade Review*, p.316, 1st March, 1906.

23. *The Pottery Gazette and Glass Trade Review*, p.1023, 1st September, 1909.

24. Leigh, Alan, draft company history, Burgess, Dorling & Leigh Ltd. Company Archives.

25. Information on the Heath family and their business, T. W. Heath & Co., latterly Woodheath (NSW) Pty Ltd, from notes written by Sydney Francis Heath in c.1985.

26. Burleigh Ware is now distributed in Australia by Lindt Trading, another small family company.

27. New Zealand International Exhibition Catalogue, 23rd March, 1907.

28. Leigh, Alan, draft article on company history, Burgess, Dorling & Leigh Ltd company archives.

29. *The Pottery Gazette and Glass Trade Review*, p.114, January, 1952.

30. *The Pottery Gazette and Glass Trade Review*, p.412, 1st April, 1910.

31. *The Pottery Gazette and Glass Trade Review*, p.923, August 1911.

32. *The Pottery Gazette and Glass Trade Review*, 1907.

33. Leigh, Alan, *Mostly Fact with a Little Help From Ann*, draft article in Burgess, Dorling & Leigh Ltd company archives states that on their marriage in 1880 Edmund and his wife lived at 6 Newport St, Burslem, with Edmund's parents. By 1881 they were living in Emberton Street, Wolstanton and by c.1888 at 203 Waterloo Road. Kelly's Directory of 1894 gives Edmund's address as Holly Lodge, Wolstanton whilst the 1896 edition indicates that he had subsequently moved to *The Oaks*, Porthill. Thereafter he moved to *Mansion House* then *Radford House* in Stone, Staffordshire According to his obituary in the *Staffordshire Sentinel*, on moving to Stone, he let *The Oaks* to the Red Cross for use as a depot.

34. Leigh, Alan, draft article on company history, Burgess, Dorling & Leigh Ltd Company Archives.

35. A *'Private Wages'* book dated from c.1914, Burgess, Dorling & Leigh company archives, indicates regular payments until 1919 to a 'Miss B'. These payments may have been made to Mathilda Burgess as a result of the partnership agreement after Richard S. Burgess' death in 1912. Edmund Leigh bought out the Burgess' interest in the company in 1919.

36. *The Pottery Gazette and Glass Trade Review*, 1st April and 2nd September, 1912, reported that *'Burgess & Leigh, Middleport Pottery, Burslem, are celebrating the Jubilee of their firm'*.

37. *The Pottery Gazette and Glass Trade Review*, p.967, 2nd September, 1912.

38. *The Pottery Gazette and Glass Trade Review*, 1913.

39. Ben Ford in conversation with the author, January 2002.

40. Information on the Heath family and their business, T. W. Heath & Co., latterly Woodheath. (NSW) Pty Ltd, from notes written by Sydney Francis Heath in c.1985

41. *Provisions of Military Service (Review of Exceptions)*, document, October 1917, Burgess, Dorling & Leigh Ltd Company Archives. The nature of Kingsley's disabilities are not disclosed but it seems that they can only have been minor as his obituary in the *Evening Sentinel*, Monday, 6th December, 1954, states that he was a keen sportsman, enjoying cricket, football and playing tennis for Stone Tennis Club in Staffordshire.

42. *The Pottery Gazette and Glass Trade Review*, 1918.

43. *The Pottery Gazette and Glass Trade Review*, 28th September, 1918.

44. Private collection.

45. *The Pottery Gazette and Glass Trade Review*, 2nd September, 1918.

46. Aldin's designs were used by Burgess & Leigh in 1925 on a similar series entitled *Merrie England*, see Chapter Four.

47. *The Pottery Gazette and Glass Trade Review*, advertisement in supplement, April 1914.

CHAPTER FOUR

1. *The Pottery Gazette and Glass Trade Review*, 1919.

2. *The Pottery Gazette and Glass Trade Review*, 1919.

3. *The Pottery Gazette and Glass Trade Review*, 1923.

4. *The Staffordshire Sentinel*, Monday, 7th January, 1924.

5. Letter of condolence, Burgess, Dorling & Leigh Ltd Company Archives.

6. *The Staffordshire Sentinel*, Monday, 7th January, 1924.

7. *The Pottery Gazette and Glass Trade Review*, p686, 1st April, 1924.

8. MacCarthy, Fiona, *A History of British Design 1830-1979*, pp.45-46 (George Allen & Unwin Ltd, 1979).

9. Dennison, Carmel, *Burslem People and Buildings*, p.13 (Burslem Development Trust 1996).

10. *The Pottery Gazette and Glass Trade Review*, p.592, 1st April, 1921.

11. Spours, Judy, *Art Deco Tableware*, p.184 (Ward Lock 1988).

12. Copeland, Robert, *Spode's Willow Pattern and Other Designs After the Chinese*, pp.53-57 (Studio Vista, 2nd ed. 1990).

13. Copeland, Robert, *Spode's Willow Pattern and Other Designs After the Chinese*, p.39 (Studio Vista, 2nd ed. 1990).

14. Connie Rogers, author of *An Illustrated Encyclopaedia of British Willow* to be published by Schiffer in 2004, has helped with information on the *Willow*-type patterns and the Burleigh *'Dillwyn' Willow*. Rogers corresponded with Edmund Leigh in November, 1983, for an article she

was then writing for *Willow Transfer Quarterly*. Valuable information has also been received from collector Nancee Rogers.

15. Leigh, Barry, correspondence with the author, 17th March, 2003.

16. Information from Connie Rogers and Robert Copeland. The pattern is closest to that shown on an unmarked plate in Figure 28, p.157, in *Copeland's Spode's Willow Pattern and Other Designs after the Chinese* (Studio Vista, 2nd ed. 1990).

17. Connie Rogers has identified this pattern.

18. Letter from Barry Leigh to Conrad Biernacki, the editor of the *Willow Transfer Quarterly*, July 1984 stated *'The pattern has only been produced in plain blue since 1940, though prior to that date it was printed variously in pink, blue or brown and in some cases parts of the print were hand enamelled in other colours.'*

19. *The Antique Collector*, Bumpus, Bernard, *'Cecil Aldin's Pottery Designs'*, August 1988.

20. Some of these shapes were to be tube-lined by Charlotte Rhead.

21. Quoted by Spours, Judy *Art Deco Tableware*, p.42 (Ward Lock 1988).

22. Leigh, Alan, draft article on company history, Burgess, Dorling & Leigh Ltd Company Archives.

23. Leigh, Alan, draft article on company history, Burgess, Dorling & Leigh Ltd Company Archives.

24. *The Pottery Gazette and Glass Trade Review* advertisements reveal that the agency was replaced in 1931 by John C. Boyle and in 1934 by Oakley, Jackson & Farewell, both of Toronto.

25. See information on Charles Wilkes, Chapter Two.

26. The vase is now in the collection of the Gladstone Pottery Museum, Longton, Stoke-on-Trent.

27. Barry Leigh remembers the last thrower employed during the late 1930s as 'young Enoch' whose father, also Enoch, worked for the firm. A shape Barry Leigh remembers young Enoch throwing was a squat ink well.

28. Information from Ernest Bailey, c.1982.

29. A letter dated 9th October, 1953, now in private family papers, from Denis Leigh to Charles Wilkes on the death of his wife supports this: *'You, I know, will be pleased to hear that quite a number of your old models are still selling very freely, particularly Flower Jugs and Bowls.'*

30. Written to Bernard Bumpus between May 1981 and April 1983 for *Charlotte Rhead, Potter and Designer* (Kevin Francis 1987).

31. Henrywood, Dick, correspondence with the author, January 2002.

32. Production difficulties resulted in only three jugs being made.

33. Coupe, Elizabeth, *Collecting Burleigh Jugs* (Letterbox Publishing 1999) writes: *'Mr [Edmund] Leigh suggests that Ernest Bailey modelled this himself from a pattern of a jug produced by the firm some twenty years earlier. He remembers as a boy that there were two vases of this pattern on his bedroom mantelpiece.'*

34. Bailey in correspondence with Bernard Bumpus, 1982.

35. A name remembered by Elsie Johnson, February 2002.

36. Casey, Andrew, *20th Century Ceramic Designers in Britain*, Chapter 3, p.72, *The Original Bizarre Girl, Clarice Cliff* (Antique Collectors Club 2001).

37. Information from Bernard Bumpus.

38. *The Pottery Ladies*, directed by Jenny Wilkes, Metropolis Pictures Production for the Arts Council, in association with Channel 4 Television, 1985.

39. Henrywood, R. K., *Relief-Moulded Jugs* (Antique Collectors' Club 1984).

40. Research by Steve Davies.

41. Research by Steve Davies.

42. *The Antique Collector*, Bumpus, Bernard, *'Flower Jugs of the Thirties'*, August 1984.

43 Trudy Jones, daughter of Ernest Bailey, told the author, 2002, that she wrote to Sir Stanley regarding this issue. In a telephone call, he informed her that he had no memory of such a jug being modelled.

44. *The Pottery Gazette and Glass Trade Review*, p1203, 1st September, 1936.

45. *The Pottery Gazette and Glass Trade Review*, p1203, 1st September, 1936.

46. Bumpus, Bernard, *Flower Jugs of the Thirties*, published in *The Antique Collector*, August 1984. It is remembered by Stan Johnson, a former employee, that Burgess & Leigh also produced musical jugs during the late 1930s. However, none has yet come to light.

47. Information from Bernard Bumpus.

48. Certainly, this is believed by Wilkes' descendants who own examples from the Verona range.

49. Research by Steve Davies.

50. A scrapbook of Wilkes in a private collection shows a similar Chinese design used as reference material.

51. Dorfles, Gillo, *Kitsch: An Anthology of Bad Taste*, quoted by Spours, Judy, *Art Deco Tableware*, Chapter Six, p.149, *Novelty and Kitsch* (Ward Lock 1988).

52. A similar, though more traditional shape, incorporating a leaf motif was also registered with number 766417 in 1931 for the Canadian market. It is not known whether this was ever produced.

53. *The Pottery Gazette and Glass Trade Review*, p.457, 1st April, 1932.

54. Johnson, Stan, retired Glost Fireman, in conversation with the author, 2002.

55. Letter of reference written by C. H. Birchall, his teacher, 12th July, 1920, now in family papers.

56 Letter of reference written by C. H. Birchall, his teacher, 12th July, 1920, now in family papers.

57. *Leek Post and Times*, reviews of amateur dramatic productions, c1948, family papers.

58. Newspaper cuttings in family scrapbook. Queen Mary purchased several items of Burleigh Ware at the British Industries Fair of 1933.

59. Bennett lived in Buxton in Derbyshire; Endon in Staffordshire; the picturesque Lower Yew Tree Farm in Over Alderley, Macclesfield, Cheshire; Blithely near Rugeley in Staffordshire; and finally Market Drayton in Shropshire.

60. Anthony Bennett, Harold's son, in conversation with the author, 2002.

61. Anthony Bennett, Harold's son, in conversation with the author, 2002.

62. Research by Steve Davies.

63. Spours, Judy, *Art Deco Tableware*, pp.101-3 (Ward Lock 1988).

64. Burgess, Dorling & Leigh Ltd Company Archives.

65. Bumpus, Bernard, 2001.

66. Coupe, Elizabeth, *Collecting Burleigh Ware, A Photographic Guide to the Art Deco Tablewares of Burgess & Leigh*, p.14 (Letterbox Publishing 1998)

67. Research by Steve Davies.

68. The name had been used on an earlier 1920s pattern.

69. *The Pottery Gazette and Glass Trade Review*, 2nd September, 1935.

70. Bumpus, Bernard, *Collecting Rhead Pottery, Charlotte, Frederick, Frederick Hurten*, p.17 (Francis Joseph 1999).

71. Leigh, Alan, draft article on company history, Burgess, Dorling & Leigh Ltd Company Archives.

72. See Chapter Two.

73. Bumpus, Bernard, *Collecting Rhead Pottery, Charlotte, Frederick, Frederick Hurten*, p.22 (Francis Joseph 1999).

74. Batkin, Maureen, *Gifts for Good Children, Part II, 1890-1990*, p.51 (Richard Dennis).

75. A factory notebook indicates that this was produced for the US agency, Fondeville.
76. Batkin, Maureen, *Gifts for Good Children, Part II, 1890-1990*, pp.51-2 (Richard Dennis). Batkin gives details of early 1930s ranges, *School Time, Bed Time* and later 1970s series, *Rupert Bear*.
77. A design by David Copeland, Art Director 1963-83.
78. *The Pottery Gazette and Glass Trade Review*, p.453, 2nd April, 1934.
79. *The Pottery Gazette and Glass Trade Review*, 1933, report of BIF trade review.
80. From interviews with Mr Stan and Mrs Elsie Johnson and Mr Ben Ford, 2002-2002.
81. *The Pottery Gazette and Glass Trade Review*, 1st August, 1935.
82. Leigh, Alan, draft article on company history from 1933-1938, Burgess, Dorling & Leigh Ltd Company Archives.
83. Elsie was to marry glost fireman Stan Johnson.
84. Johnson, Stan, transcript of interview for the Potteries Museum, 13th January, 2000.
85. Research by Steve Davies.
86. Johnson, Stan, retired glost fireman, Burgess & Leigh, interviewed 13th January, 2000 by the Potteries Museum.
87. Elsie Johnson in conversation with the author, 2001. Ben Ford remembers the Lodge man lived in another terraced cottage.
88. Taped interview with Kath Wilson and Sue Golding, John Ecclestone for the National Trust Sound Archive, 15th January, 2000.
89. Taped interview Ben Ford in conversation with John Ecclestone and Will Dorling for the National Trust Sound Archive, 18th March, 2000.
90. *The Pottery Gazette and Glass Trade Review*, 1937.
91. *The Pottery Gazette and Glass Trade Review*, 1935.

CHAPTER FIVE
1. Leigh, Barry, Taped interview with Jeremy Miln, Will Dorling and John Ecclestone for the National Trust Sound Archive 6th May, 2000.
2. Information in a document dated 1940 regarding *'the temporary deferment of calling up of a man liable to serve in the armed forces'*, Burgess, Dorling & Leigh Ltd. company archives.
3. Details from *'Concentration of Production, Pottery Trade'* document in Burgess, Dorling & Leigh Ltd Company Archives.
4. Godden, G. A., *Encyclopaedia of British Pottery and Porcelain Marks* (Barrie & Jenkins, 2000).
5. *The Pottery Gazette and Glass Trade Review*, p.759, 1st June, 1939.
6. *The Pottery Gazette and Glass Trade Review*, p.397, Export Notes, July 1942.
7. Letter from Edmund Leigh in the possession of Elizabeth Coupe states: *'Toby Jugs of other wartime leaders were modelled but as far as we are aware none of these went into production.'*
8. Letter from Edmund Leigh in the possession of Elizabeth Coupe.
9. Letter from Edmund Leigh in the possession of Elizabeth Coupe.
10. Smith, Ronald A., *Images of Greatness* (Kevin Francis Books 1989).
11. *Concentration of Production, Pottery Trade*, document dated 1941, Burgess, Dorling & Leigh Ltd Company Archives.
12. Leigh, draft article on company history, Burgess, Dorling & Leigh Company Archives.
13. Burgess & Leigh 1951 Centenary Leaflet, *A Century of Progress*, Burgess, Dorling & Leigh Ltd Company Archives.
14. Niblett, Kathy, *Dynamic Design, The British Pottery Industry 1940-1990* (Potteries Museum & Art Gallery 1990).
15. Leigh, Alan, draft article on company history, Burgess, Dorling & Leigh Ltd Company Archives.
16. Leigh, Alan, draft article on company history, Burgess, Dorling & Leigh Ltd Company Archives.
17. Burgess & Leigh Centenary Leaflet, *A Century of Progress 1851-1951*, Burgess, Dorling & Leigh Ltd Company Archives.
18. *The Evening Sentinel*, Wednesday, 3rd July, 1946.
19. Hildyard, Robin, Senior Curator, Ceramics and Glass Collection, Victoria and Albert Museum, in correspondence with the author 2002.
20. Davies, Steve, information supplied by his mother who worked as a toby jug paintress at the Middleport Pottery during the 1940s and 1950s.
21. Gardner, Juliet, *From the Bomb to the Beatles, the Changing Face of Post-War Britain*, p.53 (Collins & Brown).
22. Gardner, Juliet, *From the Bomb to the Beatles, the Changing Face of Post-War Britain*, p.48 (Collins & Brown).
23. *The Pottery Gazette and Glass Trade Review*, pp.1088-1091, July 1951.
24. Letter to Kingsley Leigh from Chairman, Henry Johnson, Burgess, Dorling & Leigh Company Archives.
25. Ben Ford in conversation with the author 2002.
26. Hallinan, Lincoln, illustrates one with the brand name *Ivory Ware in Royal Commemoratives* (The Shire Book 1997).
27. It reads: *'The Great Gothic Chair Made For Edward I Stands In Westminster Abbey. Adam Was The Name Of The Workman, Cost 11 Shillings. Master Walter The Painter Decorated It. 'The Stone Of Destiny Was Placed Under The Seat. Ready On March 27th 1300. Has Been Issued For All Coronation Services Since. With The Exception Of Queen Mary In 1553. At Coronations It Is Covered With A Cloth Of Gold. Elizabeth II Crowned June 2nd 1953. Burleigh Ware England'*.
28. Leigh, Alan, draft article on company history, of Burgess & Leigh, Burgess, Dorling & Leigh Ltd Company Archives.

29. Leigh, Alan, draft article on company history, Burgess, Dorling & Leigh Ltd Company Archives.
30. Leigh, draft article on company history, Burgess, Dorling & Leigh Ltd Company Archives.
31. Leigh, draft article on company history, Burgess, Dorling & Leigh Ltd Company Archives.

CHAPTER SIX
1. Quoted in *Medical Ceramics*, Vol. 1, 1969 by J. K. Crellin, held by the Wellcome Institute of the History of Medicine. Thanks to Bryony Kelly of the Museum of the Royal Pharmaceutical Society of Great Britain.
2. Leigh, Alan, draft article on company history, Burgess, Dorling & Leigh Ltd Company Archives.
3. *The Pottery Gazette and Glass Trade Review*, p1147, September 1969.
4. Copeland, David, in conversation with the author, 3rd March, 2003.
5. Nunn, Chris, freelance designer for Burgess & Leigh during the 1980s-90s, in conversation with the author, 3rd March, 2003, thought that the pattern might have been taken from antique pottery at Kedleston Hall, a Palladian mansion in Derbyshire built for the Curzon family. However, archivist Jill Banks confirmed that there is no written evidence at the Hall to support this theory.
6. Minutes, Shareholders' Meetings, Burgess, Dorling & Leigh Ltd Company Archives.
7. Leigh, Alan, draft article on company history, Burgess, Dorling & Leigh Ltd Company Archives.
8. Leigh, Barry, Taped interview with Jeremy Miln, Will Dorling and John Ecclestone for the National Trust Sound Archive, 6th May, 2000.
9. Leigh, Alan, draft article on company history, Burgess, Dorling & Leigh Ltd Company Archives.
10. Smith, Ronald A., *The Premier Years of Margaret Thatcher*, pp.56-8 (Kevin Francis) *'Mr E T Bailey, who was for many years one of the senior artists at Burgess & Leigh, modelled a most unusual commemorative piece which he called Spirit of Britain…. only 24 were made. The first one was sent to the South Atlantic Fund to raise vitally needed money, the second was sent to and accepted by Mrs Thatcher.'*
11. Copeland, David, in conversation with the author, 13th March, 2003.
12. Research by Steve Davies.
13. Leigh, Barry, Taped interview with Jeremy Miln, Will Dorling and John Ecclestone for the National Trust Sound Archive, 6th May, 2000.
14. Leigh, Barry, Taped interview with Jeremy Miln, Will Dorling and John Ecclestone for the National Trust Sound Archive, 6th May, 2000.
15. Leigh, Alan, draft article on company history, Burgess, Dorling & Leigh Ltd Company Archives.
16. Quoted from correspondence from Stoke-on-Trent Environmental Services, 25th May, 1982, held by Wood, Goldstraw & Yorath, architects of Hanley, Stoke-on-Trent.
17. Wilson, Kath, and Goulding, Sue, Taped interview with John Ecclestone for the National Trust Sound Archive, 15th January, 2000.
18. *The Sentinel*, February 24th 1998.
19. *The Sentinel*, February 24th 1999.

CHAPTER SEVEN
1. *The Sentinel*, Litchfield, Michael, *'Pottery given up for dead is still alive and kicking'*, 17th May, 2000.
2. For details of Elizabeth Coupe's collectors' books, see Selected Bibliography. The Burleigh Ware International Collectors' Club has since folded owing to a lack of time rather than enthusiasm. A Friends Of Burleigh Club founded by Burgess, Dorling & Leigh in 2000 has also ceased for the same reason.
3. *The Sentinel*, Litchfield, Michael, *'Pottery given up for dead is still alive and kicking'*, 17th May, 2000.
4. The China Box Company sales leaflet, 1998.
5. Quote, *The Saving of Middleport Pottery*, information sheet, Burgess, Dorling & Leigh 2001.
6 Quote, *The Saving of Middleport Pottery*, information sheet, Burgess, Dorling & Leigh 2001.
7. *The Sentinel*, *'Three groups battle to take over failed ceramics firm'*, 4th August, 1999, Paul Bateman, head of corporate recovery, KPMG, quoted.
8. *'Collect It!'* Jones, Gwyn, *'Burleigh Ware, A Unique Heritage'*, pp.10-12, December 1999.
9. Wilson, Kath and Goulding, Sue, Taped interview with John Ecclestone for the National Trust Sound Archive, 12th Janury, 2000.
10. Johnson, Elsie, retired freehand paintress, in conversation with the author, 2002.
11. Friends of Burleigh Newsletter, No 1, October 2000.
12. See Appendix for a list of Burgess, Dorling & Leigh Flower Jug reissues.
13. *The Antique Dealer*, Shoop, Fiona, *'Why it's Risky Mixing the New with the Old'*, pp.26-7, No 75, April 2001.
14. See Chapter Five.
15. See Chapter Four.
16. The *Sweden* was built in 1921 by the Anderton Company and restored by present owner Colin Bowes. The *Buckden* was built for the Grand Union Canal Carrying Company in 1936 and is being restored by John and Sue Yates.
17. Walshaw, Roger, a temporary Security Guard at the Middleport Pottery, said the words in conversation with Rosemary Dorling.

A hand-worn newel post, the patination of a century.

MARKS

Identification of early Burgess & Leigh products may be difficult as not all were marked. One of the earliest marks used throughout the nineteenth century was a simple 'B & L', perhaps alongside a design name or registration mark or number. This mark is either printed or impressed. Other impressed marks include the words 'Burslem', 'England' and 'Ivory' (denoting glaze colour). Shape numbers are also sometimes impressed, as is the date of potting. When a datemark is not present, it is possible to ascertain an approximate year of manufacture from Burgess & Leigh's printed marks. On moving to the Hill Pottery in 1868 the beehive mark, previously used by Samuel Alcock & Co Ltd, was adapted to incorporate the initials 'B & L'. Between 1868 and 1878, when Burgess and Leigh were in partnership with Lowndes-Goode, 'B, L & Co' was sometimes used. Initials may also appear in a garter mark or in pattern cartouches.

From 1889 several new marks were introduced incorporating the Middleport Pottery name. 'Royal Semi-Porcelain', or sometimes 'Semi Porcelain', denotes a type of fine earthenware body promoted at the turn of the century. By the early 1900s, the first of several variations of a globe mark was in use. The inclusion of 'Burleigh' in all marks indicates a date of post 1903, when the brand name was registered. 'Limited' may appear after 1919. In c1929 a new printed beehive mark was introduced with foliage around, 'Est'd 1851' and either 'England' or 'Made in England' beneath. In the late 1930s, the beehive mark was again redesigned. An accompanying letter B appears between c1941-52 and 'Ironstone', a new earthenware body, after 1960. From the late 1960s, cartouches were again used for printed patterns. Those with the Burleigh brand name have remained in use since 1999 when the company became Burgess, Dorling & Leigh Ltd. Since then other printed marks may incorporate the initials B, D & L.

Pre-1868 beehive mark used by S. Alcock & Co. at the Hill Pottery, printed from a copperplate engraving acquired by Burgess & Leigh.

Special mark used on a royal commemorative item, 1911.

Adaptation of mark used by Keeling & Co whose patterns and shapes Burgess & Leigh acquired in 1937.

Original *Asiatic Pheasant* pattern cartouche with B & L initials, c.1862 – c.1984. This example with impressed date 1888.

BL&Co used between 1868 and 1878. *Antique* refers to the shape name.

Simple pattern cartouche with pattern name *Old Derby*, probably adapted by Burgess & Leigh from an acquired copper engraving. B&L Ltd from 1919.

Burleigh beehive mark with backstamp of retailer, Lawley's, incorporating *Seville* pattern name, hand-painted pattern number and painter's mark, c.1934.

Adaptation of earlier *Asiatic Pheasant* pattern mark to incorporate the Burleigh name, from 1984.

One of the earliest marks, a printed B&L. Here with *Farmers Arms* pattern name, c.1870.

Burleigh Ware mark, here incorporating the *Paisley* pattern name, used from c.1920.

Simple printed pattern name *RIVIERA*, registered number and painter's mark, c.1934.

Simple mark used on David Copeland's *Chequers* pattern, from 1975.

Beehive mark with B&L, *Norman* pattern name and registration mark for 1872.

Variation of the globe mark with BURLEIGH WARE brand name above and ENGLAND beneath. Signed Rhead and used on her early designs, c.1926-28.

Re-design of the Burleigh beehive mark in c.1939. (With 'Ironstone' after 1960.)

Decorative Burleigh pattern cartouche used on the *Felicity* pattern from 1980.

Nineteenth-century mark with B&L monogram.

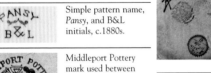

Redesign of beehive mark, c1929. Here, signed Rhead, with pattern number, painter's mark and original price label. Used on Charlotte Rhead's designs from c.1929 to c.1931.

One of the few printed marks to incorporate the name of the designer, Art Director, Harold Bennett, on a turkey dish, c.1939.

Pattern cartouche for the *Flora* pattern previously produced by Davenport. This mark from from the 1990s.

Simple pattern name, *Pansy*, and B&L initials, c.1880s.

Middleport Pottery mark used between c.1889 and c.1920. *Brampton* pattern name.

Burleigh beehive mark with ENGLAND beneath, Bennett's signature, painter's mark and pattern number. Used during 1930s, this example from c.1933.

Decorative mark used on *Davenport Hunting Scenes* pattern, from c.1940.

Decorative Burgess & Leigh pattern cartouche used on the *Burgess Chintz* pattern from the 1990s.

Burgess & Leigh lion mark, 1890s to early 1900s.

Simple BURLEIGH MADE IN ENGLAND mark, here with *ZENITH* tableware shape name, registered 1931.

BURLEIGH MADE IN ENGLAND mark with *BALMORAL* shape name and registered number. Pattern number 8207 indicates a date in the early 1950s.

Decorative Burgess & Leigh pattern cartouche used on the *Dovedale* pattern, 1990s.

Special mark used on a commemorative item, 1898.

Burleigh beehive mark with decorative pattern backstamp for *Pan*, pattern number and painter's mark, 1932.

Special beehive mark used on 1951 commemorative mug.

Printed mark used by The China Box Company established by William and Rosemary Dorling, 1992-1999.

Globe mark in use by the early 1900s; here with *Daisy* pattern name and registered number for 1889.

Burleigh beehive with MADE IN ENGLAND and special commemorative mark for Dame Laura Knight's coronation mug, 1937.

Simple Burleigh mark used from the 1960s, this example from an advertising ware item.

Garter mark incorporating the initials B & L and the name of the *Danish Fern* pattern previously produced by Davenport, c.1890s.

Variation of the globe mark with additional sash reading Middleport Pottery and Burleigh pattern name registered in 1903.

Burleigh Ware mark used from c.1910, with and without BURSLEM, ENGLAND. B, D & L for Burgess, Dorling & Leigh, from 1999.

Burleigh beehive with MADE IN ENGLAND and *BALMORAL* shape name, registered 1937.

Burleigh *Calico* cartouche, designed by David Copeland, engraved by Tom Blaize, used on UK pattern from c.1968.

Adaptation of earlier mark by Burgess, Dorling & Leigh to include Burleigh brand name and name of commissioning US retailer, Martha Stewart, 2002.

236

PATTERNS

Information on Burgess & Leigh patterns has been compiled from reports and advertisements in *The Pottery Gazette and Glass Trade Review* as well as from miscellaneous documents, notebooks, ledgers, sales catalogues and a number of descriptive (largely un-illustrated and un-dated) pattern books held in the Burgess, Dorling and Leigh Ltd company archive. The lists are by no means definitive owing to gaps in the archive and difficulties in interpreting those records remaining. Further patterns will continue to come to light but it is hoped that the information will be of interest.

Pattern Numbers
Approximate dates of pattern numbers deduced from Burgess & Leigh's undated pattern books. (N.B. The pattern book covering the period 1903 – 1919 includes a new sequence of pattern numbers beginning in c.1911 and commencing with number 1200.)

Central and Hill Potteries:
1862 - 1888:   1- 2000

Middleport Pottery:
1889 – 1902:   2001 - 3180

Middleport Pottery Burleigh Ware
1903 – 1910:	3181 - 4004
1911 – 1925:	1200 - 3900
1926 – 1939:	3901 - 6440
1940 – 1950:	6441 - 7000
1951 – 1963:	7001 - 9000
1964 – 1985:	9001 - 9428

Burgess & Leigh's Nineteenth Century Engraved Patterns
(*Indicates that the pattern was first produced before 1888. Pattern numbers shown where known.)

Acacia
Alexandra
Amherst Japan*
Apple Blossom* 2130, 2131
Apsley Plants
Arcadia
Argos*
Argyle*
Asiatic Pheasant*
Aster, 2171-3, 2175, 2193-7, 2246-7, 2226
Athol (reg'd 1898)
Austral, 2202
Autumn Belle, 2680, 2700
Ava
Barberini Vase* (reg'd 1866)
Begonia
Bishop's Border*
Blackberry*
Bouquet*
Briar, reg'd 1886
Brighton*
Brooklyn
Broseley*, 1837
Burnell*
Cable*
Cactus, 2176, 2180, 2225
Castle*
Celeste
Chariots*
Chelsea
Cherry Blossom*
Cheshire, 2060, 2061
Chinese Figures*, 1785
Chinese Pekin*
Chrysanthemum, 2432, 2442
Clarence
Clematis (reg. 1893)
Clover, 2103
Clyde*
Clytie
Conway*
Cranesbill (reg.d 1892)
Cranston (reg'd 1892)
Crown Derby, 2079
Daffodil, 2009, 2135, 2137,
Daisy (reg'd 1896)
Danish Fern*
Delhi, 2106
Derby
Doris, 2114, 2117
Dresden (reg'd 1896)
Dresden Flowers (regd 1896)
Eerie (reg'd 1892), 2214, 2253
Etruscan Vases*
Fables, 2170
Ferns
Fibre*
Flamingo*
Flora*
Florentine
Florette (reg'd 1896)
Forget-me-Nots (c1897)

Fruit
Garland
Gem*
Geranium*
Greek*
Guitar*
Hawthorn* 2735
Honeysuckle*
Hop (reg'd c1890), 2029, 2083, 2084
Hyde Park (c1898)
Indian*
Ionia
Iris, 2725
Irvon (reg. 1893)
Italian*
Jeddo*
Kaiser* (reg'd 1888)
Kensington* (reg'd 1875)
Key* (border)
Landscape*
Lilac*
Lily*
Lonsdale*
Lorne*
Louis (reg'd 1897)
Louise*
Lovers*
Mabelle (reg'd 1896)
Madras
Manchester*
Matabele
May Blossom, 2073
Melita, 2199, 2200, 2250
Napier*
Neptune*
Newport
Nizon
Non Pareil (introd. 1897)
Norman* (reg'd 1872)
Nuts*, 1824
Oak
Orange, 2095, 2098, 2112
Orchids
Orient
Osprey, 2609-2612, 2617-17
Pansy*
Pansies (c1897)
Paris*
Pekin*
Persian*
Perth*
Pinks, 2676, 2694, 2715, 2727, 2728
Pomona*
Poppy,* 2085
Prairie (reg. 1890)
Premier*
Primula
Regent, Mauve, 5074, G5080
Regent, Red, 5034, G5043
Rhine*
Rococo, 2186

Rose*
Roses, 2724, 2732, 2767
Royal, 2505, 2507, 2508
Rural
Rustic* (reg'd c1886), 1895
Scale*
Seasons*
Seville*
Shirus
Siam*
Simla
Star Leaves* (border)
Suez*
Sybil, 2684
Sydenham*
Teheran*
Tottenham, 2147, 2151, 2160, 2161
Trefoil
Tunis
Venetian*
Ventnor, (reg. 1892) 2237, 2240, 2243
Verbena, 2118
Vermont (reg'd 1895)
Victoria* (reg'd c1886), 2749
Vine
Violets, 2187
Willow*
Windflower (reg'd 1885)

Popular named Burleigh Tableware Patterns of the 1930s

Pattern Name	No.	Shape	Date of Issue
Apple Tree	4884, 4885	Sheraton, Melba	1933
Ascot	5352, 5385,	Zenith	1935
Autumn	5657	London	1937
Azalea	5567	Belvedere	1936
Biarritz	5013, 5014	Zenith, London	1934
Blackberry	6216, 6314	Balmoral	1939
Blackthorn	5339-42, 5345-7	Zenith	1935
Bluebell	4829	Zenith	1933
Bouquet	4719, 4793	Zenith	1932
Briar	5202	Zenith	1934
Britain Beautiful	4857, 4858-9	Zenith, London	1933
Brocade	5044	Zenith, London	1934
Butterfly	5080	Imperial	1934
Catkins	4613	Zenith	1931
Cornflower	5203, 5285	Imperial, London	1934
Daffodil	4813/A	Zenith	1932
Dawn	4760, 4772	Zenith	1932
Diamonds	5286-7, 5337, 5454	Zenith	1935
Ellesmere		Belvedere	1937
Evensong	5663	Balmoral	1937
Evergreen	5246	Imperial	1935
Evesham	5196, 5197	Zenith	1934
Fern	4955	London	1933
Fir	5350	Zenith	1935
Florette	5468, 5469	Imperial, London	1935
Forget-me-Not	5351	London	1935
Fragrance	4972	Zenith	1933
Fuchsia	4815	Zenith	1932
Gaiety	5245	Zenith	1935
Gala	4970, 4986, 4987	Zenith	1933
Geranium	5349, 5352	Zenith, Imperial, London	1935
Golden Days	4971/A	Zenith, London	1933
Golden Gleams	5275	Imperial	1935
Halcyon	5283, 5284	Balmoral, Zenith	1935
Harebell	4439	Sheraton	1930
Harebells	5547	Zenith, London	1936
Harmony	5697	Balmoral	1937
Harvest Moon	5456	Imperial, London	1935
Hollyhock	4434	Sheraton	1930
Homestead	5783, 5784	Balmoral	1937
Iris	4812	Zenith	1932
Kew	4977, 5011	Zenith, London	1933
Laburnum	4708/A, 4709	Zenith	1932
Laburnum	5350	London	1935
Langham	5207	Imperial, London	1935
Lilactime	5033	London	1934
Lilypond	4927	Zenith, London	1933
London	5592	Imperial, Zenith	1936
Lupin	4968/A	Zenith, London	1933
Lynton	4696	Zenith	1932
Marguerite	4578	Zenith	1931
Marina	5082	Zenith, Marina	1935
Maytime	5089-90, 5252,5338, 5377	Imperial, London, Zenith	1935
Meadowland	4807	Zenith, Imperial	1932
Melrose	5696, 5841	Balmoral	1937
Mimosa	4759, 4907, 4956	Zenith, London	1932

Pattern name	No.	Shape	Date of Issue
Moiré	5878	Balmoral	1937
Moonbeams	5045, 5055	Zenith, London	1934
Narcissus	4886, 4887	Melba, London	1933
Orchard	4767-8	Zenith	1932
Pageant	4689, 4714	Suite Ware	1932
Pagoda	4589		1931
Paisley	5788, 5842, 5879	Balmoral	1937
Pan	4827, 4828	Zenith, London Imperial	1932
Pansy	5136	Zenith	1935
Poppies and cornflowers	5137	Zenith	1935
Primrose	5138	Zenith, London	1935
Primroses	5457	Imperial, London	1935
Regatta	5253-5, 5282	Zenith, Imperial	1935
Rhapsody	5665	Balmoral	1937
Riverside	5355	Imperial, London	1935
Riviera	5088	Imperial	1934
Roseland	4837, 4851, etc	Zenith	1933
Rushmere	5353, 5354	Zenith	1935
Rutland	4567	Zenith	1931
Savoy	4758, 4773	Zenith	1932
Sefton	4541	Sheraton	1930
Seville	5021	Zenith	1934
Shadows	4933	Zenith, London	1933
Shirley	4579	Zenith	1931
Spa	5276	Imperial	1935
Spring	4759	Zenith	1932
Springtime	5664/A	Zenith	1937
Spring Blossom	5508	Zenith	1936
Stuart	4925, 5004	Zenith	1933
Summertime	4582	Zenith	1931
Sunflowers	5012	London	1934
Sunflower	4835	Zenith	1933
Sunray	4924	Zenith	1933
Sunshine	4609, 4715	(Rhead suite ware)	1931
Sweetpea	4814	Zenith	1932
Tranquil	4900, 4901	Zenith	1933
Tudor	4926	Zenith	1933
Tulip	4811	Zenith	1932
Tulip Time	5081	Imperial	1934
Twilight	5662	Balmoral	1937

(N.B. Shapes usually describe dinnerware but might also denote combinations of different dinnerware, teaware and Suite ware shapes).

Un-named patterns

Many of the Burleigh Art Deco patterns were never given names but were ordered by their pattern numbers (a common practice during the 1930s). An attempt to provide descriptive names for these anonymous patterns has been made by Elizabeth Coupe, author of a collectors' guide, *Collecting Burleigh Ware, A Photographic Guide to the Art Deco Tablewares of Burgess & Leigh* (Letterbox Publishing 1998). A few examples from her expanding list are 'Autumn Leaves' (5034); 'Black Square' (5039); 'Yellow Dahlia' (4824); 'Blue Dahlia' (5067); 'Golden Wisteria' (5340); and 'Orange Tree' (5040).

FLOWER JUGS

Names, pattern numbers and dates when first entered into the Pattern Book

Early Flower Jugs

1932	York, 4731, 4732, 4733, 47354
1932	Alma, 4800, 4802, 4850,
1932	Elers, 4803, 4804, 4870, 4871, 4872, 4873

Relief-moulded Flower Jugs

Modelled

1931	Squirrel, 4801, 4808, 4849, 4904/A, 4991, 5059, 5105, 5247, 5300, 5314, 5319, 5320, 5478, 5479, 8081
1931	Parrot, 4862, 4863, 4876, 4902, 4903, 4910, 5056, 5249, 5311, 5334, 5335, 5482, 5483, 6931, 6932, 6933, 7017
1931	Dragon, 4892, 4893, 4894, 4895, 4916, 4917, 4918, 4928, 5104, 5118, 5317/A, 5318, 7013. 7014
1931	Kingfisher, 4896, 4909, 4922, 4928, 4982, 5057, 5101, 5103, 5103, 5106, 5122, 5312, 5315, 5316, 5480, 5481
1931	Kangaroo, 4911, 4912, 4929
1932	Pied Piper, 4983, 4984, 4985, 5058, 5263, 5492, 5493, 5984, 8082
1932	Flamingo, 4990, 5002, 5003, 5094, 5095, 5321, 5437
1932	Guardsman, 5061, 5062, 5096, 5119
1932	Harvest, 5063, 5064, 5076, 5356, 5362
1932	Dick Turpin or Highwayman, 5064, 5065, 5331, 5332/A, 5422, 5549
1933	Fox in Cornfield ('Stoat'), 5123, 5124, 5151

1933	Rock Garden, 5125, 5126, 5127
1933	Galleon, 5128, 5129, 5130
1933	Stork and the Fox, 5161, 5162, 5313, 5323, 5358, 5359, 5360, 5488, 5491
1934	Monkey and the Cat, 5271
1935	Honeycomb, 5418, 5423, 5424, 5452, 5484, 5485
1935	Palm ('Bird of Paradise'), 5419, 5425, 5426, 5429, 5463, 5486, 5487, 5514
1934	Pheasant, 5622, 5623, 5624, 5637, 5638
1935	Budgerigar, 6021, 6022, 6048, 6049, 6050, 6528, 6530
1938	Butterfly, 6023, 6024, 6051, 6052, 6053, 6054, 6055, 6531, 6532, 6934, 6935, 6936, 7019, 7020, 7022
1938	Pixie, 6374, 6382, 6385, 6431
1938	Vine ('Grapes'), 6375, 6376, 6378, 6379, 6381, 6527, 6529, 6536, 6637
1954	Lupin, 8218, 8219, 8220, 8221
Not listed	Fox 'and flowers'

Sporting Jugs

1934	Tennis Player, 5289, 5308, 5329, 5330, 5415
1934	Cricketer, 5290, 5333, 5417
1935	Golfer, 5291, 5309, 5416

'Stylised' Jugs

1933	Regent, 5131, 5251, 5261, 5262, 5265, 5272, 5273
1933	Zenith ('Double Lozenge'), 5155, 5156, 5157, 5158, 5175, 5190
1934	Argosy ('Galleon and Fishes'), 5163, 5164, 5165, 5250, 5256, 5324, 5325
1934	Luxor ('Leaping Gazelles'), 5166, 5167, 5168, 5248, 5257, 5326
1934	Meridian ('Totem'), 5176, 5198
1934	Ovoid, 5205, 5214
1934	Sundial and Kingfisher, 5193
1934	Troy, 5169, 5170, 5177, 5178, 5179, 5191, 5192, 5264, 5489
1934	Regent, 5131, 5251, 5261, 5262, 5265, 5272, 5273
1934	Ovoid, 5205, 5214

'City' Jugs

1936	Cambridge, 5780, 5781, 5782, 5793, 5794, 5845, 5847, 5890
1936	Oxford, 5831, 5832, 5843, 5844, 5846, 5887, 5888, 5889
1936	Venice, 5620, 5621, 5689, 5693, 5694, 5695
1936	Eton, 5625, 5626, 5627, 5628, 5690, 5691, 5692, 5694, 5695

Reproduction Period Jugs

1936	Sally in Our Alley, 5631, 5633, 5706, 6031, 7075
1936	Gretna Green, 5632, 5634, 5705, 7076
1937	The Stocks, 5949, 5950, 5957, 5958, 5975, 6144, 6145
1938	Old Feeding Time, 6032, 7074*
1938	The Village Blacksmith, 6058, 6059, 6130, 6131, 7077
not listed, c.1954	Nell Gwynn
not listed, c.1954	Tally Ho

* This is the only Alcock & Co jug to be shown in the Pattern Books

BURGESS, DORLING & LEIGH REPRODUCTIONS 1999-2002

Flower Jugs: Guardsman,*green or black; Dragon, large, red or black, and small, green and orange; Budgerigar, white or yellow glaze; Butterfly*, white or yellow glaze; Honeycomb*, in blue or orange; Flamingo; Rock Garden*, white or yellow glaze; Kingfisher; Pied Piper; Golfer*, white or yellow glaze; Tennis Player*, white or yellow glaze; Cricketer*, white or yellow glaze; Giraffe; Turkey; 'Leaping Gazelles' (Luxor), in red or green.

* Denotes miniature size also available.

Limited Editions: Butterfly (for Bloomingdales); Pied Piper special colourway for Foxy Lady Commissions; Turkey (in red) for Ross Simons; Battle of Britain plaque for Sewells of London; Vesuvius (Dragon) jug; Arms of All Nations jug.

Second World War Commemoratives: Churchill 'Bulldogs' toby jug; Churchill 'V' for Victory toby jug; Churchill character jug; miniature Churchill character jug; Churchill ashtray and cigar; Churchill and Roosevelt Loving Cup; Churchill Union Jack mug; Battle of Britain plaque.

Jubilee Ware (produced for the Golden Jubilee of Queen Elizabeth II in 2002): 1935 GR 'Royal Standard' jug; 1953 ER 'Royal Standard' jug. Items sold through Buckingham Palace shop: 1953 'Coronation' Jug; 1953 'Gothic Chair' jug; 1937 Coronation plaque; 1953 ER 'Royal Standard' jug; miniature Guardsman jug in red, white and blue colourway.

Also produced: Bottle Oven; Caravan Teaset; Honeycomb lidded box; and Honey Pot.

Other items have been produced as samples or in small numbers. They include the Argosy Jug; Monkey and the Cat jug; Charles Dickens toby jug; Shakespeare toby jug; Beefeater toby jug; Chelsea Pensioner toby jug; Edmund Leigh 1951 toby jug; Nell Gwyn jug; and items of Acorn Ware.

CHARLOTTE RHEAD PATTERNS

The Burgess & Leigh pattern book for the period 26th March, 1925 to 18th August, 1932 contains patterns with numbers from 3740 to 4837. It includes all Charlotte Rhead's commercially produced designs for the company with the single exception of no. 4908, *New Florentine*, which was evidently not put into production until after she had left.   While working for Burgess & Leigh, Charlotte Rhead also made a large number of trial pieces. These did not go into production and were not given pattern numbers though they usually carry the Burgess & Leigh backstamp and Charlotte Rhead's name on their bases.

Most patterns by Charlotte Rhead are attributed to her in the pattern book, though towards the end of her time with the company this was not always done. The following list includes all those described as tube lined with some other designs which can be attributed to her. Work that is attributed only is noted in the list that follows.

Where a pattern or shape was given a name in the pattern book, the name is shown in italics.   *Bernard Bumpus*

u.g. appears frequently in the pattern book as an abbreviation for underglaze.

3973 Suite ware, Anemone border. Tube-lined in black painted u.g. Aerographed sunset. Top pencilled black. Black edge.

3997 *Avon* fruit bowl. Tube-lined Japanese flowers. Enamelled coral, yellow sunset, 9 light green. Also yellow inside and out. Black edge. Black line inside border and footline.

3998 *Avon* fruit bowl. Tube-lined speckled fruit painted u.g. orange, shaded fawn and pink, IBB Lucy's green edge and footline in black sienna red brown.

3999 *Regina* fruit set. Tube-lined in black painted u.g. [apples in various colours].

4000 *Avon* fruit bowl. Tube-lined in black heavy fruit pattern painted u.g. K. Blue, [fruits include pomegranates, apples and black grapes].

4001 Vases, bowls etc. *Gouda* matt glaze (Miss Rhead) u.g. painted purple, pink, puce, orange, IBB Lucy's green edge and footline in black. [Design features cloud scrolls and stylised roses. The items made with this design included toilet sets.]

4002 Vases, bowls etc. matt glaze blue background (Miss Rhead). [Tubed peonies.]

4003 Suite ware. Tube-lined and enamelled. Crown Derby pattern.

4009 *Rex* fruit set and suite ware. Tube-lined in brown with fruit and grapes painted in u.g. pink, orange, fawn, blue and red-brown IBB green, mixed silver.

4010 *Avon* fruit bowl. *Regina* saucer. Tube-lined lemon fruit in brown. Fawn edge. (*Regina* saucer) orange, fawn, IBB mixed green, red brown, orange edge.

4011 Plaque. Miss Rhead. Japanese lady [she is seated on a rug].

4012 Plaque. Miss Rhead. Pheasant and fruit.

4013 Plaque. Miss Rhead. Persian design.

4014 Fruit set, *Avon* bowl, *Regina* saucer. Tube-lined strawberry pattern in brown painted, u.g. pink, IBB green, mixed green green edge narrow band.

4015 Fruit set, *Avon* bowl, *Regina* saucer. Tube-lined bilberry pattern in brown painted u.g. K. blue, shaded purple, IBB green, mixed green orange edge and narrow band on top.

4016 Bowls, vases etc. Miss Rhead. Tube-lined fruits. Matt glaze. Lustred in various coloured lustres.

4070 Bowls, etc. Embossed leaves front leaves light green, others dark green. Tubed poppy flowers painted u.g. orange, pink and blue u.g. dark green edge.

4071 Bowls etc. embossed leaves as 4070. Tube-lined fruit and grapes, painted u.g. in pink, puce, blue purple and red brown u.g. black edge.

4072 *Jacobean* bowls embossed leaves with tube-lined grapes painted u.g. in orange, K. blue, purple and green IBB. Dark green edge and foot.

4073 *Jacobean* bowls embossed leaves. Tube-lined cherries and small leaves painted u.g. in pink, purple, light green and IBB. Aero yellow outside u.g. dark green edge and footline.

[Note in pattern book] 4100-4135 Reserved for Miss Rhead's decorations.

4100 Bowls, vases etc. Miss Rhead Tube lined *Sylvan* in blue slip. Matt glaze, lustred various lustres black edge. [Ring of trees with a mountain range in the background.]

4101 Bowls, vases etc. Tube-lined *Garland* in black slip. Matt glaze, enamelled light blue, lustred orange and green blue edge. [Garlands of leaves and apples.]

4102 Sandwich sets, fan shape tube-lined fruits, painted u.g. in orange, fawn, puce, purple, light green, pink and dark green-brown stems, underglaze ivory, centre golden brown edge and line.

4103 Sandwich sets, fan-shape tube-lined basket of fruit, painted u.g. in orange, fawn, pink, puce, purple, light green and dark green-brown edge.

4104 Sandwich sets, fan shape tube-lined as *Garland* pattern in black enamelled in pale blue and pale red finished in blue. [*Garland* 4101.]

4105 Sandwich sets, fan shape, tube-lined as *Garland* pattern in black painted u.g. in orange, fawn and IBB green finished in u.g. fawn. [*Garland* 4101.]

4106 Sandwich sets, fan shape tube-lined, puce fruit in brown painted u.g. in orange, fawn, pink, puce, purple, light green and IBB green.

4107 Dessert bowl (new shape) tube-lined seeded fruits, blue grapes, puce fruit and two shaded-in green leaves (sic), golden brown edge and footline.

4108 Bowls, vases etc *Florentine* pattern. Miss Rhead tube-lined painted u.g. in various, u.g. colours painted edge pattern tube lined on cream body (slip stained). [Various fruits and leaves on a dark blue ground.]

4109 *Jacobean* bowl, embossed leaves painted u.g. Tube-lined tomatoes, enamelled dark green edge.

4110 Tea ware. Tube-lined and painted as 4000, finished in black u.g., lustred orange.

4111 Plaque large size. Tube-lined lady and parrot painted in underglaze colours. [Richly dressed young woman in profile, holding a bunch of grapes in front of a bird of the Psittacidæ family.]

4111A Plaque similar to 4111 but with crimson lustred edge.

4112 Bowls etc. Tube-lined *Persian* leaf in black, painted u.g. in purple, red, French green, light green, pink, ivory, IBB red brown lustred yellow inside and out, blue outside.

4113 Bowls etc. Tube-lined *Vine* in black on embossed leaf bowl, painted u.g. red, brown, K blue, lustred leaves dark green outside, violet blue edge and footline, matt glaze. [Fruiting vine design.]

4114 Bowls etc. Tube-lined *Cretonne* in black enamelled stems and flowers lustred in various coloured lustres, black edge and footline, orange lustre outside, matt glaze.

4115 Bowls etc. Tube-lined *Blossom* in black enamelled pink, orange, purple and blue (leaves embossed) and outside lustred dark green, black edge and footline, matt glaze. [Leaf and blossom design.]

4116 Bowls etc. Tube-lined *Aster* in black enamelled purple, blue, 14 green, embossed leaves lustred dark green, outside violet, black edge and foot, matt glaze. [Band of Aster flowers.]

4117 *Kew* small size bowl. Tube-lined *Persian* border only as 4112, no centre, lustred yellow inside and top, outside orange.

4118 Plaque large size. Tube-lined ship in black, painted in enamel colours.

4119 Fruit bowls. Tube-lined *Persian* pattern (4112) painted in new colours for F. Barlow (a retailer?).

4120 Vases, bowls etc. Tube-lined *Carnival* in black matt glaze enamelled sunset, coral, yellow and black, pale yellow inside vases, black edge.

4121 Vases, bowls etc. Tube-lined *Carnival* in black matt glaze, pencilled u.g. in Heath's mazarine blue, enamelled yellow, coral, sunset pale yellow inside vases, black edge.

4122 Blank.

4123 Vases. *New Sylvan*, tube-lined Miss Rhead, matt glaze, painted u.g. mazarine blue, enamelled purple and green, liquid gold edge traced, inside of vases turquoise.

4124 *New Garland*. Tube-lined, matt glaze, lustred in orange and yellow, enamelled in coral and 14 green, black edge.

4125 *Crescent* sandwich sets. Tube-lined *Berries* in brown, painted underglaze in blue, purple, light green yellow, band edged in fawn.

4126 *Crescent* sandwich sets. Tube-lined *Berries* in brown, painted underglaze in puce and purple leaves, dark green, light green band edged in dark green.

4127 *Crescent* sandwich sets. Tube-lined *Berries* in brown, enamelled in yellow and orange, leaves 7 green. Pale blue band, edged in garland blue.

4128 *Empire* fruit sets. Tube-lined in black, enamelled in pink, yellow, blue, 14 green, 13C, edged in 13C. [stylised sprays of flower heads.]

4129 *Empire* fruit sets. Tube-lined in black, enamelled sunset, yellow, blue and 14 green, edged in black. [Variation of 4128?]

4130 *Empire* fruit sets. Tube-lined in black, painted u.g. in pink, orange, brown, dark blue, mixed green, edged in brown. [Variation of 4128?]

4131 Bowls, etc. Tube-lined, buff body with sprays, enamelled in bright colours.

4132 *Richmond* sandwich sets and fruit sets. *Harlequin* pattern, tube-lined. [Shapes in the form of harlequin's hats, enamelled in red, blue and green.]

4133 Fruit sets. *New Jazz* pattern, tube-lined. [Stylised red flower heads, blue and orange leaves with sprigs of multi-coloured berries.]

4134 Fruit sets. *Balloons*, tube-lined.

4135 Fruit sets. *Scroll* pattern panel, tube-lined.

4334 Sandwich sets. Red sunflower, tube-lined, red and orange petalled sunflowers with blue centres.

4335 Sandwich sets. Blue sunflower, tube-lined, underglaze blue flowers.

4336 *Richmond* sandwich sets. Tube-lined, fruit sprays with blue and gold finish.

4337 *Richmond* sandwich sets. Tube-lined, fruit sprays with sunset and black finish.

4338 New round bulb bowls. Tube-lined in black, *Scroll* design enamelled in sunset and 14 green and yellow. No edge.

4339 New round bulb bowls. Tube-lined in black, triangular panels enamelled sunset, yellow, 14 green. *Garland* blue and purple. No edge.

4340 New round bulb bowls tube-lined in black. Panels with (word illegible) blue. Enamelled sunset, yellow, 14 green. *Garland* blue. No edge.

4341 New round bulb bowls. Tube lined in black, repeated over edge [i.e. flower heads extending over borders]. Enamelled sunset. *Garland* blue, 14 green and yellow. No edge.

4342 *Abbey* bulb bowls. Aerographed in assorted colours. Black edges.

4347 Miss Rhead's *New Vine* pattern for vases etc., u.g. blue grapes with matt glaze, dark green lustred leaves and orange lustred fruit.

4348 Vases and bowls. Miss Rhead's fruit band with blue Italian ornament. Painted u.g. lustred yellow. [Pomegranates, grapes and other fruits.]

4349 Miss Rhead Plaque, 10 inch. Lady's head facing left. Pink flowers, painted u.g.

4350 Miss Rhead Plaque, 10 inch. Lady's head facing right. Orange flowers, painted u.g.

4356 Square sandwich set. Ivory glaze, tube-lined, centre spray of fruit rustic border enamelled 76 yellow, 7 green, coral, orange, orange finish. [*Rutland* pattern, also used on tea wares.]

4357 Square sandwich set. Ivory glaze, Miss Rhead new loop of flowers enamelled royal blue, coral, orange and 14 green finished in orange.

4367W Suite ware etc. Ivory glaze, tube-lined, spray of fruit with rustic border enamelled with blue finish. [Variation of *Rutland* (4356).]

4416 Suite ware. Miss Rhead (birds). Tube-lined in black. Enamelled in scarlet, blue, yellow and 7 green. Ivory glaze. Scarlet edge.

The following three patterns, for children's ware, were attributed to Charlotte Rhead in the pattern book. They were printed, not tube-lined.

4419 Dogs.

4420 Cats. This pattern was originally titled Frogs. Presumably samples were made which were not very successful, so the design was changed to Cats.

4421 Chickens.

4422 Suite ware As for 4416 but coloured blue all over.

4423 Vases. Miss Rhead [no description].

4466 [Suite ware?] Miss Rhead, sponged blue and white.

4470 Sandwich sets. Miss Rhead. Wreath pattern in black, green and sunset. Cream background. Green edge and handle.

4471W Sandwich sets. Miss Rhead. Tulip panel in centre in black. Painted in blue, pink, puce, green and orange. [This designs was also used for Suite ware, on a wide range of useful items including teapots in three sizes.]

4472 W Sandwich sets. Miss Rhead. *Iris* tubed in black and sponged blue. Ground painted in puce, purple, orange and green.

4473 W Sandwich sets. Miss Rhead. *Tulip* panel at corner in sponged blue, painted in blue, pink, puce, orange and green.

4474 W Sandwich sets. Plaid corners, painted in red, black, orange and green. Finished in green.
.

4480 Teaware, etc. Miss Rhead. Red flowerpot design.

4497 Miss Rhead. Powder blue and fruit. [Lemon shaped fruits in pink and yellow and dark leaves on a powder blue ground vases.]

4507 Vases. Miss Rhead. [*Scroll* design].

4567 Suite ware. Tube-lined. Miss Rhead cross sticks and groups of flowers [large daisies] flowers in coral, blue, turquoise and pink orange sticks and orange band orange edges etc. Tea and dinner ware to be printed, cans and saucers.

4587 Miss Rhead. Lustre ware with central tube-lined pattern and coloured bands.

4609 Suite ware, *Sunshine*. Rhead. Black edges (series of black dashes and black dots) outside blown strong yellow. [Among the articles made in this pattern was a 54 piece dinner service.]

4615 Bowls, small size. Miss Rhead. Red flowers (nasturtiums).

4615 Bowls, small size. Miss Rhead. Landscape.

4628 Suite ware. Rhead. u.g. painting on matt glaze, pattern as small size bowl. Outside of bowls to be blown pale green, blue and buff. [Presumably the pattern was similar either to 4615 or 4616.]

4663 Vases and bowls etc. Rhead. Matt glaze, vases and bowls blue then enamelled in red and liquid gold.

The following patterns, 4672-4700A, were not tube-lined.

Only 4672 and 4698-4700A are attributed to Charlotte Rhead but the other patterns appear to be parts of the same series.

4672 New vases. Tigers, blown u.g., blue, yellow tigers, lustred in silver palm leaves, orange lustre inside, silver edges. Tigers to be masked in u.g. black by Rhead matt glaze.

4673 New vases. Swallows, blown underglaze, blue at top and matt green at bottom. Swallows in bronze lustre and stippled gold on water wares stippled gold top and bottom. Matt glaze.

4674 New vases. Owls, blown underglaze brown shaded leaves traced in scoured gold and stippled at top. Matt glaze.

4675 New vases. Parrots, blown underglaze, blue ground and green parrots. Leaves in silver and stippled in gold top and bottom. Orange lustre inside. MOP lustre. Ordinary glaze.

4676 New vases. Owls, blown underglaze blue shaded leaves traced in silver and silver edges.

4677 New vases. Parrots Blown underglaze pale green ground and coloured parrots stippled in scoured gold top and bottom and silver leaves orange lustre inside gold edges MOP lustre overall and inside ordinary glaze 2 kiln fires.

4678 New vases. Tigers. Blown underglaze blue (dark tigers). Lustred in bronze lustre (word illegible) stippled in scoured gold and stippled at bottom of grass. Gold edges. Matt glaze.

4678A Silver trees, bronze tigers. Silver edges etc.

4690 New vases Swallows. Shaded in u.g. pink. Lustred all over in orange lustre. Silver swallows.

4691 Swallows. Blown blue-green. Silver swallows.

4692 New vases Elephants. Blown u.g. light blue. Light blue elephants and pink ground.

4697 Bonbon trays. Sprays of berries printed in black and enamelled in coral. Handles enamelled in coral, black and scoured gold.

4698 Bonbon trays Rhead. As for no. 4697, but bonbon trays with puce handles.

4700 Suite ware. Printed on-glaze in black Rhead Bird and leaves enamelled in green and coral and finished in scoured gold. Black edges.

4700A Bonbon trays printed onglaze in black. Rhead. Bird and leaves enamelled in green and coral but scoured gold handles.

4715 *Sunshine*. Black edges blown yellow. Presumably a variation of 4609.

4752 [pencil entry with sketchy illustration of pattern] Plaques and vases. Rhead [*Florentine*. Curvilinear geometric design, lustred in brown or dull green and brown. Mottled brown ground].

4753 Plaques only. Ship in centre Rhead. [Perhaps a variation of 4118.]

4767 Suite ware, *Zenith*. Rhead. *Orchard*. Tube-line in blue freehand apples, green leaves blue edges.

4768 Suite ware, *Zenith*. Rhead. *Orchard* as above only black tube-line, orange apples and green leaves, orange edges.

4789 Vases etc. Rhead. Laurel Band. No edges, green

body [pencil entry with illustration of a band (marked blue) of laurel leaves. In fact the ground colour is mottled brown].

4809 Vases, jugs etc. Mottled u.g. in blue etc. Lustred all over. Markings at top [pencil design in the pattern book – stylised flower heads with spiralling outlines and finished with gold spirals].

4809A As for no. 4809, without the markings [gold spirals].

4816 [Pencil entry] Vases. Rhead. *Florentine* new way [Central zigzag band above a smaller band of leaf forms.]

4831 Vases etc. Rhead as 4809, blue ground, pink lustre outside then fired, enamelled in purple and silvered silver edges two fires.

4832 Vases etc. As above only yellow lustre outside and green inside then fired enamelled in blue and silvered silver edges, two fires. Rhead. *Tudor*.

4833 Vases etc. Rhead. *Tudor* square enamelled in coral and black, half leaves in gold [*Trellis* pattern between bands of elongated leaves and scrolling foliage].

4834 Vases etc. Rhead as above only green panels (lustre) no enamel colour.

4837 end of pattern book.

The following design appeared in the next pattern book. It was evidently not produced until after Charlotte Rhead had left Burgess & Leigh.

4908 Vases, Rhead. *New Florentine*. [Brown or green lustred sunbursts separated by blue bands, all within bands of brown diamond shapes. Mottled brown ground].

SELECTED BIBLIOGRAPHY

Baker, Diane, *Potworks, The Industrial Architecture of the Staffordshire Potteries* (Royal Commission on Historical Monuments, 1991).
Batkin, Maureen, *Gifts for Good Children, Part II, 1890-1990* (Richard Dennis Publications, 1996).
Bumpus, Bernard, *Charlotte Rhead, Potter & Designer* (Kevin Francis Publishing, 1987).
Bumpus, Bernard, *Collecting Rhead Pottery, Charlotte, Frederick, Frederick Hurten* (Francis Joseph, 1999).
Casey, Andrew, *20th Century Ceramic Designers in Britain* (Antique Collectors Club, 2001).
Copeland, Robert, *Spode's Willow Pattern and Other Designs After the Chinese* (Studio Vista, 1990).
Coupe, Elizabeth, *Collecting Burleigh Jugs* (Letterbox Publishing, 1999).
Coupe, Elizabeth, *Collecting Burleigh Ware, A Photographic guide to the Art Deco Tablewares of Burgess & Leigh* (Letterbox Publishing, 1998).
Coysh, A. & Henrywood R., *Dictionary of Blue and White Printed Pottery 1780-1880* (Antique Collectors Club, Vol. 1 1982, Vol 11, 1989).
Elliott, Gordon, *The Design Process in British Ceramic Manufacture 1750-1850* (Staffordshire University Press, 2000).
Fuller, Lance, *Trade in Copperplate Engravings, An Investigation of the Second-Hand Market*, Staffordshire University MA Thesis, 2000, Spode Museum Trust Archives.
Godden, G. A., *Encyclopaedia of British Pottery and Procelain Marks* (Barrie & Jenkins, 2000).
Graham, Rev. Malcolm, *Cup and Saucer Land*, 1908 (republished Staffordshire and Stoke-on-Trent City Archive Service, 2000).
Hampson, Rodney, *Pottery References in the Staffordshire Advertiser 1795-1865* (The Northern Ceramic Society, 2000).
Henrywood, R. K., *Relief-Moulded Jugs* (Antique Collectors' Club, 1984).
Hopwood, Irene and Gordon, *The Shorter Connection, A Family Pottery 1874-1974* (Richard Dennis Publications, 1992).
Hodgkiss, B., *Mother Burslem* (Churnet Valley Books, 2001).
Kowalsky, Arnold A. & Dorothy E., *Encyclopaedia of Marks On American, English, European Earthenware, Ironstone and Stoneware 1780-1980* (Schiffer Publishing Ltd, 2002).
Morris, Donald, *The Potteries, A Collection of Nostalgic Photographs* (Brampton Publications, 1990).
MacCarthy, Fiona, *A History of British Design 1830-1979*, (George Allen & Unwin Ltd, 1979).
Riley, Noël, *Gifts for Good Children, Part I 1790 – 1890* (Richard Dennis Publications, 1991).
Spours, Judy, *Art Deco Tableware* (Ward Lock, 1988).

EXHIBITION CATALOGUES AND PERIODICALS

Britain Can Make It, Exhibition Catalogue, V&A Publications, 24th September, 1946.
The British Galleries 1500-1900, A Guide Book, Diane Winch, (V&A Publications, 2001).
Dynamic Design, The British Pottery Industry 1940-1990, Kathy Niblett, (The Potteries Museum & Art Gallery, 1990).
potteries.org website, Steve Birks
The Staffordshire Potteries As An Empire Asset and Illustrated Souvenir of the Royal Visit, J. Child, ed. (The Manchester Courier, 1913).
True Blue, Transfer Printed Earthenware, Gaye Blake-Roberts, ed. Exhibition Catalogue (Friends of Blue, 1998).

The Antique Collector
The Antique Dealer
The British Journal of Commerce
Collect It!
Journal of Ceramic History (City Museum & Art Gallery)
The Pottery Gazette and Glass Trade Review
The Pottery and Glass Record
The Staffordshire Sentinel
Tableware International

GENERAL INDEX